AF609422

Internet Shutdowns in Africa

Digital Africa series, edited by Tony Roberts

Digital Africa explores how digital technologies have opened new spaces for the exercise of democratic rights and freedoms in Africa, as well as how repressive regimes have used digital technologies to monitor, diminish, or remove those rights. The series foregrounds vital new research from across the continent, and it combines empirical rigor with theoretical sophistication in order to offer new, more nuanced perspectives on the interactions between digital technology and social life on the continent. In so doing, it offers an important, in-depth corrective to existing studies of the relations between digital technologies and social and political power, studies that have overwhelmingly focused on the Global North.

Each volume is co-edited by the series editor in collaboration with an established scholar in the field, and each features comparative and rich case studies authored by ECRs and other African scholars involved in the African Digital Rights Network. Thanks to contributors' diverse disciplinary and professional backgrounds, each chapter offers uniquely practical suggestions for policy, legislation, and practice.

Titles include:

*Digital Citizenship in Africa: Technologies of Agency and Repression*
*Digital Disinformation in Africa: Hashtag Politics, Power and Propaganda*
*Digital Surveillance in Africa: Power, Agency, and Rights*
*Internet Shutdowns in Africa: Technology, Rights and Power*

# Internet Shutdowns in Africa

## *Technology, Rights and Power*

**Edited by**
**Felicia Anthonio and Tony Roberts**

ZED

LONDON • NEW YORK • OXFORD • NEW DELHI • SYDNEY

ZED Books
Bloomsbury Publishing Plc, 50 Bedford Square, London, WC1B 3DP, UK
Bloomsbury Publishing Inc, 1359 Broadway, New York, NY 10018, USA
Bloomsbury Publishing Ireland, 29 Earlsfort Terrace, Dublin 2, D02 AY28, Ireland

BLOOMSBURY and Zed Books are trademarks of Bloomsbury Publishing Plc

First published in Great Britain 2025

Copyright © Felicia Anthonio and Tony Roberts, 2025

Felicia Anthonio and Tony Roberts have asserted their right under the Copyright, Designs and Patents Act, 1988, to be identified as Editors of this work.

Series design by Toby Way

This work is published open access subject to a Creative Commons Attribution-NonCommercial-NoDerivatives 4.0 International licence (CC BY-NC-ND 4.0, https://creativecommons.org/licenses/by-nc-nd/4.0/). You may re-use, distribute, and reproduce this work in any medium for non-commercial purposes, provided you give attribution to the copyright holder and the publisher and provide a link to the Creative Commons licence.

Bloomsbury Publishing Plc does not have any control over, or responsibility for, any third-party websites referred to or in this book. All internet addresses given in this book were correct at the time of going to press. The author and publisher regret any inconvenience caused if addresses have changed or sites have ceased to exist, but can accept no responsibility for any such changes.

A catalogue record for this book is available from the British Library.

Library of Congress Cataloging-in-Publication Data
Names: Anthonio, Felicia, editor, author. | Roberts, Tony, 1963- editor, author.
Title: Internet shutdowns in Africa : technology, rights and power /
edited by Felicia Anthonio and Tony Roberts.
Other titles: Digital Africa (Series)
Description: New York : Zed Books, 2025. | Series: Digital Africa series | Includes bibliographical references and index. | Summary: "Authored entirely by African researchers, this open access book provides ten in-depth case studies of state-sponsored internet shutdowns across all regions of Africa. In so doing, it offers the first-ever comparative analysis of how African states use internet shutdowns as tools to close civic space, suppress opposition, and maintain power, all of which produces actionable recommendations"– Provided by publisher.
Identifiers: LCCN 2025020908 (print) | LCCN 2025020909 (ebook) |
ISBN 9781350464285 (hardback) | ISBN 9781350464292 (paperback) |
ISBN 9781350464308 (epub) | ISBN 9781350464315 (pdf)
Subjects: LCSH: Internet–Access control–Political aspects–Africa. | Internet–Access control–Government policy–Africa. | Right to Internet access–Africa.
Classification: LCC HM851 .I5835 2025 (print) | LCC HM851 (ebook) |
DDC 005.8/30096–dc23/eng/20250430
LC record available at https://lccn.loc.gov/2025020908
LC ebook record available at https://lccn.loc.gov/2025020909

ISBN: HB: 978-1-3504-6428-5
PB: 978-1-3504-6429-2
ePDF: 978-1-3504-6431-5
eBook: 978-1-3504-6430-8

Series: Digital Africa

Typeset by Integra Software Services Pvt. Ltd.
Printed and bound in Great Britain

For product safety related questions contact productsafety@bloomsbury.com.

To find out more about our authors and books visit www.bloomsbury.com and sign up for our newsletters.

*This book is dedicated to the digital rights activists around the world who commit their time and expertise to tirelessly monitoring and documenting internet shutdowns and their devastating impacts on human rights, raising the alarm, and engaging in research and advocacy to #KeepItOn. Without your dedication and diligence, this book would not be possible.*

# Contents

# Illustrations

## *Figures*



## *Tables*

# Contributors

**Harold Adjaho** is an IT consultant and founder of Grand Hosters, a cloud and internet services company based in Benin. He has a background in software development, systems architecture, and IT management, and has contributed to civic tech and open data projects across West Africa. A strong advocate for internet freedom and digital rights, he is a former fellow of Internews training program (focused on internet shutdown monitoring and censorship) and of the FFGI in Burkina Faso as an expert trainer in internet governance. He previously served as president of the Internet Society Benin Chapter, the Bloggers Association of Benin, and the Google Developers Group of Cotonou. He also leads projects within the IGBANET organization and is a founding member of the Benin DNS Forum, which organizes the annual national event on DNS and Internet development. He also works as a media commentator and tech educator.

**Dr Qemal Affagnon** defended his PhD at the university of Abomey-Calavi, in Benin Republic. It was a case study of 3 online radios in Benin on how they contribute to reduce the digital divide regarding content production. Since then, Dr Qemal Affagnon has maintained an interest in the strategic power of Internet and joined Internet Sans Frontières, a non-profit organization whose objective is to lead advocacy efforts against internet shutdowns in West Africa. This practical experience has significantly enforced his academic career, pursuing collaborations with both civil society and academic colleagues. Dr Affagnon's work has been published in journals, among others European Scientific Journal, International Journal of Progressive Sciences and Technologies, International Journal of Advanced Research, Journal of Strategic Innovation and Sustainability and The Algerian Journal of Political Sciences and International Relations.

**Felicia Anthonio** is a digital rights researcher, advocate and expert, with over a decade of experience championing media and internet freedom globally. As #KeepItOn Campaign Manager at Access Now, she leads the coalition's advocacy – over 345 organizations – against internet shutdowns worldwide. Her work directly challenges authoritarian regimes, empowers activists and mobilizes communities to resist digital authoritarianism. Her publications are featured by Yale University, CIPESA, and Bloomsbury Collections. She hosted The Kill Switch podcast; was featured in The Shutdown, a BBC World Service documentary. Felicia is a member of US-based Open Technology Fund's (OTF) Advisory Council and a board member of the World Expression Forum (WEXFO), Norway. She worked at the Media Foundation for West Africa. She is a member of the African Digital Rights

Network. She holds a Masters in Lettres, Langues et Affaires Internationales, l'Université d'Orléans and a B.A. French and Psychology from the University of Ghana.

**Yohannes Eneyew Ayalew** is a Postdoctoral Fellow at 'Three Generations of Digital Human Rights' project at the Faculty of Law, The Hebrew University of Jerusalem. Prior to that, he was a Sessional Academic and Tutor at the Faculty of Law, Monash University, Australia. Dr Ayalew is an inaugural Majority World Initiative (MWI) Scholar at Yale Law School. He holds a PhD in Law at the Faculty of Law, Monash University, Australia and dual Master of Laws (LLM) degrees, one in Public International Law from Addis Ababa University, Ethiopia and the other in International Human Rights Law from the University of Groningen, The Netherlands. His research interest spans in the areas of Digital Human Rights, Balancing Digital Human Rights, African Human Rights Law, International Human Rights Law and Third World Approaches to International Law (TWAIL).

**Ababacar Diop** is President of Jonction, a digital rights advocacy organization based in Dakar, Senegal. Ababacar Diop is a lawyer and former Commissioner at the Senegalese Commission for the Protection of Personal Data (CDP), an independent administrative authority responsible for the enforcement of Senegal's law on the protection of personal data. He holds a Specialized Diploma in Economic, Social, and Cultural Rights from the Henry Dunant University College in Geneva, Switzerland. Diop is also the Senegalese representative of CREIS (Coordination Center for Research and Teaching in Computer Science) where he conducts research on the challenges of new information and communication technologies in society. Diop collaborates with several international organizations, including Privacy International and Global Partner Digital based in London, CIPESA based in Uganda, and Paradigm Initiative based in Nigeria. He is a member of several African civil society networks, including the Francophone African Civil Society Organization (OSCAF), headquartered in Benin.

**Khattab Hamad** is a Sudanese researcher and digital rights advocate committed to advancing internet freedom, countering disinformation, and amplifying marginalized voices. Through his work with Global Voices, the citizen media network, he brings unreported digital rights events in Sudan to the forefront, promoting greater global solidarity. As an active member of the #KeepItOn coalition, Khattab campaigns against internet shutdowns and for the protection of digital rights around the world. Khattab also serves as the Sudan ambassador for the Open Observatory of Network Interference (OONI), where he contributes to research efforts on internet censorship and surveillance. He is a 2020 fellow of the Optima Fellowship at Internews. Moreover, he contributed to anti-disinformation efforts by working at Beam Reports as a Lead Disinformation Researcher and at Code for Africa as an Investigative Data Analyst. Khattab holds a bachelor's degree in telecommunication engineering.

**Charles Kajoloweka** is a frontline human rights activist, Founder, and Executive Director of Youth and Society (YAS), a human rights and governance watchdog in Malawi. He is also a founder of the Malawi's Centre for Business & Human Rights, a non-profit fostering corporate accountability on human rights. With 15 years in civil society activism, he is also a co-founder of the National Anti-Corruption Alliance (NACA), and the Civil Society Coalition on Migration. Charles holds a Master's degree in Human Rights and Democratization in Africa from the University of Pretoria, South Africa. A graduate in Bachelor of Arts Degree from Mzuzu University, he is also a recipient of the prestigious Young African Leaders Initiative from the University of Virginia (USA), and the International Anti-Corruption Academy, Austria. Charles has also served as a country author for the Africa digital rights report, Londa. His other contributions include a Book Chapter on State of Corruption in Africa.

**Thobekile Matimbe** is a human rights lawyer and Senior Manager, Partnerships and Engagements at Paradigm Initiative (PIN). She is committed to advancing digital rights and inclusion in Africa and beyond. She is an avid researcher with civic engagement and human rights advocacy expertise. She is a Board Member of the Global Network Initiative, a Membership Officer for the Africa Digital Rights Network, and an Oversight Group Member of the African Internet Rights Alliance. She is also an Open Internet for Democracy Leader, participating in several regional and global digital rights processes and coalitions. Thobekile manages projects at Paradigm Initiative, including the Digital Rights and Inclusion Forum (DRIF), a multistakeholder forum on digital rights in the Global South and the publication of the state of digital rights and inclusion in Africa report, Londa.

**Kassem Mnejja** is a digital rights researcher and advocate focusing on internet shutdowns, digital repression, and the role of technology in state control across the Middle East and North Africa (MENA). He is the MENA Campaigner at Access Now, where he works on regional advocacy and campaigns, and contributes to research on how digital violations impact communities during conflict and crisis. His work spans advocacy, campaigning, policy, and collaboration with grassroots groups to support civil society in documenting abuses, resisting online repression, and defending at-risk communities. He is also a Nonresident Fellow at the Tahrir Institute for Middle East Policy (TIMEP), where his research explores the intersection of technology, warfare, and authoritarianism in the region.

**Susan Mwape** is a governance and digital rights advocate with over 15 years of experience in civil society engagement, research, election observation, and women's empowerment in Africa. She is the Founder and Executive Director of Common Cause Zambia, where she leads initiatives on democratic strengthening, civic technology, and digital rights. Susan has contributed to a number of publications on Electoral Integrity, APRM and Digital Rights. She serves on Zambia's National Governing Council for the African Peer Review Mechanism and is the Southern Africa Communication Champion for the APRM under the African Union. She is the Country Director for Pivoting in Heels Zambia. In this volume, Susan contributes a chapter on Zambia, focusing on electoral integrity and its intersection with internet shutdowns in Africa.

**Juliet Nanfuka** is a Ugandan digital rights researcher and communications expert dedicated to advancing internet freedom, digital inclusion, and media rights across Africa. She has worked on various initiatives aimed at helping individuals and organizations to advocate for an internet that is free, fair and open in Africa. She is a contributing writer for the Africa Digital Rights Network (ADRN) and has also written for the Institute for New Economic Thinking (INET), the Center for International Media Assistance (CIMA) and various other international publications. She is a member of the UNESCO Information for All Programme (IFAP) Working Group on Information for Development. Juliet works with the Collaboration on International ICT Policy for East and Southern Africa (CIPESA), a leading think tank shaping digital rights and internet governance in the region.

**Lea Mehari Redae** is a Lecturer of International Humanitarian Law at Addis Ababa University's (AAU) School of Law. She founded the AAU International Humanitarian Law Clinic in 2020, a centre within the School of Law that studies African armed conflicts and their humanitarian consequences from an African perspective. With a background in international humanitarian law, human rights law, and policy analysis, she has held various impactful roles such as a Lecturer, an Associate, a Policy Advisor and a Humanitarian Affairs Advisor in a prominent international humanitarian organization, and as an Associate Researcher at a Pan African think-tank focusing on peace and security in Africa. She holds an LL.M. in International Humanitarian Law and Human Rights from the Geneva Academy and an LL.M. in Business Law and LL.B from AAU School of Law. Her areas of research include African perspectives on armed conflicts, laws, and policy.

**Tony Roberts** is a Research Fellow at the Institute for Development Studies (IDS) UK. After a period as lecturer in Innovation Studies at the University of East London, Tony founded and led two international development agencies working in Central America and Southern Africa. When he stood down as CEO of Computer Aid International, he completed a PhD in the use of digital technologies in international development (Royal Holloway, University of London). After one year working as a Research Fellow at the United Nations University, in Macao, China, Tony joined IDS in 2016 where his research has focused focuses on digital inequality and digital rights. He co-founded the African Digital Rights Network for whom he now edits online reports and is the Series Editor of this Zed Books collected edition series "Digital Africa" for which he previously co-edited "Digital Citizenship in Africa", "Digital Disinformation in Africa" and "Digital Surveillance in Africa".

**Nompilo Simanje** is a lawyer by profession and an expert on the intersection of technology, the law, and human rights. She has years of experience in advocacy, research and capacity building aimed at promoting media freedom, freedom of expression, access to information, and the right to privacy. She currently works as the Africa Advocacy and Engagement Lead at the International Press Institute where her work includes monitoring and collecting data on press freedom threats and violations across the continent, including threats to journalists' safety and gendered attacks against journalists both online and offline to inform evidence-based advocacy.

**Arsène Tungali** is Executive Director of Rudi International, an organization working at the intersection of technology and human rights based in the DRC. He is a contributing writer with CIPESA, Paradigm Initiative as well as with the Africa Digital Rights Network (ADRN). He has collaborated on ICT policy development processes within ICANN and AFRINIC and was appointed in 2018 to serve on the UN's IGF MAG. He holds a Master's degree from Kigali Independent University and has certificates from Stanford University and University of Delaware, a fellow of US State Department's Mandela Washington Fellowship for Young African Leaders.

# Chapter 1

## An introduction to critical internet shutdowns research in Africa

Tony Roberts and Felicia Anthonio

Put simply, an internet shutdown is an intentional disruption of online or mobile communications. Shutdowns intentionally prevent the free flow of information and communication and obstruct social, economic and political life online. Each internet shutdown typically violates the fundamental human rights of millions of citizens, including their rights to freedom of expression, trade and commerce, democratic debate, and civic participation online.

Forty-one African countries imposed at least 193 internet shutdowns between 2016 and 2024. Shutdowns are usually ordered by the state and implemented by private companies: mobile phone operators or internet service providers. Whole nations can be rendered unable to communicate with family or friends, engage in online commerce or employment, and may find themselves unable to access essential services, online education, healthcare or emergency services. Internet shutdowns can have crippling financial repercussions on income, trade and national economies, and make community participation and peaceful democratic engagement impossible online.

Internet shutdowns in Africa are becoming more frequent and more sophisticated, despite repeated resolutions and statements aimed at ending the practice by the African Commission on Human and People's Rights (ACHPR), the Economic Court of Justice of the Economic Community of West African States (ECOWAS) and the United Nations. As the authors in this book explain, the perpetrators of internet shutdowns are using the novel technical affordances of mobile and internet infrastructures to diversify the types of internet shutdown and improve the precision of their targeting to impact chosen groups or regions. In recent years foreign states, military regimes and warring parties have also resorted to the use of internet shutdown as a weapon of war, by targeting and destroying telecommunications infrastructure or impeding the entry of essential resources such as the fuel necessary to maintain connectivity.

The authors in this volume provide multiple examples of governments using internet shutdown to crack down on peaceful protest, disrupt political opposition in elections, and commit human rights violations with impunity. We also provide examples of internet shutdowns imposed to protect the integrity of annual school examinations. Whatever the justification provided by the state, chapter authors describe the devastating impact of internet shutdowns on people's ability to express themselves, communicate with loved ones, engage in civic and political life and conduct business in a world where citizens increasingly depend on mobile money, the gig economy and online transactions for their livelihoods.

To date, the literature on internet shutdowns in Africa has predominantly been descriptive and documentary with insufficient attention paid to the role of power in giving rise to internet shutdowns or to the effects of these shutdowns on power relations. This book has five objectives: (i) to produce the most comprehensive documentation to date of the incidents of internet shutdowns in the African countries included in the study, (ii) to provide the most expansive assessment of how those internet shutdowns have impacted citizen's social, economic and political rights, (iii) to conduct the most extensive analysis to date of how power relations both give rise to internet shutdowns and are affected by them, (iv) to record the forms of resistance that citizens across Africa are using to circumvent, challenge and end internet shutdowns, and (v) to provide actionable recommendations to mitigate and end future rights-violating internet shutdowns.

To achieve these objectives the country case study chapters take the following form: authors begin by outlining for the reader the political history of state media controls in their country prior to the digital age. They then document the current digital landscape and detail the number and types of internet shutdowns that have occurred in recent years, before describing the impact of shutdowns not only on the most commonly discussed civil and political rights but also on the relatively neglected social, economic and cultural rights that every person is guaranteed in law. The second half of each chapter then aims to provide the most sustained conceptual analysis of internet shutdowns in each country using the three lenses of technology affordances, digital rights and power analysis.

This book addresses critical questions of *why* internet shutdowns happen, *which* human rights they violate, *what* power interests are served, and *what* can be done to mitigate and prevent them. To answer these questions authors interrogate the state's claims that internet shutdowns serve the 'national interest'. They do this by analysing who benefits, and who pays the social, economic and political price of internet shutdowns? Authors analyse how the affordances of infrastructure technologies enable powerholders to violate citizens' social, economic and political rights in ways that reproduce and amplify unequal power relations. The result is the most thorough account to date of the impact of shutdowns on fundamental rights and underlying power interests.

We centre concepts of power in our analysis not only because internet shutdowns are imposed by the most powerful state and corporate actors on those who they have power over but also because they are often imposed to limit countervailing power – most often during elections or civic protests. Internet shutdowns are often designed to affect power relations by limiting the development of counter-power in the form of opposition actors who wish to peacefully protest, communicate policy alternatives online or use social media channels to contest elections. The chapters in this book suggest that internet shutdowns are most often imposed by incumbent leaders to extinguish perceived threats to existing powerholders and to assist regimes to retain power. Although internet shutdowns are most-often implemented by states and corporations and their impositions necessarily violate the freedoms and rights of citizens, there has been surprisingly little sustained power analysis in the existing literature on internet shutdowns.

This is the first book dedicated to internet shutdowns across Africa. In it, African researchers expand the existing evidence base by producing rich case studies of eleven African countries: Zimbabwe, the Democratic Republic of Congo (DRC), Zambia, Ethiopia, Sudan, Nigeria, Chad, Senegal, Burkina Faso, Algeria and Uganda. It is the first time that African activist-scholars have come together from across the continent's subregions to provide country-specific case studies and in-depth analysis of the drivers, dimensions and direction of internet shutdowns in Africa. By engaging researchers from the countries that they are analysing, this study was able to draw upon their deep contextual knowledge of local politics, and legal and political cultures, to produce a deeper level of analysis than would otherwise have been possible.

The rest of this introductory chapter is organized as follows. The next section provides some historical background on media censorship in Africa before outlining the landscape of internet shutdown by charting their frequency and providing a typology of different forms of shutdown. We then outline our research approach and conceptual framework. We provide a brief review of what is already known about internet shutdowns and gaps in the existing literature before providing an overview of the country case study chapters. We conclude with a summary of findings.

## *Background*

Internet shutdowns are not the first media shutdowns in Africa. The internet may be the new frontier of information censorship and media control in Africa, but states have a long history of repressing voices perceived to be a threat to existing powerholders. The chapters in this book provide evidence that, prior to the digital age, other forms of media controls and shutdowns were a common means of defending the interests of incumbent power. Authors document how colonial powerholders often shut down media platforms that gave voice to anti-colonial narratives. This included newspaper shutdowns (see Chapter 2 on Zimbabwe), magazine shutdowns (see Chapter 7 on Nigeria), radio and TV shutdowns (see Chapter 3 on DRC) and even fax machine shutdowns (see Chapter 6 on Sudan).

Media shutdowns in Africa have colonial roots. The authors in this book will show that repressive media controls were often introduced to Africa by colonial powers to serve imperial power interests and opposition newspapers and radio stations were shut down. However, after independence, incoming post-colonial administrations often themselves imposed media shutdowns to further the power interests of their political parties. Today some contemporary African governments use digital media shutdowns to retain power and curtail countervailing power inimical to their interests. From this perspective, internet shutdowns can be understood as a continuity of media repression explained by contesting power interests. To capture this data and make it part of their analysis, each chapter in this book begins by locating internet shutdowns in the context of a brief political history of state media controls in that country. This approach reveals a number of interesting patterns across the countries studied, which we will return to in the concluding chapter of this book.

The first state-ordered digital repression in Africa followed soon after the introduction of the internet. In February 1996 the Zambian government threatened to prosecute local Internet Service Provider, Zamnet, for publishing an online edition of *The Post* newspaper which it had banned offline (Nyarko and Ilori, 2022). The banning of the online version of an offline publication clearly demonstrates the continuity of information controls and censorship between the analogue and digital eras. In 1996 the percentage of populations with internet access was extremely small but a decade later the use of digital media was growing rapidly, especially with the advent of social media.

The first nationwide internet shutdown in Africa was in Guinea in 2007 (Okunola, 2018). The media began covering internet shutdowns in earnest in 2009, when Iranian authorities clamped down on broadcast, mobile phones and internet access in response to contested elections results (Anderson, 2009). However, the global media coverage of internet shutdowns reached new heights when authorities in Egypt completely shut down the internet during the Egyptian revolution in 2011 (Marchant and Stremlau, 2020). These internet shutdowns were seen as part of an authoritarian response by the state to repress political mobilization online and offline, and although media coverage and academic research accelerated around the impact on civil and political rights, relatively little attention was initially paid to the social and economic impacts of internet shutdowns.

The next section provides some documentation of the frequency of internet shutdowns in Africa before we explain our choice of research approach and conceptual frame.

## *Increasing frequency of shutdowns in Africa*

There is a wide variety of internet shutdown experiences within Africa. As Table 1.1 shows, there were 193 recorded internet shutdowns in Africa between 2016 and 2024. Although shutdowns have taken place in the majority of Africa's fifty-five countries, it is important to note that there are fourteen African countries that have no recorded case of internet shutdowns as of the end of 2024. There are another twelve countries in Africa that have only ever had one internet shutdown (nine of whom have not experienced one in the last three years). Twenty-five African countries have experienced between two and eight shutdowns. However, Ethiopia alone has experienced thirty shutdowns – more than any other country on the continent; Sudan has the next highest volume with twenty-one shutdowns; and Algeria has had fourteen. These top three countries have had internet shutdowns every year since 2018.

There is not only diversity in frequency of shutdowns across Africa but also diversity in triggers and types of shutdown. Although Algeria has experienced a high volume of internet shutdowns with fourteen since 2016 as Chapter 11 on Algeria in this volume shows, with the exception of 2019 these internet shutdowns were all designed to prevent cheating in school exams.

Table 1.1 also shows that although the total number of internet shutdowns per year has increased over time since 2016 it may have plateaued and there are some

**Table 1.1** Incidence of Internet Shutdowns in Africa 2016–24

| | Countries | 2016 | 2017 | 2018 | 2019 | 2020 | 2021 | 2022 | 2023 | 2024 | Total |
|---|---|---|---|---|---|---|---|---|---|---|---|
| 1 | Ethiopia | 3 | 2 | 6 | 4 | 5 | 3 | 1 | 4 | 2 | **30** |
| 2 | Sudan | | | 1 | 3 | 2 | 5 | 4 | 2 | 4 | **21** |
| 3 | Algeria | 1 | 1 | 1 | 6 | 1 | 1 | 1 | 1 | 1 | **14** |
| 4 | Chad | 1 | | 2 | 1 | 2 | 2 | | | 2 | **10** |
| 5 | Libya | 1 | | | | | | 4 | 3 | | **8** |
| 6 | Senegal | | | | | | 1 | | 4 | 3 | **8** |
| 7 | DRC | 1 | 2 | 3 | 1 | | | | | | **7** |
| 8 | Uganda | | | | | 1 | 3 | 1 | 1 | 1 | **7** |
| 9 | Tanzania | | | | | 1 | | | 2 | 3 | **6** |
| 10 | Guinea | | | | | 2 | | | 2 | 1 | **5** |
| 11 | Kenya | | | | | 2 | | | 1 | 2 | **5** |
| 12 | Mali | 1 | | 2 | | 2 | | | | | **5** |
| 13 | Mauritania | | | | 1 | | | | 2 | 2 | **5** |
| 14 | Nigeria | | | 1 | | | 2 | 2 | | | **5** |
| 15 | Togo | | 1 | 1 | | 3 | | | | | **5** |
| 16 | Cameroon | | 2 | 1 | 1 | | | | | | **4** |
| 17 | Egypt | 2 | | | 1 | 1 | | | | | **4** |
| 18 | Burkina Faso | | | | | | 1 | 2 | | | **3** |
| 19 | Equatorial Guinea | | 2 | | | | | | | 1 | **3** |
| 20 | Gabon | | | | 1 | | 1 | | 1 | | **3** |
| 21 | Mozambique | | | | | | | | 1 | 2 | **3** |
| 22 | Sierra Leone | | | 1 | | | | 2 | | | **3** |
| 23 | Somaliland | | 1 | | | | | 1 | 1 | | **3** |
| 24 | Tunisia | 2 | | | | | | 1 | | | **3** |
| 25 | Zimbabwe | 1 | | | 1 | | | 1 | | | **3** |
| 26 | Benin | | | | 2 | | | | | | **2** |
| 27 | Eritrea | | | | 1 | | | | | 1 | **2** |
| 28 | Eswatini | | | | | | 2 | | | | **2** |
| 29 | Morocco | | 1 | | | | 1 | | | | **2** |
| 30 | Burundi | | | | | 1 | | | | | **1** |
| 31 | Comoros | | | | | | | | | 1 | **1** |
| 32 | Côte d'Ivoire | | | 1 | | | | | | | **1** |
| 33 | Guinea Bissau | | | | | | | | | 1 | **1** |
| 34 | Liberia | | | | 1 | | | | | | **1** |
| 35 | Malawi | | | | 1 | | | | | | **1** |
| 36 | Mauritius | | | | | | | | | 1 | **1** |
| 37 | Niger | | | | | | 1 | | | | **1** |
| 38 | Republic of Congo | | | | | | 1 | | | | **1** |
| 39 | South Sudan | | | | | | 1 | | | | **1** |
| 40 | The Gambia | 1 | | | | | | | | | **1** |
| 41 | Zambia | | | | | | 1 | | | | **1** |
| | Total | 14 | 12 | 20 | 25 | 23 | 26 | 20 | 25 | 28 | **193** |

Source: authors using data from Access Now Shutdown Tracker Optimisation Project.

reversals where civic resistance and changes in government have stemmed the tide of shutdowns.

## *What was our approach to analysing shutdowns?*

Methodologically, the research contained in this book was carried out using a range of qualitative methods, which included desk-based secondary analysis of existing data and articles, and primary research in the form of semi-structured interviews with purposefully selected key informants. The research was produced by the African Digital Rights Network and was carried out with researchers most of whom are part of the #KeepItOn network coordinated by leading digital rights organization Access Now (see List of Contributors). The researchers were selected by the editors based on their deep contextual knowledge of the countries and expertise on internet shutdowns. In common with the other books in this 'Digital Africa' series we provide a platform for activist researchers to deepen their analysis and to articulate their research with support from academic researchers. We chose to include researchers not based at universities because we do not believe that academics have a monopoly of knowledge about this subject. We therefore purposefully selected a range of activists, analysts and academics to bring a plurality of experience, perspectives and expertise to bear on the studies.

Our intention from the outset was both to produce detailed descriptive accounts of the internet shutdowns in each country and to use those documentary accounts as data for further critical and conceptual analysis. This critical approach to studying internet shutdowns draws on the approach of Kuo and Marwick (2021) as developed in our previous books *Digital Disinformation in Africa* (Roberts and Karekwaivanane, 2024) and *Digital Surveillance in Africa* (Roberts and Mare, 2024). We begin by grounding each study in the historical and technological context and are attentive to both the continuities and discontinuities between preceding analogue practices and contemporary digital practices. We believe that any comprehensive analysis needs to include documenting the immediate 'first-order effects' such as closing civic space and violating human rights but that it is also important to analyse the 'second-order effects' on unequal power relationships by asking 'who benefits?' and 'what power interests are served?' by digital practices. We argue that critical studies of internet shutdowns should not be neutral but rather should take a normative position against human rights violation in favour of social justice, and that this commitment leads to a responsibility to provide recommendations and practical guidance for action that intends both to mitigate and to overcome rights-violating internet shutdowns. Informed by these objectives, the next section reviews concepts of power, rights and technology from the existing literature that researchers might find useful for analysing internet shutdowns in Africa.

**First- and second-order effects of internet shutdowns.** We encouraged the authors in this book not only to go beyond documenting the incidence and types of internet shutdowns in their country but also to go beyond assessing their immediate *first-order effects* on human rights. We asked them to consider why states were prepared to violate human rights in order to achieve their ultimate goals. So, we asked authors to analyse what we call here the *second-order* effects of internet shutdowns – the achieved goals or intended goals of violating citizens' fundamental human rights. To do this we suggested conducting different forms of power analysis to understand who benefits from internet shutdowns and what power interest they serve. This builds on the approach developed to study other aspects of digital authoritarianism in our previous studies on digital disinformation (Roberts and Karekwaivanane, 2024) and digital surveillance (Roberts and Mare, 2024). Authors in this volume come primarily from the digital rights community and were naturally drawn to analyse the first-order effects of internet shutdowns using a human rights framework. However, this approach can lead to a focus on the symptoms of the disease and direct attention away from its causes. If internet shutdowns are to be ended, we argue, it is essential that we have an accurate diagnosis of their root causes to prescribe the most appropriate responses. For this reason, we encouraged researchers not to start their analysis with the shutdown event and end with the immediate first-order effects. Instead, we asked them to start with the historical and political context that gave rise to the internet shutdown and, after having assessed the triggering issues and the important first-order effects on citizens' rights and livelihoods, to persist with their analysis to identify the second-order effects on power relationships and the response in terms of resistance by citizens. This process-tracing approach is illustrated in Figure 1.1.

In this approach, we argue that these five dimensions of internet shutdowns are key to understanding the drivers, effects and responses to internet shutdowns and are useful in informing action to end rights-violating shutdowns. This five-dimensional approach is based on the following premises that are illustrated by the case studies in this book. The historical context for internet shutdowns is prior forms of media shutdown:

(i) Internet shutdowns are precipitated by and respond to other events such as protests
(ii) Internet shutdowns are responses to perceived threats to incumbent power
(iii) The first-order effect of internet shutdowns involves violation of fundamental human rights
(iv) The second-order effect of internet shutdowns aims to reinforce existing power
(v) Internet shutdowns often stimulate resistance and expressions of countervailing-power

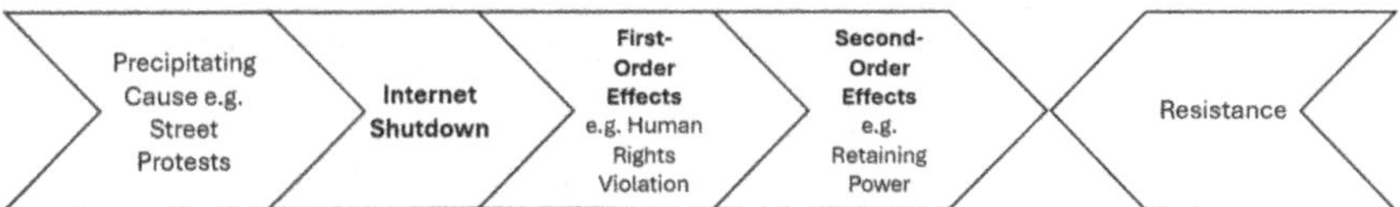


**Figure 1.1** First- and Second-Order Effects of Internet Shutdowns.

Source: authors

## Literature review

This literature review is organized in five sections. It first reviews how internet shutdowns are defined by scholars and how they are typologized before then reviewing the existing contextual literature on internet shutdowns in Africa to identify strengths and gaps. We then review the conceptual literature on technological affordances, human rights, and theories of power to provide a framework for analysing the drivers, dynamics and directions of internet shutdowns in Africa.

### Defining internet shutdowns

An internet shutdown is defined by Access Now (2016) as 'an intentional disruption of internet or electronic communications, rendering them inaccessible or effectively unusable, for a specific population or within a location, often to exert control over the flow of information'. It is important to note that in most African countries mobile cellular networks are the primary means of accessing the internet, so it is an effective means to disconnect citizens. During total internet shutdowns, access to both the mobile internet and broadband connectivity is completely cut. This is usually ordered by a government actor but implemented by a private company: a mobile phone company or internet service provider.

> An internet shutdown happens when someone – usually a government – intentionally disrupts the internet or mobile apps to control what people say or do. Shutdowns are also sometimes called 'blackouts' or 'kill switches'.
>
> Access Now (2016)

However, not all internet shutdowns are total outages. Partial internet shutdowns can be used to target specific geographical regions, particular networks (e.g. mobile phone networks) or certain websites or platforms such as Facebook or Twitter. The affordances of network infrastructure technologies provide increasingly sophisticated possibilities to the state and internet companies to target specific geographies, websites or groups of users with increasing precision. Shutdowns can be imposed nationwide, or they can be targeted to a specific neighbourhood, region or province. This raises the possibility of keeping the internet on in the central business district whilst imposing an internet shutdown in a region that opposes the government. Targeted shutdowns can be more difficult to detect and verify, particularly in remote regions and areas that are isolated from the outside world such as conflict zones that may not be accessible to journalists and human rights defenders for reasons of safety or government-imposed restrictions.

### Typology of internet shutdowns

Not all internet shutdowns are the same. There is a wide range in the frequency, duration and type of internet shutdowns experienced across Africa. This section provides a typology of internet disruption that will help the reader interpret the country case studies that follow.

Internet shutdowns can take many forms, depending on their objective and the technical means available to the perpetrator. Early internet shutdowns in Africa were complete shutdowns of all internet connectivity to all citizens nationwide. However, partial disruptions have become more common where only a specific social media platform is shut down, or only one region of the country is disconnected. Another form of internet disruption that falls short of a complete shutdown is a deliberate slowing down of the internet speed which is known as 'throttling'. Understanding the technical process of shutdowns is important for resistance as it can help pinpoint who is to blame and where to apply political pressure. When it is not clear what type of shutdown is happening or who is responsible it is difficult to attribute, anticipate or circumvent, making a line of accountability difficult to establish. The next section reviews what we know from the existing literature about the different types of internet shutdown.

Access Now (2022) identifies eight types of internet shutdowns classified by the technical means, or mechanisms, that authorities use to implement them. These can form part of a framework to analyse their scope, impacts and consequences.

1. **Fundamental infrastructure shutdown**: this refers to a shutdown implemented using a mechanism that is outside of the communications system itself, or that is caused by physical damage to the communications infrastructure. An example would be shutting down the power grid in an area in which opposition groups were concentrated (see Chapter 5 on Ethiopia in this volume).
2. **Routing**: this involves manipulating internet traffic routing to shut down all communications to and from specific nodes in the networking. One example is the eve of the 2016 election in The Gambia where routing of information at the country's international internet gateways caused an internet shutdown.
3. **DNS manipulation**: Domain Name System manipulation is related to routing but focuses on the addressing of specific internet domains. Perpetrators can manipulate servers to re-direct traffic away from intended domains like WhatsApp and towards servers either controlled by the perpetrators or that don't exist, thus causing a shutdown of the targeted services. DNS manipulation was suspected in Chapter 10 on Burkina Faso in this book.
4. **Filtering**: Perpetrators of internet shutdowns can use commercial filtering appliances, provided by private companies such as BlueCoat, Cisco and others, as well as transparent proxy devices to block access to forty commonly used communications platforms, such as Facebook, Twitter, or WhatsApp. This may have been the method used to enforce the Twitter (now X) ban discussed in Chapter 7 on Nigeria in this book.
5. **Deep Packet Inspection** (DPI): Authorities typically use DPI to carry out online surveillance, but if they use DPI online on key network trunks or backbones, they can also utilize the technology to cause internet shutdowns. Like filtering, DPI technologies are provided by private companies and require

close vendor involvement to implement and maintain on a national scale. OONI data has shown that Egyptian ISPs used this technique in 2016.

6. **Rogue infrastructure attack**: A rogue infrastructure attack happens when a perpetrator introduces a mechanism (usually temporary) to clone network infrastructure such that users connect their devices to the rogue infrastructure instead of the legitimate one, putting their communications in the hands of the operator of the rogue node. It is most often implemented on radio frequency-based networks, such as mobile cellular telecommunications, and WiFi.
7. **DDoS attacks**: Perpetrators use DDoS (Distributed Denial of Service) and other DoS (Denial of Service) attacks to target the communications of specific platforms, or even the internet communications of an entire country, as was the case in November 2016 when those behind the Mirai botnet tried unsuccessfully to shut down the submarine cable that connects the country of Liberia to the internet.
8. **Throttling**: Refers to the act of artificially restricting, but not stopping, the flow of data through a communications network. Throttling makes it appear as though internet access or a platform or service is available, but the level of interference is enough to make the service or resource effectively useless, for example by slowing 4G mobile communications to 2G speeds. Throttling was employed in Sudan and Zimbabwe shutdowns covered in this book.

This typology is useful for understanding the different types of internet shutdowns being deployed across Africa. As the chapters in this book illustrate, different types of internet shutdown are evolving within countries – moving from crude nationwide shutdowns to more targeted geographies or platform-specific shutdowns in order to more precisely punish opponents. Further refinement of these methods may make it possible to keep powerful economic allies online, thereby avoiding their economic costs, while still frustrating the organizing capacity of political opposition groups in working-class areas.

## *Internet shutdowns in Africa*

Although this is the first book to address internet shutdowns in Africa, there have been a number of notable studies, some of them by African authors. Ayalew (2019) analyses internet shutdowns in Ethiopia using a human rights framework. He shows how the 'cloak of national security' is used by the state to impose internet shutdowns to further the much narrower interest of a political party and ethnic group. Ayalew also demonstrates the impact on the national economy and on the right to information and freedom of expression and shows that internet shutdowns in Ethiopia are often timed to coincide with episodes of conflict and protest. Perpetrators often impose shutdowns to quell opposition protests, silence dissent or repress opposition party activities during elections. Nyarko and Ilori (2022) have shown how internet shutdowns have enabled authorities to cover up human rights abuses with impunity, both online and offline. A range of studies have documented the impact of internet shutdowns on social (Ilori, 2021), economic (CIPESA, 2017) and political life (Shandler, 2018).

In a special section of the *International Journal of Communication*, Marchant and Stremlau (2020) examined the causes and effects of internet shutdowns in Africa but also introduced some novel perspectives on what counts as an internet shutdown. Bergere's (2020) article in that special section looked at how the affordances of the technical infrastructure of the internet was enabling African governments to introduce new internet taxes that limit freedom of information and communication. Parks and Thompson (2020) note how restrictive legislation in Tanzania was causing 'internet slowdowns.' This nuanced approach led Marchant and Stremlau (2020) to argue that a diverse 'spectrum of shutdowns' might be a more useful frame of reference than a binary on/off conception of shutdowns. In the same special section Mare (2020) reflects critically on why private mobile and internet companies comply with government instructions to shut down the internet, given the loss of income and violation of rights that result from their actions. Ultimately, he concludes that, in the case of Zimbabwe, private operators comply in order to retain their operating licences, which are issued by the state, and to protect their staff from threats of arrest. Rydzak et al. (2020) extend the analysis to include a consideration of how internet shutdowns in Africa are often followed by escalations in citizens' resistance and mobilization against this rights-violating injustice.

Anthonio (2022), in her paper for Yale Law School, also uses a rights-based approach to analyse how internet shutdowns threaten fundamental human rights in Africa. She argues that shutting down the internet prevents communication with family and friends during crises, cloaks human rights abuses during conflict, amplifies the spread of false information and rumours and causes severe loss of income and economic damage. Anthonio and Roberts (2023) provide a historical overview since the first full African internet shutdown in Guinea and analyse more recent case studies from Ethiopia, Nigeria and Uganda to show how internet shutdowns limit digital citizenship and democratic participation and make recommendations for ending shutdowns and opening civic space.

The next section reviews the existing literature on the 'affordances' of technology for action.

## *Affordances*

Although censorship and information controls existed for decades before the internet, the technical configuration of the internet and mobile phone networks provides new action possibilities for repressive governments and their corporate partners. To analyse the difference that digitalization makes possible for media shutdowns, we find the concept of affordances helpful. The concept of affordances helps us to answer the question of what is new about internet shutdowns when compared with historical newspaper shutdowns or media blackouts in times of war or conflict. It also helps us to analyse in what ways internet shutdowns are qualitatively distinct from preceding forms of information control and censorship.

Affordances are defined as the 'new action possibilities' that a specific technology enables, invites or facilitates (Gibson, 1977; Norman, 1988; Roberts, 2017). The internet affords us the new action possibility of instantly messaging multiple recipients, globally, repeatedly at negligible marginal cost – sending them text, images and video. Affordances make new actions possible, but they do not determine them (Hutchby, 2001); a cup makes possible conveying liquid to the mouth, but a cup can also be used to hold pens. This is because technologies have 'interpretive flexibility' allowing them to be appropriated for purposes not envisaged by the original designer. Surveillance (over-seeing) cameras are deployed by law enforcement, but they can also be used by activists to capture footage of police violence in forms of 'sousveillance' (under-seeing) as a form of citizen power to resist police abuse of power (Mann, Jason and Wellman, 2003).

The technical infrastructure of the internet provides specific affordances for shutdowns, that is to say that it enables 'new action possibilities' for the state to shut down, throttle or otherwise restrict citizens' action possibilities to access information, communicate freely, and peacefully assemble and associate online (Bergere, 2020; CIPESA, 2017). As these rights are fundamental to producing counter-narratives and to building counter-power, it is clear that internet shutdowns afford powerholders new action possibilities in the contestation of power that increasingly takes place online.

## *Human rights*

A right is legally defined as a power or privilege held by the general public as the result of a constitution, statute, regulation, judicial precedent or other type of law (Cornell, n.d.). The fundamental human rights that all people are entitled to were codified and agreed by nations worldwide in the Universal Declaration of Human Rights (UDHR, 1948). Rights, including the right to privacy and to freedom of expression, political association and assembly, were further elaborated and expanded in the International Covenant on Civil and Political Rights (ICCPR, 1976) and rights including the right to work, to education and to take part in the cultural life of the community were articulated in the International Covenant on Economic, Social and Cultural Rights (ICESCR, 1976). African Union treaties on human rights include the African Charter on Human and Peoples' Rights (ACHPR, 1979) and the Maputo Protocol on the Rights of Women in Africa. International human rights law has been integrated into constitutions and domestic law to various degrees in countries across the continent.

Not only the state but also the private sector has a responsibility to promote and protect human rights. Businesses have a corporate responsibility to respect human rights under the UN Guiding Principles on Business and Human

Rights (often referred to as the Ruggie Principles) (UNHR, 2011). The OECD Guidelines for Multinational Enterprises (OECD, 2001) states that private business enterprises of any size or type should avoid infringing the human rights of others and should address adverse human rights impacts with which they are involved (ibid.). The United Nations recommends that businesses should have in place policies and processes designed to allow them to fulfil these obligations, including (a) a policy commitment to meet their responsibility to respect human rights; (b) a human rights due diligence process to identify, prevent, mitigate and account for how they address their impacts on human rights; (c) processes to enable the remediation of any adverse human rights impacts they cause or to which they contribute (UNHR, 2011). This is relevant here as many state-ordered internet shutdowns are implemented by private internet service providers of telecommunication companies. Publishing transparency reports about the incidence of service disruption are one means to facilitate impact mitigation and redress.

## *Digital rights*

Digital rights are existing human rights when using digital technologies such as mobile phones and the internet. Often digital rights are thought to refer narrowly to the right to information and communication (or the right to internet access) and sometimes discussion of digital rights is artificially limited to civil and political rights, such as the right to privacy or to freedom of expression. However, digital rights refer to the full range of civil, political, economic, social and cultural rights that all people are entitled to in international law. The United Nations Human Rights Commission has made it clear that 'the same rights that people have offline must also be protected online' (UNHRC, 2016).

There is an extensive literature focused on the application of human rights in digital contexts (Klang and Murray, 2005; Jorgensen, 2006; Andreassen and Crawford, 2013) much of which pre-dates the term 'digital rights'. This literature provides a rights-based framework that all countries have adopted into law and which can therefore be useful for analysing the introduction and impact of new technologies and phenomena including digital citizenship, digital disinformation, and internet shutdowns.

Digital rights are important because rapid technical changes have outpaced laws and regulation. Existing legal and regulatory frameworks were written in the pre-digital age and did not anticipate the challenges of algorithmic bias, digital surveillance or digital authoritarianism more widely. Governance is complicated by the fact that African citizens predominantly use digital platforms that are based in the United States or China, making it practically impossible for African governments to tax, regulate or otherwise govern the digital platforms on which social, economic and political life increasingly take place. Research shows that these foreign companies use technologies that are biased against women (Eubanks, 2019) and Black people (Noble, 2018), and which are used to systematically surveil citizens to produce data profiles used to target individuals and manipulate elections (Zuboff, 2019).

## *Internet shutdowns and digital rights*

Existing studies of internet shutdowns in Africa have focused primarily on their impact on citizens' civil and political rights, especially their effect on the right to expression. However, both the effects of internet shutdowns and the provisions of international human rights law extend beyond civil and political rights. In this book we show that internet shutdowns violate not just the rights codified in the International Covenant on Civil and Political Rights (ICCPR, 1976) but also the rights codified in the International Covenant on Economic. Social and Cultural Rights (ICESCR, 1976). For example, although researchers have begun documenting the enormous economic costs of internet shutdowns to business and commerce, to date this damage to livelihoods and freedom of trade has rarely been framed in the language of citizens' economic rights.

In this book we argue that it is useful analytically to frame the negative impacts of internet shutdowns as violations of citizens' social, economic and political rights. This is for three related reasons: firstly, because governments have clear obligations in international law to respect, protect, and promote those rights as signatories of the various conventions. Secondly, because it holds open the possibility for strategic litigation of the type pursued successfully in the ECOWAS court in West Africa, and thirdly these rights and legal obligations provide the potential basis for powerful alliances between business actors and civil society organizations to challenge the legitimacy of internet shutdowns and hold powerholders accountable. The next section reviews types of power analysis that can be used to better understand the power interests in play.

## *Concepts of power*

Although human rights are universal, the ability to exercise them is stratified. Everyone has the same human rights in theory; however, a person's ability to enjoy those rights in practice is often a function of power, including the power relations of gender, race and class. Nyamnjoh (2007) has argued that 'rights-talk' is insufficient to enable us to understand a world in which there are clear hierarchies in citizens' ability to exercise those rights. If a person's right to privacy or free expression is affected by their social status, gender, sexuality, age, party membership or ethnic group, then it can be argued that understanding these power relationships is at least as important as understanding human rights in any analysis.

It has also been argued that rights-based approaches provide an insufficient framework for critical analysis because they often focus attention on individual rights rather than social justice, and that although rights-based approaches may be very effective in diagnosing a problem, they do not provide any guidance when it comes to prescriptions for collective action (Cornwall and Nyamu-Musembi, 2004). Scholars point out that human rights themselves are the outcome of active processes of rights claiming and that gaining, defending and expanding them over time often requires an on-going power struggle of concerted collective action (Petit and Wheeler, 2005; Andreassen and Crawford, 2013).

It is for these reasons that we include power as well as rights in our framework for analysing internet shutdowns. This section reviews some concepts of power that can be useful for that purpose. As editors we wanted to encourage an assessment of power relations on internet shutdowns without being prescriptive in imposing specific concepts of power on authors. We wanted authors to be guided by their empirical data, their experiential knowledge and their research question(s) as to which conceptual lens they employed to analyse the interplay of power, rights and technology as it relates to internet shutdowns in Africa. After discussing a number of potentially useful concepts of power, authors made their own selections. Some of those chosen by multiple authors are reviewed briefly in the following sections.

**Power interests:** it is common to talk of governments protecting vested interests without specifying whether those are, for example, economic, political, gender or ethnic power interests. There are often multiple actors including government, private companies, regulators, courts and civil society organizations who have different power interests for supporting, facilitating or opposing elements of digital authoritarianism such as internet shutdowns. A comprehensive analysis of power interests requires building a table of actors (Schmeer, 1999; IIED, 2005) and detailing the different power interests of each actor as part of understanding the dynamics of the situation. Schmeer (1999) and IIED (2005) provide guidance about how to conduct power analysis to identify the different power interests in play in any particular scenario. Table 1.2 is for illustration only and does not relate to an actual empirical case. Expressions of power are reviewed in a section below.

**Table 1.2** Examples of Power Interests

| Stakeholder | Power interests | Expression of power | Source of power |
|---|---|---|---|
| **President** | Retaining military and sovereign power | Power over | Sovereign political |
| **Political party** | Retaining domination of ethnic group | Power over | Political |
| **Private company (Telco/ISP)** | Maximizing economic power | Power over | Wealth/Profit |
| **Regulator** | Balancing power interests | Power to | Legal |
| **Civil society organization** | Building collective power | Power with | Associational |
| **Citizen** | Maintaining autonomy, freedom and agency | Power within | Social capital |

Source: authors.

Power analysis is complicated by the fact that holders of political power are often holders of economic, media or other kinds of influencing power, making disaggregation problematic. In their power analysis some scholars use one form of power as their primary lens to provide in-depth understanding about that particular power interest. Other scholars chose as their analytic focus the intersection of two or more dimensions of power. bell hooks (1997, 2000) uses concepts like 'white-supremacist-capitalist-patriarchy' in her work to remind herself that power systems are interlocking systems of domination such that power analysis also needs to be intersectional.

## *The powercube*

Gaventa (2006, 2019) provides the 'powercube' as a three-dimensional framework for analysing the levels, spaces, and forms of power operating in any setting (as illustrated in Figure 1.2). The powercube is helpful for structuring a systematic analysis of the types of power operating in any space, including digital spaces. The powercube builds on Lukes' (1974; 2005; 2021) concepts of power, and on Cornwall's (2002) concepts of space, to enable a detailed analysis of how power operates in different spaces. The model is helpful in unpacking how different *forms* of power (visible, hidden, invisible) operate in different spaces (closed, invited, claimed) and at different levels (global, national, local) (see also Baltiwala, 2019). The powercube has been used in hundreds of studies of the spaces for community organizing and interaction with state actors (Gaventa, 2019) but only recently has it been applied to understand how power operates in digital spaces (Roberts and Hernandez, 2019; Faith, 2022).

**Spaces:** There are three *spaces* of power in the powercube framework. 'Closed spaces' are where decisions are taken behind closed doors by existing powerholders and vested power interests, where it is difficult or impossible for other citizens to be heard or influential. 'Invited spaces' are where representatives selected by powerholders are invited to participate in decision-making but under rules predetermined by the powerholders. Such spaces are common at all levels from global to national to local, and while they are not free of power relationships, they do provide opportunities for some contestation of power and interests. 'Claimed or created spaces' are created by less powerful actors either offline or online. In claimed or created spaces less powerful actors can co-determine the agenda and use the safe space provided to rehearse resistance, call power to account, or launch strategic litigation to claim rights.

**Forms:** There are three *forms* of power in the powercube model. 'Visible power' refers to the known rules and transparent mechanisms of decision-making. 'Hidden power' on the other hand refers to obscured and backstage mechanisms used by powerholders to determine who gets a seat at the decision-making table and what issues are on and off the agenda. 'Invisible power' is often called the most insidious form of power and refers to the powerful effect of dominant social norms and beliefs that cause people to internalize certain values and to consciously or

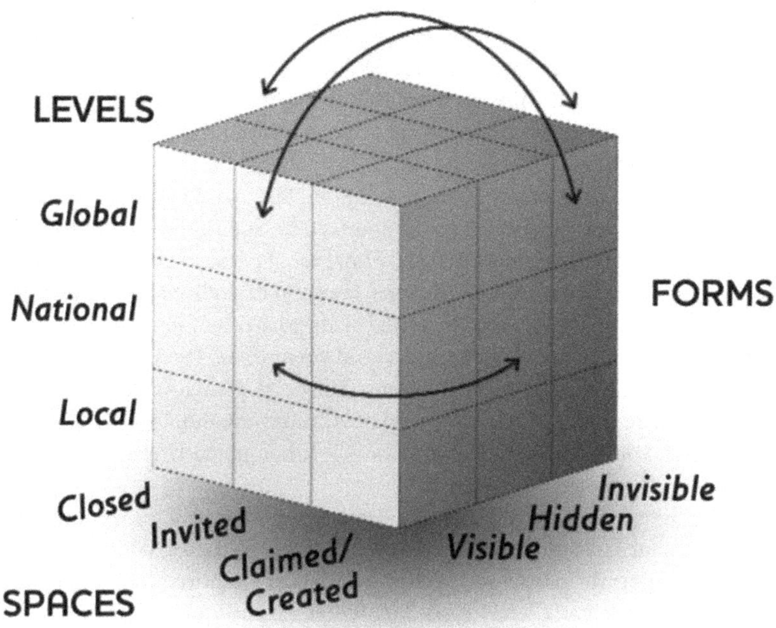


**Figure 1.2** Gaventa's Powercube.
Source: Gaventa, J. (2006) Powercube.

unconsciously self-censor, making some things taboo, unthinkable or unsayable. An example of this relevant to this book is state repression of dissenting views and opposition protests that leads to a 'chilling effect' whereby citizens become afraid to speak out and begin to self-censor what they say or post.

**Levels:** The three dimensions of levels, spaces, and forms of power may prove to be useful in analysing internet shutdowns. It may be that the people imposing shutdowns are global, national or local powerholders; their decisions may be very visible or hidden or deploying invisible power and may take place in closed or invited spaces. Citizens may be claiming new spaces to resist shutdowns, mobilize counter-power and campaign at local or global levels. In some countries shutdowns have become so frequent that they are normalized, leading to what we might term 'shutdown realism' where citizens internalize shutdowns as normal and justified, and where a 'chilling effect' results in citizens self-censoring their online comments to those they feel are acceptable to powerholders.

### *Agency and resistance*

Whilst it is a function of this book to provide rich case studies of how structural power relationships shape and are shaped by internet shutdowns, we intend to also highlight the agency (and counter-power) of those resisting internet shutdowns. To accomplish this, we argue that any comprehensive analysis of internet shutdowns requires attention both to the state's deployment of structural 'power over' to control narratives and opposition mobilization but also countervailing power in the form of collective citizen agency ('power with') mobilized to circumvent, challenge and hold state/corporate power to account.

In his classic study of power Lukes (1974; 2005; 2021) argued that agency is inherent to all power relationships. Agency is a person's ability to act in the world in pursuit of their values and interests. However, a person's ability to act is always constrained by the power of social norms, laws and disciplinary mechanisms. Most of the literature on agency is concerned with goal-orientated agency: a person's ability to act in pursuit of their values and preferences (Sen, 1999). However, a person's free agency is always constrained by social structure, by laws and norms and by power relations. A person's gender, ethnicity, wealth, literacy, ownership of media outlets or command over armies will fundamentally shape what they are able to do in the world.

Some theories of power see empowerment as increases in agency, especially by groups that have hitherto lacked that agency (Alkire, 2008; Kabeer, 1999). Here it is important not to see agency as a binary resource that a person either completely has or completely lacks but rather as a resource that people have to different degrees in different aspects of their life and at different times in their life. Even the prisoner in solitary confinement has some agency about how to react: whether to acquiesce or to resist (Sartre, 1943). Foucault, who is often presented as the straw man of structuralist conceptions of power, clearly argues (Foucault, 1995: 220) that 'the other (the one over whom power is exercised) [must] be thoroughly recognized and maintained to the very end as a person who acts'. As we will see in the chapters that follow, even when the internet is completely shut down, citizens have agency and resistance is fertile. 'Expressions of power' are one way of theorizing citizen agency as counter power.

## *Expressions of power*

Power is often defined as the ability to exert influence or 'power over' others, but it can be useful analytically to have more nuanced categories of power. Collective agency from below is also a form of power ('power with' others). From this perspective there is space to consider the power of even the most oppressed groups. VeneKlasen and Miller (2002) are among scholars who have defined and elaborated additional 'expressions of power' such as 'power within' (an internal sense of feeling able to effect change), 'power with' (collective power to act with others) and 'power to' (power to act in the world and change it) (Baltiwala, 2019). These agency-based expressions of power can be helpful in thinking through how to resist internet shutdowns and how to overcome authoritarian 'power over' (McGee, 2020). This book provides case studies of state-imposed internet shutdowns, but it also seeks to be attentive to the agency of citizens in evading or mitigating internet shutdowns. Expressions of power have not previously been applied to study internet shutdowns, but they may be appropriate for analysing forms of resistance to rights-violating shutdowns.

The next section provides an overview of the chapters that follow, including their approach to power analysis.

## *Chapter summaries*

In the chapters that follow, African authors analyse internet shutdowns in their own countries triggered by elections, protests, conflict, school exams and in retaliation for social media platforms censoring politicians. The chapters expand our empirical knowledge of the shutdowns by providing a range of rich case studies upon which other researchers can build.

In Chapter 2, Nompilo Simanje analyses how authorities in Zimbabwe cut off internet access during protest in 2019. She argues the shutdowns were intended to quell anti-government protests by removing rights to online association and expression. Simanje analyses the interplay between technological advancements, the exercise of government power, the violation of fundamental rights and citizen resistance in response. Simanje situates the internet shutdown within the long history of media controls in Zimbabwe starting under colonial rule. She identifies gaps in the existing literature about the power interests served by internet shutdowns. The author provides a rich case study and conducts a power analysis of the type of internet shutdown, the kinds of rights infringed, and the power interests advanced.

In Chapter 3, Arsène Tungali provides a fresh analysis of the longest full internet shutdown ever recorded in the Democratic Republic of the Congo (DRC). Tungali shows how, ahead of the 2018 election, the government-imposed shutdown negatively impacted the social, economic and political rights of 5 million citizens. The chapter carefully illustrates the wide range of impacts: families were unable to communicate, businesses were forced to close and the space for digital citizenship was closed almost entirely. The author highlights the scope and scale of the twenty-day long internet blackout, its impact on the electoral process and the wider effects on the ability of citizens to engage in online education, seek healthcare information, access legal services or take part in online deliberation and debate. The author uses interviews with citizens affected by shutdowns to analyse the power interests of the Congolese government and the impact on a wider than usual range of fundamental human rights.

In Chapter 4, Susan Mwape highlights the partial internet shutdown and social media restriction that occurred during the August 2021 elections in Zambia. The author focuses on the counter-power of civil society in pushing back against the anticipated shutdown, examining various advocacy and litigation efforts adopted in and outside the country. Mwape goes further, to analyse citizens' response to the social media restriction especially civil society and the youth. The author discusses in detail the role of state power and control, analysing the motivation of the political powerholders to repress dissent and maintain political power. She also uses key informant interviews to analyse forms of citizen agency and resistance and makes actionable recommendations to prevent reoccurrence of shutdowns in the future.

In Chapter 5, Yohannes Eneyew Ayalew and Lea Mehari Redae analyse the use of internet shutdowns as a weapon of war during the state-sponsored ethnic conflict in Ethiopia. No other African country has endured as many internet shutdowns in the last decade as Ethiopia. The authors provide the most comprehensive documentation of internet shutdowns in the country to date, before focusing in on three case studies from the Wollega insurgency (2019 to present); Tigray conflict (2021–2) and the armed conflict in the Amhara State (2023 to present). The authors address the impacts of internet shutdowns on the human rights and well-being of civilians as well as analysing which human rights are affected. Based on a qualitative analysis of recorded shutdowns and interviews with key informants, this chapter illustrates how internet shutdowns have been designed to curtail political discourse and participation, and to conceal atrocities and human rights violations.

In Chapter 6, Khattab Hamad focuses on Sudan, a country that experienced seventeen internet shutdowns between 2016 and 2023 – the second highest number in Africa. The chapter sets out to understand why the internet is so frequently disrupted in Sudan and provides the most detailed documentation to date of the frequency, duration and types of shutdowns. Importantly, it goes beyond this detail to study the sequence of events that precipitate shutdowns (such as popular uprisings of people's power), as well as providing an analysis of the impacts of internet shutdowns on human rights and power interests. The chapter documents abuse of media power to advance colonial power interests but also continuity in post-independence government censorship to advance their own power interests. Hamad shows how, in the digital era, social media-enabled citizens circumvent state-controlled media and make rights claims. However, this was perceived as a threat to the power of the President who frequently imposed internet shutdowns to retain his grip on power.

In Chapter 7, Thobekile Matimbe and Charles Kajoloweka analyse government-mandated internet disruptions in Nigeria between 2016 and 2023. They document the reasons offered by governments for adopting such measures and show how they violate international human rights law. Using desk research and online survey results from Nigerian citizens affected by internet shutdowns, the authors seek to understand the impact of shutdowns on a range of fundamental human rights. The chapter is unique in discussing the seven-month Twitter ban – the nationwide blocking of internet access to the micro-blogging platform Twitter (now known as X). The platform was effectively shut down in 2021 in retaliation for the company blocking posts made by the President that contravened the platform's terms of service by threatening violence. The chapter analyses the impact of the shutdown on millions of Nigerian citizens in terms of social, economic and political rights. The authors also analyse the implication of regional internet shutdowns in Zamfara State which were also imposed in 2021 by the Nigerian Communications

Commission citing national security concerns aimed at curbing waves of banditry activities in the region.

In Chapter 8, Qemal Affagnon sheds light on how authoritarian rulers in Chad have used internet shutdowns to suppress rights in the last decade and analyses the repercussions on citizens lives, human rights and on power relationships. Affagnon explores how authorities have violated citizens' social, economic and political rights in order to advance their own political interests of staying in power. The author provides a rich case study of a country which has received relatively little attention in the existing literature and welcome insight and analysis about how the imposition of internet shutdowns can deny citizens' rights to access information, communicate with colleagues and family members and thereby undermine their citizenship, affecting their ability to make informed choices and participate in the social and political life of the community. The author provides the most comprehensive documentation of internet shutdowns in Chad to date, analysing their duration, type, and the form of justification offered by the government for each shutdown.

In Chapter 9, Ababacar Diop discusses how recent internet shutdowns have tainted Senegal's otherwise good human rights record and why authorities resorted to these repressive measures to silence dissent and crack down on anti-government protests that began in 2021. The author argues that the shutdowns were politically motivated to preserve the interests of those in power amid tightened control of the online space by the incumbent government in the lead up to the country's presidential elections in 2024. Senegal had no record of internet shutdowns prior to 2021 and in many ways was a leader in human rights and enabling digital citizenship. Diop discusses how five internet shutdowns in just three years transformed the digital landscape of Senegal violating citizens' constitutional and digital rights. The author traces the impact of internet shutdowns across multiple dimensions of citizens' social, economic and political lives. He also highlights how citizens have mobilized to resist and challenge shutdowns and makes recommendations to mitigate and prevent them in future.

In Chapter 10, Harold Adjaho assesses the mobile internet shutdowns that occurred in Burkina Faso in November 2021 and January 2022 and how they made visible the flaws in democracy in this West African nation. The author highlights significant implications of these internet shutdowns in terms of democratic governance, their violations of the justice systems and human rights, as well as their impact on social and economic development in Burkina Faso. The author improves our understanding of the causes and impacts of internet shutdowns by analysing the underlying strategy to answer fundamental questions including: How and why did these internet shutdowns occur? What power interests motivated the internet shutdowns and how do they affect the rights of Burkinabe citizens? What were the socio-political and economic consequences of the shutdowns for Burkinabe citizens? What are the broader implications in terms of digital rights, freedom of expression and democratic governance?

In Chapter 11, Kassem Mnejja highlights how Algerian authorities have implemented internet shutdowns during school exams in every one of the last eight years. The chapter examines the reasons put forward by the Algerian authorities to justify the imposition of shutdowns in times of school exams as well as the damage and effects shutdowns have on a wider range of people's rights and the country's economy. Mnejja attempts to answer the following research question: How do exam-related internet shutdowns affect individual rights, economic stability, and broader societal dynamics in Algeria? To address this question, the conceptual framework integrates theories of media dynamics, power structures and digital rights, considering the historical context of media control in Algeria influenced by colonial legacies and post-independence governance. The chapter further adopts a human rights-based approach by comparing testimonies with detailed literature review, including the rights to work and business, education, healthcare, political association and expression and their intersection with digital rights. The chapter concludes with recommendations to end internet shutdowns and secure digital rights in Algeria.

In Chapter 12, Juliet Nanfuka examines how social media has provided an opportunity to amplify voices and narratives which were previously suppressed in the traditional media, highlighting how social media continues to challenge traditional power structures and political discourse in Uganda. She uses this perceived threat to incumbent power – the President has been in power for over twenty years – to explain why internet shutdowns were implemented ahead of recent elections. Nanfuka assesses the impact of the shutdowns on family life, economic development, and civic and political rights and freedoms. The author analyses how technology is used to further the political interests of a small ruling elite at the expense of the fundamental human rights of millions of Ugandans that are guaranteed in the constitution, international conventions and domestic law. She argues that internet shutdowns have been used cynically to entrench state power and to disrupt any form of counter-power. The chapter ends with a series of actionable recommendations to circumvent, mitigate and prevent future internet shutdowns.

An analysis of the lessons learned from these case study chapters is presented in the concluding chapter at the end of this book.

## *Bibliography*

Access Now (2016), *Internet Shutdowns and Elections Handbook: A Guide for Election Observers, Embassies, Activists, and Journalists*, https://www.accessnow.org/guide/internet-shutdowns-and-elections-handbook/

Access Now (2022), *A Taxonomy of Internet Shutdowns: The Technologies Behind Network Interference*, https://www.accessnow.org/wp-content/uploads/2022/06/A-taxonomy-of-internet-shutdowns-the-technologies-behind-network-interference.pdf

ACHPR (1979), *African Charter on Human and Peoples' Rights*, Addis Ababa: African Union. https://au.int/en/treaties/african-charter-human-and-peoples-rights

Alkire, S. (2008), 'Concepts and Measures of Agency', Working Paper 9. Oxford: OHPI.

Anderson, K. (2009), 'Iran Blocks TV, Radio and Phones – But Web Proves More Difficult', *Guardian*, https://www.theguardian.com/technology/2009/jun/15/iran-jamming-technology-tv-radio-internet

Andreassen, B. and Crawford, G. (2013), *Human Rights, Power and Civic Action: Comparative Analyses of Struggles for Rights in Developing Societies*, London: Routledge.

Anthonio, F. (2022), *The Kill Switch: How Internet Shutdowns Threaten Fundamental Human Rights in Africa and Beyond*, New Haven, CT: Yale Law School, https://law.yale.edu/sites/default/files/area/center/isp/documents/anthonio_kill-switch.pdf

Anthonio, F. and Roberts, T. (2023), Internet Shutdowns and Digital Citizenship, in T. Roberts, and T. Bosch (eds), *Digital Citizenship in Africa: Technologies of Agency and Repression*, London: Zed Books.

Ayelew, Y. (2019), 'The Internet Shutdown Muzzle(s) Freedom of Expression in Ethiopia: Competing Narratives', *Journal of Information & Communications Technology Law*, 28 (2): 208–24.

Baltiwala, S. (2019), *All about Power: Understanding Social Power and Power Structures*, CREA, https://reconference.creaworld.org/wp-content/uploads/2019/05/All-About-Power-Srilatha-Batliwala.pdf

Bergere (2020), '"Don't Tax My Megabytes": Digital Infrastructure and the Regulation of Citizenship in Africa', *International Journal of Communication*, 13: 4309–26.

Birhane, A. (2020), 'The Algorithmic Colonisation of Africa', *Scripted* 17(2), https://script-ed.org/article/algorithmic-colonization-of-africa/

CIPESA (2017), 'A Framework for Calculating the Economic Impact of Internet Disruptions in Sub-Saharan Africa'. Collaboration on International ICT Policy for East and Southern Africa, https://cipesa.org/2017/09/economic-impact-of-Internet-disruptions-in-sub-saharan-africa/

Cornell (no date), *Rights*, Cornell Law School, Legal Information Institute, https://www.law.cornell.edu/wex/category/legal_education_and_writing?page=23

Cornwall, A. (2002), 'Making Spaces, Changing Spaces: Situating Participation in Development', IDS Working Paper 170, Brighton, Institute of Development Studies.

Cornwall, A. and Nyamu-Musembi, C. (2004), 'Putting the "Rights-Based Approach" to Development into Perspective', *Third World Quarterly*, 25 (8): 1415–37, http://www.jstor.org/stable/3993794

Eubanks, V. (2019), *Automating Inequality: How High-Tech Tools Profile, Police, and Punish The Poor*, New York: Picador.

Faith, B. (2022), 'Tackling Online Gender-Based Violence; Understanding Gender, Development, and the Power Relations of Digital Spaces', *Gender, Technology and Development*, 26 (3): 325–40.

Foucault, M. (1995), *Discipline and Punish: The Birth of the Prison*, New York: Vintage Books.

Freyburg, T. and Garbe, F. (2018), 'Blocking the Bottleneck: Internet Shutdowns and Ownership at Election Times in Sub-Saharan Africa', *International Journal of Communication*, 12: 3896–916.

Gaventa, J. (2006), 'Finding the Spaces for Change: A Power Analysis', *IDS Bulletin*, 37(6): 23–33.

Gaventa, J. (2019), 'Applying Power Analysis: Using the "Powercube" to Explore Forms, Levels and Spaces', in R. McGee and J. Petit (eds), *Power, Empowerment and Social Change* (117–38), London: Routledge.

Gibson, J. (1977), 'The Theory of Affordances', in R. Shaw and J. Bransford (eds), *Perceiving, Acting, and Knowing*, London: Oxford University Press.

Giddens, A. (1995), *A Contemporary Critique of Historical Materialism*, Stanford, CA: Stanford University Press.

Hayward, C. (1988), 'De-facing Power', *Polity*, 31 (1): 1–22.

hooks, b. (1997), 'Culture, Criticism and Transformation', Media Education Foundation Transcript, https://www.mediaed.org/transcripts/Bell-Hooks-Transcript.pdf

hooks, b. (2000), *Feminist Theory: From Margin to Centre*, London: Pluto Press.

Hutchby, I. (2001), 'Technologies, Texts and Affordances', *Sociology*, 35(2): 441–56.

ICESCR (1976), International Covenant on Economic, Social, and Cultural Rights.

ICCPR (1976), International Covenant on Civil and Political Rights.

IIED (2005), *Stakeholder Power Analysis*. International Institute for Environment and Development, https://policy-powertools.org/Tools/Understanding/docs/stakeholder_power_tool_english.pdf

Ilori, T. (2021), 'Life Interrupted: Centering the Social Impacts of Network Disruptions in Advocacy in Africa', Global Network Initiative, https://globalnetworkinitiative.org/wp-content/uploads/2021/03/Life-Interrupted-Report.pdf

Jorgenson, A. K. (2006), 'Critical Globalization Studies. Contemporary Sociology', 35 (6): 629–30. https://doi.org/10.1177/009430610603500654 (Original work published 2006).

Kabeer, Naila (1999), 'Resources, Agency, Achievements: Reflections on the Measurement of Women's Empowerment', *Development and Change*, 30 (3): 435–64.

Klang, M. and Murray, A. (Eds). (2005). *Human Rights in the Digital Age* (1st ed.). London: Routledge-Cavendish, https://doi.org/10.4324/9781843146278

Kuo, R. and Marwick, A. (2021), 'Critical Disinformation Studies: History, Power, and Politics'. *Harvard Kennedy School (HKS), Misinformation Review*, https://doi.org/10.37016/mr-2020-76

Lukes, S. (1974; 2005; 2021), *Power: A Radical View*, London: Macmillan.

Mann, S., Jason, N. and Wellman, B. (2003), 'Sousveillance: Inventing and Using Wearable Computing Devices for DataCollection in Surveillance Environments', *Surveillance & Society*, 1(3): 331–55.

Marchant, E. and Stremlau, N. (2020), 'A Spectrum of Shutdowns: Reframing Internet Shutdowns from Africa', *International Journal of Communication*, 14, 4327–42.

Mare, A. (2020), 'Internet Shutdowns in Africa: State-Ordered Internet Shutdowns and Digital Authoritarianism in Zimbabwe', *International Journal of Communication*, 14: 4244–63.

Mburu Nyokabi, D., Diallo, N., Ntesang, N., White, T. and Ilori, T. (2019), 'The Right to Development and Internet Shutdowns: Assessing the Role of Information and Communications Technology in Democratic Development in Africa', *Human Rights Journal*, 147–72.

McGee, R. (2020), 'Rethinking Accountability: A Power Perspective', in R. McGee and J. Pettit (eds), *Power, Empowerment and Social Change*, London: Routledge.

Noble, S. (2018), *Algorithms of Oppression: How Search Engines Reinforce Racism*, New York: New York Press.

Norman, D. (1988), *The Design of Everyday Things*, New York: Basic Books.

Nyamnjoh, F. (2007), *Insiders and Outsiders: Citizenship and Xenophobia in Contemporary Southern Africa*, London: Zed Books.

Nyarko, G. and Ilori, T. (2022), 'Litigating Internet Shutdowns in Africa: A Guide on Approaching the African Commission on Human and Peoples' Rights and the African Court on Human and Peoples' Rights', Optima, https://internews.org/wp-content/uploads/2022/08/Guide-on-Litigating-Internet-Shutdowns-in-Africa.pdf

OECD (2001), *OECD Guidelines for Multinational Enterprises: Global Instruments for Corporate Responsibility*, Paris: Organisation for Economic Co-operation and Development, https://www.oecd.org/en/publications/2001/11/oecd-guidelines-for-multinational-enterprises-2001_g1ghgb46.html

Okunola, A. (2018), 'A Timeline of Internet Blockages in Africa', Tech Cabal, https://techcabal.com/2018/05/03/a-timeline-of-internet-blockages-in-africa/#:~:text=Guinea%20(February%202007),protests%20calling%20for%20his%20resignation

Parks, L. and Thompson, R. (2020), 'The Slow Shutdown: Information and Internet Regulation in Tanzania from 2010 to 2018 and Impacts on Online Content Creators', *International Journal of Communication*, 14: 4288–308.

Petit, J. and Wheeler, J. (2005), 'Developing Rights?', *IDS Bulletin*, 36 (1): 1–8.

Roberts, T. (2017), 'Participatory Technologies: Affordances for Development', in J. Choudrie, M. Islam, F. Wahid, J. Bass and J. Priyatma (eds), *Information and Communication Technologies for Development. IFIP Advances in Information and Communication Technology*, 504: 194–205, Springer, https://link.springer.com/chapter/10.1007/978-3-319-59111-7_17

Roberts, T. and Bosch, T. (2023), *Digital Citizenship In Africa: Technologies of Agency and Repression*, London: Zed Books, https://www.bloomsburycollections.com/monograph?docid=b-9781350324497

Roberts, T. and Hernandez, K. (2019), 'Digital Access Is Not Binary: The 5 'A's of Technology Access in the Philippines', *Electronic Journal of Information Systems in Developing Countries*, 85 (4): e12084.

Roberts, T. and Karekwaivanane, G. (2024), *Digital Disinformation in Africa: Hashtag Protest, Power and Propaganda*, https://www.bloomsburycollections.com/monograph?docid=b-9781350319240&st=digital±disinformation

Roberts, T. and Mare, A. (Eds) (2025), *Digital Surveillance in Africa: Power, Agency and Rights*, London: Zed Books.

Roberts, T. and Mohamed Ali, A. (2021a), 'Opening and Closing Online Civic Space in Africa: An Introduction to the Ten Digital Rights Landscape Reports', in T. Roberts (ed.), *Digital Rights in Closing Civic Space: Lessons from Ten African Countries*, Brighton: Institute of Development Studies, https://doi.org/10.19088/IDS.2021.005; https://opendocs.ids.ac.uk/articles/online_resource/Digital_Rights_in_Closing_Civic_Space_Lessons_from_Ten_African_Countries/26430283?file=48079486

Roberts, T. and Mohamed Ali, A. (2021b), 'Opening and Closing Online Civic Space in Africa: An Introduction to the Ten Digital Rights Landscape Reports', in T. Roberts (ed.), *Digital Rights in Closing Civic Space: Lessons from Ten African Countries*, Brighton: Institute of Development Studies, https://opendocs.ids.ac.uk/opendocs/handle/20.500.12413/15964

Rydzak, J., Karanja, M. and Opiyo, N. (2020), 'Internet Shutdowns in Africa| Dissent Does Not Die in Darkness: Network Shutdowns and Collective Action in African Countries', *International Journal of Communication*, 14: 24.

Sartre J. (1943), *Being and Nothingness*. Washington, DC: Washington Square Press.

Schmeer, K. (1999), *Guidelines for Conducting a Stakeholder Analysis*. Bethesda, MD: Partnerships for Health Reform, Abt Associates Inc.

Shandler, R. (2018), 'Measuring the Political and Social Consequences of Government-Initiated Shutdowns', https://www.usenix.org/system/files/conference/foci18/foci18-paper-shandler.pdf

Sen, A. (1999), *Development as Freedom*, New York: Alfred Knopf.

UDHR (1948), *Universal Declaration of Human Rights*.

UNHCR (2016), 'Human Rights Council Thirty-second session Agenda item 3', United Nations A/HRC/32/L.20, https://www.article19.org/data/files/Internet_Statement_Adopted.pdf

UNHR (2011), *Guiding Principles on Business and Human Rights*, https://www.ohchr.org/sites/default/files/documents/publications/guidingprinciplesbusinesshr_en.pdf

VeneKlasen, L. and Miller, V. (2002), *A New Weave of Power, People and Politics*, Oklahoma: World Neighbours.

Zuboff, S. (2019), *The Age of Surveillance Capitalism: The Fight for a Human Future at the New Frontier of Power*, New York: PublicAffairs.

# Chapter 2

## Zimbabwe's 2019 internet shutdown

## The interplay of technology, rights and power

Nompilo Simanje

### *Introduction*

This chapter analyses Zimbabwe's longest ever internet shutdown in January 2019 with specific attention to the motivations of the powerholders who implemented the shutdown and the agency of citizens resisting its implications on fundamental human rights. This internet shutdown, which occurred amidst protests in the country, lasted for six days, and internet access was only restored following a court order by the High Court of Zimbabwe. The Cost of Shutdown Tool[1] projected that Zimbabwe lost at least USD 5.7 million per day in direct economic costs, for every day that the internet was shutdown (Nanfuka, 2019). The timing of internet shutdowns also hampers the documentation and blocks the communication of human rights violations. During this shutdown in Zimbabwe, the Zimbabwe Human Rights NGO Forum (2019) documented several human rights atrocities which included seventeen extra judicial killings, arbitrary arrests and cases of rape and sexual violence perpetrated by state security agents.

However, this was not the first time that the Zimbabwean authorities had restricted access to the internet and other digital platforms. If anything, this was an extension of the government's modus operandi in its attempts to control access to information as has been noted in its influence over traditional media. While internet shutdowns may seem like a new phenomenon in Zimbabwe, with the first partial internet shutdown having been recorded in July 2016 (Mare, 2020), Zimbabwe is, however, not new to censorship and true to Kperogi's (2022) words '*internet censorship is intimately linked with the wider censorship practices in the mainstream media*'.

State control of the media has also been noted through its influence of the public broadcaster, the Zimbabwe Broadcasting Corporation (ZBC) which was established in 1980. Several studies have concluded that the ZBC is not a true public broadcaster but instead a state-controlled broadcaster whose editorial policy has been influenced by the government (Masuku, 2011).

Closer attention should however be paid to internet shutdowns because, in this digital age, internet access plays a significant role in every facet of society, be it legal, health, education, business or politics. Internet shutdowns have grave implications for the socio-economic and political landscape of any country, including the realization of socio-economic, civil and political rights.

This chapter therefore seeks to address the following question:

*How did the 2019 internet shutdown in Zimbabwe reflect the interplay between the exercise of government power over technology, and the potential infringement on fundamental rights?*

The remaining sections of this chapter will be organized as follows: the next section will provide a political history of media controls in Zimbabwe. It will also provide a review of information from existing publications about the 2019 shutdown in Zimbabwe and identify gaps in that literature before reviewing concepts of power, rights and technology that can be used to analyse internet shutdowns. Findings from a web-based survey of fifteen people representing civil society, the media and academia and secondary data analysis will also be analysed as part of this case study through the lens of technology, power and rights. The chapter will conclude with some tentative recommendations for key stakeholders and conclusions.

## *Background*

The history and context of internet shutdowns in Zimbabwe cannot be approached in isolation from the overall regulation of the media landscape and the information ecosystem in the country. State control has been noted in various stages of media development including both in the colonial and post-colonial era. Ever since the colonial period, the media has been subjected to varying degrees of control by successive governments (Moyo and Chabwinja, 2018). In all these stages, what is clear has been government attempts to regulate citizens' access to information, mainly as a means of consolidating power, protecting government interests and minimizing criticism.

**1888–1979** During colonial rule, Zimbabwe's media was controlled by Britain to serve its imperialist power interests. The Rhodesian press primarily catered for the white community to facilitate their loyalty to the colonial mission and safeguard the economic interests of the British South African Company. Entertainment news through newspapers like the *Bantu Mirror* targeted the black community to 'channel their thoughts away from politics' (Willems, 2014).

During the leadership of Zimbabwe's first Prime Minister Ian Smith, between 1964 and 1979, there was forced closure of several media outlets that were not aligned to the regime's interest, and these included the *African Daily News*, *The Central African Examiner* and other African nationalist publications that were critical of the regime (Windrich, 1979). Favourable media was relied on to disseminate propaganda and disinformation to counter the narrative of Uhuru[2] from the growing liberation movement.

The censorship and control of the media was also complemented by legislative developments in attempts to further entrench colonial rule and limit media freedom and freedom of expression. Such laws included the Official Secrets Act in 1970 and the Law and Order Maintenance Act (LOMA). The Official Secrets Act was designed to prevent the disclosure of state secrets and counter espionage, but its provisions went, and still go, beyond that to unjustifiably limit fundamental rights (Veritas, 2016). While the Official Secrets Act has remained in force to date, LOMA was repealed in 2002 and replaced by the Public Order and Security Act (POSA). POSA was later also replaced and repealed in 2019 by the Maintenance of Peace and Order Act (MOPA) which also governs demonstrations, gatherings and processions and impacts freedom of assembly and expression (ICNL, 2019).

**1980–2007** Zimbabwe attained its independence on 18 April 1980, and in the immediate post-liberation period, the government continued to control the media and ensure that it served political party interests as well as Shona ethnic power interests. Chabikwa (2024) reveals coordinated disinformation campaigns that state aligned actors launched to propagate a narrative that Gukurahundi was a national security necessity and not a war. Gukurahundi is the term used to describe state-sponsored violence that targeted Ndebele-speaking civilians in Matebeleland and Midlands provinces between 1983 and 1987. State media and a network of social media accounts were relied on to spread this disinformation.

Media freedom under the colonial rule was regarded as comparable to the post-colonial era (Moyo and Chagwinja, 2018). In the post 2000 period Zimbabwe featured prominently among countries that maintained tight controls on information channels (Kperogi, 2022).

State control was also noted in the telecommunication industry with only the Posts and Telecommunications Corporation of Zimbabwe (PTC) having monopoly in the industry. Econet Wireless challenged this monopoly through a constitutional challenge based on the right to information and the court ruled in its favour in 1995 allowing Econet to be allocated a mobile telecommunications licence (Velamuri, 2003). In 2000, Capital Radio Challenge also approached the court and challenged provisions of the Broadcasting Act. Muzulu (2020) notes that state monopoly over the airwaves started breaking between 1994 and 2000 because of these constitutional court orders.

Of note, was the enactment of the 2002 Access to Information and Protection of Privacy Act (AIPPA) and the Protection of Order and Security, 2002 which were viewed as part of the Zimbabwean government's onslaught of independent press in Zimbabwe (Mukasa, 2003). Post the enactment of AIPPA, several newspaper shutdowns were noted. Newspapers critical of the government, such as the *Daily News*, closed after bombs exploded at their offices and the government refused to renew their licence (Moyo and Chabwinja, 2018). Arrest, intimidation and harassment of journalists immediately followed the enactment of AIPPA (Moyo, 2014).

In summing up the environment, (Melber, 2004) highlighted that

> the current situation in Zimbabwe under the ZANU-PF government shows increasing signs of abuse of power by those in political control. They also

> direct their desire to suppress criticism towards the media. Press organisations in private ownership have been closed and journalists have been physically harassed, arrested and expelled. Laws are abused to regulate and manipulate public opinion by a policy of banning.

**2008–16** As digital media started taking root in Zimbabwe, so did increased state control, including arrests for online expression. In 2008, Zimbabwe experienced a political shift due to the establishment of the Government of National Unity (GNU) following a contested general election. Media credibility was already limited due to state ownership and control, which was resulting in the media being openly biased in favour of the ruling ZANU PF party (Moyo, 2010). During this election, citizens actively used the internet and mobile phones in the campaigning and monitoring process of the contested election. This signalled the increased uptake of digital technologies and ICTs in Zimbabwe.

In 2010, the then main opposition political party, Movement for Democratic Change (MDC), introduced an audio service across three mobile network operators, Econet Wireless, Netone and Telecel, which allowed citizens to engage with the opposition on its policies, events and news round-up. Three days after the launch of this program, the government advised the mobile operators to cut off the service or risk losing their business licences. Econet Wireless is reported to have complied and blocked the service while the other lines remained open (*The Zimbabwean*, 2010). Chuma (2018) notes that the MDC had also devised the strategy of sending out regular SMS briefings to communicate directly with the public as the media broadcasting remained closed to voices other than those of the ruling party (Chuma, 2018).

The Postal Telecommunications Regulatory Authority of Zimbabwe (POTRAZ) also banned the use of the Blackberry smartphone in 2011 due to its encryption features which were believed to be a security concern as they restricted the government's capacity to monitor and intercept communications in terms of the Interception of Communications Act (*Newsday*, 2011). The then Constitution did not provide for the right to privacy and privacy of communications, as is the case with the current 2013 Constitution that explicitly provides for the right to privacy in Section 57, including the privacy of communication. Ahead of the 2013 elections, POTRAZ is reported to have ordered the blocking of bulk text messages from Kubatana Trust of Zimbabwe which distributed civil society and human rights information through bulk text messages sent through the international gateway system (IT Web Africa, 2013).

In 2014, Edmund Kudzayi, was arrested for allegedly using a pseudonym 'Baba Jukwa' on Facebook since 2013 to post sensitive information relating to state officials and politicians (Tvelt, 2014). While the charges were later withdrawn, the government enforced digital censorship in various ways, including facilitating the removal of the Facebook page of 'whistleblower' Baba Jukwa in 2014 (Madenga, 2021).

The enactment of the 2013 Constitution with an extensive Bill of Rights was a significant development, with the Constitution also providing in Section 61 for freedom of expression and freedom of the media.

It is through the increased reliance on social media platforms like Facebook and WhatsApp that digital activism found its roots in Zimbabwe, which birthed online movements like the #ThisFlag Movement and the #Tajamuka/Sesijikile Movement. The #ThisFlag movement started in 2016 after one Pastor Evan Mawarire published a video that trended online bemoaning the failing economic situation in the country and highlighting the symbolism behind the Zimbabwean flag (Karekwaivanane and Mare, 2019). The #Tajamuka campaign was another movement which translated to English meant 'we are rebelling'. Stemming from the above, in July 2016, the Zimbabwean government blocked access to the social media platform, WhatsApp (Freedom House, 2016).

Following this social unrest, the government proposed the introduction of the Computer Crime and Cyber Crime Bill which was believed to be an attempt to restrict access to social media, monitor private communications, and restrict access to information online as a way of stifling calls for political and economic reform (Freedom House, 2016). The law was later enacted in 2021 as the Cyber and Data Protection Act.

### *2017–23*

Zimbabwe experienced a political shift in November 2017, when the then President Robert Mugabe was ousted through a military coup and replaced by current President Emmerson Mnangagwa. Hundermark (2022) argues that the Mnangagwa regime continued the legacy of his predecessor Robert Mugabe which included violent crackdowns on protests pushing citizens to embrace alternative forms of activism including online campaigns.

In 2017 when access to the internet and mobile network was down for a day, the government and internet service providers attributed it to severed cables in South Africa, but some observers suspected government involvement (Marchant and Stremlau, 2020).

The January 2019 internet shutdown was imposed during a time when there were ongoing protests over an increase in fuel prices. This increase in the cost of fuel was one indicator of the general increase in the cost of living (Amnesty International, 2019).

However, several changes have been noted, including the 2019 repeal of the Access to Information and Protection of Privacy Act and its replacement with the Freedom of Information Act 2020, the Zimbabwe Media Commission Act, 2020 and the Cyber and Data Protection Act, 2021. While this was a significant milestone in Zimbabwe's law reform, the Media Institute of Southern Africa (MISA, 2020) noted that there is still a need to reform other laws and align them to the Constitution, such as the Official Secrets Act, Interception of Communications Act among others, which have provisions that continue to undermine fundamental rights.

In principle, media plurality and diversity started to improve in Zimbabwe significantly in 2020, as the Zimbabwean government licensed six private television stations while eight community radio stations were also licensed in 2021. Diversity concerns were still raised (MISA, 2020).

On 20 February 2022, Netblocks (2022) documented internet throttling[3] in Zimbabwe, mainly affecting the capital city Harare, on a day when major opposition political party, Citizens Coalition for Change was hosting a political rally ahead of the by-elections. Ahead of the 2023 general elections, internet throttling was also reported on 22 August 2023, the eve of the elections, with an internet slow down being recorded on Netone, Telone, Econet and Liquid (MISA, 2023).

The history of internet restrictions in Zimbabwe has therefore been centred around political and economic upheavals, with these restrictions being relied on by the government to limit access to information and restrict the capacity of the citizens to mobilize.

The above narrative shows how powerholders, across different eras in colonial and post-colonial Zimbabwe, have abused their authority to control the media and subsequently regulate the exercise of fundamental rights like media freedom, freedom of expression, access to information and freedom of assembly and association. The shutting down of the internet is therefore not because of the technology itself or alleged risks that it poses but rather it is merely the modern version of newspaper shutdowns, media blackouts, blocking of bulk SMS etc.

It is in that regard that this chapter will use the concepts of power and rights to analyse the 2019 internet shutdown. Before the analysis, the next section will describe the circumstances surrounding the 2019 internet shutdown for the reader who is unfamiliar with the context.

## *Unpacking the 2019 Internet Shutdown*

On 18 January the government ordered a total internet shutdown, which lasted six days, with internet access being restored on 24 January, following an order of the High Court (Access Now, 2019). However, as highlighted above, Zimbabwe has a history of internet restrictions spanning across several years. Chimedza (2024a) notes that Zimbabwe has experienced eight notable internet restrictions either as internet shutdowns or as throttling.

The January 2019 internet shutdown, however, remains one of the major internet shutdowns in Zimbabwe's history of internet restrictions. It started off as a partial internet shutdown on 15 January, restricting access to platforms like Facebook, WhatsApp and Twitter in response to ongoing protests at the time. This was the second day of the stay-away, a form of general strike or protest where people were told to 'stay away' from work. Karombo (2019) notes that Zimbabweans resorted to using Virtual Private Networks (VPNs) to circumvent the block and continue accessing these platforms, while others resorted to using alternative messaging platforms like Telegram.

One of the mobile network operators, Econet Wireless, released a statement highlighting that they had been ordered to shut down the internet totally. The directive was issued by the then Minister of State Responsible for National Security in the President's Office, supposedly acting in terms of the Interception of Communications Act (MISA, 2019). The reasoning behind this government's

**Table 2.1** History of Internet Shutdowns in Zimbabwe

| Date of internet shutdown | Circumstance associated with the internet shutdown |
|---|---|
| 1. July 2015 | There were ongoing national stay-away protests against government corruption and economic mismanagement. Reports of internet disruptions and partial blocking of social media platforms, including WhatsApp. (Chimedza, 2024b) |
| 2. July 2016 | Internet disruption and slow down recorded ahead of a planned nationwide protest against the government's economic policies. Access to social media platforms and messaging applications especially WhatsApp and Facebook was restricted for several hours. (CIPESA, 2016) |
| 3. August 2018 | In the aftermath of the 2018 harmonized elections, protests and violence erupted, leading to intermittent disruptions of internet connectivity. Access to social media platforms such as Facebook, Twitter, and WhatsApp were temporarily blocked for several hours. (Internet Society Pulse, 2024) |
| 4. January 2019 | The government ordered a nationwide blackout following widespread protests against fuel price increases and economic hardships. This shutdown lasted for six days and is the focus of this chapter. |
| 5. February 2022 | Media reports confirmed a significant slowing of internet service for several hours on Sunday 20 February 2022, as a major political opposition rally was held in the capital city, Harare. (*Zimbabwe Independent*, 2022) |
| 6. March 2022 | Reports of a series of internet disruptions amidst protests organized by opposition political parties (Human Rights Watch, Zimbabwe Events of 2022) |
| 7. August 2023 | Ahead of the 2023 harmonized elections, NetBlocks, a network measurement organization reported that the quality of internet access was degraded on 22 August 2023, the eve of the election. |

Source: author.

approach was the need to promote public order and national security, with some media reports (*The Herald*, 2019) referring to the Arab Spring as an example to justify the need to control access to the internet. The Arab Spring was a series of protests and uprisings in the Arab world that started off in Tunisia before spreading to other countries including Egypt (Douglas and Khouri, 2014). Social media networks were relied on during the Arab Springs by activists to organize demonstrations, amplify their demands and share information.

This shutdown was also country-wide, affecting all Zimbabweans. DataReportal (2019) highlighted that, as of January 2019, mobile subscriptions were 13.04 million, amounting to 76 per cent of the population while internet penetration was 40 per cent, which translated to 6.08 million internet users. This was the total number of people that were impacted by the internet shutdown. Marchant and Stremlau (2020) indicated that due to general limited access to the internet and poor quality of internet, some communities especially in rural and marginalized communities do not experience the full impact of internet shutdown.

During the time when the internet was shut down, several human rights violations also occurred and the capacity to raise awareness widely was limited. Zimbabwe NGO Forum (2019) documented a total of 1803 human rights violations and reported that these were mainly perpetrated by officers from the Zimbabwe National Army and the Zimbabwe Republic Police. These violations included 954 cases of arbitrary arrests, seventeen extra judicial killings and 586 cases of assault, among others.

Information gathered from medical sources which indicated that the nature of injuries treated in medical centres in Belvedere, Manresa and Parktown in Harare between 14 and 16 January included those resulting not only from gunshots, but also from beatings with boots, blunt instruments such as wooden logs, abrasions from being dragged on tarmac, and from sharp and penetrating objects (Amnesty International, 2019). Citizens were, however, also able to communicate through direct calls and text messages.

Madziwa (2021) highlighted that delivery of healthcare in the Bulawayo metropolitan province was also disrupted because of the internet shutdowns. This included the failure by patients to access health information online, failure to communicate with their physicians and failure to make online payments for medical bills. For the physicians, the negative impact included failure to conduct telehealth consultations and failure to access patient records online, among others. Both patients and the physicians demonstrated strong reliance on emails and WhatsApp as platforms for communication, both of which were inaccessible because of the internet shutdown.

From the education sector, Tarisayi and Munyaradzi (2021) highlighted that teachers bemoaned the disruption of their research and communication amongst themselves, with the school administration and management of sporting activities across the schools.

Small businesses in Zimbabwe were reported to have lost an estimate of $12 million per day since the imposition of the internet shutdown (Chimhanga, 2019). The country also lost millions of dollars in delayed revenue inflows as import and export processing had been slowed down due to the internet shutdown (Telecompaper, 2019).

This internet shutdown also restricted the citizens' online participation in democratic debate and interactive dialogue. This was coupled with the restricted exercise of freedom of assembly and association online and the limited access to information that was in the public interest in such a period of unrest (Matshazi, 2019).

Following the January 2019 internet shutdown, the Media Institute of Southern Africa and the Zimbabwe Lawyers for Human Rights filed an urgent application before the High Court of Zimbabwe, challenging the warrant that was relied on to order the internet shutdown (Veritas, 2019). In its interim order, the High Court suspended forthwith the directives or warrants issued by the Minister of State or the Director-General of POTRAZ, shutting down internet communications, and ordered the ISPs to unconditionally resume full and unrestricted internet services to all subscribers.

## *Literature review*

Several articles and reports have been published on the January 2019 internet shutdown in Zimbabwe, covering various thematic areas including its implications on digital rights and its impact on the economy, as well as the political and business interests served.

With regard to power, Baltiwala (2018) identifies five different expressions of power, which include the power to, power over, power within, power under and power with. Power over, is the direct or indirect control over other people. 'Power to' is an expression of counter-power or agency and resistance demonstrated by the citizens individually to challenge other forms of power. On the other hand, 'power with' is the power to confront and challenge injustice by finding, mobilizing and joining hands with others who face the same injustice, or care about the same cause, hence a reflection of collective power. These expressions of power will be analysed in this chapter in the context of the 2019 internet shutdown in Zimbabwe.

SALC and MISA (2020) focused on navigating litigation during internet shutdowns in Southern Africa and highlight the necessary aspects to consider when developing a litigation strategy which would include mapping the applicants, the respondents, the requisite procedures, among others. Their report also broadly highlights the socio-economic impacts of internet shutdowns and regional and international human rights frameworks that apply to the internet. By proposing strategic litigation as one of the mechanisms that can be relied on to address internet shutdowns, this report demonstrates the concept of agency and resistance by highlighting the legal mechanisms at national, regional and international levels that people affected by internet shutdowns can rely on to challenge them. MISA and SALC demonstrate that government power should not go unchecked but rather that there are mechanisms that can be utilized to facilitate checks and balances.

A further review by Mare (2020) focused on how state-ordered internet shutdowns in Zimbabwe point to digital authoritarianism while highlighting why the private sector complies with directives to shut down the internet. Digital authoritarianism is the use of digital technologies by those who hold power to restrict the democratic space and curtail the use of mobile and internet tools in online civic engagement (Roberts and Bosch, 2021). Mare (2020) noted that private telecommunications operators and internet service providers comply with government partly to abide by their licensing obligations, for fear of political harassment and victimization and because of threats of arbitrary imprisonment. Mare relied on the political economic logic of internet shutdowns.

Mare (2020) highlighted that the government derives its power over the private sector by owning and controlling four of the five international gateways. He further notes that there is demonstrated capture of the regulator of the telecommunications sector, POTRAZ, by the political elites, which undermines its independence and enables the state to abuse its power and impose internet shutdowns. In so doing, Mare's account can be interpreted as using the concept of 'power over' which is one of the expressions of power used to analyse the power relations between the government, companies and citizens. As highlighted above, this was the case of the 2019 internet shutdown as the government issued a directive ordering the mobile network operators and internet service providers to shut down the internet. This concept is also highlighted from the perspective that the private sector also complies with government directives to safeguard their economic interests.

Other reports have focused on human rights violations that were perpetrated during the 2019 internet shutdown. The Zimbabwe Human Rights NGO Forum (2019) for example, documented the atrocities that were perpetrated by state actors when the internet was shut down. The internet shutdown created an enabling environment for state actors to further abuse their power through arbitrary arrests and extra judicial killings among other human rights violations. This demonstrates the continued urge by state authorities to safeguard their political power and political interests in the face of resistance.

Kperogi (2022) grounded his research on the concept of agency and resistance by unpacking what he termed 'protest journalism and citizen dissidence on social media'. This is when citizens use the power of social media to confront state oppression. However, because of this, states respond through censorship by shutting down the internet.

Building on the above, this chapter will assess the interplay between technology, the exercise of government power, and digital rights. This will be guided by the concepts of power interests and expressions of power to analyse the 2019 internet shutdown.

## *Methodology*

This chapter combined desk research, qualitative analysis of academic and media reports on the 2019 internet shutdown with primary data from a web-based survey of fifteen people. The survey was administered through Google forms as an anonymous form that did not collect any personally identifying information. The consent and anonymity policy also highlighted that the feedback from the survey was going to be used only for the purposes of this book chapter.

The survey targeted various actors from the media, civil society, academia and the private sector who were carefully selected based on their expertise and sectors they represent, to reflect a multi-stakeholder approach and diversity in the feedback. The survey was administered for a period of two weeks in May 2024. This survey assessed the primary reasons behind the 2019 internet shutdown and their justification, the impact of the shutdown including on human rights and based on previous trends with internet restrictions in Zimbabwe, whether there would be other internet shutdowns in the future. The survey participants also shared their opinions on how the 2019 internet shutdown demonstrated the interplay between technology, power and rights and their recommendations to stakeholders.

## *Findings*

The survey participants highlighted that the government indicated that the internet shutdown was imposed for the protection of public order and safety. While the aforementioned reasons were acknowledged as having been the official position from the government, other survey respondents believed the shutdown was aimed at cracking down on protests and limiting the capacity of the citizens to mobilize. This demonstrated that internet shutdowns were a response to citizen agency and resistance, with the government entrenching its political interests.

> The government had no right to limit access to information during the critical time. It was important for citizens to know what was going on and be in a better place to know which places to avoid during the protest time. Shutting down the internet interfered with this.
>
> Civil society representative

The above was feedback from a survey respondent representing civil society whose approach was viewed from the rights perspective. The respondent was also of the opinion that the reasons proffered to justify the internet shutdown were not reasonable and justifiable as the protests did not pose any legitimate threat to public order or national security. In that regard, the internet shutdown is believed to have failed the three-pronged test on the limitation of fundamental rights.

> It was not clear which places were safe from state security during the protest time when the state security was setting dogs and firing live ammunition on protesters and doing dragnet arrests to see who had been violent during the fuel price hike protests and who was looting. The State actually posed a security risk to the public.

The above was feedback from a survey respondent who emphasized that shutting down the internet during ongoing protests posed a risk to the physical security of the citizens. This response stemmed from a rights perspective, highlighting how the internet shutdown affected the right to physical security. Further rights that were reported to have been unjustifiably impacted by the internet shutdown included freedom of expression, media freedom and socio-economic rights.

The above implications on fundamental rights were also earlier reiterated in a 2019 article by a local journalist who noted that

> The Internet shutdown flew in the face of President Emmerson Mnangagwa's assertion that Zimbabwe is open for business. The shutdown greatly weakened investment prospects in Zimbabwe because no serious investor would invest in a country that shuts down the internet at the slightest whiff of unrest … Additionally, the shutdown constrained not only the flow of information around the protests, but it restricted the flow of business-related information and communications including Internet-based banking services and transactions.

The above analysis of the internet shutdown was based on the concept of affordances by highlighting that the internet is an enabler for socio-economic and political rights, hence shutting down the internet restricts the realization of those rights.

One of the survey respondents from the civil society sector focused the preservation or consolidation of power by state actors through internet shutdowns. The survey respondent highlighted that government exercises power over both citizen rights and businesses. The respondent highlighted the following:

> In context, Zimbabwe went through a coup in 2017 and even though elections were held in 2018, the military remained in control of government and their preferred candidate was in power. The government of Zimbabwe in 2019 was therefore heavily controlled by the military and can be described as authoritarian. In an authoritarian government, I believe power is heavily skewed towards the state with very little accountability or restraints with the power the government holds. The government therefore has power over citizens and civilian institutions. The directive to shut down the internet violated the rights of citizens. Any digital rights, technological innovation or transformation processes can only exist and grow where there is a conducive environment. The power dynamics existent in 2019 meant that the rights of people mediated by technology can be violated with impunity in an authoritarian environment.

Commenting on the court's decision from the litigation process, MISA Zimbabwe (2019) highlighted that the court did not consider whether the government has the right to completely shut down the internet and, if so, whether the Interception of Communications Act is the proper law to effect internet shutdowns or any other disruptions of communications. This brings in a different angle on the power dynamics, especially from the perspective of power interests which was also raised as part of the administered survey. The failure by the court to explicitly address the constitutional aspects of the court application is another demonstration of the concept of power interests.

> The judicial avoidance in addressing the legality or illegality of internet shutdowns in Zimbabwe also provides a platform for further abuse of power by the State to impose internet shutdowns. They didn't bother to follow due process and arbitrarily ordered the internet shutdown. This was confirmed by the judgement.

The above feedback was shared by a representative from academia to demonstrate the abuse of political power by the Executive in complete disregard of due process. The fact that an official without the requisite authority issued a directive ordering the shutdown of the internet is a highlight of the abuse of power to protect certain interests. While the Interception of Communications Act was recently amended, one of the survey respondents indicated that

> The blatant discretion in the Cyber and Data Protection law which amends the Interception of Communications Act and gives unfettered power to the Minister

> to order any other measures with regard to communications can be seen to empower ordering Internet shutdowns. This should be amended.

The above was feedback from a survey respondent and through this observation, the respondent also shows that powerholders also entrench their interests through legislation which allows them to exercise their powers without the requisite oversight mechanisms. This is an example of hidden power exercised in closed spaces where parties with vested interests can maintain power and privilege by removing key issues from public discussion or oversight (Institute of Development Studies, 2009).

With internet shutdowns, one aspect that is clear is the correlation among the different concepts regarding power, technology and rights. Through the lens of affordances, it is clear that technology is an enabler for several fundamental rights. Technology is providing platforms for citizens to exercise rights like media freedom and freedom of expression, access to information and freedom of assembly and association. However, state power can also interfere with the enjoyment of these rights.

> The shutdown demonstrated how government uses power to muzzle free speech.

The above was feedback from a survey respondent who is part of the media sector. This brings in a very key aspect around state power and fundamental rights; more so, that while fundamental rights might be guaranteed for example through the Bill of Rights in the Constitution, due to power interests, the enjoyment of such rights can be limited.

> The government's decision to shut down the internet demonstrated the power that authorities possess to control and restrict these rights through technological means. It highlights the potential misuse of power by governments to curtail civil liberties and maintain control. From a different angle, this event demonstrated how detrimental it can be to have a government that has control of telecommunication services in Zimbabwe.

The above was feedback from a survey respondent from the media sector who highlights the interrelationship between all the concepts pertaining to technology, power and rights. This was aptly highlighted by a survey respondent from the diplomatic community who highlighted that 'Tech can only flourish if politics allow'. However, this does not mean state power will go unchecked, hence bringing in the concept of agency and resistance.

## *Power interests and the 2019 internet shutdown*

The Zimbabwean government through various officials including the Minister of Information have proffered various reasons for why they consider internet shutdowns to be lawful, justifiable and necessary. These reasons include that internet shutdowns are necessary to maintain public order, they prevent the use of social media to propagate false information, they prevent violence and conflict and because human rights are not absolute.

During the 2019 partial internet shutdown, on 19 January 2019, the then Zimbabwean Minister of Information, Senator Monica Mutsvangwa, addressed the media, and presented a paper titled: 'Information as a threat to national security' (*The Chronicle*, 2019). The Minister justified internet shutdowns as necessary to regulate and manage information, safeguard national security, remove the negative effects of the information revolution including the use of social media by opposition parties and civil society to depict the country as failing. Using the lens of power, it can be noted that internet shutdowns are a way of entrenching state monopoly and power over political narratives while suppressing dissenting or opposing views. At the same time, it was also a violation of rights to freedom of expression, media freedom and freedom of assembly and association.

Speaking at the 2022 Internet Governance Forum in Addis Ababa Ethiopia, the Minister of Information, Monica Mutsvangwa, is reported to have said the following about the lawfulness of internet shutdowns,

> Shutdowns during conflicts could be attempts by governments across the world to prevent the use of digital platforms and social media to spread propaganda and fake news which may result in more bloodshed, loss of life and even genocide .... there is a need to maintain connectivity and free access at all times but balancing the right of the population to digital access and the right of the population to safety and peace.
>
> (*The Herald*, 2022)

From the above, it is clear is that the government intended to tighten control of the internet to limit access to information by the citizens and protect government power interests by minimizing 'negative reportage'. While national security is a common justification for internet shutdowns, the concept is regarded as overbroad in its definition and therefore susceptible to abuse (UNESCO, 2021). In light of the above, it is clear that what is claimed as national interest is actually partisan interests of certain public officials, political elites or political parties. This is particularly so in light of the above impact of the 2019 internet shutdown on access to information, access to health, access to education and the negative impact on business and economic interests. The narrative of promoting 'national interest' is therefore difficult to justify and instead what is clear is the promotion of narrower power interests.

Chari (2024) aptly describes this phenomenon by highlighting that internet shutdowns are mainly instituted by African governments for political preservation and yet are rationalized as a necessity to protect national security, state security and for the preservation of the moral and societal fabric.

CIPESA (2019) also demonstrates this correlation of power and internet shutdowns by highlighting that 77 per cent of the countries that imposed internet shutdowns were categorized as authoritarian under the Democracy Index produced by the Economist Intelligence Unit (1998). The list of authoritarian regimes included Zimbabwe.

## *Affordances, citizen resistance and agency*

It has been noted that governments with democracy deficits, regardless of the numbers of their citizens that use the internet, fear the power of the internet in enabling citizen organizing and empowering ordinary people to speak truth to power (CIPESA, 2019). This also showcases another key aspect regarding technology, power and rights – being the way technology has also empowered citizens toward the full realization of their rights and enabling them to demand accountability from their governments. For example, Chabikwa (2024) notes that state-controlled media had effectively silenced any discussion of the Gukurahundi genocide that was perpetrated in the early 1980s in the Zimbabwean media, but the advent of social media provided a relatively free online civic space where citizen discussion of Gukurahundi and demands for justice could not be completely supressed.

In August 2020, the hashtag #ZimbabweanLivesMatter went viral on Twitter worldwide. The hashtag was launched to critique the repression, human rights abuses and economic mismanagement perpetrated by the Zimbabwean government on its citizens. At its peak, the hashtag was used in more than 700,000 tweets a day demonstrating powerful public criticism (Karekwaivanane, 2024).

Social media affords citizens the ability to exercise the right of association and assembly to dissent and protect in ways not safe in physical space in Harare. Social media affords citizens the ability to circumvent state media and establishment political parties and raise the alarm about human rights violations; digital technologies afford citizens the ability to reach a global audience instantly, repeatedly, affordably and using text, images and video. In doing so, digital tools expand the ability of citizens to exercise, defend and expand their digital rights. Using the lens of expressions of power, social media enables citizens to build collective 'power with' and to exercise agency or 'power to' hold government to account.

To interfere with that citizen power, governments have resorted to internet shutdowns and in other instances arrests for online expression. For example, in July 2020, prominent investigative journalist Hopewell Chin'ono was arbitrarily arrested for allegedly inciting violence following posts that he made on social media, calling on citizens to participate in the anti-corruption demonstrations that took place on 31 July 2020 around the country (Front Line Defenders, 2021). This had also been the case of Zimbabwe in 2016, wherein WhatsApp was blocked during the #ThisFlag movement, or the 2019 internet shutdown during protests.

This sentiment was also shared by one of the survey respondents who acknowledged that 'the 2019 internet shutdown in Zimbabwe disempowered civic groups from organizing against the government'.

Amnesty International (2019) summed up Zimbabwe as 'open for business, closed for dissent' as it exposed the instruments of suppression used by the Zimbabwean authorities to disperse assemblies, silence dissent and clamp down on protestors and ordinary people calling on the state to improve their livelihoods and demanding accountability during the national stay-away that led to the January 2019 internet shutdown. 'Zimbabwe is open for business' is the mantra used by President Emmerson Mnangagwa to sum up his foreign policy in 2018 focused on economic growth (Ndimande and Moyo, 2018).

In the same light, citizens have also used their agency to come together, which is an expression of 'power to', using strategic litigation to form 'power to' so as to hold the government to account for its abuse of power through the imposition of internet shutdowns. Following the internet shutdown, Zimbabwe Lawyers for Human Rights (ZHLR) and Media Institute of Southern Africa (MISA) approached the court in a strategic litigation matter. This demonstrated the principle of 'power to' by highlighting the agency or counter-power that lies in civil society actors that ensure that there is sufficient oversight on government power. The government argued that Section 6 of the Interception of Communications Act authorizes the Minister to impose an internet shutdown; so while the internet shutdown impacted the realization of fundamental rights, that limitation of the rights was lawful. The Court's decision was that the Minister of State who issued the warrant did not have the authority or was not conferred such powers by the President who has the mandate to assign the administration of the Act to the Minister (Veritas, 2019).

Mare (2020) notes that this 'ruling has serious implications in terms of reconfiguring the unequal power relations between state and nonstate actors because, despite the assumed "capture" of the judiciary by the political elite, the ruling by judge Owen Tagu is one of few incidences in which the courts have called the government to order'. In light of this, while civil society actors demonstrate agency by approaching the courts and the courts act as arbitrators, the ability of the court to also uphold justice is also another expression of power.

According to Veritas (2019), government statements following the court decision highlighted that 'the Act as it stands is not only consistent with the Constitution but gives Government the power, albeit through the correct official to impose an Internet shutdown and/or to interrupt social media applications whenever it believes such action to be justified'. The government's argument was therefore that it derives power from existing legislation and, in particular, the Interception of Communications Act. This position sought to rely on the expression of 'power over' the citizens using legislation, although in this case it was challenged by another expression of power, being 'power to'.

## *Recommendations*

This chapter has highlighted the various expressions of power in the context of internet shutdowns and in particular, learning from the 2019 internet shutdown in Zimbabwe. From the lens of agency and resistance, which is the expression of 'power to' and 'power with', there are several viable measures to consider for preventing internet shutdowns in Zimbabwe or to push back against internet shutdowns. One of the avenues that has already been explored is strategic litigation, as noted in the case of *MISA Zimbabwe and Zimbabwe Lawyers for Human Rights versus Minister of State for National Security and Others* highlighted in this chapter.

From the above perspective, civil society and the media can also raise awareness among members of the public on the implications of internet shutdowns on both the human rights and the socio-economic landscape to cultivate citizen agency in the advocacy against internet shutdowns. In addition, civil society have an oversight role to play in ensuring that government exercise of power over technologies and access to technologies does not go unchecked. This can also include building the capacity for monitoring and documenting human rights atrocities committed during internet shutdowns as noted by Chimedza (2024b).

The absence of legal clarity on the legality or illegality of internet shutdowns in Zimbabwe creates an opportune environment for abuse of power by state actors to overregulate technology including through imposing internet shutdowns. In that regard, both state and non-state actors should consider advocating for legal reform that introduces checks and balances where other actors, for example, the Minister has unfettered powers to exercise discretion with regard to ICTs while also explicitly highlighting the illegality and disproportionate of internet shutdowns like the 2019 total internet shutdown in Zimbabwe.

As noted in this chapter, when states impose internet shutdowns they also demonstrate their power over the private sector. However, as a key measure to consider, the private sector should disclose any requests by state authorities to restrict internet access. This should be included as part of human rights policies in these companies, guiding the private sector on how to handle government requests. Mobile network operators and Internet Service Providers should also be guided by the United Nations principles on business and human rights. Mare (2020) also highlights that the same litigation approach utilized by civil society actors may also empower private telecommunication operators and internet service providers to resist future government orders on the basis of legal precedent.

## *Conclusion*

This chapter set out to answer the research question of how the 2019 internet shutdown in Zimbabwe reflects the interplay between the exercise of government power over technology, and the potential infringement on fundamental rights. This question was answered from the concept of power assessing the aspects of power interests, expression of power and agency and resistance. When this internet shutdown was viewed from the perspective of power interests, it was evident that internet shutdowns do not serve national or public interests but rather the political interests of a few, especially in light of shutdowns' grave implications on human rights.

Internet shutdowns in Zimbabwe are not isolated developments but rather they demonstrate the continued exercise of government power to regulate the media, information dissemination and the exercise of fundamental rights. Such exercise of state power has also been noted in the regulation of traditional media during the colonial and post-colonial era in Zimbabwe. Legislative developments have also been relied on to consolidate that power as noted in laws like the Interception of Communications Act, Official Secrets Act and the Presidential Powers (Temporary Measures) Act among others.

From the perspective of expression of power, it was clear that governments believe that they derive the power to shut down the internet from legislation, including that human rights are not absolute. In that regard, when governments shut down the internet, they will be exercising their power over the internet and over the citizens.

However, through agency and resistance, citizens also derive power from the internet which enables them to mobilize and challenge forms of censorship and suppression. Further, as noted through regional and international standards that Zimbabwe is a party to, internet shutdowns are not a reasonable, justifiable and proportionate limitation to fundamental rights; more so, total internet shutdowns like the 2019 one. This enables citizens to rely on national, regional and international mechanisms including strategic litigation to challenge internet shutdowns. In conclusion, the concepts relating to power, rights and technology, in as far as internet shutdowns are concerned, are intertwined.

## *Notes*

1 The Cost of Shutdown Tool estimates the economic impact of an internet disruption, mobile data outage or application restriction.

2 The Swahili term for freedom or independence.

3 Internet throttling is the practice of intentionally slowing down internet speeds (without shutting it down completely), making it difficult or impossible for users to upload or download information. Throttling can also target specific services, applications and platforms, rendering them unusable.

## *Bibliography*

Access Now (2019), *Zimbabwe Orders a Three-Day Countrywide Internet Shutdown*, https://www.accessnow.org/press-release/zimbabwe-orders-a-three-day-country-wide-internet-shutdown

Access Now (2021), *Internet Shutdowns and Elections Handbook: A Guide for Election Observers, Embassies, Activists and Journalists*, https://www.accessnow.org/guide/internet-shutdowns-and-elections-handbook/

Amnesty International (2019), 'Open for Business, Closed for Dissent: Crackdown in Zimbabwe during the National Stay Away 14–16 January', https://www.amnesty.org/en/documents/afr46/9824/2019/en/

Baltiwala, S. (2018), 'All About Power: Understanding Social Power and Power Structures, Creating Resources for Empowerment in Action', CREA, https://creaworld.org/wp-content/uploads/2020/07/All-About-Power.pdf

Chabikwa, R. (2024), '(Re)writing History: Discursive Practices of Gukurahundi Disinformation on Twitter', in T. Roberts and G. H. Karekwaivanane (eds), *Digital Disinformation in Africa: Hashtag Politics, Power and Propaganda*, London: Bloomsbury Publishing.

Chari, T. (2024), 'Internet Shutdowns in Africa, Triggers and Rationalization', in T. D. Oyedemi and R. A. Smith (eds), *Media in Africa: Issues and Critiques* (1st edn). London and New York: Routledge, https://doi.org/10.4324/9781003352907

Chimedza, B. (2024a), 'Fighting Back Against Internet Shutdowns in Zimbabwe', *Internet Society Pulse*, https://pulse.internetsociety.org/blog/fighting-back-against-internet-shutdowns-in-zimbabwe

Chimedza, B. T. (2024b), 'Building the Capacity for Monitoring and Documenting Human Rights Violations during Internet Shutdowns: A Zimbabwe Needs Assessment Report', https://www.linkedin.com/posts/bright-chimedza-207282142_needs-assessment-internet-shutdowns-in-zimbabwe

Chimhanga, K. (2019), 'Amid Civil Unrest, Internet Shutdowns Are Making Zimbabwe's Economic Crisis Worse', https://advox.globalvoices.org/2019/01/29/amid-civil-unrest-internet-shutdowns-are-making-zimbabwes-economic-crisis-worse

Chuma W. (2018), 'The Politics of Media Policy Making in a Contested Transition', *International Journal of Communication*, 12: 2387–405.

CIPESA (2016), 'Zimbabwe Becomes the Latest Country to Shut Down Social Media', https://cipesa.org/2016/07/zimbabwe-becomes-the-latest-country-to-shut-down-social-media/

CIPESA (2019), 'Despots and Disruptions: Five Dimensions of Internet Shutdowns in Africa', https://cipesa.org/2019/03/despots-and-disruptions-five-dimensions-of-internet-shutdowns-in-africa/

Data Reportal (2019), 'Digital in Zimbabwe', https://datareportal.com/digital-in-zimbabwe

Douglas, C. and Khouri, R. (2013), *The Arab Uprisings: Causes, Consequences and Perspectives: An Extended Discussion of a Panel Discussion with Rami Khouri*. Kennesaw State University, Georgia, United States of America, http://icat.kennesaw.edu/docs/pubs/RK_Final_Paper.pdf

Economist Intelligence Unit (2020), *Democracy Index 2019: A Year of Democratic Backsliding and Popular Protest*, https://www.democracywithoutborders.org/12764/eiu-report-2019-a-year-of-democratic-setbacks-and-popular-protest/

Freedom House (2016), 'Zimbabwe: Government Proposes Tighter Controls over Social Media', https://www.africa-newsroom.com/press/zimbabwe-government-proposes-tighter-controls-over-social-media?lang=en

Frontline Defenders (2021), 'Charges against Human Rights Defender and Journalist Hopewell Chin'ono Nullified', https://www.frontlinedefenders.org/en/case/human-rights-defender-hopewell-chinono-detained-and-charged

Human Rights Watch, *Zimbabwe Events of 2022, World Report 2023*, https://www.hrw.org/world-report/2023/country-chapters/zimbabwe//

Hundermark, C. (2022), '*#ZimbabweanLivesMatter vs #ThisFlag*: A comparative discourse analysis of two social media movements in Zimbabwe', Masters in Media Studies, University of Cape Town, South Africa, https://open.uct.ac.za/bitstreams/8924464f-82ad-4bd2-92de-a1303ddcbe02/download

Institute of Development Studies (2009), Powercube: Understanding Power for Social Change, https://www.ids.ac.uk/projects/powercube-understanding-power-for-social-change/

International Centre for Not-for-Profit Law (2019), 'Practical Guide: Zimbabwe's Maintenance of Peace and Order Act' (Chapter 11: 23).

Internet Society Pulse (2024), 'Fighting Back against Internet Shutdowns in Zimbabwe', https://pulse.internetsociety.org/blog/fighting-back-against-internet-shutdowns-in-zimbabwe

IT Web Africa (2013), 'Zimbabwean Regulator "Blocks" Bulk SMS as Election Nears', https://itweb.africa/content/WnpNgM2AEDR7VrGd

Karekwaivanane, G. and Mare, A. (2019), '"We Are Not Just Voters, We Are Citizens!": Social Media, the #ThisFlag Campaign, and Insurgent Citizenship in Zimbabwe', in *Social Media and Politics in Africa: Democracy, Security and Surveillance*, London: Zed Press.

Karekwaivanane, G. and Msonza, N. (2021), 'Zimbabwe Digital Rights Landscape Report', in T. Roberts (ed.), *Digital Rights in Closing Civic Space: Lessons From Ten African Countries*, 43–60, Brighton: Institute of Development Studies.

Karekwaivanane, G. H. (2024), 'Disinformation on a Shoestring: Examining the Anatomy and Strategies of the Pro-State Network in the Zimbabwe Twitterverse', in International Centre for Not-for-Profit Law.

Karombo, T. (2019), *Zimbabweans Switch to Telegram as Social Media Remains Down*, ITWeb, https://itweb.africa/content/DZQ587VPb5QqzXy2

Kemp, S. (2019), Digital 2019 Zimbabwe, https://datareportal.com/reports/digital-2019-zimbabwe

Kperogi, F. A. (2022), *Digital Dissidence and Social Media Censorship in Africa*, London: Taylor & Francis.

Madenga, F. (2021), 'From Transparency to Opacity: Storytelling in Zimbabwe under State Surveillance and the Internet Shutdown', *Information, Communication & Society*, 24(3): 400–21, https://doi.org/10.1080/1369118X.2020.1836248

Madziwa, P. K. (2021), 'Effects of Network Disruptions on Health Service Delivery among Private Practicing Physicians in Bulawayo Metropolitan Province, Zimbabwe, https://internews.org/wp-content/uploads/2022/08/Network-Shutdowns-and-the-Health-Delivery-System-in-Zimbabwe.pdf

Marchant, E. and Stremlau, N. (2020), 'A Spectrum of Shutdowns: Reframing Internet Shutdowns from Africa', *International Journal of Communication*, 14: 4327–42.

Mare, A. (2020), 'State Ordered Internet Shutdowns and Digital Authoritarianism in Zimbabwe', *International Journal of Communication*, 14: 4244–63.

Masuku, J. (2011), *The Public Broadcaster Model and the Zimbabwe Broadcasting Corporation (ZBC): An Analytical Study*, South Africa: Stellenbosch University.

Matshazi, N. (2019), *Digital Rights Lessons from Zimbabwe's Internet Shutdown*, Zimbabwe: Media Institute of Southern Africa.

Melber, H. (Ed.) (2004), *Media Public Discourse and Political Contestation in Zimbabwe*, Uppsala, Sweden: Nordiska Afrikainstitutet.

MISA Zimbabwe (2019), 'High Court Sets Aside Internet Shutdown Directives', https://zimbabwe.misa.org/2019/01/21/high-court-sets-aside-internet-shut-down-directives/

MISA Zimbabwe (2020), 'New Information Law Should Set Pace for Repeal of Other Draconian Laws', https://zimbabwe.misa.org/2020/07/02/new-information-law-should-set-pace-for-repeal-of-other-draconian-laws

MISA Zimbabwe (2023), 'Internet Degrade on the Eve of Elections', https://zimbabwe.misa.org/2023/08/22/internet-degrade-on-the-eve-of-elections/

Moyo, D. (2010), 'The New Media as Monitors of Democracy: Mobile Phones and Zimbabwe's 2008 Election', *Journal for Communication Studies in Africa*, 29, https://journals.co.za/doi/pdf/10.10520/EJC144878

Moyo, L. (2014), 'Freedom of the Press, the Zimbabwean Situation up to 2009', *Mediterranean Journal of Social Sciences*, http://dx.doi.org/10.5901/mjss.2014.v5n27p1543

Moyo, L. and Chabwinja, T. (2018), 'Media and Democracy in Zimbabwe', Alice, South Africa: Department of Communication, University of Fort Hare.

Mukasa, S. D. (2003), 'Press and Politics in Zimbabwe', *African Studies Quarterly*, 7 (2–3): http://www.africa.ufl.edu/asq/v7/v7i2-3a9.pdf

Muzulu, P. (2020), 'End ZBC's Honeymoon', ZimEye, https://www.zimeye.net/2020/11/28/end-zbcs-honeymoon/

Nanfuka, J. (2019), CIPESA and Open Net Africa join public call against internet shutdown in Zimbabwe

Ndimande, J. and Moyo, G. K. (2018), 'Zimbabwe Is Open for Business: Zimbabwe's Foreign Policy Trajectory under Emmerson Mnangagwa', *Afro Asian Journal of Social Sciences*, IX (II): 1–25. https://www.researchgate.net/publication/327982537_'ZIMBABWE_IS_OPEN_FOR_BUSINESS'_ZIMBABWE'S_FOREIGN_POLICY_TRAJECTORY_UNDER_EMMERSON_MNANGAGWA

Netblocks (2022), 'Internet Slow Down Limits Coverage of Zimbabwe Opposition Rally', https://netblocks.org/reports/internet-slowdown-limits-coverage-of-zimbabwe-opposition-rally-oy9Ykoy3

*Newsday* (2011), 'BlackBerry Services Remain "Banned"', https://www.newsday.co.zw/telecommunications/article/242158/blackberry-services-remain-banned

Roberts, T. and Bosch, T. (2021), 'Case Study: Digital Citizenship or Digital Authoritarianism', Paris: Organization for Economic Cooperation and Development.

Share, F. (2019), 'Minister Calls for Laws Regulating Social Media', *Chronicle*

Slade, B. V. (2017), The Law of General Application Requirement in Expropriation Law and the Impact of the Expropriation Bill of 2015, *De Jure Law Journal*, 50 (2): 346–62.

Southern Africa Litigation Centre and Media Institute of Southern Africa (2020), 'Navigating Litigation during Internet Shutdowns in Southern Africa', https://www.southernafricalitigationcentre.org/wp-content/uploads/2019/08/SALC-Internet-Shutdown-Guide-FINAL.pdf

Tarisayi, K. S. and Munyaradzi, E. (2021), 'A Teacher Perspective on the Impact of Internet Shutdown on the Teaching and Learning in High Schools in Zimbabwe', *Human Behaviour & Emerging Technologies*, 3 (1): 169–75, https://doi.org/10.1002/hbe2.230

Telecompaper (2019), 'Zimbabwean Internet Shutdown Costs Government Millions of Dollars in Lost Revenue', https://www.telecompaper.com/news/zimbabwean-internet-shutdown-costs-government-millions-of-dollars-in-lost-revenue–1277071

*The Chronicle* (2019), 'Minister Calls for Laws Regulating Social Media', https://www.chronicle.co.zw/minister-calls-for-laws-regulating-social-media/

*The Economist* (1998), 'Judgement Day', https://www.economist.com/business/1998/10/08/judgment-day

*The Herald* (2019), 'The Case for Internet Shutdowns', https://www.herald.co.zw/the-case-for-internet-shutdown/

*The Herald* (2022), 'Conflict-induced Digital Shutdowns Lawful', https://www.herald.co.zw/conflict-induced-digital-shutdowns-lawful/

*The Zimbabwean* (2010), 'Technology-Shy ZANU Blocks MDC Voice', https://www.thezimbabwean.co/2010/06/technology-shy-zanu-blocks-mdcs/

Tvelt, M. M. (2014), 'Facebook Politics in Zimbabwe', https://africasacountry.com/2014/07/facebook-politics-in-zimbabwe-who-is-baba-jukwa

UNESCO (2021), *Global Toolkit for Judicial Authorities, International Legal standards on Freedom of Expression, Access to Information and Safety of Journalists*, https://unesdoc.unesco.org/ark:/48223/pf0000378755

Van Zyl, G., (2013), 'Zimbabwe Regulator "Blocks" Bulk SMS as Election Nears', ITWeb, https://itweb.africa/content/WnpNgM2AEDR7VrGd

Velamuri, S. R. (2003), *Resisting Political Corruption: Econet Wireless Zimbabwe (Research Case Study) (June 2003)*, Social Science Research Network, https://papers.ssrn.com/sol3/papers.cfm?abstract_id=1009452

Veritas (2016), *Constitutional Alignment: The Official Secrets Act and Freedom of Expression, Constitution Watch 15*, https://www.veritaszim.net/node/1764

Veritas (2019), Court Watch 1/2019, *The Internet Shutdown: The High Court's Ruling of 21st January*, https://www.veritaszim.net/node/3397

Willems, W. (2014), 'Producing Loyal Citizens and Entertaining Volatile Subjects: Imagining Audience Agency in Colonial Rhodesia and Post-Colonial Zimbabwe', in S. Livingstone and R. Butsch (eds), *Meanings of Audiences: Comparative Discourses* (pp. 80–96), London: Routledge.

Windrich, E. (1979), 'Rhodesian Censorship: The Role of the Media in the Making of a One-Party State,' *African Affairs*, 78 (313): 523–34, http://www.jstor.org/stable/721756

Zimbabwe Human Rights NGO Forum (2019), 'On the Days of Darkness: An Updated Report on the Human Rights Violations Committed between 14 January 2019 and 5 February 2019', https://www.veritaszim.net/node/3514

# Chapter 3

## Internet shutdowns in the Democratic Republic of Congo

Arsène Tungali

### *Introduction*

On 30 December 2018, Congolese citizens were invited to elect a new president as well as members of the national and regional parliaments. For the next twenty days, until a few hours before the final results were announced, the internet was shut down across the country. The government claimed the shutdown was necessary for reasons of 'national security' to prevent electoral speculation and the sharing of false results. However, the analysis presented in this chapter suggests that it was not the public interest that was served by the imposition of the internet shutdown but the narrower power interests of the incumbent political party. This chapter will focus on understanding what was at stake in the various internet shutdowns that the Democratic Republic of Congo (DRC) has experienced, with a focus on what human rights were affected and what power interest were served.

The 2019 shutdown negatively impacted the social, economic and political rights of 5 million citizens, including their right to access and share information, in addition to their ability to enjoy the benefits of technology in sectors such as education (especially, online education), health (remote medical care), culture (cultural dissemination such as through social media activities), justice (access to legal services), security and humanitarian aid (risk prevention and emergency coordination) (Kasamira, 2023). This chapter provides context for the reader by documenting the history of internet shutdowns that occurred in the country between 2011 and 2019.

The chapter focuses on one main research question 'What human rights were violated by the state's imposition of internet shutdowns in the DRC and what power interests were served?' To answer the question, desk-based analysis of existing literature on internet shutdowns was combined with primary data from interviews with ten Congolese citizens who experienced internet shutdowns in the cities of Kinshasa, Bukavu and Goma. It is worth noting that, given the sensitivity of the subject, interviewees' real names are not disclosed, and pseudonyms are used to protect them. The majority of quotes were translated by the author, from their original French into English.

The chapter is comprised of six sections organized as follows: the next section presents the country's political and historical background with specific attention to the country's media and ICT development landscapes. The third section provides a case study description of historical network disruptions including the dates, the type of shutdowns, and the justifications provided by the state. Section four reviews the existing literature review on network disruptions and describes the two main conceptual frameworks that will be used to analyse the findings (the concepts of rights and power interests). Section five focuses on presenting the findings from the interviews as well as an analysis responding to the main research question, while looking at the effects of internet disruptions on citizens using the lenses of human rights and power interests. The chapter will end with a conclusion and recommendations arising from the analysis for policy, practice and further research.

## *Country historical background*

The DRC is the second largest country in Africa with an area of 2,345,000 km$^2$ located in the heart of the continent; its population is estimated at 99 million and its GDP per capita stands at USD 653,7 (World Bank, 2022). This section will present the country and the media landscape under various regimes to provide context of media controls prior to the internet era.

The country that we know of today as the DRC has a history in terms of name changes. It started by being called the Congo Free State (at the time, a Belgian King's private domain, between 1885 and 1908), then became a colony of Belgium (at the time, Belgian Congo) before gaining independence on 30 June 1960 and being called the Democratic Republic of Congo. The country then underwent a series of name changes, starting with the Democratic Republic of the Congo, then Zaire under President Mobutu and back again to the Democratic Republic of Congo (DRC), under President Kabila (the Father), which is the official name as of today (Lemarchand, n.d.).

### *The pre-independence period (1885–1960)*

The media were strictly controlled by the Belgian colonial administration. The media were used to serve the power interests of the colonizer and undermine any perceived threat to the incumbent power (Africa Museum, n.d.). Media content did not reflect the concerns of the majority population and disinformation was used to misrepresent the growing movement for national liberation. The country became independent in 1960 with Joseph Kasavubu as President and Patrice Lumumba as Prime Minister. Soon after independence, the country declined into chaos with divisions along ethnic lines as tensions between both leaders arose. The media were still influenced by the colonial legacy and became a divisive force separating groups along ethnic and regional lines (Kabemba, 2015).

### *The country under President Mobutu (1965–97)*

Mobutu Sese Seko came to power following a coup in 1965 and established an autocratic one-party state. Mabutu is known for being the longest ruling President of the country, with thirty-two years in power. When he assumed power, Mobutu brought both the print and electronic media under state control. The media were used for propaganda to serve the power interests of the post-colonial administration and to attack any perceived opposition groups who might constitute a threat to his power. At one point, in early 1975, the media were forbidden to refer to anyone other than Mobutu by name; others were referred to only by the positions they held (Young and Turner, 1985).

In early 1990, the liberalization of political activities was followed by an explosion in private media activities, in both print and audio-visual format (Kabemba, 2015). The same year, in response to public pressure, President Mobutu terminated the one-party regime and many of its controls, and dozens of newspapers and other media emerged. Many new media were outspoken in their opposition to the regime – and the near anarchy of Mobutu's last years there were significant abuses of press freedom (International Media Support, 2003).

In their report, Amnesty International (1993) shares that more than ten newspapers were founded since 1990, with no restriction in the beginning. But when they started being critical of the President and his partisans, the government began to censor them. Journalists started being imprisoned and printing companies were destroyed by government agents. In the Shaba region, newspapers from the opposition were closed, by order of the local governor, from 1992. In Kinshasa, in January 1992, offices of *La Reference*, and in November the same year, the printing company, *Terra Nova*, were set on fire. The same also occurred for *Phare* and *Potentiel* that year in December as well as the home of Leon Moukanda Lunyama, head of *Umoja* almost facing the same situation. These incidents were a sign that those who were trying to exercise their freedom of expression as part of their job were being punished.

Rebel forces of the Alliance des forces démocratiques pour la libération du Congo (AFDL) led by Laurent-Desiré Kabila took over the country after a military coup in 1997, forcing Mobutu into exile in Morocco where he died. Kabila declared himself President in 1998, after reaching Kinshasa, the capital city.

### *The DRC under the Kabilas (1998–2018)*

He had a penchant for confiscating radio and TV stations (International Media Support, 2003). Human Rights Watch (HRW) reported that the new authorities, after taking over Kinshasa, decided to 'nationalize' Télé Kin Malebo (TKM), a private television station belonging to Ngongo Luwowo, a former official under Mobutu. They thought that 'Luwowo abused his position as Minister of Information under Mobutu to misappropriate material destined for the national television station. The managers of TKM responded that they had all the documents attesting they legally bought their equipment but this did not help to overrun the governmental decision to confiscate this media (Human Rights Watch, 1997).

One of the newest decisions from the Information minister, Raphael Ghenda, was to 'prohibit the broadcasting of promotional advertisements by private radio and television stations', for the reason that he wanted to 'put an end, without further delay, to the disorder and anarchy reigning in the commercial sector'. The new power claimed that these stations belonged to Mobutu partisans and that, as they did not pay any taxes, a new 'tax equivalent to 30% of their turnover could be introduced and that this money would be used to finance public broadcasting channels' (Human Rights Watch, 1997).

At that time, the media in Congo were governed by the 1996 Media Law Relative to the Freedom of Expression which guaranteed freedom of expression, although promulgated during the one-party state period. Despite the fact that freedom of the press was guaranteed by law, journalists were harassed, kidnapped and imprisoned (Kabemba, 2015). The written press was the most threatened in 1997, the year Kabila took office. The press group *Le Soft* saw their office ravaged by soldiers on 17 May; *La Reference Plus*, the main outlet of Kinshasa, saw its chief editor called to respond to the intelligence service about an article they published 'alleging a conflict between two candidates for the post of Presidential Security Adviser'. Later that year, *Le Potentiel* received threats from intelligence services, and *Le Phare* was detained over a published article. Human Rights Watch thought that 'The expected consequence of these attacks and intimidation visits seemed to be a process leading to self-censorship in the private press' (Human Rights Watch, 1997).

When Laurent-Desiré Kabila was assassinated in 2001, his son, Joseph Kabila Kabange, the then national army head, became President and served until January 2019. His eighteen-year tenure coincided with the dawn of DRC's digital age, and between 2011 and January 2019 his administration initiated the largest number of network disruptions (including internet shutdowns) in the history of the DRC. He left the country with a number of concerns and a legacy ranging from security, the economy, poverty, corruption and crisis within the education system (Aljazeera, 2018). During his term in office, on several occasions the government decided to impose shutdowns on the transmitters of a number of broadcasters, including that of Radio France Internationale (RFI), the UN-backed Radio Okapi and main stations close to the political opposition (Fledler and Frère, 2018).

### *The DRC under President Tshisekedi (2019 to date)*

Antoine-Felix Tshisekedi Tshilombo was declared the winner of the December 2018 elections and was inaugurated in January 2019. The transfer from President Joseph Kabila marked the first peaceful transition of power in the DRC's history. Under President Tshisekedi's first term (2019–23), the media landscape flourished, with dozens of new TV, radio and online media companies operating across the country. As of 2023, it is reported that the DRC had more than 7,000 professional journalists, 540 newspapers (of which only about fifteen are published regularly), 177 TV channels, more than 4,000 radio stations and thirty-six online media.

To date, the DRC has four main telecom companies, namely, Vodacom, Orange, Airtel and Africell. DataReportal (2023) reports a total of 48 million active cellular mobile connections in early 2023, with this figure equivalent to 48 per cent of the total population. The same report highlights that the country recorded a total of 23 million internet users at the start of 2023, when internet penetration rate stood at 23 per cent. Only the state radio and TV broadcaster, *Radio Télévision Nationale Congolaise (RTNC)*, the UN's *Radio Okapi* and *Top Congo FM* reach the entire country. The print media is almost non-existent outside the capital, Kinshasa (Reporters Without Borders, 2024).

Despite media liberalization under President Tshisekedi, violations of media freedom were recorded and media rights entities such as Reporters Without Borders (RWB) and Journalistes en Danger (JED) issued statements urging the President to follow through on promises to reform the media landscape and put a stop to the closure of stations and attacks on journalists (IFEX, 2019).

The DRC held its most recent general elections on 20 December 2023 and saw the incumbent president, Felix Tshisekedi, announced as winner for a second term by the Highest Court and officially inaugurated on 20 January 2024. Under the first term, President Tshisekedi showed commitment to improving the human rights situation and the development of the technology landscape such as by enacting progressive laws in both sectors; he did not impose any internet shutdowns or network disruption during his first term nor during the 2023/24 general election cycle.

In terms of concluding this section, it is important to note the various forms under which power interests were playing, from the time of colonialism until now. The dynamics, motives and reasons behind media shutdown throughout the recent history of the country are similar whereas, during the colonial time, the colonizer sought to oblige citizens to serve the interests of Belgium, making sure the narrative was controlled and that no one would ever speak against them or raise awareness of the fact they were exploiting the natural resources as well as the people of the Congo. After independence, the media shutdowns or threats to freedom of expression that occurred were meant to serve the interests of President Mobutu who made sure he stayed the master over everything, that he remained the leader who controlled and served his own interests. By controlling the media, he became powerful and managed to stay in power for thirty-two years; during his entire tenure, the media comprised mainly print, radio and TV. The next leadership was the Kabila family who, from father to son, ruled over the country for over twenty years. It was under Kabila that the country embarked on its widespread technology era, increasing his influence and being in the position of better controlling the narrative through print, radio, TV and information and communication technologies. In order to maintain himself in power, Kabila inaugurated the first and all the series of network disruptions the country has ever experienced, including internet shutdowns, slowdowns (throttling), as well as SMS, as presented in the next section. The last internet shutdown he orchestrated led to the inauguration of a new era under President Tshisekedi who has been, so far, more open with internet-freedom friendly policies and practices.

## *Case study description*

This section will review the existing literature on internet shutdowns in the DRC. It will start with a literature review section looking at various definitions of the concept of internet shutdowns as written about by various authors, then will provide a detailed account of the different instances where an internet shutdown or network disruption has happened in the DRC, building a case study for later analysis and ending with a literature review of the concepts of human rights and power that will be used in framing the analysis of internet shutdowns.

## *Literature Review*

### *Definitions*

There is no settled definition of a network disruption; however, Rydzak (2018) suggests it is 'the intentional, significant disruption of electronic communication within a given area and/or affecting a predetermined group of citizens'. In the introduction to this volume Anthonio and Roberts suggest that the term 'internet disruptions' is a collective term, and shutdowns, technical failures and throttling are all types of internet disruptions. Network disruption may be intentional or accidental. In light of that, it is worth noting that this chapter is concerned with intentional, state-imposed internet disruptions.

There is literature on other forms of network disruptions that are rather due to technical issues that lead to limited or no access to the network for a certain period of time. This can be an issue with a submarine cable being damaged, such as the four fibre-optic cables that were damaged on the shores of Côte d'Ivoire in March 2024 (Jeune Afrique, 2024); or the two cables that were damaged in August 2023, in the Congo River canyon, an area notorious for such incidents (Jeune Afrique, 2023). However, in such cases, there is always wide coverage and technical explanation of the incident to justify why users cannot access the internet.

### *Assessing theories around internet shutdowns*

Psaila (2024) wrote that the United Nations Human Rights Council has recognized, through a report that, the internet is a catalyst for the enjoyment of a variety of rights, including the right to freedom of expression. Along those lines, Garbe (2021) suggests that internet access has potential as a means to challenge authoritarian rule due to its decentralized and low-cost affordances that help citizens and opposition supporters overcome traditional collective action problems by circumventing state control over traditional media.

Rydzak (2018) further shared that shutdown requests (or the law authorizing them) could restrict telecom companies' ability to publicly acknowledge the existence of the disruption and that civil society groups have been calling for transparency regarding these disruption orders, and for companies or the government to let people know that there is a scheduled interruption. It can also be the case that disruption orders are anonymously leaked out, as in August 2017 for the case of the DRC, where the media obtained a copy of the letter from the Regulator to operators asking them to conduct a throttling.

Research from CIPESA (2019) confirms that ISPs are implementing shutdown directives as part of licensing requirements that oblige them to abide by all orders from governments, including disrupting their services; that some providers such as Millicom, Vodafone and Orange – as well as platform operators such as Facebook, Google and Twitter – are increasingly releasing transparency reports on government shutdown orders, demand for user's data and requests for interception of communications support. CIPESA further shares that most telecom operators in Africa do not issue transparency reports, and those that do often publish heavily redacted versions that make it impossible to see how they are protecting the privacy of their users and promoting freedom of expression online.

### *Internet disruptions in authoritarian regimes*

Network disruptions are somehow linked to the political system in place in a country. CIPESA (2019) shares that the network disruptions experienced in 2019 all show that the fewer democratic credentials a government possesses, the higher the likelihood that it will order internet disruptions. The report shows that all the African countries that disrupted the internet access that year are categorized as authoritarian under the Democracy Index published by the Economic Intelligence Unit (EIU). The report also shares that countries that disrupt internet access have some of the lowest internet usage figures (percentage of people using the internet in the country): the DRC was at 8.6 per cent in 2019 and, citing a report by CIPIT, countries with an internet penetration rate of less than 20 per cent are more likely to disrupt the internet during protest than those with high rates.

As noted by Garbe (2021) above, CIPESA (2019) also shares in their report that conventional wisdom might suggest that low-internet usage countries would be the last to disrupt internet access as they might consider the population online too small to threaten public order or national security. On the contrary, it appears that African governments with democracy deficits, regardless of the number of citizens that use the internet, recognize – and fear – the power of the internet in strengthening citizen organizing and empowering ordinary people to speak truth to power.

## *History of internet shutdowns in the DRC*

The DRC has a very long record of intentional, government-initiated internet shutdowns and other forms of network disruptions in its history, all of which happened during President Joseph Kabila's regime. The first took place in 2011 and the most recent one in 2019, during the election period (under the rule of

Kabila), until a few hours before the results were announced and before the new president took office.

The following section lists and provides details about the number of times the DRC has recorded network disruptions, according to various sources, as at the time of writing this chapter. Details such as the date, the duration, as well as, when applicable, the reasons put forward by the government as they try to justify it are presented.

### *1 SMS blocking from 3 to 28 December 2011*

DRC experienced its first shutdown of the digital era during the 2011 Presidential elections. The disruption affected telephone short messaging service (SMS) and lasted twenty-five days. President Kabila was running for another term of office when, according to Reporters Without Borders (RWB, 2011), mobile phone operators received an order from the Deputy Prime Minister and Minister of Interior and Security, on 3 December 2011, to suspend SMS services 'until further notice' in order to 'maintain public order and protect the safety of property and people'. This SMS blocking occurred because the government thought that among the messages circulating, some of them were calling for 'looting, vandalism and hatred between provinces, ethnic groups and tribes' and, as a response, there was the need to 'ensure a successful culmination of the electoral process' (Agence Ecofin, 2011).

### *2 SMS and internet shutdown from 20 January to 8 February 2015*

Telecommunication companies (telecoms) and other internet service providers were ordered to block access to SMS and the internet on 20 January, inaugurating a shutdown that would last for a total of eighteen days. SMS was restored on 7 February and internet access on 8 February. The Minister of Communication shared that he was engaging with the Media Regulatory body (CSAC) to examine the responsibility of certain media in 'glorifying illegal acts' responsible for the damage caused during the demonstrations and that services were cut for national security reasons. The Parliament was discussing an amendment to the electoral law as suggested by the government but opposition leaders started a strike that, according to official sources, led to the death of three citizens. They claimed that 'making the organization of elections subject to a population census, as provided for in this text, would delay the presidential election scheduled for 2016, resulting in the President staying longer in power' (Radio Okapi, 2015c).

### *3 Social media blockage from 18 to 19 December 2016*

President Kabila, in power since 2001, was supposed to step down on 20 December 2016, according to the Constitution which didn't allow him another term; but he attempted to manoeuvre a plan to stay longer, leading to protests across the country. To operationalize the shutdown, internet operators received a letter signed by the Telecoms Regulator (ARPTC) asking them to block the sharing of images, videos and voice access throughout social media sites across the network, an operation they were asked to perform on 18 December at midnight, and if they failed to implement a partial cut, they should consider a total blocking of access to social media sites. This nationwide shutdown lasted one day, or twenty-four hours.

*4 Image sharing restricted over social media sites on 7 August 2017*

On 7 August 2017, internet service providers were asked to restrict sharing of images over social media sites and the letter to operators, signed by the Telecoms Regulatory president, contained the following: 'to prevent abusive sharing of images through social media between clients of your networks, I ask you to take the necessary technical measures to restrict the capacity to transfer images to the bare minimum'. This order came ahead of a two-day nationwide general strike called by the main opposition party, which was demanding the publication of the electoral calendar (Amnesty International, 2017).

Elections that were supposed to happen on 20 December 2016 were yet to be organized – no calendar or timeline was shared. The government, through the Telecommunications minister, justified the action, declaring 'there is a lot of messages altering the truth and calling for violence shared over social media' (Radio Okapi, 2017), following a day of violence in several neighbourhoods in the capital Kinshasa, as well as in the central cities of Matadi and Boma, images of which were shared widely on social media. The duration of this shutdown has not been documented.

*5 Internet and SMS shutdown for three days, from 31 December 2017 to 2 January 2018*

This shutdown is to be added to the list of those orchestrated by the government in response to protests against President Kabila staying in power after his Constitutional last term. The Catholic Church announced a nationwide 'peaceful protest' on Sunday and asked their believers to 'march with bibles, rosaries and crucifixes in hand after mass this Sunday morning' (RTBF, 2017). The Congolese authorities, through the Telecommunications Minister, ordered telecoms operators to 'suspend SMS and Internet until further notice, for security reasons' (Paris Match, 2018). Internet was restored on 3 January 2018.

*6 Internet shutdown from 20 to 24 January 2018, lasting three days*

This shutdown happened ahead of the planned Sunday protests by the Catholic Church, three weeks after a similar protest on New Year's Eve, expressing their disapprobation for President Kabila's plan to stay in power. This demonstration was backed up by the head of the Muslim community in the DRC calling on authorities to authorize the march to take place (News 24, 2018). It has been reported that this

**Table 3.1** Internet Shutdowns in the DRC since 2011

| No | Date | Duration | Trigger | Type of shutdown | Govt Justification |
|---|---|---|---|---|---|
| 1 | 2011 | 25 days | | SMS blocking | Maintaining public order and security of citizens after elections |
| 2 | 2015 | 18 days | Protests by the opposition against a law that could favour the political regime and delay the planned elections | SMS and internet | National security reasons |
| 3 | 2016 | 1 day | Protests against the president staying longer beyond the legal term of office | Sharing of multimedia content over social media, leading to the blockage of the use of social media | For national security reasons |
| 4 | August 2017 | No data | Ahead of a two-day general protest by the opposition demanding the publication of the electoral calendar | Throttling (restricting the transfer of images to the bare minimum over social media) | The government thought there were messages altering the truth and calling for violence shared over social media |
| 5 | 2017/18 | 3 days | Protests by the Catholic Church against the president staying in power beyond the legal term of office | SMS and internet | For security reasons |
| 6 | January 2018 | 3 days | Second cycle of protests by the Catholic Church, supported by the Muslim community | Internet shutdown (on targeted cities with high number of protests) | For security reasons and to ensure public order |
| 7 | February 2018 | 10 hours | Third cycle of protests by the Catholic Church | Internet and SMS | For security reasons and ensure public order |
| 8 | December 2018/ Jan 2019 | 20 days | The day after general and contested elections | Internet shutdown | To counter the spreading of fake results before the official announcement |

Source: author.

was a multi-regional shutdown that mostly affected the cities of Goma, Bukavu and Kinshasa where protests were high.

*7 Internet and SMS shutdown on 25 February 2018 for almost ten hours*

This time, again, internet connectivity as well as SMS were shut down across the country. Ordered ahead of the third cycle of the series of protests by the Catholic Church, asking for strict respect of the agreement. In December 2017, the Catholic Church hosted peace talks between the government and the opposition leaders, which resulted on 31 December in the signing of the 'Saint Sylvestre agreement'. This agreement highlighted, for the first time, a clear plan as to how the country would be managed until general elections that would condone the exit of President Kabila. All previous protests were a way to asking the government to abide by this agreement and allow a sharing of power, during a transitional period, until elections were organized before December 2017 (Afrique Magazine, 2017).

*8 The long-lasting shutdown: starting 31 December 2018*

The DRC under President Kabila finally organized general elections on 30 December 2018 after all the internal and international pressure he had received. But the day after, Netblocs (2018) reported major outages affecting mobile and fixed-line connections, and a full blackout in Lubumbashi and parts of the capital Kinshasa, as well as mobile connectivity in Goma and other regions. The reason offered by the government was that fake results started to be shared over social media, a situation that could lead to chaos. This was the longest internet shutdown and lasted twenty days, until a few hours before the final results on 19 January, announcing Felix Tshisekedi as the newly elected president.

On 24 January 2019, Congolese citizens experienced the first-ever historical and peaceful transition of power (inauguration) between President Kabila who, after eighteen years, handed over the reigns of the country to President Tshisekedi (RFI, 2019). There have been no further internet shutdowns since in the DRC.

Table 3.1 provides a visual summary of all shutdowns in the DRC including (where known) the events that preceded the shutdowns, the type of shutdown and its duration, and the justification offered by the government.

## *Review of concepts and theories*

The following section reviews some of the concepts and theories that can be used to frame an analysis of the impacts and drivers of internet shutdowns: rights, power and interests.

### *Human rights*

According to the United Nations (UN), human rights are entitlements inherent to all human beings, regardless of race, sex, nationality, ethnicity, language, religion or any other status. Human rights include the right to life and liberty, freedom from slavery and torture, freedom of opinions and expression, the right to work and to access an education, and many more.

Speaking about 'human rights', Orend (2002) suggests that one cannot say it without saying both 'human' and 'rights'. He suggests that the importance of drawing attention to the 'human' component of it is to introduce a core concept: that of a right-holder, who very simply, is the person who has the right in question. He adds that for the longest time, a person was considered a right-holder only if they possessed certain select characteristics, like being an able-bodied, land-owning adult male. The contemporary idea of 'universal' human rights, by contrast, suggests that every human being – man or woman, rich or poor, adult or child, healthy or sick, educated or not – holds human rights; we are all members of the human community, and so hold any and all of those rights referred to as 'human rights'.

In the introduction to this book Roberts and Anthonio remind us that the fundamental human rights that all people are entitled to were codified and agreed by nations worldwide in the Universal Declaration of Human Rights (1948) after being proclaimed by the UN General Assembly in Paris on 10 December 1948, as a common standard of entitlements for all peoples. These rights were then further elaborated and expanded in the International Covenant on Civil and Political Rights (ICCPR, 1966) and the International Covenant on Economic, Social and Cultural Rights (ICESCR, 1966). The African Union has elaborated treaties on human rights, the most predominant one being the African Charter on Human and People's Rights (ACHPR, 1981). The ICCPR deals with civil and political rights such as the rights to freedom of movement; equality before the law; freedom of opinion and expression; peaceful assembly; freedom of association. Whereas the ICESCR promotes and protects economic, social and cultural rights including the right to work in just and favourable conditions; the right to education and healthcare and the right to enjoy the benefits of cultural freedom and scientific progress.

Businesses have a corporate responsibility to respect human rights and that state-owned and private business enterprises of any size or type have an obligation to protect and promote the human rights of others and should address adverse human rights impacts with which they are involved (UN Guiding Principles on Human Rights, n.d.). It is in light of their responsibility as described above that some businesses produce 'transparency reports' which, according to Access Now's Transparency Index, 'is one of the strongest ways for technology companies to disclose threats to user privacy and free expression. Such reports help users understand a company's policies and safeguards against government abuses. Disclosures illuminate the scope and scale of online surveillance, internet shutdowns, content removal, and a host of other practices impacting fundamental rights' (Access Now, 2021).

In the DRC, telecom companies have never challenged any request of disruption received from the government; they always abide by the government's instructions and act whenever asked to, despite the fact that they have, as businesses, the responsibility to respect the human rights of their clients.

### *Digital rights*

Digital rights are all existing human rights when they occur in digital contexts. Digital rights apply to the use of digital technologies to exercise, defend or claim rights as well as to the exercise, defence or expansion of rights using digital tools and spaces. In the introduction to this book, Roberts and Anthonio point out that 'often digital rights are thought to refer narrowly to the right to information and communication (or the right to internet access)'. They further shared that the reason that there is a separate field of digital rights is that existing human rights law was written in the pre-digital age and could not anticipate some of the challenges to human rights brought about by the complexity and rapid-changing nature of the digital era. However, international law is clear that 'the same rights that people have offline must also be protected online' (UNHRC, 2019).

### *Concepts of power*

This section reviews some concepts of power that can be useful for analysing processes of digital authoritarianism such as digital disinformation and internet shutdowns.

### *Power interests*

In the introductory chapter to this volume Roberts and Anthonio wrote that it is common to talk of governments pursuing their power interests without specifying whether those interests are economic, political, gender or ethnic, for example. They further suggested that there are often multiple actors: government, private companies, regulators, courts, and civil society organizations who have different power interests for supporting, facilitating, or opposing elements of digital authoritarianism such as internet shutdowns. This chapter will assess which power interests gave rise to internet shutdowns in DRC.

Before going to that, let's look at this concept. According to Kurbalija (2016), 'internet governance' establishes the multistakeholder model which provides that different stakeholders, including the government, the private sector and civil society, among others, have to sit at the same table, on equal footing, to discuss and decide on the present and future of the internet. This includes, in this specific case, any action that can undermine people's ability to access the internet. Each stakeholder has a specific mission or agenda in the governance of the internet: the government looks at the security aspect, among others, because they are responsible of the well-being and security of their citizens. The private sector (here, internet service providers) will look at investing in building the infrastructure to provide connectivity, in partnership with the government, who must ensure the business and legal ecosystems are permissive. Civil society will fight for human rights, looking at issues such as access to the internet, accessibility, education, internet freedoms, etc. All of these stakeholders are very important if the internet has to operate and serve as a tool for good. In a later section, the power relations between different stakeholders in the DRC will be discussed.

*Modes of shutdown*

The technologies used to implement internet shutdowns can be used as part of a framework to analyse their scope, impacts and consequence. Jigsaw, a project of Google, argues that there are six modes of internet shutdown: throttling, IP blocking, mobile shutoffs, DNS interference, server name blocking and deep packet inspection. In practice, governments often implement shutdowns using a combination of these tactics. And shutdowns themselves are often dynamic, escalating from partial shutdowns impacting just a few sites and services to total blackouts before receding again (Jigsaw, 2020).

- **Throttling**: The internet does not have to be shut off to be made unusable. Instead, ISPs can slow – or 'throttle' – connections to the point that loading websites becomes impractical or impossible. State-mandated bandwidth throttling can be particularly hard to identify and verify, making it an attractive option for governments seeking to conceal their actions.
- **IP Blocking**: Devices connected to the internet, including phones, computers and the servers that host websites, locate each other across the web by means of unique keys called IP addresses. ISPs can use these addresses to target shutdowns with almost surgical precision, blocking specific websites and platforms in narrow geographic locations, while still allowing particular individuals in affected regions unfettered access.
- **Mobile Data Shutoffs**: In many low-income countries, where access to computers is limited but smartphone ownership is common, a shutdown of mobile data services is sufficient to achieve the goals of a complete shutdown while leaving some connection to the global web intact.

This section presented and reviewed the concept of human rights, including understanding digital rights as a particularity under the digital age, then the concept of power, highlighting that power interests between various stakeholders need to be understood in order to understand the decision leading to internet shutdown orders. The shutdowns that the DRC has faced and that are being discussed in this chapter will be assessed in the next section, using the concepts of both power and human rights as a framework to analyse the DRC case study.

## *Findings/Analysis*

This section will present findings from ten in-depth interviews with key informants to complement the case study description before using the above-mentioned conceptual frameworks to analyse the primary and secondary data about internet shutdowns in the DRC.

*How is a disruption operated and the role of the private sector*

From the early section that listed the various internet shutdowns the DRC has experienced; it is clear from the mentioned sources that the order has always come or gone through the telecoms minister who then directs the request (or rather the order) to the Telecoms Regulator (ARPTC) who will then speak to internet service providers (telecom companies or other private ISPs) for them to act or operate the shutdown. In most cases, the order has been made public (through the media) or the public has found a way to be informed that this is a government-ordered disruption (through leaked documents).

Garbe (2021) suggested that state ownership of an ISP could justify the fact that they can easily order a shutdown with no resistance. However, this is not the case for the DRC since all four main operators are fully private-owned and the state has no share in any of them; here, they are obliged by the law to abide to such requests from the state (DRC Télécoms and ICT Act, 2020), although they also have the duty to respect human rights recognized globally, as a business as per the UN Guiding Principles. Operators (private sector), have the final role to action the shutdown and therefore fail to provide their customers (end users) with the service they paid for, while also violating their human rights. This is where power interests play again between the various stakeholders, some holding considerably more power than others, and using it to violate others' rights.

Operators also hold the technological power (being the ones to action the switch), whilst also being mindful of their financial interests and the constraints (to their shareholders) that they need to uphold (as businesses, they too lose a lot of money when the service is not provided); while end users (citizens and human rights defenders) have no power at all but try to uphold their interest through protesting for their right to freedom of expression and of assembly, access to information etc. and holding the government accountable for their decisions. However, the government holds the political power, including the fact they give/withhold operating licences to/from the operators as a way to uphold their political interests. In the end, their political power (including military and policing powers) is able to trump these other power interests.

CIPESA (2019), quoted in the literature section, shared that all countries that ordered network disruptions are classified as authoritarian states. The DRC has been listed as an authoritarian country under President Kabila's regime, which could justify why it has recorded an important number of network disruptions. Britannica (n.d.) defines authoritarian regimes as systems of government that have no established mechanism for the transfer of the executive power and do not afford their citizens civil liberties or political rights. Since the end of colonialism, the DRC has not had the opportunity to experience a political transfer of power through fair and largely non-contested elections, until the 24 January 2019 inauguration, which saw President Kabila handing power to President Tshisekedi. Ever since, the country has experienced no internet shutdowns and President Tshisekedi has organized elections in 2023, five years later, in accordance with the law that gave him a second mandate.

### *Human rights violations*

This section argues that all the internet shutdowns and other network disruptions documented in this chapter involved the violation of users' human rights. This was the case not only for Congolese citizens but for the millions of foreigners and visitors who happened to be in the country at that time. In the next sections, I provide explanations, backed by interviews from affected users, on what and how rights were violated during each of the shutdowns.

There, human rights are divided into two categories, starting with analysis of the shutdowns that violated the economic, social and cultural rights of users, and then their civil and political rights.

### *Economic, social and cultural rights*

Under international law, states have a duty to respect, protect and fulfil the economic, social and cultural rights of its citizens. Under the ICESCR (1966), the state must ensure citizens fully enjoy, among others, their right to education and the enjoyment of the benefits of cultural freedom and scientific progress.

During the 2011 SMS blocking that lasted twenty-five days, many voices of protest were raised, including those of Reporters Without Borders (RWB, 2011). In their letter to Congolese authorities, they mentioned that, in addition to the rights violated, the blocking has affected election observers, human rights activists who use SMS to issue alerts and, most importantly, those with hearing impairment who cannot make phone calls.

It is worth noting that, at this point in time, VoIP[1] platforms (such as WhatsApp) were not as widely spread as they are today and the internet penetration rate was still very low – only 1.2 per cent of the Congolese population was using the internet (World Bank, 2011) – and still expensive due to less infrastructure deployment across the country. That means, citizens were relying primarily on SMS to communicate.

During the 2015 SMS and internet shutdown that lasted eighteen days, citizen's rights were heavily affected. The inhabitant of Kinshasa (no name) quoted in this news article shared that with no access to social networks, 'we have no access to reliable information' and that these acts are 'really setting us back another 20 years'. Another one shared 'we're now forced to call, although calls cost more than texting' or this student 'you can't live a month without the internet! It enabled us to do our homework, browse websites' (Radio Okapi, 2015a).

The above quotes can be interpreted that Congolese citizens rely on social media and online press coverage to access information because it is easy and quick. During the shutdown, they were obliged to rely on traditional media such as radio and TV to have access to information, taking people back to the time where internet access was still a luxury due to its cost and lack of wide coverage. It is a fact that these media restrictions do not allow for comments nor for listeners to provide their views, as a way to exercise their right to participate in debates and conversations about public life and hold political leaders accountable, which they could easily do through social media platforms.

A student that I interviewed, Gakuru, a humanitarian worker in Goma, reflected on how his remote schooling was affected and how his right to education was violated:

> Man, when I think about how I almost failed to pass my exam due to the internet shutdown in January 2018! Imagine, I was in the middle of my masters' studies with a foreign university and I had to prepare for an exam that I had to take two days after the Internet was shutdown. I had to cross the border to Gisenyi (a city in Rwanda) in order to access the internet and pass my exam because there was no way to postpone it. This resulted into me being stressed up, I had to spend money to cross the border, to pay for food at a restaurant in order to use their public Wi-Fi.

Like many others in a similar situation in Goma at that time, Gakuru's right to access education was affected and he almost failed his exam. He also had to spend unplanned expenses for the travel and stay in Gisenyi, which affected his economy. The reader will recall that the January 2018 shutdown occurred as a response from the government to public protests against the then-president staying longer in power; this was a power issue – the government (big power) against the people (less power). As said in previous sections, it is important to highlight that the partisan power interests of the governing regime were prioritized over the right to education for students, over the right to free expression and communication of all citizens, and over the right to conduct business on the part of the ISPs and all of the online businesses that rely on the internet. This is arguably an abuse of power that serves not the national interest but the narrow interest of a regime wishing to retain power.

I also interviewed a woman who was relying on a mobile app to check the progress of her pregnancy. Francine, 37, shared:

> I was seven months pregnant in December 2018 at the time of our general elections that were followed by a full internet shutdown. As a habit, all the data related to the evolution of my pregnancy since month 1 were kept in this mobile app; I have been using it since I was pregnant with my first baby, six years before. Suddenly, with no internet, it was hard and painful to still load and get the advice such as my dietary needs, my fitness activity, or even some essential advices on keeping my baby safe in my womb. I wish I had known a shutdown would happen; I would have kept hand-written notes as well.

Francine's story is just one out of many on how internet disruptions can impact people's ability to access online medical care, diet or even fitness advice. Her right to healthcare was violated. Some Congolese citizens use online data and apps to control and check some of their vital signs before they decide on the necessity to consult a doctor. The internet is a source of multiple information services that support the wellness of its users and this has become part of their daily lives – until there is a network disruption. To put things in context, in 2015, the internet penetration rate was at 3.8 per cent in the DRC (World Bank, 2015), many people were connected and it was the first time they experienced an internet shutdown, coupled with no access to SMS communication. It is not only citizens' health rights that were impacted, their economic rights were also affected, as the next interview shows. One interviewee, Franck, a tech entrepreneur in the city of Goma, described the 2015 shutdown as an abuse of government power:

> I remember that situation. Because they are more powerful than us, the government prevented us from all means of easy and cheap communication options we could have. In my habits, I only use SMS and data bundles for easy and low-cost communication. I can tell you that for the duration of the shutdown, I wasted a lot of money because I could only rely on landline calls that were very expensive,

Ilori (2021), speaking on the social impact of internet shutdowns in the DRC, quoted a user who was affected by the fact that mobile money services were interrupted despite some individuals gaining their living from such activities. Another interviewee recognized that, given the low rate of internet penetration in the country (about 30.6 per cent), fewer people actually felt the consequences, but such consequences could be faced by entrepreneurs who relied on digital services to earn a living and support their family, who could not because there was no network.

Thousands of small businesses in the DRC generate income using mobile money and were devastated by the shutdown. I interviewed Sylvie, a female owner of a mobile money transfer shop in Kinshasa. She recalled what happened to her business during the twenty-one-day internet shutdown:

> Many people come to top up their mobile money wallets because they want to be able to directly pay for their data, SMS or call bundles, even at night when shops are closed. For twenty days, I had fewer clients because many of them rely on data bundles to communicate and do other stuff, but due to the unavailability of the Internet, my business was affected. Just a few would top up and buy call bundles because it is expensive.

Not only were her customers' rights to communicate and access information affected, but Sylvie's economic right was also affected, negatively impacting her business and therefore her income as an entrepreneur in financial services.

Thinking that these disruptions only affect those who have internet access could be biased because the impact goes beyond just those who have access. The country's economy at large is impacted, therefore affecting even those who do not use the internet. In their report, CIPESA (2019) shares that internet disruptions, however short-lived, affect many facets of the national economy and tend to persist far beyond the period in which access is disrupted. It is estimated in that report that the DRC would lose up to USD 16,093,684 for a five-day total shutdown that included apps such as Twitter, Facebook and WhatsApp in 2019.

Al Kitenge, a Congolese business analyst, in an interview with the UN radio, shared that 'Cutting off the Internet sends a very bad message to the whole world and to technology and business developers. We're showing people that if you invest entirely in technology, one day or other, for purely political reasons, you can be halted, and you'll lose an incredible amount of money' (Radio Okapi, 2015a). Mr. Kitenge is identifying political power interests as the real motivation for the shutdown, as opposed to the 'national security' reason claimed by the government.

As already noted in this chapter, ISPs, although they are the ones that operate the shutdown after the order from political authorities, are also economically affected. Reporters Without Borders highlight the economic power interest of ISPs by sharing that there are also financial repercussions on mobile operators who suffer daily losses of around USD 150,000 (RWB, 2011).

Internet access is also increasingly central to social life, as another interviewee, Francoise, 36, employed by a private company in the city of Bukavu, explained to me:

> I cannot imagine my life without platforms like WhatsApp today. I am a member of various groups including one with my family members, church fellows, former classmates and even with my colleagues at work. All I need is a connectivity which, if used only for WhatsApp, costs me less than USD 10 per month to be connected and speaking with all those people instantly. Imagine now when the internet is disrupted as used to happen under Kabila's term, my life would stop and I would lose so much, including spending way more on landline calls.

I met Francoise in 2024, nearly six years after the country experienced its last internet shutdown, reflecting on how her economic rights could be affected if this were to happen now that the internet penetration rate has increased and social media platforms are widely used in the country for communication and business such as e-commerce.

### *Civil and political rights*

Under international law, states have a duty to respect, protect and fulfil the civil and political rights of their citizens. Under the ICCPR (1966), the state must ensure citizens fully enjoy, among others, their right to participate in democratic political processes, freedom of expression, association and religion.

The internet has empowered citizens to enjoy many of the freedoms they are not able to enjoy when they are offline. Through social media and blogging, they are freely expressing themselves and therefore contributing to the debate and conversations that are shaping their lives and well-being. Through online platforms such as WhatsApp, it is easy to unite people within groups and offer them platforms to exchange views, to organize and unite for a given cause.

One interviewee, Muhindo, a member of a citizen movement operating in the city of Goma, explained how their organization used the internet as part of civic engagement:

> In our collective, we have decided to solely use WhatsApp communication, for reliability and cost-effectiveness, in a group with all our members gathered. It is easy to organize, strategize and plan our next demonstration or physical meeting that way. During an internet shutdown, our effectiveness in fighting for the causes we care about was negatively affected due to no group chat and communication.

In other words, their right to political participation was negatively affected, therefore making it hard for them to speak on behalf of those citizens who cannot speak for themselves. The eastern part of the DRC has lately seen the birth of many citizen movements, which are unregistered informal associations whose sole mission is to hold decision-makers accountable through public demonstrations, loudly speaking out against issues affecting citizens in their areas. One focus of citizen action was to demand an end to internet shutdowns in the DRC.

This is where citizen power is clearly demonstrated in the sense that they use the internet to build forms of counter-power, exercising their right to assembly online and to organize to hold powerholders accountable. But here again, the decision to change or to listen lies in the hands of those who hold the political power; sometimes it works, sometimes it doesn't produce expected results. When demonstrations can no longer be carried out online due to an internet shutdown, resistance goes onto the streets.

### *Challenging shutdowns in the DRC*

This section explores the agency of Congolese citizens and international reporters in response to internet shutdowns. The term counter-power is sometimes used to describe the countervailing agency that citizens use to resist the authoritarian or repressive power of elites (Graeber, 2004; Gee, 2011). This section uses concepts of counter-power and citizen agency to analyse how civil society organizations have worked to help citizens to circumvent, challenge or evade intentional internet disruption imposed by powerholders.

Whenever there was a network disruption, Congolese citizens would speak up against it and were supported by human rights organizations. During the 2011 SMS shutdown, Reporters Without Borders reminded the minister in a letter that 'the fundamental rights to freedom of communication and the free flow of information are being flouted by this measure, the impact of which is all the greater because SMS messaging is a dominant form of communication in a country where internet penetration rate is only 1 per cent' (RWB, 2011). During the August 2017 internet throttling, human rights organizations such as Amnesty International raised their voices, calling this action an 'attack on freedom of expression, in the DRC' (Amnesty International, 2017).

During the January 2018 targeted shutdown, Blaise Ndola, a digital rights activist, quoted in an article by Internet Without Borders (IWB) said 'It is unacceptable for the government to shut down the internet every time the security services are about to commit serious human rights violations by suppressing demonstrations'. In the same article, Julie Owono, Executive Director of that entity urged internet service providers to 'dissociate themselves from censorship in the DRC by refusing to obey the Congolese government's illegal demands' (IWB, 2018a).

Internet shutdowns often provide cover for authorities to disguise the commissioning of human rights violations (Access Now, 2023). Often when the internet is disrupted during or after violent protests, the government doesn't want what's happening to be disseminated over social media platforms because this could raise serious international human rights implications. This could justify why, during August 2017, 'throttling' rather than a complete shutdown was employed. The internet service providers were asked by the Telecoms Regulator (Amnesty International, 2017) to 'restrict the capacity to transfer images to the bare minimum' over social media because human rights activists and citizens at large were taking and posting pictures/videos of the violent repression of protesters, which could depict what was really happening. Similarly, in 2016 when operators were asked to stop users' ability to share multimedia contents over social media for national security reasons, as there were huge protests against President Kabila staying in power longer than the Constitution permitted (RFI, 2017).

This clearly shows the power imbalance between the government being too powerful and the citizens, who are weak and obliged to face the consequences of government actions, which include violation of their most basic human rights and access to information, but most importantly, freedom of expression. In such a situation, citizens have no avenue to make their voices heard, no way to claim their rights – they are powerless.

On that line, for the February 2018 shutdown, Reporters Without Borders (2018) issued a statement where they condemned this action saying that 'Preventing the flow of information does not limit the violence, nor does it conceal the repression of these demonstrations. The Congolese people must not be deprived of their fundamental right to be informed.'

Two days before this happened, another entity, Internet Without Borders (2018b) had issued a statement to the government asking them not to resort to an internet shutdown in preparation for the march supported by the country's Catholic Church on 25 February 2018, reminding them that this would not come without consequences. Among them, IWB mentions human rights, the economic cost, as well as the need for the government to honour their international human rights' engagements and obligations.

Under the International Covenant on Civil and Political Rights (ICCPR, 1966), the State has the duty to ensure citizens are able to participate in the democratic political process. The Congolese government was failing to secure citizens' rights to political participation every time they resorted to a network disruption.

Interviewees suggested that this was conscious powerplay to stifle counter-power and prevent citizens from speaking up, hold protests or organizing. Kataliko, 28, a human rights activist told me:

> When we are preparing for a protest, social media platforms help us gather support and communicate about our plans such as dates, venues and itinerary for our public demonstrations. Knowing that, the government will shut down the Internet to prevent us from better organizing, better coordinating the activities on the ground and better communicate the outcome of our actions or results.

*Circumventing internet shutdowns*

Due to the number of disruptions Congolese citizens faced between 2011 and 2019, various human rights entities have been working to support local activists with knowledge on how to circumvent an internet shutdown, such as by using a Virtual Private Network (VPN) or other alternative connectivity schemes to stay connected. The use of VPNs increased during that time and citizens in cities like Goma managed to acquire SIM cards from neighbouring country, Rwanda, that they can use to stay connected whenever everything is offline in the DRC.

In the case of Claudine, 27, who was a university student in Goma during the 2017–19 shutdowns, she told me 'I always have a VPN in my phone ready to be activated when the shutdown is not total. This was suggested to me by a friend who posted on his social media page that he managed to stay online when the rest of us were offline and struggling. The VPN has saved me a number of times.'

Many Congolese citizens learnt the benefits of using VPNs through advice and campaigns led by digital rights activists and have managed to have them installed on their mobile phones, ready for the next time any such situation should occur.

> A VPN (Virtual Private Network) creates a secure portal between devices, providing an encrypted connection to the internet no matter where you are. When you use a VPN, your computer or phone is connected to a VPN's server, located overseas. It allows you to virtually break through the borders of your country where an unethical, government-created internet shut down could be taking place.
> (Collins, 2021)

Under harsh circumstances, citizens become very creative because they have to fight for their rights to access information and use the internet even when there is an internet shutdown going on. Jean Claude, a 32-year-old journalist in Goma, demonstrated creative ways to circumvent the shutdowns. He would travel from his house and spend the day close to the Rwandan border. He told me

> I managed to buy an MTN SIM card from Rwanda and loaded it with internet bundles; but since the network cannot be used at my house which is far from the border, I made a decision to spend time close to the border. Throughout the duration of the 2019 shutdown, because I had stories to be published by

my media, I would spend my days at a coffee shop close to the Rwandan border and use that SIM card to be online and work.

Jean Claude, like many other citizens who rely on the internet to make their living, had to find ways to survive an internet shutdown. When there is a total internet shutdown, you cannot use a VPN and if your internet connection is through providers based in the DRC, these will have received the order to cut you off. This comes with additional expenses, making your financial situation harder but you find a way to be online.

### *Power interests around network disruptions in the DRC*

Network disruptions in the DRC, from the first one (2011) to the last (2019), reveal at least two forms of power interests: on one side, the state (government, the Telecoms Regulator and operators) that holds the political power and authority to decide, and on the other side, the population (individual citizens, internet end-users including small internet-based businesses), including civil society organizations that are the expression of collective agency (or forms of counter-power). On each side, there is a justification (or a specific interest) for the action being taken.

In order to expand on the above, it is important to recall an important concept presented in the literature. The multistakeholder model promoted by the internet governance concept, which assumes that stakeholders sit around the table on an equal footing to discuss and agree on matters of mutual interest, is operated differently in the DRC, especially when a network disruption has to be ordered: the government will never think to include civil society entities in that decision and justify it as a matter of national security. The internet service providers will receive, from the Regulator, an order to execute. Civil society, on their part, will bring forward the concept of human rights that, as per the UN Declaration, requires states to respect their citizens' human rights, which are violated when a network disruption is being executed.

In the DRC, all network disruptions whose analyses are the subject of this chapter happened during the administration of President Joseph Kabila. The first disruption happened because the opposition party was contesting the way elections were organized; they held public protests to speak out and channel their opposition to the results that would come out of those elections. Rather than using another way to respond to their queries, the state resorted to an SMS blocking as a way to stifle dissent. Here, the state holds total power: the political authority, the army and all security forces including the fact that they control the media and the telecoms industry. In fact, as shown in the literature, the state grants to the latter their operating licences (Article 41, Telecoms and ICT Law) as per the DRC law, and they have the duty to abide by any such request from the government, when national security is being mentioned.

The same plan is being activated for the other reported network disruptions that the DRC has recorded. Under President Kabila, the DRC was considered an autocratic country (CIPESA, 2019) and has always sought to show how powerful it is – for such a regime, freedom of expression and of opinion are not respected and citizens will protest against the decision, but this one will be lifted only when the state sees fit. President Kabila had to disrupt the network almost every time opposition leaders, supported by the population, were in disagreement with his decisions, especially, when he was manoeuvring to stay in power longer than the Constitution allowed him to.

### *The DRC with no network disruption*

Since the last full internet shutdown that inaugurated President Tshisekedi's first term (January 2019), Congolese citizens haven't experienced any network disruption. Many people believe that it is because President Tshisekedi has publicly shown his willingness to 'use technology as a lever for good governance and for social development' (PNN, 2025), with various initiatives including new and progressive legislations, creating technology-related offices within the government but also introducing technology in service provision in a number of entities.

To better illustrate how this new way of serving (not shutting down the internet) is positively experienced on the ground, I met with Benita, a Congolese college student in Kinshasa, who shared how, for her entire life, she has only really fully enjoyed the internet for the last five years and, as a millennial, she had a very bad experience when she started using the internet:

> I am 24 today and started using a mobile phone in 2014. I experienced my first internet shutdown a year later with the 2015 occurrence. I did not understand what happened to my phone as I could not browse and download my favourite hits, until I spoke to my brother who explained what was going on. I felt very bad, for a first experience. I then experienced the subsequent ones with the same level of pain until the 2019 one which luckily was the last one.

For the 2023 general elections, when citizens like Benita feared an internet shutdown, the government publicly declared, through the Interior Minister, Peter Kazadi: 'We will not cut the internet connection. We are not in a war situation. Tomorrow, there will be a morning, a noon and an evening. We're all going to sleep peacefully in our own homes. We have not envisaged such a measure' (Actu7, 2023). Unlike the 2018 elections, there was no internet shutdown and there haven't been any since, up to the publication of this chapter.

## Conclusion

This chapter sets out to answer the question of 'What human rights were violated by the state's imposition of internet shutdowns in the DRC and what power interests were served?'. The chapter began with a historical review of how successive colonial and post-liberation governments in the DRC each used media controls to serve almost the same power interests, making sure they controlled the narrative and that no one could challenge their power; this resulted in those governments staying longer in power with no respect for democratic principles such as those of allowing citizens to choose their leaders (through elections) and to exercise their freedoms. This provided valuable context for understanding President Kabila's use of media controls in the digital age, since all reported shutdowns happened during his regime. His predecessors operated in the pre-digital age, exercising their influence through newspapers, radio and TV, whereas for him, digital technologies were added to the elements he needed to control in order to establish his power and serve his personal interest.

An analysis of the series of shutdowns from 2011 to 2018 challenges the government's claims that internet shutdowns were motivated by the public interest. Analysis of primary and secondary data sources suggests that they were motivated by Kabila's personal interests in retaining power. The chapter documents a clear pattern of shutdowns timed to suppress the counter-power of opposition protests whenever citizens called power to account. Interviews from affected citizens as well as declarations from civil society organizations gave a clear pattern of the triggers and consequences of these shutdowns. The analysis further shows how the impact of shutdowns violated not only citizens' civil and political rights including their right to freedom of expression, freedom of association, access to information or even access to health, but also the social, economic and political rights of millions of citizens, damaging the economy, well-being of citizens and democracy. It has also been demonstrated that operators, although not able to share their perspectives for fear of reprisals, lost huge amounts of money whenever they positively responded to the government request.

The above analysis gives rise to the following question: what can be done now that the DRC has a relative democratic opening to improve internet governance by ensuring that the wider 'public interest' in keeping the internet on is not sacrificed to serve the narrow 'elite interests' in retaining power? In my tentative effort to respond to that question, I draw the following recommendations.

It is recommended that the *DRC government* should learn from the harm that network disruptions have caused to citizens, including how they have affected the country's economy and decide to never resort to that practice again. The government should also use the power of technology to support the country's economic development through the establishment of good relationships with the private sector, especially internet service providers, who work at expanding the network.

It is recommended that the *Parliament*, which has acted very passively when internet shutdowns were ordered, should review existing legislations that make it easy for the government to use internet shutdowns, with no respect for citizens' and international human rights. They, in fact, should adopt legislation that makes shutdowns illegal by enshrining in the law the right to unfettered information and communication offline and online.

It is recommended that *operators*, as important actors in connectivity and business partners to the government, discuss important revisions of their licence agreements, which would allow them to stand strong and uphold their obligations to serve their customers with no interruption and uphold their international human rights obligations. They should also consider filing transparency reports about all shutdown requests and joining their clients (end-users) to challenge shutdowns in the court.

It is recommended that the *Congolese citizen* (end-users) should continue using technology in a way that helps them enjoy their human rights and their political participation by holding the government accountable of their actions, which is a good way to improve democracy. Human rights defenders (local and international) should continue playing their role of watchdogs and always speak out whenever there are plans to violate their human rights through practices such as network disruptions.

It is, however, important to note that this chapter has not covered all aspects related to internet shutdowns in the DRC and I would like to call on other researchers to look at other avenues, such as researching what citizens on one side and internet service providers on the other can really do to challenge internet shutdown orders from autocratic governments. It is also important to look at articles in Congolese legislation that pave the way for network disruptions and suggest rewording or changes to be submitted to the parliament for revision.

## *Note*

1 VoIP: abbreviation for voice over Internet protocol (= a system that allows you to use your computer as a telephone, and your Internet connection as a telephone line): Most VoIP services have the ability to transfer your current phone number to your new service (Cambridge Dictionary).

## *Bibliography*

Access Now (2021), 'Transparency Reporting Index', https://www.accessnow.org/campaign/transparency-reporting-index/

Access Now (2023), 'Evading Accountability through Internet Shutdowns', https://www.accessnow.org/wp-content/uploads/2023/03/Evading-accountability-through-internet-shutdowns.pdf

ACHPR (1981), 'African Charter on Human and People's Rights', https://au.int/en/treaties/african-charter-human-and-peoples-rights

Actu7.cd (2023), 'Élections 2023: "On ne coupera pas la connexion internet le jour du vote" (Peter Kazadi)', https://actu7.cd/2023/12/19/elections-2023-on-ne-coupera-pas-la-connexion-internet-le-jour-du-vote-peter-kazadi/

Africa Museum (n.d.), 'Colonial Cinema on the Brink of the Decolonisation of the Belgian Congo: Propaganda, Censorship and Contrasting Vision with Reality (1940–1960)', https://www.africamuseum.be/en/learn/history_articles/colonial_cinema_1940-1960

Afrique Magazine (2017), 'L'accord de la Saint-Sylvestre: en attendant un miracle', https://afriquemagazine.com/l-accord-de-la-saint-sylvestre-en-attendant-un-miracle

Agence Ecofin (2011), 'RD Congo: les SMS sont de retour … sous haute surveillance', https://www.agenceecofin.com/securite/3012-2717-rd-congo-les-sms-sont-de-retour-sous-haute-surveillance

Al Jazeera (2018), 'DRC: What Is Joseph Kabila's Legacy after 18 Years in Power?', https://www.aljazeera.com/news/2018/12/25/drc-what-is-joseph-kabilas-legacy-after-18-years-in-power.

Amnesty International (1993), https://www.amnesty.org/fr/wp-content/uploads/2021/06/afr620111993en.pdf (see pp. 10–11).

Amnesty International (2017), 'DRC: Bloc on Social Media Images an Appalling Attack on Freedom of Expression', https://www.amnesty.org/en/latest/news/2017/08/drc-block-on-social-media-images-an-appalling-attack-on-freedom-of-expression/

Britannica (n.d.), 'Authoritarianism', https://www.britannica.com/topic/authoritarianism

CIPESA (2019), 'Despots and Disruptions: Five Dimensions of Internet Shutdowns in Africa', https://cipesa.org/wp-content/files/briefs/report/Despots-And-Disruptions_March-20.pdf

Collins, M. (2021), 'How to Stay Connected during Internet Blackout', MysteriumVPN, https://www.mysteriumvpn.com/blog/internet-shutdown

DataReportal (2023), 'Digital 2023: The Democratic Republic of the Congo', https://datareportal.com/reports/digital-2023-democratic-republic-of-the-congo

Fledler, A. and Frère, M. S. (2018) 'Press Freedom in the African Great Lakes Region: A Comparative Study of Rwanda, Burundi, and the Democratic Republic of Congo, 2018', https://www.researchgate.net/publication/325574820_Press_Freedom_in_the_African_Great_Lakes_Region_A_Comparative_Study_of_Rwanda_Burundi_and_the_Democratic_Republic_of_Congo

Garbe, L. M. (2021), 'Authoritarian Survival in the Digital Age – Internet Access and Control in African Autocracies' https://www.e-helvetica.nb.admin.ch/api/download/urn%3Anbn%3Ach%3Abel-2263842%3ADis5105.pdf/Dis5105.pdf

Gee, T. (2011), *Counter Power: Making Change Happen*. Oxford: World Changing.

Graeber, D. (2004), *Fragments of an Anarchist Anthropology* (2nd pr. ed.), Chicago: Prickly Paradigm Press.

Human Rights Watch (1997), 'Non-respect des droits', https://www.hrw.org/legacy/french/reports/drc1997/d.htm

ICCPR (1966), 'International Covenant on Civil and Political Rights', https://treaties.un.org/doc/treaties/1976/03/19760323%2006-17%20am/ch_iv_04.pdf

ICESCR (1966), 'International Covenant on Economic, Social and Cultural Rights', https://www.ohchr.org/en/instruments-mechanisms/instruments/international-covenant-economic-social-and-cultural-rights

IFEX (2019), 'DRC President Urged to Act on Promises to Reform Media Landscape', https://ifex.org/drc-president-urged-to-act-on-promises-to-reform-media-landscape/

Ilori, T. (2021), 'Life Interrupted: Centering the Social Impacts of Network Disruptions in Advocacy in Africa', Global Network Initiative, https://globalnetworkinitiative.org/wp-content/uploads/2021/03/Life-Interrupted-Report.pdf

International Media Support (2003), '*DRC Media Environment Assessment Report*', https://www.mediasupport.org/wp-content/uploads/2012/11/ims-drc-assessment-2003.pdf

IWB (2018a), 'The DRC Should Respect Its Commitments by Stopping Internet Shutdowns', https://internetwithoutborders.org/the-drc-should-respect-its-commitments-by-stopping-internet-shutdowns/

IWB (2018b), 'Empêcher la prochaine coupure Internet en RDC', https://internetwithoutborders.org/empecher-prochaine-coupure-internet-rdc-lettre-ouverte-gouvernement/

Jeune Afrique (2023), 'En RDC, comment la rupture d'un câble sous-marin ralentit Internet', https://www.jeuneafrique.com/1471723/economie-entreprises/en-rdc-comment-la-rupture-dun-cable-sous-marin-ralentit-internet/

Jeune Afrique (2024), 'Coupure internet en Afrique: la panne aurait-elle pu être évitée?', https://www.jeuneafrique.com/1548880/economie-entreprises/coupure-internet-en-afrique-la-panne-aurait-elle-pu-etre-evitee/

Jigsaw (2020), The Internet Shutdowns Issue, https://static.googleusercontent.com/media/jigsaw.google.com/en//static/images/current/04-internet-shutdowns/the-current-by-jigsaw-issue-004-internet-shutdowns.pdf

Kabemba C. (2015), 'The State of the Media in the Democratic Republic of the Congo,' EISA, Institute of the Advancement of Journalism.

Kasamira L. (2023), 'As Digital Censorship Concerns Cloud DR Congo's Crucial Election, Elsewhere in Francophone Africa, Internet Shutdowns Also Threaten Livelihoods and Democracy', https://www.equaltimes.org/as-digital-censorship-concerns

Kurbalija, J. (2016), *An Introduction to Internet Governance*, Malta: Diplo Foundation.

Lemarchand, R. (n.d.), 'The Congo Crisis', *Encyclopedia Britannica*, https://www.britannica.com/place/Democratic-Republic-of-the-Congo/The-Congo-crisis

Netblocks (2018), 'Evidence of Internet Shutdowns in DRC Amid Election Unrest', https://netblocks.org/reports/evidence-of-internet-shutdowns-in-drc-amid-election-unrest-PW80YLAK

News 24 (2018), 'DRC Blocks Internet Ahead of Banned Protests', https://www.news24.com/News24/dr-congo-blocks-internet-ahead-of-banned-protests-20180121

OHCHR (1966), 'International Covenant on Civil and Political Rights', https://www.ohchr.org/en/instruments-mechanisms/instruments/international-covenant-civil-and-political-rights

OHCHR (2011), 'Guiding Principles on Business and Human Rights', https://www.ohchr.org/sites/default/files/documents/publications/guidingprinciplesbusinesshr_en.pdf

Orend, B. (2002), *Human Rights: Concept and Context*, Peterborough, ONT: Broadview Press, https://books.google.cd/books?hl=fr&lr=&id=yfSgCvlyTaoC&oi=fnd&pg=PA7&dq=what+are+human+rights&ots=TVCo78N3iz&sig=Au1dtVsxNL-6c9nrasK3dwWp3u4&redir_esc=y#v=onepage&q=what%20are%20human%20rights&f=false

*Paris Match* (2018), 'RDC: Internet rétabli après des marches anti-Kabila', https://www.parismatch.com/Actu/International/RDC-Internet-retabli-apres-des-marches-anti-Kabila-1430132

PNN (2025), 'Plan National du Numérique – Horizon 2025', https://presidence.cd/services/1/plan_national_du_numerique_horizon_2025

Psaila B. S. (2024), '"UN Declared Internet Access a Human Right" – Did It Really?', https://www.diplomacy.edu/blog/un-declares-internet-access-human-right-did-it-really/

Radio Okapi (2015a), 'Al Kitenge: "Si l'État n'avait pas paniqué, il n'aurait pas coupé les communications d'entreprises"', https://www.radiookapi.net/actualite/2015/01/22/al-kitenge-si-letat-navais-pas-panique-il-naurait-pas-coupe-les-communications-dentreprises

Radio Okapi (2015b), 'Lambert Mende annonce le rétablissement d'Internet dans les "heures qui viennent"', https://www.radiookapi.net/actualite/2015/02/06/rdc-lambert-mende-annonce-le-retablissement-dinternet-dans-les-heures-qui-suivent

Radio Okapi (2015c), 'SMS et Internet coupés en RDC', https://www.radiookapi.net/actualite/2015/01/20/sms-internet-coupes-en-rdc

Radio Okapi (2017), 'Accès aux réseaux sociaux: la restriction sera levée "d'ici quelques jours", annonce Emery Okunji', https://www.radiookapi.net/2017/08/10/actualite/societe/acces-aux-reseaux-sociaux-la-restriction-sera-levee-dici-quelques-jours

Reporters Without Borders (2011), 'After Disputed Election, SMS Messaging Suspended until Further Notice', https://reliefweb.int/report/democratic-republic-congo/after-disputed-election-sms-messaging-suspended-until-further

Reporters Without Borders (2018), 'RSF dénonce le nouveau black-out Internet en RDC', https://rsf.org/fr/rsf-d%C3%A9nonce-le-nouveau-black-out-internet-en-r%C3%A9publique-d%C3%A9mocratique-du-congo

Reporters Without Borders (2024), 'Democratic Republic of the Congo', https://rsf.org/en/country/democratic-republic-congo

RFI (2017), 'RDC: pourquoi le gouvernement a limité l'accès aux réseaux sociaux', https://www.rfi.fr/fr/afrique/20170810-rdc-gouvernement-acces-reseaux-sociaux

RFI (2019), 'RDC: revivez la prestation de serment du nouveau président Felix Tshisekedi', https://www.rfi.fr/fr/afrique/20190124-direct-rdc-suivez-investiture-nouveau-president-felix-tshisekedi

RTBF (2017), 'RDC: Internet coupé "pour des raisons de sécurité" et check-points multiples dans Kinshasa', https://www.rtbf.be/article/rdc-internet-coupe-pour-des-raisons-de-securite-et-checks-points-multiples-dans-kinshasa-9800499

Rydzak, J. (2018), 'Disconnected: A Human Rights-Based Approach to Network Disruptions', Global Network Initiative, https://globalnetworkinitiative.org/disconnected-human-rights-network-disruptions/

Télécoms and ICT Law (2020), 'La Loi sur les Télécommunications et les TIC en RDC' https://www.primature.cd/public/wp-content/uploads/2022/04/Loi-N%C2%B020-017-du-25-novembre-relative-aux-Te%CC%81le%CC%81com_08-12-020.pdf

UDHR (1948), 'Universal Declaration of Human Rights', https://www.ohchr.org/sites/default/files/UDHR/Documents/UDHR_Translations/eng.pdf

UN Guiding Principles on Business and Human Rights (n.d.), https://www.business-humanrights.org/en/big-issues/governing-business-human-rights/un-guiding-principles/#:~:text=The%20UN%20Guiding%20Principles%20on,abuses%20committed%20in%20business%20operations

UNHRC (2019), 'OHCHR and privacy in the digital age', https://www.ohchr.org/en/privacy-in-the-digital-age/international-standards

World Bank (2011), 'Utilisateurs d Internet (% de la population) – Congo, Dem. Rep.', https://donnees.banquemondiale.org/indicateur/IT.NET.USER.ZS?contextual=aggregate&end=2011&locations=CD&start=2011&view=bar

World Bank (2015), 'Utilisateurs d'Internet (% de la population) – DRC', https://donnees.banquemondiale.org/indicateur/IT.NET.USER.ZS?contextual=aggregate&end=2015&locations=CD&start=2015&view=bar

World Bank (2022), 'Congo Democratic Republic', https://data.worldbank.org/country/congo-dem-rep?view=chart

Young C. and Turner E. (1985), *The Rise and Decline of the Zairian State*, Madison, WI: University of Wisconsin Press, p. 169.

# Chapter 4

## Weaponization of the internet during Zambia's 2021 election

Susan Mwape

### *Introduction*

This chapter assesses the impact on human rights of the first internet shutdown in Zambia's history and analyses which power interests were served and how citizens resisted the restrictions. Prior to 2021, Zambia had never experienced an internet shutdown or any major social media restriction, although specific investigative news websites that were perceived to be hostile to the government experienced blockages between 2012 and 2016. However, on election day, 12th of August 2021, the Zambian government imposed a nationwide internet shutdown that had a significant impact on the social, economic and political rights of millions of citizens.

Zambia's history of state control over mainstream media and routine repression of journalists had fuelled the use of relatively safe online spaces to critique government policies and call for change. The popularity of social media platforms such as Facebook, Twitter and WhatsApp became an Achilles heel to the political elites in power as citizens took to social media to challenge the status quo. In 2020 Covid-19 restrictions on social gathering resulted in the shrinking of civic space offline, which meant that citizens could no longer freely mobilize outside of government buildings to protest about matters affecting their well-being; this led to social media becoming the primary outlet for public protests and platforms for expression.

This chapter will highlight the partial internet shutdown that occurred in 2021 during the elections of 12 August in Zambia. It will highlight civil society's role in pushing back against the shutdown, including the advocacy and strategic litigation efforts that were made by stakeholders. The chapter will highlight and analyse citizens' response to the social media restrictions, especially civil society and the youth, and the efforts made by government to repress such action. The main research question this chapter will address is, 'Which human rights were impacted and whose interests were advanced by the Zambian government's decision to restrict the internet during the 2021 elections?'

The role of government power and control will be analysed through close attention to the motivation and strategies of the political elites in preventing dissent and maintaining power. Further, the affordances of social media platforms will be analysed with regard to how they presented new action possibilities for citizens agency and for state repression when compared to the limitations of traditional civic engagement avenues.

A qualitative research approach is adopted, combining desk-based analysis of existing studies with primary data, specifically key informant interviews with government officials, CSOs, activists and citizens on the social media restrictions of 2021. Additional analysis is made of legal documents, media reports and social media posts.

The remainder of this chapter is organized as follows: the next section will provide the reader with contextual history about media restrictions in Zambia before detailing the case study of the 2021 internet shutdown. I then review the existing literature on concepts of power, rights and agency to provide a framework for analysing the case study. Following the analysis, a section is dedicated to studying the agency of citizens who resisted the shutdowns, before making some concluding remarks and recommendations.

## *Background*

Zambia is located in central southern Africa; it is a landlocked country that has had to contend with numerous political tensions. Pre independence Zambia was called Northern Rhodesia. It is among the first countries that reverted to multi-party democratic rule in the early 1990s. The 1991 elections ushered in the Movement for Multi Party Democracy (MMD), which replaced the United National Independence Party (UNIP) that had governed the country for twenty-seven years since independence in 1964. Under the leadership of President Kaunda, UNIP had been the sole legal party in Zambia from 1973 to 1990.

Pre-independence, the British colonial administration ran the Northern Rhodesia Central Africa Broadcasting Station (CABS). The broadcasting authority began broadcasting as a means of providing social control, as the radio would provide the necessary distraction and 'impart to the African, the right kind of knowledge'. Thakar (2021) demonstrates that as the media was all controlled by the colonial administration, information was churned out on those terms. This methodology ensured the power interests of the colonial administration whose programming promised a better life but placed the onus on the listeners.

In the post-independence era, the Kaunda administration developed a ubiquitous eavesdropping state security apparatus that spied on citizens and bugged communication lines such as telephones (Sardanis, 2014: 89). By extension, the media environment was repressive and state-owned, including the national broadcaster Zambia National Broadcasting Corporation (ZNBC), *Daily Mail* and *Times of Zambia*, which were all perceived as the ruling party mouthpieces.

The reintroduction of multiparty politics in Zambia brought about hope for a more enabling environment that would encompass media autonomy, and that the state-owned media would be free and independent to play its role professionally. This hope was escalated by the strongest opposition party, the MMD, which criticized UNIP for not creating a conducive environment for free press and freedom of speech.

According to Ndawana et al. (2021), since the country's return to multiparty democracy in the 1990s, efforts to deregulate the media that started under the MMD administration proved futile. Successive governments were reluctant to actualize the idea of a free and independent media. In fact, the government opted to regulate the media and maintained a hostile legal framework by not passing the access to information legislation. Media self-regulation efforts were thwarted. Although civil society organizations joined the advocacy efforts, demanding the enactment of access to information legislation, politicians remained adamant in refusing to pass the law, stating that journalists would abuse the law as far as going to their bedrooms to fish out information. This was merely a figure of speech that suggested the media would gain access to their most private information and air it out.

What remained clear was the fact that access to information (ATI), as far as policymakers were concerned at the time, was a tool that would be used by the media to abuse the ruling elites. They fought all efforts made by stakeholders to bring the bill to parliament. They often overlooked the importance of ATI to every citizen and the extent the legislation went to in contributing to development and decision-making by both politicians and citizens. The internet shutdown was testimony to how ATI was affected, as citizens could not access news, receive timely information that would aid the voters in crucial decision-making. After much advocacy and campaigning among stakeholders, the Access to Information Act was passed in December 2023 and officially published in June 2024.

In 2013 a famous online investigative news website run by the Zambian Watchdog had its website blocked by the government in Zambia. The Watchdog proprietors opted to take their news to Facebook where it became even more popular. It was not long before the Facebook page, which served as a secondary news dissemination platform, was deactivated (*Lusaka Times*, 2013). The Deputy Minister of Labour was quoted at an event expressing the government's satisfaction that the Zambia Watchdog had been blocked, as it had been causing a lot of confusion (Committee to Protect Journalists, 2013). The proprietors were later able to circumvent the blockade and still have the website accessible in Zambia.

To date it was never established whether there had been an order given by government to shut down the Facebook page. The hunt for the Watchdog persisted with a few journalists getting arrested and interrogated by the police. Investigative journalists Thomas Zgambo, Wilson Pondamali and Clayson Hamasaka had their homes raided on allegations of suspected drugs. They were then arrested for sedition and in additional charges, Clayson Hamasaka was arrested for being in possession of obscene materials. The police confiscated their computers and phones, after which they were later accused of being behind the news updates on the Zambian Watchdog. The matter was taken to court where all three were acquitted.

In September 2016 armed state operatives raided Hai Telecommunications, a web-hosting company in search of Watchdog Newspaper Servers. Some equipment was allegedly taken from Hai Telecommunications Ltd; however, no further reports were made by the authorities on the outcome of the raid. The Committee to Protect Journalists (CPJ, 2013a) reported that, similar to the Zambian Watchdog, government went on to block another online news platform, Zambia Reports, in July 2013. It was not clear what circumstances caused the blockage of the website within Zambia. The news site had been critical of the government and often expressed critical views, albeit without breaking the law. Zambia Reports filed a complaint to the ICT Regulator regarding the blocking of its website but did not get any response. In response to the blocking of the Watchdog, the *Post Newspaper* quoted the Vice President at the time, Dr Guy Scott, saying that, 'The Zambian Watchdog deserved to be blocked for inciting people to hatred'.

The Zambian state has a long history of media shutdowns that has included shutting down newspapers, television stations and websites. According to Sally Burnheim (1999), the first official act of internet censorship in Africa occurred in February 1996 when the Zambian government succeeded in removing a banned edition of *The Post* from the newspaper's website by threatening to prosecute the country's main internet service provider (ISP), Zamnet.

The offending edition of *The Post* was banned under the Preservation of Public Security Act because it contained a report based on leaked documents which allegedly revealed secret government plans for a referendum on the adoption of a new constitution. A presidential decree warned the public that anyone caught with the banned edition, including the electronic version, would be liable to prosecution. It remained on the newspaper's website for two days until the police warned Zamnet that it too would be liable to prosecution. Burnheim posits that the government's action in banning the offending edition was rendered futile when a US reader published *The Post* edition on his own internet site. Thus, anyone with internet access could still read the banned paper and, because it was located on a computer in the United States, it was outside the jurisdiction of the Zambian authorities. The Zambian government also tried to pressure Zamnet to cease publishing *The Post* on the internet. However, Zamnet stood its ground and instead encouraged the government to publish its media on the internet as well.

*The Post* was an independent newspaper that uncovered and exposed many government misdeeds. Over the years, *The Post* became a thorn in the flesh of successive governments. It presented a platform that spoke truth to power and also held power accountable. Following the arrest of *The Post* newspaper proprietor Fred Mmembe, Muchena (2016) alleged that *The Post* were victims of the state's attempts to silence critical media that spoke truth to power. In 2017, under the Patriotic Front (PF) government led by Edgar Lungu, *The Post* was closed down and later liquidated by the Zambia Revenue Authority (ZRA), which is the national tax authority for non-compliance with tax regulations. However, *The*

*Post* management accused the government of using state machinery to shut the newspaper down because it had unearthed the 2016 election rigging plans.

What began as playful, leisurely platforms such as Facebook and Twitter fast became an avenue for expression, communication and information outlets. These were platforms where government policies, kleptocracy, poor service delivery, lack of transparency and accountability became topics that were debated online daily by the citizenry, who used the same platforms to not only mobilize like-minded people but also to speak truth to power and challenge their civic leaders.

The shrinking civic space offline in the country was as a result of the government's hostility towards those that expressed any form of dissent. This only made social media even more popular as it remained the safest space for citizens to mobilize, advocate and inform each other without facing the wrath of the law that was often used to intimidate, detain and arrest citizens. The police and government agencies threated those that suggested going against the status quo with detention and arrests.

An influential television station, Prime TV, was closed in April 2020 by the Independent Broadcasting Authority (IBA) who accused the station owner of spurning their requests to broadcast free public service announcements on the TV station during the Covid-19 pandemic. Prime TV was fast becoming a leading platform for political discourse and gave access to various stakeholders and opposition parties who were often not permitted to feature on the national broadcaster. CPJ (2020) reported that the revocation of the Prime TV's broadcast licence confirmed the government's aim to silence a key independent media house that had at times been critical of the government's stance on governance issues.

The government made a number of attempts to restrict internet access in some parts of the country. Freedom House (2020) observed that in 2020 internet users in Southern Province experienced a two-day connectivity disruption amid nationwide political tensions. While the disruption was blamed on the seasonal rains, opposition parties alleged that it was government engineered, due to the ongoing political tensions that had arisen in the run up to the 2021 elections. In addition, journalists and citizens were arrested for expressing themselves online. In February and March 2020, police arrested Kelly Nawezhi, Prince Kaliza, Joel Banda and Akapelwa Simat for their activity on various Facebook and WhatsApp groups that each administered. The four were charged with various crimes, including proposing violence on social media, distributing pornography and criminal libel. Elizabeth Mubanga, who is married to the popular Zambian musician Afunika, was arrested in February 2020. She was alleged to be the source of a viral audio clip claiming that water in Copperbelt Province was contaminated with chemicals. Mubanga was charged with seditious publication with intent to cause fear and alarm, and released on police bond (CPJ, 2020).

In June 2020, a group of youth gave police notice of its intention to hold a peaceful protest against injustices and failure by government to meet their needs. The youth were to protest against the high costs of living and unemployment, among other issues. A few days before the set protest date, the police spokesperson issued a statement that no permit had been granted for any youth protest and that the police would arrest any protesters (*Lusaka Times*, 2021). The protesters informed the nation that they would go ahead and still hold the protest with or without the police permit, after which the Minster of Home Affairs warned the protesters, saying those who challenged the state's authority would only have themselves to blame (Mbewe, 2020).

On the set date of the protest, police in heavy riot gear were seen conducting motorized and foot patrols around the central business district in search of the youth who opted to outsmart the waiting police by streaming the protest online. The Inspector General of Police was quoted as saying that they knew where the online protest was taking place and that those that were apprehended would only have themselves to blame. However, the protest ended uninterrupted and no police caught up with the protesters.

The online protest changed the narrative of how people in Zambia opted to exercise their rights and freedoms. Instead of taking to the street and getting beaten up and arrested they opted to assemble online. In accordance with the statements made by Chama Fumba, one of the protest organizers, 'it has the potential to change how protests will be conducted, there are two streets, the physical streets and social media streets'.

## *The digital era*

The digital era began in 1994 when the country first connected to the internet through ZAMNET which served as the country's first ISP. The Zambia ICT Policy (2006) was the first ICT policy developed in the country that recognized the role that the ICT sector could play in bridging the developmental divide.

As the legal and regulatory environment in the country underwent several changes, in 2019 the government introduced the Constitution of Zambia (Amendment) Bill, No. 10 of 2019. It was dubbed Bill 10 and sought to revise a number of provisions including the electoral system. Overall, the bill, if passed, would weaken oversight of the executive by the legislature, judiciary and other state institutions. The government was heavily condemned by civil society and various stakeholders for sponsoring such a bill. Renowned Constitutional lawyer, Professor Muna Ndulo advised that if the Bill was enacted it would install a constitutional dictatorship and undermine democracy in Zambia (Ndulo, 2020). In December 2020 the bill did not garner a two-thirds majority in Parliament and fell through.

Following the failed Constitutional (Amendment) Bill No. 10 of 2019, the government went on to enact several cyber laws in 2021. These included: the Cyber Crimes and Cyber Security Act (2021), E-Government Act (2021), Data Protection Act (2021), The National Cyber Security Policy (2021) and Postal and Courier services Policy (2021). The Electronic Communication and Transactions Act (2021) was repealed.

The Cyber laws were passed amidst public outcry. Stakeholders pointed out that some of the provisions in the Cybercrimes and Cybersecurity Act (2021) were inimical to some fundamental human rights including freedom of expression and access to information. A coalition of Civil Society Organizations (CSOs) petitioned some of the provisions that were contained in the Cyber Crimes and Cyber Security Act (2021). The CSOs argued that, in addition to threatening the right to freedom of expression, it also granted the Minister of Information, the ICT Regulator and law enforcement agencies excessive powers over the broad provisions that threatened the civic space, especially for those that used online communication platforms (MISA, 2016).

Zambia had 5.48 million internet users by 2021; the country's total population was 18.65 million. There was a 300 thousand (13 percent) increase in the number of social media users between 2020 and 2021 (Data Reportal, 2021). The rise of social media in Zambia revolutionized the manner in which citizens engage with governance issues. Key among the governance issues was the police abuse of the Public Order Act, a piece of legislation that governs public gatherings. Additionally, issues of access to information, media freedoms, mis/disinformation were among the governance issues that were gaining traction in online discourse. After the November 2021 elections, the United Party for National Development (UPND) government established a new Ministry of Technology and Science. The role of the Ministry would be to guide ICT's policy formulation and implementation. In 2022, the Ministry of Technology and Science began stakeholder consultations on the draft law.

## *Country case description*

Zambia has experienced numerous internet restrictions and partial shutdowns In addition to platform censorship and website blockages over the years. Notably, most network interferences have occurred during election periods and in areas facing political disputes, as was seen in 2016 and 2021.

Table 4.1 outlines the key internet restrictions, dates and durations.

**Table 4.1** Internet Restrictions and Partial Shutdowns

| Year | Occurrence | Duration |
|---|---|---|
| 2013 | The Zambian Watchdog online newspaper website blocked | 3–10 Days |
| 2013 | Zambia reports online news website blocked | Duration unconfirmed |
| 2014 | The Zambian Watchdog online newspaper website blocked | Over a month |
| August 2016 | Mobile broadband disruption in southern and north-western province | 48–72 hours |
| September 2016 | Armed state operatives raid Hai Telecommunications, a web-hosting company, on suspicion of keeping Zambian Watchdog servers. This was part of the effort towards shutting down the Watchdog newspaper | Duration unconfirmed |

| Year | Occurrence | Duration |
|---|---|---|
| 2017 | 2017 State forces Zamnet to block edition of *The Post* newspaper online | Unconfirmed |
| February 2020 | Internet inaccessible in southern province | 2 Days |
| August 2021 | ZICTA blocks social media and communication platforms including Facebook, Twitter, Messenger and WhatsApp | 2 Days |

## *The 2021 shutdown*

The 2021 internet shutdown was not a full shutdown of the entire internet but rather a partial shutdown of the main social media platforms used by Zambian citizens. On 12 August 2021, a social media restriction was imposed by the government on popular social media platforms including Facebook, Instagram, Twitter (now X) and WhatsApp which became inaccessible in the country until a court ruling served to the ICT regulator on 13 August 2021 ordered their unblocking. The internet was only restored on 14 August 2021. Chapter One Foundation filed for a judicial review against the ICT regulator on 13 August 2021. The Court ordered the regulator to restore the internet. A consent judgment was later entered in March 2022 where the Zambia Information Communication Technology Authority (ZICTA), the ICT Regulator, agreed not to act outside its legal authority in future.

## *2021 elections*

The 2021 elections were highly contentious elections in Zambia. They were held in the context of Covid-19 and the two front runners, Patriotic Front (PF), which was the ruling party, and United Party for National Development (UPND), the Opposition Party at the time had clashed several times. The UPND presidential Candidate Hakainde Hichilema, popularly known as HH, had been arrested for treason and was released after interventions from the international community led by the Commonwealth.

HH used social media, particularly X (formerly Twitter), to engage and mobilize support, especially from the youth who started referring to himself as 'Bally', a colloquial term that loosely translates as Dad or Father. His online popularity grew so much that his campaign slogan became 'Bally will Fix It'.

In the run-up to the 2021 elections, citizens took to online platforms to express themselves, raise awareness and protest various actions that were not to their satisfaction. Prior to the election day, Common Cause Zambia, a civil society organization in Zambia that works to promote good governance and digital rights, collaborated with the global #KeepItOn Coalition, a global movement that has international membership and works towards fighting internet shutdowns globally, and issued an open letter to the president and published a statement appealing to the government not to shut down the internet (Access Now, 2021b). The government dismissed as malicious claims made by Common Cause Zambia that there was a looming possibility of an internet shutdown in Zambia. The Permanent Secretary in the Ministry of Information dismissed as false and calculated to cause alarm any statement suggesting an imminent shutdown.

As the election day drew closer, the same spokesperson, Amos Malupenga, was quoted in the media saying, 'Government expects citizens to use the internet responsibly. But if some people choose to abuse the internet to mislead and misinform, government will not hesitate to invoke relevant legal provisions to forestall any breakdown of law and order as the country passes through the election period.'

The 2021 general elections in Zambia were against the backdrop of the Covid-19 pandemic. The elections were held in the context of Covid-19. As the campaign period was gaining momentum, in June 2021 the Electoral Management Body (EMB) banned all physical political party campaign activities because they were drawing big crowds and going against the Covid-19 preventive measures. This followed a report made by the Zambia National Public Health Institute which warned that, if the number of Covid-19 cases increased, the Zambia National Public Institute would have to recommend stringent restrictions such as lockdown, disaster declaration and even suspension of elections.

At the beginning of the political party campaigns most parties opted to use what they called 'campaign roadshows', where contesting candidates sat in vehicles playing music and driving through neighbourhoods with megaphones, canvasing for votes and sharing their party manifestos. As the campaigns went on, the roadshows began drawing huge crowds of people who were following the entertaining music, defying all Covid-19 preventive measures and protocol. As a result, the EMB used its regulatory powers to suspend physical campaign activities in some provinces affected by violence while the police enforced the Public Order Act and Covid-19 Standard Operating Procedures (SOPs).

The application of the restrictions by the EMB was selective as the ruling party was accused of holding political party campaigns under the guise of national duties, which were drawing scores of people who disregarded Covid-19 SOPs. For example, the president would launch a bridge, which is official government business, but supporters clad in political party regalia would attend the launch.

Following the ban on campaign rallies, political parties shifted their campaigns to online platforms where they mobilized online concerts and canvassed for votes. This move was not without challenges for the political parties in that it created a number of limitations based on the fact that internet penetration in the country was below 50 per cent, which meant a huge demographic was not reachable through online platforms. Data Reportal (2021) indicated that there were 5.48 million internet users in Zambia and only 2.60 million active social media users (see Table 4.2). The cost of data to access these video live streams was high for a sustained audience and, finally, the slow internet that was experienced whenever the opposition parties had their online campaigns, compounded by questionable power outages, raised concerns among stakeholders, who concluded that these were schemes aimed at blocking opposition political parties from reaching

**Table 4.2** Internet and Social Media Statistics: Zambia 2021

| Total population | Mobile connections | Internet users | Active social media users | Internet users % of population |
|---|---|---|---|---|
| 18.65 Million | 16.73 Million | 5.48 Million | 2.60 Million | 29.4% |

Source: www.datareportal.com/digital-in-zambia

the voters. In addition, the cost of data to access the internet was prohibitive, compounded by an erratic electricity supply; it was clear that a large number of voters was being left out.

## *Conceptual framing*

This chapter seeks to examine the extent to which the Zambian government weaponized the internet through social media restrictions, website blockages to suppress dissent and control information flow. This section will review the existing literature on concepts of rights, power and agency that will later be used to frame my analysis of the Zambian case study.

The concept of rights is paramount in comprehending the implication of state restrictions on internet access and freedom of expression online. Gani (2015) posits that the right to freedom of expression is increasingly understood to encompass digital freedoms, which include not only the right to access information but also the right to express oneself freely on the internet. Article 19 of the Universal Declaration of Human Rights guarantees that individuals have the right to receive, seek and impart information through any media, including the internet (United Nations, 1948).

Despite the foregoing, governments often justify internet censorship by invoking national security concerns, maintaining public order or curbing online hate speech and misinformation (Keller, 2020). This brings in the question of balance between state control and individual rights especially where political participation is concerned. The case of Zambia where powerholders continuously implement measures such as social media restrictions and website blockages can be perceived as restricting the rights of citizens' access to information, expressing political opinion, especially during periods of political instability or elections (Zikode, 2019).

It is crucial to understand the dynamics of internet censorship in order to grasp the concept of power. Michel Foucault's theory of power relates to his perception of surveillance control and discipline, which has been widely applied to understand how states leverage digital technology to assert control over populations (Foucault, 1977). States have increasingly been using the internet as a tool for surveillance and as a platform to exercise disciplinary power, controlling and manipulating what is heard, seen and shared. In the case of Zambia, the states' use of social media restrictions can be interpreted as authoritarian control in the digital sphere (Lyon, 2007).

In an increasingly interconnected world, internet governance becomes a critical dimension of state power. According to Zuboff (2019), the weaponization of digital tools by the state can be viewed as a form of 'surveillance capitalism', wherein the state manipulates or restricts access to digital platforms in order to shape political behaviour and maintain control over the electorate. The Zambian government's pattern of shutting down social media platforms during politically charged moments (e.g., elections) can be seen as an effort to curtail dissent. This state of digital authoritarianism is increasingly common in many African countries, where regimes use internet restrictions as a tactic for entrenching political control and curbing potential challenges to their authority (Puddephatt, 2020).

The concept of agency refers to the ability of individuals and groups to act autonomously and resist forms of control or coercion. In the context of internet censorship, agency becomes a central theme in understanding how citizens engage with or resist state imposed restrictions. Digital platforms, including social media have become a critical space for citizens to assert their agency, especially in countries where traditional means of political engagement are limited or heavily controlled (Appadurai, 2001). In Zambia, social media users and activists have developed strategies to bypass censorship and continue to engage in political discourse, government's attempts to restrict access to websites and platforms may momentarily disrupt the flow of information but it also highlights the resilience and adaptability of citizens seeking to assert their rights and political agency (Sullivan, 2021).

Citizens in Zambia found themselves at the mercy of powerholders that control the keys to the internet gateway, leaving them vulnerable to abrupt shutdowns and other forms of censorship. Internet shutdowns infringe citizens' rights to freedom of expression and undermine their access to information. They also impact on social, economic and cultural rights – as they affect people's ability to access online education and healthcare and to work, if they are gig-workers or work virtually.

The 2021 partial internet shutdown that occurred in Zambia can be linked to heightened citizen engagement in political discourse using online platforms. Prior to the shutdown, the Permanent Secretary in the Ministry of Information was quoted by the media (*Lusaka Times*, 2021): 'Government, therefore, expects citizens to use the internet responsibly. But if some people choose to abuse the internet to mislead and misinform, Government will not hesitate to invoke relevant legal provisions to forestall any breakdown of law and order as the country passes through the election period.' This statement was issued by a government official, despite the fact that the constitution of Zambia (2016) guarantees freedom of expression, freedom of association and freedom of assembly.

Conversely, Principle 5 of the Declaration of Principles on Freedom of Expression and Access to Information in Africa affirms human rights online. 'The exercise of rights to freedom of expression and access to information shall be protected from interference both online and offline, and states shall interpret and implement the protection of these rights in the declaration and other relevant international standards accordingly.'

Section 29, 38 and 58 of the Cybercrimes and Cybersecurity Act (2010) empowers law enforcement officers to legally intercept communication through a central monitoring and coordination centre. It pressurizes service providers to use electronic communication systems that are capable of supporting lawful interception. Further, it criminalizes production, possession and circulation of any obscene materials or any objects that corrupt morals.

The existence of repressive laws such as the Public Order Act in the country also contributes to unfettered powers in some of the 'closed spaces' where decisions are made without any consideration of human rights violations. The 2021 shutdown is a clear case where a decision was made and implemented in violation of the fundamental human rights guaranteed in Article 19 of the Universal Declaration of Human Rights and articulated in Principle 37 of the Declaration of Principles on Freedom of Expression and Access to Information in Africa, which promotes and protects the right to freedom of expression and article 19 of the International Covenant on Civil and Political Rights, which protects this right to freedom of expression.

The case of Zambia will be used to examine its historical precedence to censorship going back as far as 1996. We will highlight the tireless efforts of governments aimed at dominating online narratives. Although some ISPs such as ZAMNET attempted to maintain strength under duress, authorities have been relentless in mounting pressure in order to censor opposing voices as a means of retaining power.

In the case of Zambia, the internet restriction on election-day gave rise to a citizen resistance. Despite the numerous threats and warnings issued, citizens self-mobilized and shared VPNs openly, using platforms like telegram and those that were still functional. The courage and resilience of citizens in pushing back against censorship and shutdown was manifest in the action taken by Chapter One Foundation that sued the ICT Regulator and got a court order for internet restoration.

In light of the long-winded journey that has witnessed blocking of websites, content take downs, internet restrictions that ended up in litigation, it remains clear that those in power continue to exert pressure and seek to silence dissenting voices.

## *Definition and types of internet shutdowns*

This statement was issued by a government official, despite the fact that the constitution of Zambia (2016) guarantees freedom of expression, freedom of association and freedom of assembly.

According to Access Now there are many types of internet shutdowns; for example, during blanket shutdowns, or total internet blackouts, access to the internet or all telecommunication services is completely cut, usually by a government actor. In contrast, partial shutdowns target specific types of networks (for example, mobile networks) or services such as social media and messaging apps. An internet shutdown can also take the form of throttling, when internet speeds are intentionally slowed down for the purpose of making it harder – or even impossible – for people to upload, download, or access information. One of the tactics commonly used by governments is downgrading mobile internet speeds from 4G and 3G levels to 2G.

Prior to the August 2021 Election Day, there were observations made of suspected attempts to throttle the internet. According to journalist Brenda Zulu (Zulu, 2024), citizens reported that there were often unscheduled power interruptions and slow network which made it difficult to stream videos online let alone campaigns that were being streamed online, due to Covid-19 health measures.

This frames citizens as being at the mercy of those that have control over the internet gateway, who can use their power at any time to shut down the internet or throttle access to the internet, consequently stifling the right to freedom of expression and access to information. While studies have shown that internet shutdowns violate human rights (OHCHR, 2022), in the case of Zambia we saw the rise of people power. Once there was an anticipation of a potential shutdown, efforts were made by civil society to prepare human rights defenders, media and citizens on how to measure availability of the internet using tools such as OONI Measurement Tool and also the use of VPNs. Pure VPN (2021) reported a rise in the use of VPNs in Zambia in 2021 and using Google analytics they noted a visible increase in Zambia traffic.

This chapter will use the concepts of rights and power to answer the question of which human rights were impacted and whose interests were advanced by the Zambian government's decision to restrict the internet during the 2021 elections.

## *Analysis*

The power interests that drove the 2021 internet shutdown in Zambia was largely by governmental authorities whose intention was to stifle dissent and control information flow. For instance, the Freedom Online Coalition (FOC), expressed concern at the escalation of state sponsored interruption of access to and dissemination of information online (FOC, 2017). It cannot be overlooked that most disruptions occur during politically driven dissent, elections and protests that border on socio-economic issues leading to political discontent.

The internet increasingly became a threat to the government as more citizens began demanding accountability and mobilized online when restrictive laws such as the Public Order Act were used to police offline physical spaces. Once citizens were able to hold online protests that received massive support, the opposition political parties equally capitalized on online spaces to mobilize, campaign and rally support, leading the government to perceive the internet as a threat to its power.

The events that led to the August 2021 shutdown began systematically. Heightened political activities were undertaken by political parties and civil society advocacy against the infamous Constitutional Amendment Bill No. 10 of 2019, which sought to remove parliamentary oversight over the Executive among other detrimental clauses.

The proposed Constitutional Amendment Bill No. 10 of 2019 came out of the ruling party (Patriotic Front) dominated conference, which did not include key stakeholders such as the leading opposition parties and civil society. The endless protest campaigns online and offline against the enactment of Bill 10 led to the government use of Covid-19 pandemic health measures as a means to prevent citizens from mobilizing. The Minister of Home Affairs warned against holding protests against Bill 10 since government had banned public gatherings in view of Covid-19 (*Zambia Daily Mail*, 2020). Despite all efforts made, the Constitutional Amendment Bill No. 10 did not see the light of day. It failed to garner a two-thirds majority, as opposition members walked out of parliament in protest when it was tabled (Sakala, 2020).

In March 2021, President Edgar Lungu signed three laws, including the Cyber Security and Cyber Crimes Act, The Data Protection Act of 2021 and the Electronic Communication and Transactions Act of 2021 (NAZ, 2021). The rapid enactment of the laws, especially the Cyber Security and Cyber Crimes Act, was viewed as a backup measure by power holders to exert power over telecommunications companies and ISPs to restrict the rights of citizens, media, human rights defenders and civil society expression and association online. The president had made numerous threats that he would deal with people who abused social media. In February 2021 during a public address, President Lungu said security agents would soon begin arresting social media abusers following the introduction of the cybercrimes and cyber security law (Malakata, 2021).

In the run up to the 2021 elections, the Electoral Commission of Zambia (ECZ) banned physical campaign road shows as they were drawing huge crowds that were listed as Covid-19 super spreaders. It was noted that every time opposition parties held online rallies, the network was extremely slow with endless buffering. Conversely, when the ruling party held its online rallies the network was often stable and streams were flawless.

This banning of campaign activities by the ECZ drew a dangerous line between upholding standard health procedures but also violating constitutional guaranteed principles such as freedom to exercise political rights, freedom of movement and freedom of assembly. Undeniably, the Covid-19 SOP gave the ruling party undue advantage over the other competing parties and violated the constitution by depriving citizens a level playing field that provided fair and equal access to information throughout.

Ultimately, by 12 August 2021 popular social media platforms Facebook, Instagram, Twitter and WhatsApp were completely shut down. To date, Zambians have been left in the dark about the reasons behind the shutdown and also who ordered it.

The partial shutdown in itself, besides infringing citizens' rights to access information and freedom of expression, led to loss of business, although there are no clear statistics on the extent to which citizens were affected. The watershed election had a record 71 per cent voter turnout which saw massive queues. Citizens went to queue as early as 1.00 am. on election day and some queued for twenty hours. Although the citizens used their individual and collective agency and made efforts to share VPNs to encourage fellow citizens to circumvent the restriction and exercise their rights, the state countered these efforts by blocking some VPNs that were publicly shared. Although the citizens' resistance highlights the strong counter power, the dynamics that came into play when the government pushed back showed the extent of power struggles that exist in the digital space. The agency and counter power require innovation and adaption for those resisting power.

The shutdown had adverse effects on business that depend on social media platforms. For instance, bloggers who monetize their accounts and depend on web traffic lost income, causing a breach of citizens fundamental economic right to work as enshrined in the Universal Declaration of Human (1948) and the Covenant on Economic Social and Cultural Rights (1966). Similarly the use of VPNs at the time of the shutdown led citizens to use insecure VPNs which could have led to loss of finances, hence some of the banks urged their customers not to use their banking applications and internet banking while using VPNs (Digital Safe, 2021).

The shutdown was perceived as the government's abuse of its power over its citizens; however, it led to galvanizing the collective agency of citizens' action. Citizens resisted government action through circumvention. A lot of agency and efforts to build 'power with' others to exert power to hold government accountable was observed among the citizens and CSOs. Common Cause Zambia collaborated with the BBC Media Action and the Zambian Bloggers Network began preparing citizens, human rights defenders, media and CSOs for any potential shutdowns by building capacity and sharing safe VPNs in preparation for any potential shutdown that they anticipated. The organization further rallied the support of the international community through the #KeepItOn Campaign Coalition which provided support in calling on the Zambian Government to keep the internet on before, during and after the elections (Access Now, 2021a).

## *Holding Power Accountable: legal resistance*

In August 2021 virtual conversations on the ills of internet shutdown were continuously held, pressuring the government to keep it on. The government's power over ISPs and Telecommunication companies represses the companies' obligation to protect their customers' rights. Shutting down social media was challenged through legal means by CSOs led by Chapter One Foundation who sued the ICT regulator ZICTA, seeking a court order for restoration of all services.

The notice of application was filed in the High Court by Chapter One Foundation, who contended that the decision by the regulator was illegal, unreasonable and outside the ICT regulators' mandate. The Court ruled that ZICTA did not have the legal power to implement a shutdown and forced it to restore the internet. In 2022, a consent judgment was entered between ZICTA and Chapter One Foundation where ZICTA agreed not to act outside its legal powers going forward and that it would provide reasons for any shutdown within thirty-six hours in future.

The landmark judgment presented a shift in power relations – the perception that citizens had of the judicial system and their ability to hold power accountable. For decades the Zambian state had acted with impunity, imposing media shutdowns on newspapers, television stations and websites. For the first time citizen agency and collective 'power with' had created an effective form of counter-power that successfully challenged the state's 'power over' companies and citizens. The legal precedent meant that power had shifted and future governments could not expect to act with impunity. The Court ruled that the regulator had exceeded its legal power and that the shutdown was illegal. It is an important element of human rights law that powers must be 'legal, necessary, and proportionate'. In this case it was unnecessary, illegal and disproportionate. The judgment will serve as precedence for future injustices and shutdowns and give rise to citizens' agency in pushing back against repressive laws and unwarranted internet shutdowns and network interference. The legality of shutdowns will also be challenged because precedence has been set.

## *Conclusion*

In answering the research question, 'Which human rights were impacted and whose interests were advanced by the Zambian government's decision to restrict the internet during the 2021 elections?' it was found that the Zambian government's imposition of an internet restriction during the 2021 elections impacted the rights of access to information, freedom of expression and enjoyment of economic social and cultural rights. This action primarily served the interests of those in power by potentially limiting public scrutiny, dissent and the dissemination of alternative viewpoints during a critical democratic process. The implication on various rights and interests included:

### *Impact on rights*

**Freedom of Expression:** The internet shutdowns restricted citizen's ability to freely express their opinions, share information and engage in discourse online. This affected the democratic process by limiting the diversity of viewpoints available to the public on Election Day and in the post election environment.

**Access to information:** Access to timely and accurate information is crucial during elections. The internet shutdown hampered access to news updates, election results and other critical information necessary for informed decision-making by voters.

**Communication rights:** Citizens rely on the internet for communication through social media, messaging apps and email. The shutdown disrupted these channels, hindering the ability of individuals, civil society groups and media organizations to communicate effectively and fully participate in the electoral process at such a crucial time.

*Whose interests were served?*

*Government authorities* Most internet shutdowns are imposed by those with incumbent power, in order to weaken the organizing power of opposition. It is most often a means of maintaining power and repressing counter-power. However, in this case Zambians used their agency to challenge the 'power over' of the state and chose to mobilize the collective 'power with' others and the 'power to' petition the court and secure legal redress. In as much as the court censored the regulator and warned against reoccurrence, it is clear that the balance of power shifted. The push back by citizens who bravely shared VPNs to enable as many citizens to exercise their human rights as possible is testimony to that shift. Although the internet shutdown aimed to stifle dissenting views, there were criticisms of electoral processes and allegations of misconduct or exposure of electoral fraud. Restricting online communication limited citizens' ability to communicate effectively, access real-time data, mobilize support, organize and even communicate some of the life-threatening situations that came about as the electoral process ensued.

In summary, the internet shutdown during Zambia's 2021 elections underscored the tension between protecting national security and ensuring fundamental rights such as freedom of expression and access to information. While governments may justify such actions on grounds of maintaining public order or security, they can also undermine the transparency and fairness of democratic processes.

The question of government control and citizens' rights in Zambia remains symbiotic. Incumbent political power in Zambia continues to silence voices and violate citizens' rights to free expression. However, citizens are using online space to hold power to account and the successful use of strategic legislation to ask the court to hold the state accountable in law is evidence that a new space of power contestation has opened. This is a testimony to the tensions that continue to exist between government and citizens in the digital age.

In a democratic dispensation, shutdowns can only serve the interests of those in power at the expense of democratic rights and socio-economic development. By doing so, citizens' increasing appetite to resist shutdowns is a clear example of the importance of defending fundamental rights and holding the government accountable while calling power back to the people.

This chapter presented evidence that citizens' civil and political rights to freedom of information, communication, speech, assembly and association were infringed by the illegal internet shutdown. The chapter also provided evidence that additional economic, social and cultural rights were violated when the government exceeded its legal power to implement the shutdown. Zambian citizens used their collective power through civil society to hold the government to account. The High

Court of Zambia ruled that the state had exceeded its powers in implementing the internet shutdown. It is clear in this case that the internet shutdown was neither legal, necessary nor proportionate. The digital rights of citizens to share information, communicate freely and to enjoy unhindered participation in civic and political life must persevere in future Zambian elections.

## *Key recommendations*

There is a need to review existing policies that are inimical to the enjoyment of human rights and freedoms in Zambia, such as the Cybercrimes and Cybersecurity Act (2021). Existing laws and policies should adhere to international human rights standards. This includes providing legal justifications and notifying the public in advance whenever possible (Access Now, 2020).

The Government should engage in meaningful dialogue with stakeholders, including civil society, experts and citizens, in policy formulation for managing public order and security concerns without resorting to internet restrictions and shutdowns. This collaborative approach can lead to more effective and rights-respecting responses.

More efforts should be made to promote digital literacy, cyber security awareness, and resilience among citizens and institutions. According to the Brookings Institute, empowering individuals and communities to navigate online spaces safely and responsibly can reduce the perceived need for broad-scale shutdowns during crises (Brookings Institution, 2021).

The role of Telecommunication companies and ISPs in ensuring that networks are operational is crucial, even more so during times of political strife. In the face of shutdown orders often made by powerholders who want to control communication or supress citizens' agency, companies should challenge these orders through legal channels. Transparency remains critical and companies should publicly disclose their source of orders. That way ISPs can protect their users' rights and their corporate integrity. Institutions should adhere to existing international human rights frameworks, such as those outlined by the United Nations Human Rights Council, which emphasize that any restrictions on internet access must be lawful, necessary and proportionate. Upholding these standards ensures that internet shutdowns are used only as a last resort and for the shortest time possible (UN Human Rights Council, 2018).

## *Bibliography*

Access Now (2020), 'Internet Shutdowns: Trends, Legal Standards and the Way Forward', Access Now, https://www.accessnow.org/wp-content/uploads/2023/03/Evading-accountability-through-internet-shutdowns.pdf

Access Now (2021a), 'Internet Shutdowns and Elections Handbook', Access Now, https://www.accessnow.org/guide/internet-shutdowns-and-elections-handbook/#section

Access Now (2021b), 'Open Letter to President Edgar Changwa Lungu: Keep the Internet Open throughout the Upcoming Elections and Thereafter', https://www.accessnow.org/wp-content/uploads/2021/08/KeepItOn_-open-letter-Zambia.pdf

Access Now (2022), 'Taxonomy of a Shutdown: 8 Ways Governments Restrict Access to the Internet and How to #KeepItOn', https://www.accessnow.org/publication/internet-shutdown-types/

Access Now (n.d.), Fighting Internet Shutdowns around the World, www.accessnow.org/campaign/keepiton/

Access Now (n.d.), 'What is an Internet shutdown', https://www.accessnow.org/guide/internet-shutdowns-and-elections-handbook/#section-I

Alison, S. (2020), 'Audacious Zambian protesters outsmart the police', *Mail* and *Guardian*, https://mg.co.za/africa/2020-06-26-audacious-zambian-protesters-outsart-the-police/

Appadurai, A. (2001), 'Deep Democracy: Urban Governmentality and the Horizon of Politics', *Environment and Urbanization*, 13 (2): 23–43.

Basil, J. (2021), 'To VPN or Not to VPN', https://www.techtrends.co.zm/?s=to+VPN

Brookings Institution (2021), 'The Future of Internet Freedom: How to Prevent Shutdowns in Africa', Brookings Report (URL not available).

Burnheim, S. (1999), 'The Right to Communicate, Internet in Africa. Censorship and Control: Obstacles to Growth', Article 19, https://www.article19.org/data/files/pdfs/publications/africa-internet.pdf

CCMG (2021), Preliminary statement on the 2021 General Elections, CCMG Zambia, https://ccmgzambia.org/ccmg-preliminary-statement-on-the-2021-general-elections/

CCMG Zambia. 'CCMG Preliminary Statement on the 2021 General Elections', https://ccmgzambia.org/ccmg-preliminary-statement-on-the-2021-general-elections/

Chapter One Foundation is a Civil society organisation that works on Access to Justice.

Committee to Protect Journalists (2013), 'In Zambia, Harassment of Watchdog site continues', 17 July 2013, https://cpj.org/2013/07/in-zambia-harassment-of-watchdog-site-continues/

Constitution of Zambia (2016), Republic of Zambia Constitution. Lusaka: Government of Zambia, https://www.parliament.gov.zm/sites/default/files/documents/amendment_act/Constitution%20of%20Zambia%20%20(Amendment),%202016-Act%20No.%202_0.pdf

CPJ (2013a), 'Two Journalists Detained Without Charge in Zambia', https://cpj.org/2013/07/two-journalists-detained-without-charge-in-zambia/

CPJ (2013b), 'Zambia Blocks Another Website and Re-Arrests Reporters', https://cpj.org/2013/07/zambia-blocks-another-website-re-arrests-reporter/amp/

CPJ (2020), 'Zambia Cancels Broadcaster Prime TVs Licence, Police Shutter Office', https://cpj.org/2020/04/zambia-cancels-broadcaster-prime-tvs-license-polic/

*Daily Nation Zambia* (2021). 'ZICTA Sued Over Internet Shutdown', *Daily Nation Zambia*, 14 August, retrieved from https://dailynationzambia.com/2021/08/zicta-sued-over-internet-shutdown/

Data Reportal (2021), 'Digital 2021: Zambia', Data Reportal, 12 February, https://datareportal.com/reports/digital-2021-zambia

Digital Safe (2021), 'VPN Risks During Internet Shutdowns', Digital Safe (URL not available).

FOC (2017), 'Joint Statement on State Sponsored Network Disruption', Freedom Online Coalition, https://freedomonlinecoalition.com/wp-content/uploads/2021/06/FOC-Joint-Statement-and-Accompanying-Good-Practices-for-Government-on-State-Sponsored-Network-Disruptions.pdf

Foucault, M. (1977), *Discipline and Punish: The Birth of the Prison*, New York: Pantheon Books.

Freedom House (2020), 'Freedom on the Net 2020: Zambia', Freedom House Report, https://freedomhouse.org/country/zambia/freedom-net/2020

Gambanga, N. (2016), Zambian Government Suspected of causing Internet shutdown following outages in opposition strongholds, TechZim, http://www.techzim.co.zw/2016/08/zambia-government-suspected-of-causing-internet-shutdown/

Gani, R. (2015), 'Freedom of Expression in the Digital Age', *Journal of Media Law and Ethics*, 7 (1): 55–70.

Kasama, H. (2021), 'Government Dismisses Internet Shutdown Claims', ZNBC, http://www.znbc.co.zm/news/govt-dismisses-internet-shutdown-claims/

Keller, J. (2020), 'Balancing National Security and Digital Rights in Africa', *African Journal of Internet Policy*, 5 (1): 12–25.

Lesoetsa, G. (2021), 'ZICTA Sued Over Internet Shutdown', *Daily Nation*, https://dailynationzambia.com/2021/08/zicta-sued-over-internet-shutdown/

*Lusaka Times* (2013), 'Police Raid Houses and Detain Journalists Suspected of Publishing Zambian Watchdog', https://lusakatimes.com/2013/07/09/police-raid-houses-and-detain-journalists-suspected-of-publishing-zambian-watchdog/

*Lusaka Times* (2020), 'The planned Protests are illegal my office has not permited any protests - Kampyongo', *Lusaka Times*, 22 June 2020, https://www.lusakatimes.com/2020/06/22

*Lusaka Times* (2021), 'New Cyber Law Goes to Court', https://www.lusakatimes.com/2021/04/02/new-cyber-law-goes-to-court/

Lyon, D. (2007), *Surveillance Studies: An Overview*. Cambridge: Polity Press.

Mabunda, P. L. (2021), 'The Role of Traditional Leadership in South Africa: A Relic of the Past, or a Contemporary Reality?', *The Round Table: The Commonwealth Journal of International Affairs*, 110 (1): 99–100, https://www.tandfonline.com/doi/full/10.1080/03086534.2021.1985218#abstract

Malakata, M. (2021), 'Zambia to Arrest Social Media Abusers – Lungu', ITWeb Africa, 25 February, https://itweb.africa/content/j5alrMQa8dzMpYQk

Malunga, J. (2021), 'ECZ Officially Suspends Campaign Rallies, Says Election Date Wont Change', News Diggers, https://diggers.news/local/2021/06/04/ecz-officially-suspends-campaign-rallies-says-election-date-wont-change/

Mbewe, A. (2020), 'State Warns Protesters Over Bill 10', *Zambia Daily Nation*, 12 June (URL not available).

Mbewe, Z. (2022), 'COF, ZICTA Enter Consent Judgement in Internet Shutdown Case', News Diggers, https://diggers.news/courts/2022/03/22/cof-zicta-enter-consent-judgement-in-internet-shutdown-case/

MISA (2016), 'Zambia's Cyber Law Proposals Raise Concerns', Media Institute of Southern Africa, (URL not available).

Muchena, D. (2016), 'Zambia: Detained newspaper owner and staff must be immediately released immediately and unconditionally released', Amnesty International, 28 June, https://www.amnesty.org/en/latest/press-release/2016/06/zambia-detained-newspaper-owner-and-staff-must-be-immediately-and-unconditionally-released/

NAZ (2021), 'Cyber Security, Data Protection and E-Transactions Acts Passed', National Assembly of Zambia, https://www.parliament.gov.zm/

Ncube, S. (2020), 'ZICTA Fines All 3 Mobile Networks K5.4m for POOR SERVICES', News Diggers, https://diggers.news/business/2020/09/04/zicta-fines-all-3-mobile-networks-k5-4m-for-poor-service/

Ndawana, Y., Knowles, J. and Vaughan, C. (2021), 'The Historicity of Media Regulation in Zambia: Examining the Proposed Statutory Self-Regulation', *African Journalism Studies*, 42 (2): 59–76, https://doi.org/10.1080/23743670.2021.1939749

Ndulo, M. (2020), 'Cyber Law and Democracy in Zambia', *Zambia Law Journal*, 48 (2): 101–20.

News Diggers (2020) 'Those who dare the state will have themselves to blame warns Kampyongo', News Diggers, 22 June, https://diggers.news/local/2020/06/22/those-who-dare-the-state-will-have-themselves-to-blame-kampyongo-warns-youths/

Office of the High Commissioner for Human Rights (OHCHR) (2022) 'Activists: Internet shutdowns violate human rights', OHCHR, 19 August, https://www.ohchr.org/en/stories/2022/08/activists-internet-shutdowns-violate-human-rights

'Privacy International, Legality, Necessity and Proportionality', Privacy International, https://privacyinternational.org/our-demands/legality-necessity-and-proportionality#:~:text=This%20is%20the%20principle%20of,must%20be%20necessary%20and%20proportionate

Puddephatt, A. (2020), 'Authoritarianism in the Digital Age: Internet Shutdowns and Control in Africa', Global Freedom Report, (URL not available).

Pure VPN (2021), VPN Use Rises in Zambia Due to Internet Blackouts', https://www.purevpn.com/blog/vpn-use-rises-in-zambia-due-to-internet-blackouts/

Sakala, N. (2020), 'PF Drag Bill 10 Debate After Failing to Make Two Thirds Majority', https://diggers.news/local/2020/03/18/pf-drag-bill-10-debate-after-failing-to-make-two-thirds-majority/

SALC (2020), 'Authorities Escalate Attacks on Dissent by Denying Youth Leaders Right to Protest', https://www.southernafricalitigationcentre.org/2020/06/24/joint-statement-zambia-authorities-escalate-attacks-on-dissent-by-denying-youth-leaders-right-to-protest/

Sardanis, A. (2014), *Zambia: The First 50 Years*, London: I.B. Tauris.

Southern Africa Litigation Centre. 'Joint Statement: Zambia Authorities Escalate Attacks on Dissent by Denying Youth Leaders Right to Protest', https://www.southernafricalitigationcentre.org/2020/06/24/joint-statement-zambia-authorities-escalate-attacks-on-dissent-by-denying-youth-leaders-right-to-protest/

Sullivan, T. (2021), 'Digital Resistance and Censorship in Zambia', *Digital Rights Africa*, 10 (4): 88–102.

Thakar, S. (2021), 'Colonial Media Control and Information Power', *Journal of Postcolonial Studies*, 17 (3): 45–62.

United Nations (1948), *Universal Declaration of Human Rights*, New York: United Nations, https://www.un.org/en/about-us/universal-declaration-of-human-rights

UN Human Rights Council (2018), 'Report on the Promotion and Protection of the Right to Freedom of Opinion and Expression', New York: United Nations, https://digitallibrary.un.org/record/1643488?v=pdf

Zambia National Broadcasting Corporation. 'Govt Dismisses Internet Shutdown Claims', http://www.znbc.co.zm/news/govt-dismisses-internet-shutdown-claims/

Zikode, T. (2019), 'State Control and Social Media in Zambia', *African Digital Rights Review*, 6 (2): 74–87.

Zuboff, S. (2019), *The Age of Surveillance Capitalism: The Fight for a Human Future at the New Frontier of Power*. New York: PublicAffairs.

Zulu, B. (2024), 'Digital Disruptions and Political Participation during COVID-19', *Zambian Journal of Media Studies*, 12 (1): 29–41.

# Chapter 5

## Shrouded in shadows: Human rights, armed conflicts and internet shutdowns in Ethiopia

Yohannes Eneyew Ayalew and Lea Mehari Redae

### *Introduction*

Ethiopia has experienced more internet shutdowns than any other country in Africa (Access Now, 2024). Internet shutdowns in Ethiopia have been used to stifle dissent, to quell protests, to administer school exams and to wage ethnic war. This chapter focuses on three very different internet shutdown case studies that took place in Ethiopia between 2019 and 2023. Primary and secondary data is analysed through the lens of power, and rights to understand how shutdowns violate human rights to protect vested power interest, and how citizens possibly use their agency to resist, circumvent and challenge this abuse of power. From the insurgency and counter-insurgency movements in Wollega province, Oromia region, which have flared up since 2019, to the war in Tigray (2020–2) and the armed conflict in the Amhara region that erupted in August 2023, Ethiopia once again finds itself in a violent internal conflict unprecedented in its modern history. In such cases, a common reaction of the government is to shut down the internet and restrict private digital communications.

The Ethiopian government has proactively employed internet shutdowns as a tactic to curb protests and restrict the digital sphere where citizens engage in discussions about current affairs (Ayalew, 2019; Yilma, 2022). This strategy encompasses a range of measures, from blocking specific websites critical of the government to imposing geographically targeted or nationwide connectivity restrictions, be it mobile or broadband (Marchant and Stremlau, 2020; Anthonio and Roberts, 2023).

Even beyond armed conflicts, internet shutdowns have been strategically utilized to stifle political, economic and social activism in Ethiopia. Over the past fifteen years, the internet has emerged as an alternative space where digital citizens can engage in unfettered discourse, free from government control (Brhane and Eneyew, 2023). Activists have leveraged this platform to mobilize support for various political and social causes, effectively organizing protests and work strikes through social media channels.

Before discussing the nuances of internet shutdowns, it is important to highlight the issues of internet access and the digital divide in Ethiopia. While the digital divide – where individuals and communities experience an uneven distribution of access to the internet and digital technologies – remains very wide within Ethiopia, internet access has grown exponentially over the past decade. From 1.1 per cent in 2011, it rose to 28.4 per cent in 2023, according to the Ethio Telecom annual report in 2024 (Ethio Telecom, 2024). Accordingly, there are approximately 36.4 million internet subscribers in Ethiopia, which comprises 28.4% of the total estimated population of 128.3 million (Ethio Telecom, 2024).

However, the Ethiopian Prime Minister, Abiy Ahmed, made a controversial statement at a press conference addressing the issue of recurrent internet shutdowns in Ethiopia. The Prime Minister announced their policy: 'As long as it is deemed necessary to save lives and prevent property damages, the internet would be closed permanently, let alone for a week. Ethiopia will cut the internet as and when, it's neither water nor air' (AfricaNews, 2019). Although there was a supportive environment for online space in the early stages of Abiy's administration, the government has since 2018 imposed multiple internet shutdowns across the country, driving it down the path of digital authoritarianism (Brhane and Eneyew, 2023).

While the government of Ethiopia has launched an ambitious national 'Digital Strategy' (2020–5) that aspires to achieve the country's digital transformation by the year 2025, it is ironic that the same government justifies internet shutdowns by using the narrative that internet access is 'neither water nor air' (Digital Strategy, 2020).

It goes without saying that internet and communication blackouts have been a common tactic not only in authoritarian countries like Ethiopia but also in democracies such as India (Ayalew, 2021a). Quite often, internet shutdown is the hallmark of authoritarian governments around the world. Morozov in his book, *The Net Delusion*, aptly argued that 'While it's becoming clear that few authoritarian regimes are interested in completely shutting down all communications, if only because they want to stay abreast of emerging threats, censorship of at least some content is inevitable' (Morozov, 2011: 93). According to the Collaboration on International ICT Policy in East and Southern Africa (CIPESA), this claim is true in twenty-two African countries where internet disruptions were imposed from 2014 to 2019; 77 per cent of them are authoritarian and the rest are hybrid or semi-authoritarian governments (CIPESA, 2019: 4). This claim is true in Ethiopia where internet shutdowns have become a go-to tactic used by the government to respond to any violence or armed conflict happening in the country.

This chapter aims to explore the various episodes of internet shutdowns used by the government, drawing upon three case studies from the insurgency and counter-insurgency in Wollega (2019 to present); the Tigray conflict (2021–2) and the armed conflict in the Amhara Regional State (2023 to present). Despite steady growth in internet connectivity and staunch opposition from human rights activists and civil societies (CSOs), the Ethiopian government has consistently engaged in this practice. This chapter poses the following questions: (1) What are the impacts of internet shutdowns on the human rights and well-being of civilians and the community in those cases studies? and (2) Whose and which rights are affected by internet shutdowns in situations of conflict in Ethiopia and whose power interests are best served? Using a doctrinal legal research method, and a qualitative analysis of recorded shutdowns and interviews with selected experts in the field, this chapter seeks to answer these questions and examine the ways in which internet shutdowns have been implemented to curtail political discourse in conflict situations, and conceal atrocities and human rights violations, with a particular focus on those case studies in Ethiopia.

## *Conceptual background on internet shutdown and human rights*

According to Access Now's empirical data from 2022, there were at least 187 deliberate internet shutdowns in thirty-five countries worldwide, including those countries in conflict situations such as Ethiopia (Access Now, 2023a). In addition to the steady increase in the number of shutdowns, there has been a discernible uptick in their frequency over the years. Before delving into the conceptual frameworks of internet shutdowns, it is useful to demystify some of their definitions.

Internet shutdowns are known by other names such as 'internet blackouts', 'internet disruptions,' 'internet outages' or 'kill switches' (Anthonio, 2022: 7; Wagner, 2018: 3918). An internet shutdown happens when an entity, typically a government, deliberately interrupts internet services or mobile applications to regulate or restrict what individuals can communicate or access (Anthonio and Roberts, 2023: 89). A more technical, crowdsourced definition of internet shutdown was developed by digital rights experts at the conference in Brussels on 30 March 2016 (Olukotun and Micek, 2016). According to this definition an internet shutdown is:

> [a] deliberate disruption of internet or electronic communications, rendering them inaccessible or effectively unusable, for a specific population or within a location, often to exert control over the flow of information.

In this definition, the first limb of a shutdown is the *intentionality* behind it (Ayalew, 2019: 210). This means that governments, private telecoms or internet service providers (ISPs) restrict access to the internet deliberately. The second element in the definition is the *disruption* of the internet services (Wagner, 2018: 3918). The last element in the definition is the target location or population of the disruption. Sometimes this is a specific geographic region, at other times it is the entire state (Ayalew, 2021b: 9).

The participants at the African School of Internet Governance in October 2016 provided a nuanced definition of internet shutdown that builds upon and refines the definition given by Access Now (Statement on Intentional Internet Shutdowns, 2016). Accordingly, they define it as follows:

> An internet shutdown is an intentional interruption of the internet by state or non-state actors which renders the internet inaccessible or effectively unusable, for a specific population and for the purposes of exerting control over the free flow of information.

This means that not only governments can implement shutdowns, but non-state actors such as telecom companies may also be involved in blackout measures. This definition helps us understand those actors involved and perhaps responsible for internet shutdowns.

In 2022, the UN Office of the High Commissioner for Human Rights offered a systematic definition to understand internet shutdowns as 'measures taken by a government, or on behalf of a government, to intentionally disrupt access to, and the use of, information and communications systems online' (OHCHR, 2022: 2, para 4). This definition highlights the main instigators (and often perpetrators) of internet shutdowns, which are primarily governments or entities acting on their behalf, such as telecommunication companies or internet service providers. The UN report elaborates that internet shutdowns encompass not only measures that limit the ability of a large number of people to use online communications tools by restricting internet connectivity at large but also include tactics that hinder the accessibility and functionality of essential interactive communication platforms like social media and messaging services (OHCHR, 2022: 2–3, para 5).

In terms of the typology of shutdowns, the UN report identifies various types of internet shutdowns. Firstly, there are total shutdowns where access to the internet or certain services is entirely blocked (OHCHR, 2022: 2, para 5). The second type is a partial shutdown or speed throttling. In these cases, governments may still allow access to the internet, but they drastically reduce bandwidth or limit mobile services to 2G speeds. This makes meaningful internet usage almost impossible, particularly when it comes to sharing and viewing videos or live streams. The third category is a selective blackout, where only specific websites and services are restricted while access to the remainder of the internet continues (OHCHR, 2022: para 5). In all these scenarios, users can potentially bypass these restrictions using virtual private networks (VPNs). In the most severe cases, the fourth type involves shutdowns escalating to a full network blackout, severing both internet and entire telephone services and cutting any form of direct electronic communication (OHCHR, 2022: para 5). A notable instance of this was witnessed in the Tigray region by the Ethiopian government from 2020 to 2022, which included both internet and telecommunication blackouts (Access Now, 2022).

A review of the literature on the impact of internet shutdowns shows that it has a far-reaching consequence on the economy, human rights, politics and society (Ayalew, 2019: 208; Mare, 2020: 4244; Wagner, 2018: 3918), for instance, a Brookings study found that internet shutdowns have had adverse consequences on the economy, costing countries $2.4 billion in 2016 (West, 2016: 8). According to a study by Top10VPN, Ethiopia experienced a loss of $1.59 billion due to internet shutdowns in 2023, ranking it as the second-largest suppressor of internet access worldwide, following Russia (Top10VPN, 2024). In addition to the economic impacts, internet shutdowns have had widespread and debilitating social effects, including lack of access to important public health information during the pandemic, being kept in the dark about election results, economic repercussions felt by broad swathes of society, limitations on employment and educational opportunities, and lack of access to digital finance (Ilori, 2021: 12).

There are some useful approaches to conceptualize internet shutdowns. The first approach to understand internet shutdowns is through a human rights-based approach. The human rights-based approach frames internet shutdown as a phenomenon to be assessed using three inter-related pillars: substantive, process and procedural dimensions (Ayalew, 2021b: 12; Sander, 2020: 939).

As shown in Figure 5.1, the substantive dimension comprises four key components: legality, legitimacy, necessity and proportionality. These principles require states and private entities, such as telecommunications companies, to align their internet shutdown measures with international human rights law. The process dimension involves transparency and oversight mechanisms that both states and companies are expected to adhere to before implementing shutdown measures that infringe upon rights. The procedural dimension encompasses due process and remedial actions that should guide states and companies both prior to and following the imposition of shutdown measures (Ayalew, 2021a: 467).

This chapter uses this framework to situate the concept of internet shutdowns in the broader debate of international human rights law. This is because internet shutdowns impede human rights in the digital age, and the internet provides a mechanism for amplifying the exercise of rights online. Following its landmark Resolution in 2012, the UN Human Rights Council has acknowledged that human rights can be exercised on the internet: 'The same rights that people have offline must also be protected online' (Digital Human Rights Resolution, 2012: para 1). This means that digital rights hold the same protection as traditional offline human rights. Importantly, the human rights-based approach offers three pillars (substantive, process and procedural dimensions) to assess whether various types

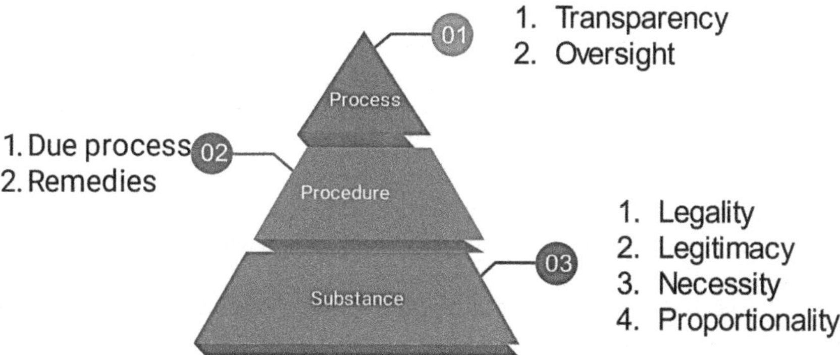


**Figure 5.1** Pyramid of the Human Rights-Based Approach.

Source: Centre for the Advancement of Rights and Democracy (CARD) report, Ayalew, 2021b: 29.

of internet shutdowns are lawful under international human rights law – which is further taken up later in the chapter. Therefore, this chapter seeks to interrogate the impact of internet shutdowns on human rights using a human rights-based approach.

While the human rights-based approach has much to commend it, it is not a panacea for all real-life problems nor does it help us understand a world where there are structural challenges and asymmetries in citizens' ability to exercise their rights (Nyamnjoh, 2007: 75). This brings us to the second approach: the concept of power dynamics. The power approach is important to demystify hierarchical and unequal power relations, including those of gender, race and class beyond a normative rhetoric of rights discourse. Without a doubt, in many countries, a person's ability to freely express their views is affected by their social status, gender, sexuality, age, party membership or ethnic group. Importantly, it is erroneous to focus analysis almost exclusively on institutional and constitutional frameworks of rights, thereby downplaying the hierarchies and relationships of inclusion and exclusion shaped by race, ethnicity, class, gender and geography, which fundamentally determine access to citizenship and rights in practical terms (Nyamnjoh, 2007: 75). Applied to internet shutdowns, it can therefore be argued that understanding these power relationships (e.g. who orders the shutdowns, whose interests are at stake, etc.) is at least as important as understanding normative human rights when analysing who controls the internet and, consequently, what can and cannot be communicated.

In sum, internet shutdown may be understood as deliberate disruption of internet or electronic communications. There are various approaches employed to conceptualize internet shutdowns. These are: human rights-based and power approaches. The next section navigates the brief episodes of internet shutdown in Ethiopia.

## *Episodes of internet shutdown in Ethiopia: an overview*

While Ethiopia has had telecommunication services since 1894, the history of the internet in Ethiopia only began in 1997 (Yilma and Abraha, 2015: 109). Soon after its introduction, the Ethiopian government began exerting control over the internet through censorship and shutdowns (Gagliardone, 2014: 279). In response, people resorted to downloading, printing and distributing news, commentaries and political manifestos as leaflets to those without internet access. Notably, mobile phones, particularly SMS, became crucial for real-time mobilization and spreading calls to action originally started on other platforms (Gagliardone, 2014: 282).

After the 2005 elections, the Ethiopian People's Revolutionary Democratic Front (EPRDF) – the then ruling party in the country – faced unexpected losses and was confronted by public protests over delayed election results. In response, the government shut down several communication channels used for mobilizing protesters, including SMS, which was suspended on 6 June 2005, and was not reinstated for approximately two years (US Department of State, 2006). This was part of a broader strategy to silence dissent and prevent the spread of alternative information and narratives. Using draconian media laws, the regime targeted media houses – mainly newspapers, radio and TV – preventing them from operating freely in the country, which subsequently led to their shutdown (Roberts, 2019: 28). This entrenched habit prompted the government to apply the same tactic in the digital space.

Over the years, the digital space has become an alternative platform for opposition voices after the government consolidated its power and restricted the civic and political space. This move by the government allowed opposition voices to effectively contest its actions by utilizing online platforms. The controversial Addis Ababa City Master Plan initiated by the Federal government sparked significant opposition, prompting Oromo youths to take to the streets in 2014. Between 2014 and 2016, youths in the Oromia and Amhara regions mounted challenges against government policies by initiating various social movements, both online and offline. In response to these digitally mobilized protests, the government implemented internet shutdowns in an attempt to quell the unrest (Ayalew, 2019: 214).

The dark side of internet shutdowns did not end there in the history of Ethiopia. Successive governments have implemented internet shutdowns as a go-to tactic to muzzle freedom of expression and human rights in the country. Between 2016 and 2021, for example, the Ethiopian government employed various justifications for shutting down the internet in Ethiopia. For instance, the government invoked national security concerns, the integrity of school exams, public order, armed conflicts, insecurity and deflecting cyber-attacks as official reasons for turning off the internet (Brhane and Eneyew, 2023: 75–7). Additionally, internet shutdowns have been implemented frequently during major events happening in Ethiopia, such as in the wake of a high-profile assassination in Bahir Dar and Addis Ababa, during the armed conflict in Tigray, and the insurgency in Wollega (Ayalew, 2021b: 1).

Unfortunately, Ethiopia has witnessed unprecedented internal armed conflicts in its contemporary history. For example, the internet was severed following the insurgency and counter-insurgency movements in the Wollega province, Oromia region, which have flared up since 2019. Similarly, the government resorted to internet and communication blackouts following the war in Tigray (2020–2) and the armed conflict in the Amhara regional state that erupted in August 2023.

Overall, the various episodes of internet shutdown in Ethiopia (Figure 5.2) show that, while the government sought to justify them through various narratives and official justifications, they appeared to be knee-jerk reactions to shut down the internet and restrict private digital communications, since the measures were neither legally rigorous nor logically tenable. The next section will discuss these case studies at length.

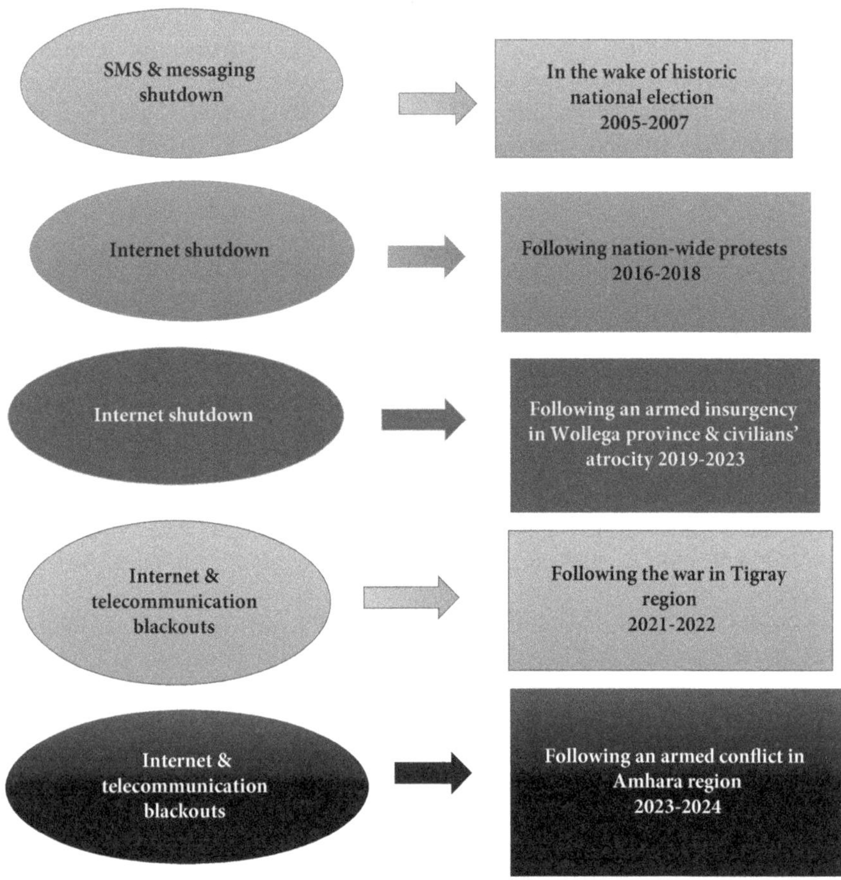


**Figure 5.2** Maps the Brief Episodes of Internet Shutdown in Ethiopia (2005–24).
Source: authors.

## *Case studies of internet shutdowns in conflict situations in Ethiopia*

Ethiopia has recently experienced a significant surge in armed conflicts in regions such as Tigray, Amhara and Wollega province in Oromia, accompanied by internet shutdowns (OHCHR, 2024: 13, para 52). A report by Access Now and the #KeepItOn Coalition on internet shutdowns in 2023 puts Ethiopia ninth in the global list of countries with the most internet shutdowns in the year, and the first in Africa (Rosson, Anthonio and Carolyn, 2024: 6). These shutdowns have profound implications for human rights, international humanitarian law, humanitarian aid, as well as democratic processes. The following section explores the duration, impact and broader implications of these shutdowns, focusing on their violation of fundamental rights and their socio-political consequences.

### *Wollega province*

Wollega province was left in the dark and disconnected from internet and telecommunication services from 2019 to 2020 due to a shutdown measure imposed by the government to crack down on the rebels, i.e. the Oromo Liberation Army (OLA) (Meseret, 2020). The people of Wollega province in Oromia region, located in the western part of Ethiopia, did not have access to the internet from 2019 to the end of March 2020 (Human Rights Watch, 2020). Regrettably, the shutdown continues unabated to this point in the province despite the government's claims of its restoration (Fana Broadcasting Corporate, 2020). According to the UN Office of the High Commissioner for Human Rights, the internet and telecommunication services have not been restored in the region due to an ongoing armed conflict between the government forces and the OLA (OHCHR, 2024: 11, para 42). Evidently, Wollega province is endowed with natural resources such as coffee, gold, platinum, coal and precious stones (Ta'a, 1993: 64). It is also one of the largest provinces in the Oromia region, where rebel forces such as the OLA once agitated to create an independent state (Ayalew, 2020).

The official justification for internet shutdown and telecommunication blackout in Wollega province is linked with suppressing the movement of rebels in the area. In his conversation with *Addis Standard*, the President of Oromia region, Shimelis Abdisa, claimed that 'investigators have determined that OLA assassins use phones to coordinate the stalking, pursuit, and murder of government officials they often target' (Zelalem, 2020: 11). While the justification has some merit in controlling the armed insurgency, the authors argue that it is neither proportionate nor legal, as the measure fails to meet the three pillars – particularly the substantive requirements – of the human rights-based approach discussed earlier in the chapter.

In terms of impact, the blackout in the province has taken a heavy toll on the lives of residents both within the province and beyond (Human Rights Watch, 2020). It prevented families from communicating, severely affected humanitarian services in the region, and contributed to an information blackout. This significantly affected the human rights of citizens in Wollega province. For example, the shutdown made it difficult to locate students who were abducted from a local university in January 2020 by effectively ending an online campaign for their rescue (Amnesty International, 2020). For those in power, mainly government officials, shutting down the internet serves as a powerful tool to demonstrate their control over the rebels in that region. Seen in light of power relationships as proposed by (Mayers (2005) and Schmeer (1999), we argue that the government sought to achieve political interests over the rebels in the region by shutting down the internet and communication in the province. The next sub-sections explore the shutdowns in Tigray and Amhara regions.

### *Tigray region*

The conflict in Ethiopia's Tigray region, which erupted on 4 November 2020, plunged the region into a state of turmoil characterized by violence, displacement and widespread human rights abuses (OHCHR & EHRC Joint Probe, 2021). As hostilities escalated between the Tigray People's Liberation Front (TPLF) and the Ethiopian Federal Government supported by Eritrean troops and regional militias, the Ethiopian government swiftly implemented a comprehensive internet and telecommunications blackout (Brhane and Eneyew, 2023: 77). This blackout, commencing at 1.00 am East Africa Time on the day the conflict began, was confirmed by NetBlocks, an organization monitoring global internet disruptions (NetBlocks, 2020).

The internet shutdown in Tigray endured for an unprecedented period, according to Access Now report published in 2024, with 1153 days of internet shutdown until 31 December 2023 – the Tigray region faced the longest uninterrupted internet blackout in the world (Rosson, Anthonio and Carolyn, 2024: 8). Throughout this extended period, more than six million residents of Tigray were cut off from the outside world, deprived of essential communication channels and denied access to vital services such as banking and telecommunications (NetBlocks, 2020). This isolation severely impeded humanitarian efforts and exacerbated an already dire humanitarian crisis, rendering it extremely challenging for aid organizations to provide life-saving assistance to those in need.

One of the most significant consequences of the internet shutdown was its obstruction of information flow. With all forms of digital communication severed, residents of Tigray were effectively silenced, unable to share information about the conflict's developments or seek help during emergencies (OHCHR & EHRC Joint Probe, 2021: 62, paras 252–67). This blackout not only prevented civilians from accessing critical updates on the evolving security situation but also hindered journalists and human rights organizations from reporting on alleged atrocities and abuses committed by both belligerent parties (Access Now, 2022; Issa, 2024).

The internet blackout in Tigray effectively silenced dissenting voices and obstructed the work of local activists, journalists and human rights defenders (Freedom House, 2023). Without access to online platforms, individuals were unable to report on human rights abuses, document atrocities, or communicate critical updates about the conflict to the outside world. One of our key informants Ahmed Bekele (not his real name) a senior human rights officer, stated 'we are unable to receive human rights related information from our branch offices where the internet is cut off'. This lack of transparency and information dissemination delayed international humanitarian responses, exacerbating the humanitarian crisis and prolonging the suffering of civilians.

The humanitarian consequences of the internet shutdown were profound and multifaceted. For instance, internet shutdowns impeded the delivery of humanitarian aid and delayed critical interventions during the crisis. From the beginning of the shutdown, it impeded international efforts to monitor and respond to the humanitarian crisis in real time. Humanitarian organizations faced severe logistical challenges in delivering aid, as communication breakdowns hampered coordination and made it difficult to assess the scale of needs on the ground (OCHA, 2020). Aid workers operating in Tigray faced significant hurdles due to restricted communication channels, impeding their ability to coordinate relief efforts effectively and leaving them unable to reach many in need of assistance. The blackout also had repercussions for the healthcare sector, limiting access to medical information and hindering efforts to combat disease outbreaks and provide essential medical care to the affected population. The inability to access timely information about security threats, disease outbreaks or emergency medical services endangered lives and intensified humanitarian suffering in the region. Moreover, there were widespread reports of sexual violence perpetrated against women and girls in conflict-affected areas, underscoring the heightened vulnerability of populations cut off from external assistance and protection (UN Human Rights Council, 2023: 25, para 134).

Despite the signing of a ceasefire agreement in November 2022, which stipulated the restoration of basic services including internet access, the Access Now (2022) report shows that the connectivity in Tigray was 'still well below pre-war levels' (Rosson, Anthonio and Carolyn, 2024: 13). The protracted nature of the blackout and the uncertainty surrounding its resolution perpetuated the suffering of Tigray's residents, prolonged their isolation and exacerbated the humanitarian crisis in the region. It was only in June 2024, that Safaricom – the only other telecommunication services provider in Ethiopia – launched its commercial operations in Tigray to commence in two phases (Safaricom, 2024). Overall, the prolonged internet blackout during the Tigray conflict represents a flagrant violation of human rights, obstructing communication, exacerbating humanitarian suffering and impeding international efforts to address the crisis effectively.

### *Amhara region*

The conflict in Ethiopia's Amhara region, which began in August 2023, involves intense clashes between local Amhara militias, collectively known as the Fano Forces, and military forces of the Federal Government after an attempt by the latter to disarm them (Associated Press, 2023). This escalation has resulted in significant violence, displacing thousands and creating a severe humanitarian crisis (Mandefro, 2023). With ongoing hostilities exacerbating the suffering of civilians, and no ceasefire or peace agreements having been reached thus far, the situation remains volatile (Bader, 2023).

The Ethiopian government has responded to the unrest in the Amhara region by imposing internet shutdowns, like in Tigray. These shutdowns, notably implemented since 3 August 2023, have severely disrupted communication channels and exacerbated tensions in the region, further complicating communication and humanitarian efforts and obstructing the flow of information about the conflict and associated human rights abuses (Bader, 2023; OHCHR, 2024: 13–14, para 52).

As discussed above, these shutdowns continue to represent a recurring pattern in Ethiopia, where internet shutdowns are used as a tool to control information flow, muzzle freedom of expression and suppress dissent during periods of unrest (Ayalew, 2019: 208).

In terms of duration and its impact, the Ethiopian government has shut down internet services in the Amhara region during periods of heightened conflict since 3 August 2023 (Internet Society, 2023). The shutdowns have had significant implications for communication within and outside the region. Residents have faced challenges in accessing crucial information, including updates on the conflict's developments, safety advisories, as well as humanitarian aid efforts.

The shutdown of the internet and the blackout of digital communication platforms have also hindered the ability of journalists and media outlets to report on the ground, limiting transparency and public awareness of the situation. Civil society organizations have condemned these shutdowns, arguing that they not only violate international human rights standards but also endanger lives by limiting access to emergency services and obstructing humanitarian aid operations. In an interview with a senior human rights officer, Kinfe Assefa (not his real name), he stated,

> Internet shutdowns infringe the human right for freedom of expression and access to information by de-platforming users. Additionally, it makes it easy for government security forces to use disproportional force without accountability as the shutdowns break the flow of information.

The shutdowns have created an environment of fear and uncertainty, where residents are unable to communicate effectively with loved ones or seek assistance during emergencies. Internet shutdowns in the Amhara region have stifled the ability of civil society organizations and activists to organize protests, mobilize communities and advocate for human rights. Social media platforms, crucial for coordinating peaceful demonstrations and disseminating information, become inaccessible during these shutdowns, effectively suppressing dissent and hindering the exercise of freedom of assembly.

Beyond the immediate curtailment of civil liberties and humanitarian concerns, the internet shutdowns in the Amhara region have had profound economic repercussions. These shutdowns are often accompanied by disruptions in telecommunications infrastructure, affecting not only residents but also local businesses and international operations such as flight services by the Ethiopian flag carrier (Sey, 2023). Local businesses and start-up businesses dependent on online transactions and communications have suffered losses due to disrupted operations and reduced customer access (Ayalew, 2022: 18). In the words of Abebe Tesfaye (not his real name), a programme manager at an Ethiopian human rights organization,

> It (the internet shutdown) affects trades, transactions, and productions of goods affecting digital operations. It also affects for example hospitals and health care activities bearing live cost to the patients limiting digitalized health systems.

This means that the internet shutdowns in the Amhara region affected not only civil and political rights but also socio-economic rights. For example, the inability to access banking services or communicate with suppliers and customers stalled economic activities, worsening hardships both in the region and across the country.

Added to that, the shutdowns have impacted educational institutions and students reliant on online learning platforms. Schools and universities have struggled to deliver educational materials, disrupting the learning process and affecting the academic activities of students in the region (Anthonio and Mandefro, 2023). The shutdowns have isolated communities, preventing residents from accessing vital services, communicating with family members, and seeking help during emergencies.

The international community has once again expressed concern over the recurring internet shutdowns in the Amhara region and other conflict zones in Ethiopia. For example, international civil societies, and various human rights organizations, have called for an immediate cessation of these shutdowns, highlighting their detrimental impact on human rights, freedom of expression, and access to information, as the next section demonstrates (Access Now, 2023b).

## *The impact of shutdowns on human rights in Ethiopia*

Internet shutdowns have posed or continue to pose a serious threat to the enjoyment of human rights and fundamental freedoms in Ethiopia, especially in the context of armed conflicts. According to a study by the Centre for the Advancement of Rights and Democracy (CARD), internet shutdowns have a profound impact not only on civil and political rights but also on socio-economic and collective rights (Ayalew, 2021b). This chapter focuses on civil and political rights in armed conflict situations.

Both under international law, including Article 19 of the International Covenant on Civil and Political Rights (ICCPR) and domestic law, i.e. Article 29 of the Ethiopian Constitution, individuals have the right to freedom of expression, access to information and peaceful assembly, both offline and online. These rights extend to all forms of media and communication, including the internet, as affirmed by various international bodies and resolutions (Digital Human Rights Resolution, 2012). It is now widely understood that the enjoyment of these human rights does not cease in situations of armed conflicts, as human rights apply in all situations (be it in peacetime and in armed conflicts). Even in situations with an officially declared State of Emergency where certain human rights are temporarily derogated or suspended due to a 'public emergency which threatens the life of a nation' as stated under Article 4 of the International Covenant on Civil and Political Rights (ICCPR), it is understood that such derogation has its own limits. The Human Rights Committee in its General Comment No. 29 provided that the derogation of rights must be limited to the extent strictly required by the exigencies of the situation (in its duration, geographical and material scope) – reflecting the need to respect the principles of necessity and proportionality in such times.

Internet shutdowns in Ethiopia directly violate these established rights. By restricting internet access, the Ethiopian government has hindered the exercise of these fundamental rights, preventing citizens from freely expressing themselves, accessing critical information, and engaging in political discourse. It has also undermined the right to seek, receive and impart information critical for their safety and well-being in situations of armed conflicts. Accordingly, any restrictions on internet access must be lawful, necessary, proportionate and non-discriminatory, conditions that often fail to be met during conflict-related shutdowns in Ethiopia (Kaye, 2019).

Internet shutdowns imposed during armed conflicts raise significant legal and accountability concerns. These shutdowns, often justified as measures to maintain national security or restore public order, have far-reaching implications for human rights, democratic principles, and international legal standards. Shutdowns often occur during armed conflicts and operations, severely restricting reporting and human rights monitoring. This lack of access to tools for documenting and quickly reporting abuses can exacerbate violence and atrocities (Office of the United Nations High Commissioner for Human Rights, 2022).

Some shutdowns may be intended to conceal human rights and international humanitarian law violations. For example, the internet shutdowns during the different armed conflicts in Ethiopia, particularly in regions such as Tigray, Amhara and the Wollega province of Oromia, constitute severe violations of civil and political rights guaranteed under international law. These shutdowns are frequently employed by the Ethiopian government as a tactic to control information flow, suppress dissent, conceal atrocity crimes and maintain authority during periods of unrest. In an interview with Desta Berhane (not his real name), a project worker at an Ethiopian rights-based non-profit, he mentioned that:

> Internet shutdowns make it difficult to monitor the human rights violations and identifying the perpetrators, to know the magnitude of the incident. It also affects the quality or accuracy of information about where, when, what and how of happenings and by whom hindering important details. Internet shutdowns pave the way for disinformation in which, from my experience, most of the conflict-related human rights violations happenings come out after days, weeks or months taken out of context and lead to further conflict, misleading the users when the internet is resumed. This also further affects my duty to report and forecast potential human rights violations to alert the concerned body. Internet shutdowns are fertile grounds for ethnic cleansing and genocide, it limits people's right to emergency reliefs.

Crucially, Ethiopia's constitution guarantees fundamental rights and freedoms, including the right to freedom of expression and access to information. However, the practical application of these rights is often compromised during periods of political unrest or armed conflict, where emergency measures, including internet shutdowns, are invoked under the guise of national security on the basis of Article 93 of the Constitution. Legal challenges within Ethiopia's judicial system to contest internet shutdowns have been limited, with decisions often being deferred to the executive under emergency provisions. The lack of judicial oversight and accountability mechanisms further exacerbates concerns regarding the legality and constitutionality of these shutdowns. The lack of judicial review means that citizens often lack the agency to challenge shutdown measures through strategic litigation before national and regional bodies.

Across the three case studies, the impact of internet shutdowns not only affects human rights – particularly civil and political rights – in conflict situations but also shapes power relationships and dynamics. This leads to our final observation on power dynamics: internet shutdowns primarily benefit those in power, including the government (the incumbent Prosperity Party), security forces, and ruling elites, by enabling control over information, suppressing dissent and maintaining political stability. Security forces gain operational advantages over protesters and dissidents while limiting accountability for their actions (NetBlocks, 2020). Using digital surveillance, intelligence agencies also exploit shutdowns to enhance monitoring and data collection, further infringing on citizens' privacy rights. Political parties in power use shutdowns during elections to disrupt opposition campaigning and media coverage, ensuring electoral dominance and suppressing opposition voices (Freyburg and Garbe, 2018: 3896). As Nyamnjoh (2007) aptly argued, hierarchical and unequal power relations are inherent in social and political interactions, influencing citizens' rights. Similarly, internet shutdowns reflect and reinforce unequal power dynamics, as they directly impact these relationships. In the three case studies we explored (i.e. Wollega, Tigray and Amhara), shutdowns were imposed by the ruling Prosperity Party-led government, executed by telecom companies (such as Ethio-telecom and Safaricom), and experienced by citizens and users in those places. These shutdowns reveal both vertical power relations between the government and citizens, and horizontal ones between telecom companies and users, illustrating the state's power over both companies and the public.

Undeniably, while Ethio-Telecom claims to be a self-funded and autonomous government enterprise, it has long maintained its position as the sole telecommunications provider in Ethiopia. This monopoly has effectively granted the government unchecked power to shut down the internet at will, often through opaque and unaccountable procedures. Recently, Safaricom entered the Ethiopian telecommunications market, breaking Ethio-Telecom's monopoly. However, Safaricom's operations so far appear to follow a similar pattern, as it too complies with government-mandated internet shutdowns. According to the UN Guiding Principles on Business and Human Rights, private telecommunications companies bear a responsibility to respect human rights (UNHROHC, 2011: 18, Principle 17). This obligation entails refraining from facilitating internet shutdowns and adhering to a human rights-based approach, as outlined earlier. Upholding these principles not only protects individuals' rights but also impacts the balance of power. We argue that the greater the autonomy of private companies, the less frequent and arbitrary internet shutdowns are likely to be, thereby fostering a stronger culture of respect for human rights, even during times of armed conflict. The upshot from this analysis is clear: both public and private telecommunications providers must honour their human rights obligations, both offline and online. This includes resisting unlawful or arbitrary shutdown orders, even when pressured by government authorities.

In sum, internet shutdowns impinge on fundamental rights and freedom of civilians in the context of armed conflicts in Ethiopia.

## Conclusion

This chapter has demonstrated the ways in which internet shutdowns have been implemented to restrict civil and political rights, curtail political discourse in conflict situations and conceal atrocities and human rights violations in three contexts, the Wollega insurgency, the war in Tigray and the Amhara conflict. Internet shutdowns during armed conflicts in Ethiopia, whether in Tigray, Amhara or the Wollega province, undermine fundamental civil and political rights, disrupt democratic processes and exacerbate humanitarian crises. This means that the lives of civilians will hang in the balance, and their rights will be shrouded in shadows. These shutdowns also represent a regressive step in the protection of human rights and hinder efforts to promote peace, accountability and socio-economic development in Ethiopia, necessitating concerted efforts from the government, civil society organizations and the international community to safeguard human rights, uphold the rule of law and ensure equitable access to information and communication technologies. While the government seeks to justify these shutdowns, none of them appear to be lawful and legitimate, and in turn, they do not pass the strict test of human rights, both under international law and domestic laws. Beyond the human rights implications, we discussed how the shutdowns in the three case studies led to unequal power relationships between those in power and the citizens.

Based on the analysis, we make the following recommendations. First, the Ethiopian government, as the primary duty-bearer of human rights, must end the practice of internet shutdowns, thereby respecting and ensuring the protection of human rights during conflict situations. Second, telecommunications companies should resist unlawful or arbitrary shutdown orders. Yet, if they implement shutdowns, they should fulfil their due diligence obligations to mitigate the harms suffered by users and provide clear explanations to the public about what occurred. Third, given that the practice of resorting to internet shutdowns continues unabated across the three case studies, the international community should exert maximum pressure on the government to cease this unlawful practice. In doing so, it should also urge the government to refrain from imposing shutdowns as part of its war efforts. To this end, multilateral organizations, such as the African Union and its human rights bodies – specifically the African Commission on Human and Peoples' Rights – should jointly or separately develop guiding principles or declarations on the impact of internet shutdowns during armed conflicts. We hope that such normative principles will serve as a blueprint to shape state behaviour not only in Ethiopia but across Africa as a whole.

Additionally, and most importantly, international organizations, such as the International Committee of the Red Cross (ICRC), should take the issue of internet shutdowns during armed conflicts seriously. Guided by the 34th

Resolution of the International Conference of the Red Cross and Red Crescent on *Protecting Civilians and Other Protected Persons and Objects Against the Potential Human Cost of ICT Activities During Armed Conflict*, adopted in October 2024, these organizations should work to develop comprehensive guiding principles and normative frameworks addressing internet shutdowns in the context of international humanitarian law and their applicability to such situations.

Given that mitigating and preventing internet shutdowns requires both legal and non-legal steps (e.g. applying circumvention tools), civil societies operating in Ethiopia should challenge the illegal actions of the government before national and international courts. Ultimately, future studies on internet shutdown should investigate the implications of shutdowns on human rights, power dynamics and citizens agency over time in Ethiopia and beyond as the impacts of shutdowns evolve over time.

## *Bibliography*

Access Now (2022, 4 November), 'Two Years of Internet Shutdowns: People in Tigray, Ethiopia, Deserve Better', Access Now, https://www.accessnow.org/press-release/two-years-internet-shutdowns-tigray/

Access Now (2023a), 'Internet shutdowns in 2022: The #KeepItOn Report', Access Now, https://www.accessnow.org/internet-shutdowns-2022/

Access Now (2023b, 12 September), 'Authorities in Ethiopia Must Restore Internet Access in Amhara', Access Now, https://www.accessnow.org/press-release/amhara-internet-shutdown/

Access Now (2024, 15 May), 'Shrinking Democracy, Growing Violence: Internet Shutdowns in 2023, Access Now, https://www.accessnow.org/internet-shutdowns-2023/

AfricaNews (2019, 2 August), 'Ethiopia Will Cut Internet As and When, "It's Neither Water Nor Air"—PM Abiy', *Africanews*, https://www.africanews.com/2019/08/02/ethiopia-will-cut-internet-as-and-when-it-s-neither-water-nor-air-pm-abiy/

Amnesty International (2020, 25 March), 'Ethiopia Universities Close as Whereabouts of 17 Amhara Students Remain Unknown', Amnesty International, https://www.amnesty.org/en/latest/news/2020/03/ethiopia-parents-fear-for-missing-amhara-students-as-universities-close-over-covid19/

Anthonio, F. (2022), *The Kill Switch: How Internet Shutdowns Threaten Fundamental Human Rights in Africa and Beyond* (Digital Future Whitepaper Series, pp. 1–29). Information Society Project, Yale Law School, https://law.yale.edu/sites/default/files/area/center/isp/documents/anthonio_kill-switch.pdf

Anthonio, F. and Mandefro, H. (2023, 22 November), 'The Human Impact of Internet Shutdowns in Ethiopia', Access Now, https://www.accessnow.org/keepiton-in-conflict-the-human-impact-of-internet-shutdowns-in-amhara-region-ethiopia/

Anthonio, F. and Roberts, T. (2023), 'Internet Shutdowns and Digital Citizenship', in T. Roberts and T. Bosch (eds), *Digital Citizenship in Africa: Technologies of Agency and Repression* (1st ed., pp. 85–115). London: Bloomsbury Publishing.

Associated Press (2023, 3 August), 'Ethiopia's Amhara Region Pleads for Help with Violent Unrest After Attempt to Disarm Local Fighters', AP News, https://apnews.com/article/ethiopia-military-amhara-violence-c487bd66bc4042bd23bb7122f05dafa0

Ayalew, Y. E. (2019), 'The Internet Shutdown Muzzle(s) Freedom of Expression in Ethiopia: Competing Narratives', *Information & Communications Technology Law*, 28(2): 208–24.

Ayalew, Y. E. (2020, 2 April), 'How Internet Shutdowns Have Affected the Lives of Millions of Ethiopians', The Conversation. http://theconversation.com/how-internet-shutdowns-have-affected-the-lives-of-millions-of-ethiopians-134054

Ayalew, Y. E. (2021a), 'From Digital Authoritarianism to Platforms' Leviathan Power: Freedom of Expression in the Digital Age Under Siege in Africa', *Mizan Law Review*, 15(2): 455–92.

Ayalew, Y. E. (2021b), *Rights Deplumed: Mapping the Human Rights Impact of Internet Shutdowns in Ethiopia* (pp. 1–42) [Research Report], Center for the Advancement of Rights and Democracy (CARD), https://www.cardeth.org/rights-deplumed-mapping-the-human-rights-impact-of-internet-shutdowns-in-ethiopia-research-report

Ayalew, Y. E. (2022), *Business Trampled Demystifying the Impact of Internet Shutdown on Start up Businesses in Ethiopia*. Center for Advancement of Rights and Democracy (CARD), https://www.cardeth.org/wp-content/uploads/2022/10/Business-Trampled-Demystifying-the-Impact-of-Internet-Shutdown-on-Start-up-Businesses-in-Ethiopia.pdf

Bader, L. (2023), *Deepening Crisis in Ethiopia's Amhara Region*, Human Rights Watch. https://www.hrw.org/news/2023/08/09/deepening-crisis-ethiopias-amhara-region

Brhane, A. and Eneyew, Y. (2023), Digital Crossroads: Continuity and Change in Ethiopia's Digital Citizenship, in T. Roberts and T. Bosch (eds), *Digital Citizenship in Africa: Technologies of Agency and Repression* (1st ed., pp. 63–83). Bloomsbury Publishing.

Collaboration on International ICT Policy in East and Southern Africa (CIPESA) (2019), *Despots and Disruptions: Five Dimensions of Internet shutdowns in Africa*, CIPESA, https://cipesa.org/2019/03/despots-and-disruptions-five-dimensions-of-internet-shutdowns-in-africa/

Digital Human Rights (2012), 'The Promotion, Protection and Enjoyment of Human Rights on the Internet', Resolution adopted by the Human Rights Council, A/HRC/RES/20/8 (2012). https://digitallibrary.un.org/record/731540?ln=en&v=pdf

Digital Strategy (2020), *Digital Strategy in Ethiopia 2025 – A Strategy for Ethiopia Inclusive Prosperity*, Prime Minister Office, https://www.pmo.gov.et/media/other/b2329861-f9d7-4c4b-9f05-d5bc2c8b33b6.pdf

Ethio Telecom (2024, 23 January), *Ethio telecom 2023/24 Semi-Annual Business Performance – Ethiotelecom*, https://www.ethiotelecom.et/ethio-telecom-2023-24-semi-annual-business-performance/

Fana Broadcasting Corporate (2020, 31 March), 'Telecom Services Restored in Oromia's Western Zones', Welcome to Fana Broadcasting Corporate S.C., https://www.fanabc.com/english/telecom-services-restored-in-western-zones-of-oromia/

Freedom House (2023), *Ethiopia: Freedom on the Net 2023 Country Report*. Freedom House, https://freedomhouse.org/country/ethiopia/freedom-net/2023

Freyburg, T. and Garbe, L. (2018), 'Blocking the Bottleneck: Internet Shutdowns and Ownership at Election Times in Sub-Saharan Africa', *International Journal of Communication*, 12: 3896–916.

Gagliardone, I. (2014), 'New Media and the Developmental State in Ethiopia', *African Affairs*, 113(451): 279–99, https://doi.org/10.1093/afraf/adu017

Human Rights Watch (2020, 9 March), *Ethiopia: Communications Shutdown Takes Heavy Toll*, https://www.hrw.org/news/2020/03/09/ethiopia-communications-shutdown-takes-heavy-toll

Ilori, T. (2021), *Life Interrupted: Centering the Social Impacts of Network Disruptions in Advocacy in Africa*. Global Network Initiative (GNI), https://globalnetworkinitiative.org/life-interrupted-network-disruptions-africa/

Internet Society (2023), *Internet Shutdown in Amhara Region, Ethiopia, August 2023*, https://pulse.internetsociety.org/shutdowns/internet-shutdown-in-amhara-region-ethiopia-august-2023

Issa, K. (2024, 3 April), 'Dying to Tell the Story: How War Has Affected the Work of Journalists in Ethiopia', *Journalists For Justice (JFJ)*, https://jfjustice.net/how-war-has-affected-the-work-of-journalists-in-ethiopia/

Kaye, D. (2019), *End-of-Mission Statement from the Special Rapporteur on Freedom of Expression to Ethiopia* [United Nations Special Rapporteur on the Promotion and Protection of the Right to Freedom of Opinion and Expression: David Kaye Visit to Ethiopia, 2–9 December 2019, End of Mission Statement], United Nations, https://ethiopia.un.org/en/27708-end-mission-statement-special-rapporteur-freedom-expression-ethiopia,https://ethiopia.un.org/en/27708-end-mission-statement-special-rapporteur-freedom-expression-ethiopia

Mandefro, H. (2023, 4 August), 'How Years of Tension in Amhara Boiled to the Surface', *African Arguments*. https://africanarguments.org/2023/08/how-years-of-tension-in-amhara-boiled-to-the-surface/

Marchant, E. and Stremlau, N. (2020), 'A Spectrum of Shutdowns: Reframing Internet Shutdowns from Africa', *International Journal of Communication*, 14: 4327–42.

Mare, A. (2020), 'State-Ordered Internet Shutdowns and Digital Authoritarianism in Zimbabwe', *International Journal of Communication*, 14: 4244–4263.

Mayers, J. (2005), 'Stakeholder Power Analysis', *International Institute for Environment and Development (IIED)*, https://policy-powertools.org/Tools/Understanding/docs/stakeholder_power_tool_english.pdf

Meseret, E. (2020, 24 March), 'Worried Ethiopians Want Partial Internet Shutdown Ended', AP News. https://apnews.com/general-news-89fd18405f659792d44ff1a26eef80dc

Morozov, E. (2011), *The Net Delusion: The Dark Side of Internet Freedom* (1st ed). New York: Public Affairs.

NetBlocks. (2020, 4 November), 'Internet Disrupted in Ethiopia as Conflict Breaks Out in Tigray Region', NetBlocks. https://netblocks.org/reports/internet-disrupted-in-ethiopia-as-conflict-breaks-out-in-tigray-region-eBOQYV8Z

Nyamnjoh, F. B. (2007), 'From Bounded to Flexible Citizenship: Lessons from Africa', *Citizenship Studies*, 11(1): 73–82. https://doi.org/10.1080/13621020601099880

OCHA (2020, 21 November), 'Ethiopia: Tigray Region Humanitarian Update – Situation Report No. 4 (20 November 2020) – Ethiopia', https://reliefweb.int/report/ethiopia/ethiopia-tigray-region-humanitarian-update-situation-report-no-4-20-november-2020

Office of the United Nations High Commissioner for Human Rights (2022), *Internet Shutdowns: Trends, Causes, Legal Implications and Impacts on a Range of Human Rights* [Report of the Office of the United Nations High Commissioner for Human Rights, A/HRC/50/55].

OHCHR (2024, 14 June), *OHCHR update on the human rights situation in Ethiopia in 2023*. OHCHR. https://www.ohchr.org/en/documents/country-reports/ohchr-update-human-rights-situation-ethiopia-2023

OHCHR and EHRC (2021), *Report of the Ethiopian Human Rights Commission (EHRC)/Office of the United Nations High Commissioner for Human Rights (OHCHR), Joint Investigation into Alleged Violations of International Human Rights, Humanitarian and*

*Refugee Law Committed by all Parties to the Conflict in the Tigray Region of the Federal Democratic Republic of Ethiopia* (2021), https://digitallibrary.un.org/record/3947207

Olukotun, D. and Micek, P. (2016, 30 March), 'No More Internet Shutdowns! Let's #KeepItOn', Access Now, https://www.accessnow.org/no-internet-shutdowns-lets-keepiton/

Roberts, T. (2019), *Closing Civic Space and Inclusive Development in Ethiopia* (IDS Working Paper 527). Falmer, UK: Institute of Development Studies.

Rosson, Z., Anthonio, F. and Carolyn, T. (2024, 15 May), 'Shrinking Democracy, Growing Violence: Internet Shutdowns in 2023', Access Now, https://www.accessnow.org/internet-shutdowns-2023/

Safaricom (2024, 10 June), 'Safaricom Officially Starts Its Commercial Operations in Tigray Region', https://safaricom.et/index.php/about-us/news-and-insights-safaricom/113-safaricom-officially-starts-its-commercial-operations-in-tigray-region

Sander, B. (2020), 'Freedom of Expression in the Age of Online Platforms: The Promise and Pitfalls of a Human Rights-Based Approach to Content Moderation', *Fordham International Law Journal*, 43(4): 939.

Schmeer, K. (1999), *Guidelines for Conducting a Stakeholder Analysis*. Partnership for Health Reform, Bethesda, MD: Abt Associates.

Sey, A. (2023, 4 August), 'Ethiopia Shuts Down Internet Services Amid Flight Suspension', APAnews – African Press Agency, https://apanews.net/ethiopia-shuts-down-internet-services-amid-flight-suspension/

*Statement on Intentional Internet Shutdowns* (2016, 17 October), African School on Internet Governance, https://afrisig.org/previous-afrisigs/afrisig-2016/statement-on-an-intentional-internet-shutdown/

Ta'a, T. (1993), 'The Process of Urbanization in Wollega, Western Ethiopia: The Case of Neqemte', *Journal of Ethiopian Studies*, 26(1): 59–72.

Top10VPN, (2024, 8 March), *The Global Cost of Internet Shutdowns*, https://www.top10vpn.com/research/cost-of-internet-shutdowns/

UN Human Rights Council (2023), *International Commission of Human Rights Experts on Ethiopia*, OHCHR, https://www.ohchr.org/en/hr-bodies/hrc/ichre-ethiopa/index

UNHROHC (2011), *United Nations Guiding Principles on Business and Human Rights*. United Nations Human Rights Office of the High Commissioner.

U.S. Department of State (2006, 8 March). *U.S. Department of State Country Report on Human Rights Practices 2005 – Ethiopia*, Refworld, https://www.refworld.org/reference/annualreport/usdos/2006/en/47377

Wagner, B. (2018), 'Understanding Internet Shutdowns: A Case Study from Pakistan', *International Journal of Communication*, 12, 3917–38.

West, D. M. (2016), 'Internet Shutdowns Cost Countries $2.4 Billion Last Year', Center for Technology Innovation at Brookings, https://www.brookings.edu/articles/internet-shutdowns-cost-countries-2-4-billion-last-year/

Yilma, K. M. (2022), '"Not Water or Air": The Legality of Network Disruptions in Ethiopia', *African Journal of Legal Studies*, 14(4): 468–90, https://doi.org/10.1163/17087384-bja10066

Yilma, K. M. and Abraha, H. H. (2015), 'The Internet and Regulatory Responses in Ethiopia: Telecoms, Cybercrimes, Privacy, E-commerce, and the New Media', *Mizan Law Review*, 9(1): 108. https://doi.org/10.4314/mlr.v9i1.4

Zelalem, Z. (2020, 20 March), 'Special Edition: Failed Politics and Deception: Behind the Crisis in Western and Southern Oromia' *Addis Standard*, https://addisstandard.com/special-edition-failed-politics-and-deception-behind-the-crisis-in-western-and-southern-oromia/

# Chapter 6

## Internet shutdowns in Sudan, power, counter-power and rights

Khattab Hamad

### *Introduction*

Since Sudan's independence, the media landscape has been characterized by a history of censorship and control. From the colonial era, when press censorship was used to stifle nationalist sentiment, to the modern digital age marked by internet shutdowns, the struggle for freedom of expression has been a defining feature of Sudanese society.

Sudan's internet shutdowns are a direct demonstration of the country's unique political climate and the challenges it has long faced. Many countries use internet shutdowns primarily for short-term control during protests or elections, but Sudan has been an exception, given the variety of shutdowns it has used, from social media-only restrictions to mobile-only outages, region-specific outages and nationwide shutdowns. These diverse experiences have made Sudan an exceptional case study for understanding the effects of internet censorship. However, people in Sudan have experienced more internet shutdowns than any other African country, except Ethiopia. These events, often implemented during periods of political instability, protest and conflict, reveal how governments control access to information to maintain power. This chapter examines three major internet shutdowns in Sudan: the 2019 and 2021 shutdowns, which lasted for thirty-seven and twenty-five days, respectively, and the notable shutdown in February 2024. Together, these events highlight the complexities of controlling communications in a volatile political environment such as Sudan.

Internet shutdown is defined as an intentional disruption of internet or electronic communications, rendering them inaccessible or effectively unusable, for a specific population or within a location, often to exert control over the flow of information (Access Now, 2023). Despite the low internet penetration in the country, the internet is a vital tool that impacts the social, economic and political situations in the country, as proven by the frequency of internet shutdowns during the last decade. Despite the slow growth in the communications sector, the internet has succeeded in establishing a field for public work and business and a space for community discussions, which makes cutting it off a matter that affects many sectors. This chapter found that the internet was cut off in Sudan twenty-one times, making it the first study to document all of these events.

The history of Sudan witnessed numerous types of internet shutdowns, varying from nationwide blackouts to targeted blockages of specific applications or websites. "Sudan has experienced twenty-on shutdown events between 2016 and 2024 (Table 1.1. introduction to this volume)". This number represents one of the African countries with the highest number of internet shutdowns. These disruptions were justified by the authorities for different reasons.

This chapter sets out to address the following research questions:

1. What human rights are affected by internet shutdowns in Sudan?
2. What power interests are served by internet shutdowns in Sudan, and what is the role of ISPs in each case?
3. What forms of civic resistance and counter-power are emerging?

Based on the background of war, political instability and national exams, understanding the contexts of internet shutdowns in Sudan is crucial to protecting fundamental rights and promoting online freedoms. Through examining internet shutdowns, this chapter aims to shed light on the challenges to ensuring citizens' rights and the authoritarian motives of the government, and suggests recommendations to overcome these challenges.

The next section of the chapter provides a brief background of the history of media censorship in Sudan, including the pre-internet era. The following section discusses the internet ecosystem in Sudan and explores the internet shutdown events. Then, the existing literature on power and human rights has been reviewed to frame the analysis of the internet shutdown in Sudan.

## *Background*

Sudan is a country in Africa with land borders of 6,780 kilometres, bordered by Egypt, Libya, Chad, Central Africa, South Sudan, Ethiopia and Eritrea, and a coastline along the Red Sea (Alredaisy, 2024). Modern Sudan was established in 1956, when it gained independence from Anglo-Egyptian rule (Kumsa, 2017).

Since 1956, Sudanese have lived through a succession of military coups, transitional periods and incomplete democratic rule (Ayferam, 2023). History recorded thirty-five military coup attempts in Sudan between 1956 and 2021 (Armstrong, 2023). This instability made it harder to establish a democratic rule, which disrupted the development of the state, created social discord, sparked wars and caused numerous human rights violations. Moreover, the colonial era itself witnessed abuses and media censorship.

### *Colonial era (1899–1956)*

Media censorship was introduced to Sudan by the colonial authorities, who used it to strengthen their hold on power and serve colonial power interests. Arabic newspapers were forced to submit their issues for censorship to the colonial intelligence service. The British authorities were fearful of the transmission of nationalist sentiment from Egypt to Sudan via the press. This led the colonial administration to bring Lebanese editors to censor the content to avoid the Egyptian influence damaging colonial power (Sharkey, 1999).

### *Nationalist era (1956–2005)*

After independence, the nationalist governments maintained the colonial practice of press censorship until the start of the internet era (Sharkey, 1999). The nationalist governments imposed censorship on the press for political reasons to hold on to power to repress reporting on corruption and limit the right to access information (Hamid, Mohammed and Ahmed, 2018). Like the colonial rulers, the media controlled what was exercised to further the powerholders' interests and suppress opposition power.

During the thirty years of rule by the National Congress Party (NCP), through a military coup in 1989 led by Omar Albashier, press freedom was systematically repressed. The NCP initially banned all newspapers. After a brief resumption of journalistic activity, certain newspapers that were working before June 1989 were prohibited from continuing operations, creating a selective publication environment (Human Rights Watch, 1996b). The NCP regime imposed censorship on regional and international newspapers, magazines and books. Any independent publications carrying reporting deemed critical of the Sudanese authority were seized, in addition to harsh censorship on international mail letters (Human Rights Watch, 1996a). During this era – before 2005 – people almost lost interest in reading newspapers due to the severe censorship, which caused financial struggles for the media houses (Reliefweb, 2002).

Not only was printed media restricted, but the government imposed a licensing policy for using satellite dishes in 1996. Also, in the same year, the fax was banned for use without a permit as a former government official was arrested for owning a fax machine (U.S. Department of State, 1996). In general, these practices indicate the ingrained idea of closing government access to information, whether in the internet era or elsewhere.

In conclusion, it seems like the NCP regime tried to impose its Islamist ideology through isolating citizens from foreign influence, even by one-way communication, such as satellite TV.

### *Digital era (2005–24)*

The internet enabled citizens to bypass the censorship of the traditional press, radio and TV by publishing directly on the World Wide Web. Over time, the government updated its practices and transferred censorship to the online sphere by including online media within the scope of its censorship. The NCP regime blocked access to several websites, including YouTube (*Sudan Tribune*, 2008). In addition, to control the social discussions around domestic issues, the government imposed internet shutdowns (*Sudan Tribune*, 2013). However, in 2020, the Telecommunication and Postal Regulation Authority (TPRA) introduced a regulation on content filtering and website blockage on the internet, which legalized the partial internet shutdown represented in website blockings (Global Voices, 2022). However, this regulation created a significant opportunity for authorities to lawfully restrict access to web content, as it granted them the power to block any website they deemed inappropriate or classified as such. The regulation even added VPN services to their filtering list.

Therefore, the regulation acts as a legal tool that could be employed by the government to justify and legalize any blocking decision, in addition to serving the authorities' interests in controlling the information flow. In contrast, due to the absence of the parliament after 2019, this regulation was not publicly discussed, so civil society did not resist it.

## *Country description*

The first piece of information that was sent via the internet in Sudan was in 1996, with 128 kbps bandwidth capacity. Then, in 1998, Sudan Telecom Co. Ltd. (Sudatel) introduced its internet service in the country as a value-added service to its basic fixed telephony services, with a 265 kbps bandwidth capacity (Sudan Internet Society, n.d.). Since then, internet capacity has started rising in the country until now. By 2024, internet penetration in Sudan stood at 28.7 per cent (Kemp, 2024) (see Figure 6.1).

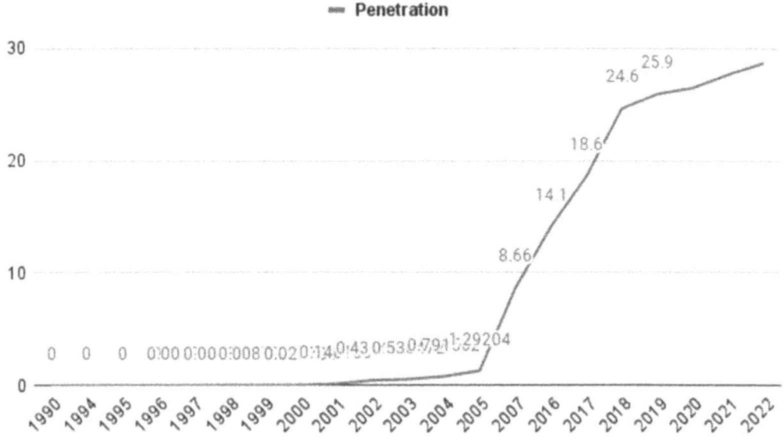


**Figure 6.1** Sudan Internet Penetration.

Source: Author via data from International Telecommunication Union[1]

The history of internet shutdowns in Sudan started earlier than in other countries in the region. The first reported case was on 22 July 2008, when the government blocked access to the YouTube website to prevent sharing a video of security forces beating and torturing minors (*Sudan Tribune*, 2008). The government also blocked YouTube twice in 2010 to stop the spread of a video showing electoral fraud, and in 2012 following the sharing of an anti-Islam video on the platform (*Sudan Tribune*, 2010; Freedom House, 2013). These partial shutdowns were specific to the YouTube platform, and the rest of the internet remained functioning.

However, the internet was completely cut off on 25 September 2013 for one day amidst protests against lifting fuel subsidies (Micek, 2013). This event was a milestone because it was the first total shutdown of the internet in the country under government orders.

Sudan's political situation has witnessed major change since 2018, when the people went on the streets against the rule of the ousted president, Omar al-Bashir, who ruled the country for thirty years. This political situation established a new era of censorship and internet shutdowns that started in December 2018 during the spark of the Sudan uprising. The government blocked access to numerous social media platforms, which lasted for sixty-eight days between December 2018 and February 2019. Platforms that were blocked included Facebook, Twitter (now X), Instagram and WhatsApp (Hamad, 2020b).

On 7 April 2019, a social media shutdown that lasted for one day was timed to coincide with planned protests in Khartoum (Freedom House, 2019). Considering that mobile networks are the most widely used in Sudan, with fixed broadband subscriptions only 29,800 by 2022,[2] the June 2019 mobile internet shutdown was the longest internet outage the Sudanese had experienced. A thirty-seven-day mobile internet shutdown was imposed following the massacre of Khartoum,[3] recording the longest nationwide mobile internet shutdown in the country (Blanchard, 2019a). The mobile shutdown of June 2019 almost paralysed all activities in Sudan. Online banking applications stopped, as well as small and medium-sized businesses that relied on the internet, and international communication related to applying to universities and travel interviews at embassies stopped (Hamad, 2020a).

Not all internet shutdowns in Sudan have been nationwide. In March 2020, the authorities shut down the mobile internet in Kassala City, eastern Sudan, in synchronization with tribal conflict (Dabanga, 2020). In September of the same year, the government shut down the mobile internet for three hours daily for eleven days, recording the first event of internet disruption 'to avoid cheating in national exams' (Emna and Samaro, 2020).

Some internet shutdowns have been motivated by sharing school exam questions and answers. In June 2021, the authorities shut down the mobile internet for another eleven days, three hours per day during the national exam sessions (Fatafta, Mnejja and Anthonio, 2021). This shutdown triggered an outcry as a large number of citizens expressed their anger because the internet cut-off times coincided with the most vital times for business and commerce. The shutdown resulted in work stopping almost completely due to the lack of access to email and

**Table 6.1** Timeline of Internet Shutdowns in Sudan

| Year | Type of shutdown | Details | Duration |
|---|---|---|---|
| 2008 | YouTube shutdown | N/A | Unknown |
| 2010 | YouTube shutdown | N/A | Unknown |
| 2012 | YouTube shutdown | N/A | Unknown |
| 2013 | Total shutdown | N/A | 1 day |
| 2018 | Social media shutdown | Facebook, Twitter (X), Instagram, WhatsApp | 68 days |
| 2019 | Mobile data shutdown | N/A | 37 days |
| 2019 | Social media shutdown | Facebook, Twitter (X), Instagram, Telegram, WhatsApp | Unknown |
| 2020 | Partial shutdown | Mobile data shutdown for a daily 3 hours during exams sessions | 11 days |
| 2021 | Total shutdown | During planned protests | 1 day |
| 2021 | Partial shutdown | Mobile data shutdown for 3 hours during exams | 11 days |
| 2022 | Total shutdown | During planned protests | 1 day |
| 2022 | Total shutdown | Prime Minister resignation | 12 hours |
| 2022 | Regional shutdown | Wad Almahi area, Blue Nile state, amid tribal conflict | Unknown |
| 2022 | National blackout | 25 October anniversary | 8 hours |
| 2024 | Kill switch | RSF takeover of telecom data centres | Unknown |

other internet services (Fatafta, Mnejja and Anthonio, 2021). Later in October of the same year, the government imposed an internet blackout that lasted twenty-five days, following a military coup (Anthonio, 2022). This case of internet blackout caused several job losses, missed educational opportunities and scholarships, as well as significant financial losses by internet-dependent businesses (Hamad, 2021). The authorities also shut down the internet on 25 December 2021, during anti-coup protests (STOP, 2022).

The year 2022 witnessed five documented shutdown events in January, June and October. In January, the throttling occurred concurrently with the Prime Minister's resignation and protests (Madory, 2022). In June, the authorities shut down the internet for eleven days, three hours daily, during national exam sessions. On 30 June, the government cut off the connectivity for twenty-five hours, in conjunction with planned protests against military rule. It is reported that nine protestors were killed during the shutdown period (Access Now, 2022). There were two further mobile internet shutdowns in October 2022; one was region-specific and the other was nationwide. The first was on 18 October, during tribal conflict in the Blue Nile region. The second happened on 25 October during the protest against the anniversary of the military coup. This shutdown lasted for only eight hours (Belson, 2023).

In April 2023, war erupted in Khartoum, the capital of Sudan (Stigant, 2023). The government immediately issued an internet shutdown order but cancelled it later on the same day (Freedom House, 2023). However, the telecommunication operators struggled to deliver their services as critical civilian and telecommunication infrastructure were destroyed due to the war. For instance, MTN Sudan mobile operator failed to deliver service due to power outages. Access to fuel to power backup generators or plants was almost impossible due to difficulty in movement during the conflict. This resulted in internet shutdowns within the telecom industry on several occasions (Hamad, 2023).

February 2024 witnessed the first military-imposed internet shutdown in Sudan's history, when the Rapid Support Forces (RSF), the 'rebel' paramilitary force fighting the Sudanese state military, took over the data centres of internet service providers (ISPs) operating in Khartoum, imposing a nationwide telecommunication blackout in the country (Access Now, 2024). The takeover of the ISPs' data centres threatens the delivery of humanitarian and emergency services (Amnesty International, 2024), which are crucial amidst the ongoing conflict. Also, it affected accessing life-saving information on safe routes used by citizens who were trapped in conflict areas. In addition, money transfers and the use of e-wallets, which many in Sudan depend on, have become more challenging (Shabaka, 2024).

## *Literature review*

Numerous think tanks, organizations, and scholars have highlighted the phenomenon of the internet shutdown in Sudan. They discussed the phenomenon in the context of disinformation, economic impact, social impact, civic resistance and human rights.

Researchers like Rydzak et al. (2020) point out how these shutdowns act as 'invisibility cloaks' for security force abuses, shrouding their actions in secrecy. This was evident during the 2019 Sudanese revolution, as documented by Alaa Daffalla (2021). Social media blockages, Daffalla argues, could lead to resistance tactics such as using VPNs, using other unblocked texting applications, and using coded language within the SMS to bypass the governmental restrictions and avoid censorship and tracking. Also, Daffalla mentioned that a complete blackout could cripple activists' ability to organize and communicate.

The motivations behind these shutdowns are complex. Research by Global Partners Digital and Access Now (2022) suggests that the government uses internet shutdowns to evade accountability for its actions, such as killing protestors. Bhatia et al. (2023) further highlight how the military weaponizes these shutdowns to spread disinformation through the traditional media, such as radio and TV, manipulating the narrative and controlling the flow of information.

The consequences of these shutdowns are far-reaching and can be devastating. They create information vacuums, as noted by Bhatia et al. (2023), denying citizens their right to online dissent and connect with the outside world. SMEX (2023) emphasizes the dangers posed to civilians caught in armed conflicts, as internet access is crucial for coordinating emergency services and staying informed. This is particularly concerning in Sudan, where Kpilaakaa (2023) warned of a looming internet shutdown during the ongoing conflict that transpired in February 2024 – a critical communication channel for mobilizing aid efforts.

Lauren Ploch Blanchard (2019b) highlights the disruption caused by human rights monitoring and pro-democracy advocacy. While the immediate effects of internet shutdowns are clear, their long-term impact is extremely concerning. These shutdowns raise questions about human rights violations and the government's motivations, as Hamad (2022a) suggests.

The economic consequences are undeniable, further deepening the humanitarian crisis. Ultimately, as Ryng et al. (2022) argue, internet shutdowns are tools used to suppress fundamental rights, including freedom of expression and assembly, all under the guise of national security, but in reality, they aim to consolidate power. The human and economic costs, however, paint a clear picture of the devastating impact these shutdowns have on the Sudanese people.

## *Conceptual framework*

Internet shutdowns are a complex interplay of power dynamics and human rights implications. While they are often employed as a tool to control information flow and repress opposition, they also have far-reaching consequences for individuals and societies. This analysis seeks to explore the intricate relationships between internet shutdowns and power structures, as well as their impact on fundamental rights.

### *Power*

Governments use internet shutdowns as a tool to control information flow and limit dissent, often during times of political unrest or elections (Howard and Hussain, 2013). This exertion of power over communication channels can reinforce incumbent power, vested power interests, and suppress counter-power and opposition power.

Power is defined as the actual or potential ability or capacity to achieve goals through a personal process in which goals and means of achieving goals are mutually determined and worked toward. Numerous scholars have divided the definition of power into 'power over' and 'power to' (Hawks, 1991).

To examine the relationship between internet shutdowns and power, we will use this framework because it offers insights into how power is exercised as a means of control and as a means of enabling or disabling action. So, driven from the contextual framework, we defined the following shapes of power to focus on:

1. Power over citizens

Governments exercise power over citizens by shutting down the internet during critical times. These shutdowns restrict citizens' access to information and communication and suppress their ability to gather. This form of power over the people allows the state to control the citizens' behaviour by controlling the flow of information and preventing the sharing of any documentation (Mare, 2020).

2. Power over ISPs

Telecommunications companies operate in countries in agreement with them based on a licence and regulatory framework. Mare (2020) argued that governments use regulatory and legal threats to maintain control over these companies, reflecting a 'power over' practice where the state imposes control on ISPs.

3. Power to control flow of information

Governments and authoritarian regimes have historically used their authority to practice the 'power concept' to restrict the flow of information, silencing voices and creating a climate of censorship. Wasserstrom and Cunningham (2018) argued how the Chinese government uses digital censorship as a way to control public opinion by selectively blocking and filtering online content. He discusses how the government manages the flow of information to reduce public dissent and protect its authority, effectively creating a 'power to control' dynamic through the internet.

4. Power to impunity

Authoritarians abuse laws and their enforcement for a variety of reasons, including impunity. Shutting down the internet allows authoritarian leaders to control the flow of information at critical times, such as protests and armed conflicts. This information often contains documentation of violations, prompting authoritarian leaders to shut down the flow of information in order to get away with it. The power to impunity empowers the authorities to deprive citizens of their rights of freedom of expression, access to information, and gathering, where these rights are considered as resistance tactics and civil society power. Amnesty described the internet shutdown in Iran as a tool of impunity (2020).

5. Power to grab power

Often, the success of any military operation depends on disrupting communications. The governments impose internet shutdowns to seize power illegally (Rowe and Mah'derom, 2023). In Sudan, the military shut down the internet during a military coup to take over power (Access Now, 2022).

6. Power to resist

Power relations means acceptance on the part of those subject to them. They also imply resistance (Barbalet, 1985). The power to resist is represented in the 'counter-power' concept against an imposed 'power over'.

### *Rights*

In 2016, the UN considered the internet as a human right (Howell and West, 2016). This was because internet shutdowns violate several human rights, including the following:

*Freedom of expression* The right to freedom of expression, enshrined in international human rights law, is often violated by internet shutdowns (United Nations Human Rights Council, 2016). The right to freedom of expression is guaranteed in international human rights law, including Article 19 of the International Covenant on Civil and Political Rights (ICCPR) and Article 9 of the African Charter on Human and Peoples' Rights (ACHPR) (United Nations, 1966 and ACHPR, 1986). By limiting access to information and the ability to communicate, authorities violate individuals' rights to voice opinions and access diverse standpoints.

*Access to information* Internet shutdowns disrupt access to information, which is a fundamental human right and crucial for personal and societal development (UNESCO, 2016). Such disruptions can have severe consequences, particularly during emergencies when accurate information is critical.

*Right to peaceful assembly and association* Internet shutdowns curb the ability to organize and participate in peaceful assemblies or associations online. This right is protected under Article 21 of the ICCPR.

*Right to work and education* The right to work and education is stipulated in Article 6 and Article 13 of the International Covenant on Economic, Social, and Cultural Rights (ICESCR) (United Nations (General Assembly), 1966, art. 3). Internet shutdowns disrupt remote work and e-commerce, impacting people's basic activities. Also, internet shutdowns restrict access to online education resources.

*Right to health* The right to health is mentioned in Article 12 of the ICESCR. This article guarantees the right of everyone to get care for both physical and mental health.

## *Methodology*

This chapter addresses the research question, 'What human rights are affected by internet shutdowns in Sudan, what power interests are served by internet shutdowns in Sudan, and what is the role of ISPs in each case? and what forms of civic resistance and counter-power are emerging?'. It approaches this question methodologically by using case studies of internet shutdowns in Sudan, such as the June 2019, October 2021 and February 2024 shutdowns. These cases have been chosen due to their prolonged periods and their devastating impact on people's lives, and offer enough data to study their implications on power and rights. Moreover, the February 2024 shutdown is the most unique case as it was the first shutdown instance to be imposed by the military in Sudan following the ongoing conflict between the Sudanese Armed Forces (SAF) and the Rapid Support Forces (RSF). As conflict intensified, the RSF took over the internet infrastructure and

**Table 6.2** The Interviewees Categorised by Occupation

| Name | Description |
|---|---|
| K.M. | ISP engineer |
| A.M. | ISP engineer |
| M.A. | A Sudanese licensed lawyer |
| M.E. | A Sudanese human rights advocate |
| N.M. | A Sudanese pro-democracy politician |
| B.M. | A Sudanese pro-democracy politician |
| M.B. | ISP engineer |

cut off the power, establishing a long era of digital darkness. The method of data collection relies on seven key informant interviews. The selection criteria for these interviewees depended on a relevance score based on their scientific and practical experience, their political standing, their influence on the course of events, their testimony to these events and their proximity to decision-making or resistance centres. Based on Access Now's definition of internet shutdowns we mentioned earlier, read with the UN declaration that internet access is a human right, we interviewed human rights experts, lawyers and civil society representatives (as shown in Table 6.2) to identify the rights that each case violated. Moreover, we conducted interviews with politicians to define the power interests that motivated the shutdown decisions. In the next three sections, the chosen conceptual framework is used to analyse the shutdowns. The collected data focus on the concepts mentioned in the conceptual framework, including power and rights. The interviews were conducted for all targeted cases.

The interviewees' consent was taken by written message via WhatsApp in the Arabic language. However, due to the anonymity policy – which requires that everybody's identity must be anonymised – the names of the interviewees have been replaced by pseudonyms.

## *Analysis*

Our case studies for this chapter are the shutdowns in June 2019, October 2021 and February 2024. We extracted data from key informant interviews to build up our findings. Furthermore, media reports are considered to support the information from the interviewees.

### *Power*

The internet has been completely cut off in Sudan in the context of exams, political unrest, military coups or conflict. The reasons for cutting off the internet vary from one event to another, but what distinguishes cutting it off during political unrest is that it is linked to power interests. The only case where it could be claimed that shutdowns are not related to power interests is exams.

According to N.M., a Sudanese politician:

> By cutting off the internet, the regime was targeting some factors, most notably weakening the ability of civil forces to organize and communicate. In 2019, this coincided with the events of dispersing the sit-in – a mass protest in Khartoum that overthrew the old president of Sudan – and calling for 30 June processions, as the regime expected a huge public reaction. In the case of October 2021, the regime's goal, by cutting off the internet, was to prevent information about the coup and resistance against it from the masses, with the aim of reducing the growing public resistance to the coup.

Here, the politician claims that powerholders were using the internet shutdown to repress the development of counter-power in the shape of what the interviewee calls '*growing public resistance*' of citizens. The interviewee suggests that the shutdown is deployed as a tool to serve the power interests of the incumbent government and to block the growing power of the opposition.

Moreover, B.M., a Sudanese politician, stated:

> the primary purpose of the internet shutdown in June 2019 was to only limit witnesses to those who experienced the Khartoum massacre at the crime scene and to stop the circulation of evidence abroad. Also, one of the purposes was to restrict any communication between demonstrators for fear of coordinating protests in response to the massacre by creating new gatherings other than the sit-in that was dispersed by force.

The politician argues that the government used the internet shutdown to exercise power over citizens to control information flow on social media. Moreover, the interviewee shows that the powerholders shut down the internet in the frame of power to impunity by depriving the people from sharing human rights violation documentation. Furthermore, the interviewee claims that the government practised power against the concept of 'power to resist' through an internet shutdown to disable the opposition's peaceful weapons.

In addition, B.M. continued:

> the aim of cutting off the internet in October 2021 was to prevent the people from flowing into the streets in advance coordination in rejection of the military coup. Before the coup, the streets were full of pro-democracy protests, which led the authorities to plan to cut off communication to evade the protests because mass movement is the greatest source of strength for democracy.

In this statement, the interviewee argues that the authority uses internet shutdown to restrict the counter-power, which appeared in response against power to grab power illegally. Moreover, it is noticed that this form of power has an impact on human rights, including the right to assembly.

However, the RSF shut down the internet in February 2024 in the frame of the conflict between the RSF and the SAF, which is different. The interviewee mentioned that 'the aim of RSF's action was to deprive the SAF, which controls the telecommunications sector' (Ahmed, 2022), which generates money to help finance the war. On the other hand, the RSF benefits from the shutdown by financing its activities via providing Star Link satellite services for a commercial fee, in addition to imposing fees on those who operate this Star Link in some areas in the Darfur region, western Sudan.

The interviewee's point of view shows how the powerholder practises power over ISPs. However, this case is unique as the powerholder (executer) here is not the government but another armed actor that resists the counter-power by isolating the government's financing channels through internet shutdown.

Also, 'Until July 2019, there was no legal text that prohibited internet shutdowns or even guaranteed the right to access the internet. Therefore, it can be said that this practice of the authorities reflects the concept of abuse of power in order to protect the regime against peaceful protesters exercising their freedom to express their will' (M.A., a Sudanese lawyer).

This statement places the Sudanese government's internet shutdowns in the context of its exercise of 'power over' citizens to maintain control over dissent. By exploiting internet blackouts during periods of political unrest – such as the 2019 Khartoum massacre or the October 2021 coup – the government prevents 'counter-power' from emerging in civil society, particularly the ability of citizens to organize and resist powerholders. This 'power' not only interferes with 'power over resistance', but also serves to maintain state impunity by restricting access to evidence of human rights abuses and silencing witnesses, effectively blocking any channel through which citizens can hold the government to account.

### *Counter-power*

Despite facing internet shutdowns, Sudanese citizens resisted governmental power through diverse strategies. Offline activism was a reaction to governmental actions, including street protests, sit-ins and acts of civil disobedience. The offline activism was employed by the pro-democracy groups to mobilize against government actions, representing an alternative communication method. Moreover, to overcome communication barriers, many turn to alternative channels like satellite internet, importing roaming SIM cards and employing bulk SMS to mobilize, maintain contact and spread information (Hamad, 2020b).

Moreover, civil society countered the internet shutdown in Sudan in collaboration with legal firms and independent lawyers. The Sudanese Consumer Protection Organization (SCPO), the United Attorneys firm and two other individuals filed suit challenging the internet shutdown on the basis of their subscription contracts with the telecom companies. The General Court of Khartoum ordered the ISPs to restore internet service to those organizations, and then restore to all citizens in an extension to this order (Hamad, 2021).

The counter-power actions of ISPs to internet shutdowns are almost non-existent. Canar, one of the largest ISPs, refused to cut off the internet in June 2019, representing the only recorded counter-power point in the telecom sector (Hamad, 2020b). However, ISPs often find themselves caught between the rights of their customers and the pressures exerted by the regulator, the TPRA. The TPRA holds significant control over the ISPs, with the authority to issue directives and impose penalties for non-compliance.

In situations of political unrest, the TPRA usually instructs ISPs to restrict or completely shut down internet access. These orders often come with legal justification based on the Telecommunication and Post Regulation Act, under which ISPs work. Consequently, ISPs are faced with a difficult challenge, either ignoring the government's orders and risking severe repercussions, or adhering to them and serving their power interests.

Despite these legal bases, civil society in Sudan shows countermeasures to internet shutdown orders, as mentioned above. The ignorance of the ISPs regarding supporting these initiatives and exploiting them for their benefit is a big question mark around the role of these companies in serving the power interests of the authorities in Sudan. No company or employee in the telecommunications companies condemned the governmental orders to cut off the internet, but Al-Fateh Erwa, the managing director of Zain Telecom in Sudan, implicitly condemned the RSF's cutting off of communications in the country, indicating the company's alignment with the authorities' interests.

It is important to know that the ISPs' board of directors usually includes a government-related person, such as Al-Fateh Erwa at Zain, who is a former minister of defence and an ambassador (Erwa, n.d.), in addition to Ibrahim Jabir at Sudatel, who is a member of the Transitional Sovereignty Council (TSC), the head of state (Sudatel, n.d.). The involvement of government officials shows a clear effort by the government to influence the ISPs' power towards their power interests.

### *Rights*

*Political rights* According to M.E., a human rights advocate:

> The internet shutdowns in Sudan violate the human rights of those who are in the country and abroad, as the internet has no limits. The main purpose of the internet cut-off in June 2019 was to limit freedom of expression and restrict the right to assembly. Therefore, this case narrowed the right to access information for the purpose of preventing the documentation of the massacre of Khartoum and creating a media blackout. Moreover, the purpose of the shutdown case of October 2021 was the same as in 2019, as it limited the freedom of expression, access to information and the right to assembly.

This feedback agreed that both shutdowns have an impact on the right to free expression and the right to assembly. It is clear that the powerholders aimed to restrict any way that empowers citizens to resist their actions, even through soft power.

*Civil rights* M.E., a human rights advocate, stated:

> The 2021 event impacted the right to health, as numerous people could not access health facilities and information during the Covid-19 pandemic. Also, it violated the right to work and education as several freelancers and those who have worked remotely since the Covid-19 pandemic lost their jobs, and some students who study remotely were forced to travel abroad to attend their lectures or exams.

This comment from our interviewee highlights the broad human rights implications of internet shutdowns, extending beyond civil and political rights to impact social and economic rights deeply as well. The right to work and the right to education were violated and financially impacted remote workers and freelancers, whilst in addition impacting remote students.

M.A., a Sudanese lawyer, posited:

> The shutdown of October 2021 occurred under the authority of the interim constitutional charter of 2019, which guaranteed the right to access the internet under Article 57/2. Thus, the right to access the internet in Sudan has become one of the constitutional rights that must be protected by the competent authorities and other law enforcement authorities. So, citizens can sue based on a violation of their constitutional rights.

In this intervention, our interviewee, who is a lawyer, clarified how this shutdown constitutes a violation of Sudan's citizens' constitutional rights, providing legal grounds for them to challenge the shutdown in court. By denying access to the internet, the shutdown restricted freedom of expression and information and impeded the exercise of constitutionally protected rights essential to democratic engagement.

However, the case of February 2024 triggered discussions. For example, M.A., a Sudanese lawyer claimed:

> The intended shutdown of communications services carried out by the RSF is considered a violation of the constitutional rights of the Sudanese. However, it is important to know that there are no penal provisions that directly criminalize such actions. However, this event may fall within the scope of war crimes and crimes against humanity. This act can also be included among the criminalized acts in Article 72 of the Criminal Code of the year 1991.

Based on this feedback, the human cost is clear, despite the fact that the legal implications of the RSF's actions are complicated. Cutting off communication services during conflicts directly impacts the lives of citizens. It restricts their ability to seek help, stay informed and connect with loved ones. So, we can conclude that this shutdown violated the right to life and the right to health.

M.E, a human rights advocate stated:

> On the other hand, the RSF shut down the internet to limit free expression and limit the flow of information about the crimes committed by the RSF, both of which concepts are human rights. The crimes of RSF in Gezira state include storming villages to loot cars, residents' property, and large sums of money, in addition to killing citizens [*Sudan Tribune*, 2024a]. Moreover, the 2024 event violates the right to life as it established a bad environment for the Human Rights Defenders, as they used to request emergency or help if they faced any danger during their work.

Also, due to the inability to access online banking applications, the internet shutdown of 2024 violated the right to life.

According to M.E, a human rights advocate:

> The work of the Emergency Response Rooms (ERRs) in supplying food, water and medications, has stopped. ERR is an initiative that was established following the eruption of the violent conflict between the RSF and the Sudanese Armed Forces to provide support to the people in conflict areas [UN News, 2024]. Also, it violated the right to education as several students shifted to studying online because of several on-campus activities due to security concerns regarding the ongoing conflict.

Here, the interviewee sheds light on the fact that, by limiting access to information and communication, the RSF has not only suppressed freedom of expression but also restricted humanitarian efforts. The inability to access online banking services has impacted essential services. Furthermore, the disruption of online education has deprived students of their right to learn and grow. These actions highlight the impact of the internet shutdown on financial rights and basic needs.

## *Conclusion*

This chapter sets out to address the following research questions: 'What human rights are affected by internet shutdowns in Sudan? What power interests are served by internet shutdowns in Sudan? What forms of civic resistance and counter-power are emerging?' The chapter focuses on the longest shutdown events of 2019 and 2021, which lasted for thirty-seven and twenty-five days, respectively, in addition to the unique shutdown of February 2024.

In conclusion, internet shutdowns served the power interests of the powerholders by restricting access to information and communication, suppressing dissent, controlling public opinion and maintaining their grip on power. Moreover, they served their political interests by suppressing protests, restricting the ability of citizens to organize, mobilize and coordinate protests.

Also, internet shutdowns empower the regimes with impunity, protecting them from accountability by limiting access to information and evidence of human rights abuses. In addition, internet shutdowns grant powerholders economic control, as when RSF shut down the internet to undermine the economic power of SAF.

In this chapter, we found that Sudanese citizens' resistance to internet shutdowns highlights the adaptability of pro-democracy movements under repressive conditions. Offline activism, including street protests, emerged as a vital response to government efforts to limit communication, allowing activists to mobilize despite restrictions. By adopting alternative communication methods like satellite internet, imported SIM cards and bulk SMS, Sudanese citizens circumvented communication barriers and maintained the flow of information. Moreover, the legal path was followed in resisting shutdown orders. This effort of information access and organized resistance suggests a strong civil society that challenges governmental power and serves as a source of hope for enhancement in the digital rights in the country.

Moreover, we found that ISPs have largely complied with government orders to enforce internet shutdowns, prioritizing regulatory compliance over citizen access to information. While some resistance, such as Canar's refusal in 2019, has occurred, ISPs are constrained by the TPRA, which holds significant control over their operations. The close ties between key ISP executives and the government further suggest that these companies serve the political interests of the authorities, often aligning with their power dynamics rather than advocating for digital rights or resisting shutdown orders for their own benefit.

Internet shutdowns in Sudan represent significant threats to human rights, undermining fundamental freedoms, including the right to freedom of expression, the right to access information and the right to assembly. Also, shutdowns threaten the right to work, the right to education and the right to health.

Between the colonial era and the modern digital era, Sudanese media were subjected to various forms of censorship and control, which reflects the historical extensions of these phenomena, whether by blocking newspapers or blocking access to the fax machine and finally by shutting down the internet.

This chapter found that the internet has been cut off in Sudan nineteen times, making it the first study to document all of these events. However, the emergence of internet shutdowns represents a new front in the negative practices of various authorities in Sudan throughout modern history, with a clear impact on human rights and democratic governance. The current war in Sudan has cut off the path towards democracy and development and introduced the internet as a means of military and political pressure, making it necessary to confront the challenges posed by cutting off the internet, protect basic rights and promote a comprehensive digital ecosystem for all citizens.

By using a human rights-centric framework, it was possible to see that internet shutdown events in Sudan violated many human rights stipulated in international conventions, including freedom of expression, the right to access information, the right to life, the right to assembly, the right to work and learn and the right to health. By using the lens of power, it was possible to identify that the authoritarian motives for cutting off the internet varied from one event to another, but they were united in working to limit the flow of information; one of the unique reasons came within the context of the war in Sudan, which was depriving the enemy of its sources of funding, of which communications is one of them. Despite the fact that Sudan is a signatory of regional and international conventions that protect the right to access the internet, power abuse usually succeeds in bypassing these legal obligations.

Moreover, to guarantee sustainable internet connection, the authorities in Sudan should reform internet-related policies by establishing legal frameworks safeguarding digital rights and prohibiting internet shutdowns. These reforms should align with international human rights standards.

Moreover, civil society plays a pivotal role in advocating for digital rights and holding authorities accountable. Stronger civil society means impactful engagement and advocacy against shutdowns. This leads us to the importance of raising the awareness of civil society members. The international community must actively engage with Sudanese stakeholders to address digital governance challenges. Diplomatic pressure, technical assistance and capacity-building initiatives can support Sudan's transition towards a more inclusive digital ecosystem.

However, the shutdown of February 2024 shed light on the importance of investment in resilient technological infrastructure. It is crucial to mitigate the impact of shutdowns on critical services and emergency response systems, especially in a war context. Diverse communication channels and decentralized networks can bolster resilience against censorship efforts.

## *Notes*

1 Individuals using the Internet. ITU. https://datahub.itu.int/data/?e=SDN&c=701&i=11624. *Data missing between 2008 and 2015.*

2 World Bank open data, https://data.worldbank.org/indicator/IT.NET.BBND?end=2022&locations=SD&start=1960&view=chart

3 The Khartoum massacre occurred on 3 June 2019, when the Sudanese security forces, including the Rapid Support Forces (RSF), used heavy gunfire and tear gas to disperse a sit-in by protestors in Khartoum, killing over 100 citizens.

## *Bibliography*

Access Now (2022), 'Internet Shutdowns and Blockings Continue to Hide Atrocities of Military Coup in Sudan', Access Now, https://www.accessnow.org/press-release/update-internet-shutdown-sudan/

Access Now (2023), *Internet Shutdowns and Elections Handbook*, Access Now, https://www.accessnow.org/guide/internet-shutdowns-and-elections-handbook/

Access Now (2024), '#keepiton in Times of War: Sudan's Communications Shutdown Must Be Reversed Urgently', Access Now, https://www.accessnow.org/press-release/keepiton-sudan-shutdown/

African Charter on Human and Peoples' Rights (1986), 'African Commission on Human and Peoples' Rights', https://achpr.au.int/en/charter/african-charter-human-and-peoples-rights

Ahmed, W. (2022), 'Will Sudan's Telecom Sector Remain Under Military Control?' SMEX. https://smex.org/will-sudans-telecom-sector-remain-under-military-control/

Alredaisy, S. M. A. H. (2024), 'The Physical Geography of Sudan: A State's Power and Threats', *International Journal of Research Publication and Reviews (IJRPR)*, 5 (1): 2814–22.

Amnesty Intrnational (2020), 'A Web of Impunity: The Killings Iran's Internet Shutdown Hid', https://iran-shutdown.amnesty.org/

Amnesty International (2024), 'Sudan: Internet Shutdown Threatens the Delivery of Humanitarian and Emergency Services', https://www.amnesty.org/en/latest/news/2024/03/sudan-internet-shutdown-threatens-delivery-of-humanitarian-and-emergency-services/

Anthonio, F. (2022), 'The Kill Switch', Yale Law School, https://law.yale.edusites/default/files/area/center/isp/documents/anthonio_kill-switch.pdf

Armstrong, M. (2023), 'A History of Sudan's Coups', Statista Daily Data, https://www.statista.com/chart/26044/sudan-coup-timeline/

Ayferam, G. (2023), 'Sudan's Conflict in the Shadow of Coups and Military Rule', Carnegie Endowment for International Peace, https://carnegieendowment.org/sada/90382

Barbalet, J. M. (1985), 'Power and Resistance', *The British Journal of Sociology*, 36 (4): 531, https://doi.org/10.2307/590330

Belson, D. (2023), 'Cloudflare. Internet Disruptions Overview for Q4 2022', https://blog.cloudflare.com/q4-2022-internet-disruption-summary/

Bhatia, K. V., Elhussein, M., Kreimer, B. and Snapp, T. (2023), 'Internet Shutdown and Regime-Imposed Disinformation Campaigns', *Communicatio*, 49 (2): 53–71, https://doi.org/10.1080/02500167.2023.2230391

Blanchard, L. P. (2019a), 'Congressional Research Service', https://sgp.fas.org/crs/row/if10182.pdf

Blanchard, L. P. (2019b), 'Sudan's Uncertain Transition', R45794, Washington, Congressional Research Service, https://sgp.fas.org/crs/row/R45794.pdf

Dabanga (2020), '"Precautionary" Mobile Internet Slowdown in Sudan's Kassala', https://www.dabangasudan.org/en/all-news/article/precautionary-mobile-internet-slowdown-in-sudan-s-kassala

Daffalla, A. (2021), 'Security & Privacy Practices and Threat Models of Activists During a Political Revolution', Kansas: University of Kansas, https://kuscholarworks.ku.edu/handle/1808/34276

Darrell, M. W. (2016), 'Internet Shutdowns Cost Countries $2.4 Billion Last Year', the Brookings institution, https://witnessradio.org/wp-content/uploads/2016/10/intenet-shutdowns-v-3.pdf

Emna and Samaro, D. (2020), 'Internet Shutdowns in Algeria and Sudan: Damaging Practices During Exceptional Circumstances', Access Now, https://www.accessnow.org/internet-shutdowns-in-algeria-and-sudan-damaging-practices-during-exceptional-circumstances/

Erwa, E. (n.d.). LinkedIn, https://www.linkedin.com/in/elfatih-erwa-1a7b491a/

Fatafta, M., Mnejja, K. and Anthonio, F. (2021), 'Internet Shutdowns during Exams: When MENA Governments Fail the Test', Access Now, https://www.accessnow.org/mena-internet-shutdowns-during-exams/
Freedom House (2013), 'Freedom on the Net', https://freedomhouse.org/sites/default/files/2020-02/fotn%202013_full%20report.pdf
Freedom House (2019), 'Freedom on the Net Sudan', https://freedomhouse.org/country/sudan/freedom-net/2019
Freedom House (2023), 'Sudan. Freedom on the Net', https://freedomhouse.org/country/sudan/freedom-net/2023#:~:text=Internet%20access%20was%20disrupted%20in,before%20reversing%20itself%20hours%20later
Global Partners Digital and Access Now (2023), 'Evading Accountability Through Internet Shutdowns', https://www.accessnow.org/wp-content/uploads/2023/03/evading-accountability-through-internet-shutdowns.pdf
Global Voices (2022), 'How the Government in Sudan Legalized Internet Categorizing and Content Filtering', https://advox.globalvoices.org/2022/08/02/how-the-government-in-sudan-legalized-internet-categorizing-and-content-filtering/
Hamad, K. (2020a), The Socio-Economic Cost of the Internet Shutdown in Sudan, https://internews.org/wp-content/uploads/2022/08/socio-economic-impact-of-shutdowns-in-sudan.pdf
Hamad, K. (2020b), Internet Shutdowns in Sudan: The Story Behind the Numbers and Statistics. Global Voices, https://globalvoices.org/2020/06/08/internet-shutdowns-in-sudan-the-story-behind-the-numbers-and-statistics/
Hamad, K. (2021), 'In Sudan, the Court Stands on the Side of Unrestricted Access to the Internet', Global Voices, https://globalvoices.org/2021/12/16/in-sudan-the-court-stands-on-the-side-of-unrestricted-access-to-the-internet/#
Hamad, K. (2022a), 'The Unfreedom Monitor, Sudan Report', Global Voices Advox, https://advox.globalvoices.org/2022/08/04/unfreedom-monitor-report-sudan/
Hamad, K. (2022b), 'Three Years After Al-Bashir Ouster, Sudan's Internet Freedom Landscape Remains Precarious', CIPESA, https://cipesa.org/2022/12/three-years-after-al-bashir-ouster-sudans-internet-freedom-landscape-remains-precarious/
Hamad, K. (2023), The Ongoing Conflict's Impact on ICT and Digital Transformation Efforts in Sudan, Gobal Voices, https://globalvoices.org/2023/10/21/the-ongoing-conflicts-impact-on-ict-and-digital-transformation-efforts-in-sudan/
Hamid, Y. B., Mohammed, R. and Ahmed, M. K. (2018), 'Sudanese Newspapers and "Fourth Estate" Role: Impacts of Censorship on Anti-Corruption Campaign', *New Media and Mass Communication*, www.iiste.orgISSN2224-3267 (Paper) ISSN 2224-3275 (Online) Vol.67, 2018,https://www.researchgate.net/publication/323515542_Sudanese_Newspapers_and_Fourth_Estate_Role_Impacts_of_Censorship_on_Anti-Corruption_Campaign
Hawks, J. H. (1991), 'Power: A Concept Analysis', *Journal of Advanced Nursing*, 16 (6): 754–62, https://doi.org/10.1111/j.1365-2648.1991.tb01734.x
Heficed (2021), 'What Is a Null Route?', https://www.heficed.com/kb/security/what-is-a-null-route/
Howard, P. N. and Hussain, M. M. (2013), 'Democracy's Fourth Wave? Digital Media and the Arab Spring', Oxford Academic, https://doi.org/10.1093/acprof:oso/9780199936953.001.0001
Howell, C. and West, D. M. (2016), 'The Internet as a Human Right', Brookings, https://www.brookings.edu/articles/the-internet-as-a-human-right/

Human Rights Watch (1996a), *Human Rights Watch World Report 1996 – Sudan*, https://www.refworld.org/docid/3ae6a8b110.html

Human Rights Watch (1996b), *Political Repression in Sudan*, https://www.hrw.org/reports/1996/sudan.htm

Kemp, S. (2024, 23 February), 'Digital 2024: Sudan', https://datareportal.com/reports/digital-2024-sudan

Kpilaakaa, J. (2023), 'Sudanese Are Using Social Media to Mobilize for Safety and Aid During Conflict', International Journalists' Network, https://ijnet.org/en/story/sudanese-are-using-social-media-mobilize-safety-and-aid-during-conflict

Kumsa, A. (2017), 'South Sudan Struggle for Independence, and Its Implications for Africa', *RUDN Journal of Sociology*, 17 (4): 513–23, https://doi.org/10.22363/2313-2272-2017-17-4-513-523

Leon, P. A. V. (2019), 'Addressing the Ultimate Form of Cybersecurity Control, a Multiple Case Study for the "Internet Kill Switch"' (Doctoral dissertation, Syracuse University).

Madory, D. (2022), '12-Hour Internet Disruption on Sunday in Sudan as the Prime Minister Resigned and the Military Regained Country of the Government', X [Post]. https://twitter.com/DougMadory/status/1478441370721337349

Mare, A. (2020), 'Internet Shutdowns in Africa: State-Ordered Internet Shutdowns and Digital Authoritarianism in Zimbabwe', *International Journal of Communication*, 14: 4244–63.

Micek, P. (2013), Update: Mass Internet Shutdown in Sudan Follows Days of Protest', Access Now, https://www.accessnow.org/mass-internet-shutdown-in-sudan-follows-days-of-protest/

Mockapetris, P. and Dunlap, K. J. (1988), 'Development of the Domain Name System', in *Proceedings of the ACM SIGCOMM '88 Conference on Communications Architectures, Protocols and Applications* (pp. 123), Association for Computing Machinery, https://doi.org/10.1145/52324.52338

OHCHR (1986), *International Covenant on Civil and Political Rights*, https://www.ohchr.org/en/instruments-mechanisms/instruments/international-covenant-civil-and-political-rights

Reliefweb (2002), Situation of Human Rights in the Sudan (e/cn.4/2002/46) – Sudan, https://reliefweb.int/report/sudan/situation-human-rights-sudan-ecn4200246

Rowe, J. and Mah'derom, S. (2023), 'Weaponizing Internet Shutdowns to Evade Accountability for Rights Violations', https://www.openglobalrights.org/weaponizing-internet-shutdowns-evade-accountability-rights-violations/

Rydzak, J., Karanja, M. and Opiyo, N. (2020), 'Internet Shutdowns in Africa | Dissent Does Not Die in Darkness: Network Shutdowns and Collective Action in African Countries', *International Journal of Communication*, 14, https://ijoc.org/index.php/ijoc/article/view/12770

Ryng, J., Guicherd, G., Saman, J. A., Choudhury, P. and Kellett, A. (2022), 'Internet Shutdowns', *The RUSI journal*, 167 (4–5): 50–63, https://doi.org/10.1080/03071847.2022.2156234

Shabaka (2024), 'Internet Shutdowns in Sudan and Senegal: The Humanitarian Fallout', https://shabaka.org/internet-shutdowns-in-sudan-and-senegal-the-humanitarian-fallout/

Sharkey, H. J. (1999), 'A Century in Print: Arabic Journalism and Nationalism in Sudan, 1899–1999', *International Journal of Middle East Studies*, 31 (4): 531–49. http://www.jstor.org/stable/176461

SMEX (2023), 'Sudan: Internet Shutdowns Fuel Human Rights Abuses', https://smex.org/sudan-internet-shutdowns-fuel-human-rights-abuses/

Stigant, S. (2023), 'What's Behind the Fighting in Sudan', United States Institute of Peace, https://www.usip.org/publications/2023/04/whats-behind-fighting-sudan

STOP (2022), 'Shutdown Tracker Optimization Project', Access Now, https://docs.google.com/spreadsheets/d/1DvPAuHNLp5BXGb0nnZDGNoiIwEeu2ogdXEIDvT4Hyfk/edit?gid=1914386612#gid=1914386612

Sudan Internet Society (n.d.), Sudan Internet and.sd Experience, https://www.itu.int/itudoc/itu-t/workshop/cctld/cctld050.pdf

*Sudan Tribune* (2008), 'Sudan Bans YouTube Website', 1 August, https://sudantribune.com/article28083/

*Sudan Tribune* (2010), 'Sudan Reportedly Blocks YouTube over Electoral Fraud Video', 21 April, https://sudantribune.com/article34622/

*Sudan Tribune* (2013), 'Sudan Cuts Internet for Next 48 Hours as Fears Mount of New Post-Friday Prayers Protests', 26 September, https://sudantribune.com/article47213/

*Sudan Tribune* (2024a), 'RSF Accused of Fresh Violations, Army Intensifies Operations in Al-Jazeera State', 3 March, https://sudantribune.com/article282863/

*Sudan Tribune* (2024b), 'Sudan Experiences Widespread Internet Outage Amidst War and Accusations', 5 February, https://sudantribune.com/article281998/

Sudatel (n.d.), Board of Directors – Sudatel Telecom Group, https://www.sudatel.sd/investor-relations/governance/board-of-directors/

UN News (2024), 'Youth-Led "Emergency Rooms" Shine Rays of Hope in War-Torn Sudan', (2024), https://news.un.org/en/story/2024/02/1146187

UNESCO (2016), UNESCO Series on Internet Freedom: 'Fostering Freedom Online: The Role of Internet Intermediaries', https://unesdoc.unesco.org/ark:/48223/pf0000231162

United Nations (General Assembly) (1966), *International Covenant on Economic, Social, and Cultural Rights*. Treaty Series, 999, 171. https://treaties.un.org/doc/Treaties/1976/01/19760103%2009-57%20PM/Ch_IV_03.pdf

United Nations Human Rights Council (2016), 'The Promotion, Protection, and Enjoyment of Human Rights on the Internet', Human Rights Council, Thirty-Second Session, A/HRC/32/L.20, http://daccess-ods.un.org/access.nsf/Get?Open&DS=A/HRC/32/L.20&Lang=E

U.S. Department of State (1996), 'Sudan Human Rights Practices, 1995', https://reliefweb.int/report/sudan/sudan-human-rights-practices-1995

Vigderman, A. and Turner, G. (2024), 'ISP Throttling: How Do You Know If You're Being Throttled?' Security.org, https://www.security.org/vpn/isp-throttling/ [Original source: https://studycrumb.com/alphabetizer]

Wasserstrom, J. N. and Cunningham, M. E. (2018), *China in the 21st Century: What Everyone Needs to Know*®. Oxford: Oxford University Press.

# Chapter 7

## A rights-based approach to assessing internet shutdowns in Nigeria

Thobekile Matimbe and Charles Kajoloweka

### *Introduction*

This chapter analyses the incidence of internet shutdowns in Nigeria and measures the reasons proffered by the government against international standards in applying a rights-based approach. The analysis seeks to answer the following questions: 'What are the forms of internet shutdowns in Nigeria? What power interests are served by them? What are their impacts on human rights? How have citizens pushed back to hold the government to account, end their occurrence and regain their rights?' The approach deployed is an analysis of primary interview evidence and secondary assessment of literature through the lens of a rights-based conceptual framework, towards recommendations aimed at strengthening policy and practice in Nigeria. The chapter particularly focuses on the Twitter (now X) ban that lasted about 222 days in Nigeria. The internet shutdown choice is premised on the long duration of the internet shutdown and broad coverage across the Nigerian population. While Nigeria has not blatantly shut down the internet, it has blocked access to Twitter across the country and disrupted mobile network services in certain states within Nigeria.

The concept of rights in the context of internet shutdowns, government interests at stake and the way forward for human rights are addressed. Internet shutdowns are usually ordered by governmental officials but involve a complex assemblage of actors, infrastructure, political drivers and regulatory discourses with national and transnational dimensions. In the next section, a historical background of Nigeria is presented, outlining the media landscape before and after independence and showing that restrictions have always been relied upon by the government of Nigeria; this is followed by a literature review and analysis of internet shutdowns in Nigeria with a particular emphasis on the Twitter ban. A case description of Nigeria unpacking the use of social media in Nigeria follows, then a literature review capturing the conceptual framework articulating internet shutdowns in Nigeria, technology concepts, and the concept of rights, power and affordances. The analysis follows, drawing from the literature reviews, with recommendations, and a conclusion is formulated.

## Background

Lying on the coast of West Africa, Nigeria borders Niger and Chad to the north, Benin in the west, Cameroon in the east and Gulf of Guinea in the south. It has a population of 229,152,217 people (Worldometer, 2024). With an estimated GDP of USD 477 billion and the gross domestic product per capita equalling USD 2.33 thousand, Nigeria is considered Africa's largest economy (Statista, 2024). However, millions of Nigerians face grim human rights threats and actual violations, courtesy of incessant security challenges, including insurgencies, kidnappings and communal and sectarian violence. There are also concerns about extrajudicial killings, torture and other abuses by state security institutions. Repression of women and the LGBTIQ+ community and targeted attacks against the media through criminal defamation laws continue to undermine civil liberties. However, in the last decade, Nigeria has experienced significant adoption of digital technology, leading to growth in internet connectivity and the country's economy. Nigeria has a long history of restriction on media freedom and freedom of speech, spanning from the colonial to the democratic era.

### *Colonial period (1850–1960)*

The history of the press in Nigeria centres on the activities of the British colonialists. Historically, the first printing press in Nigeria was established by the Christian Presbyterian mission when they arrived in Calabar in 1946. Named '*Iwe Irohin Fun Awon Ara Egba Ati Yoruba*' (translated as *Newspaper in Yoruba for the Egba and Yoruba people*), the newspaper was installed in December 1859 by Reverend Henry Townsend (Onuoha, 2021). The press aimed to increase literacy and knowledge among locals, particularly on religious matters. The Calabar empowered locals 'to exercise their power of participation in the government of their land'.

The establishment of the British colony in Nigeria in 1850 and the years to come saw proliferation of various media houses owned by Europeans. The press became a critical instrument in the independence liberation struggle by journalists (Ismael, 2011). The Anglo-African newspaper was founded by Robert Campbell in 1863. Given its critical stance against colonization, the paper was deemed too critical of British authorities and never enjoyed government patronage and business before its closure. The paper's editor, Andres Thomas, in his editorials of March 1881 is quoted: 'We are not clamouring for immediate independence, but it should always be in mind that the present order of things will not last forever. A time will come when the colonies on the west coast will be left to regulate their own internal and external affairs.' The newspapers served as radical platforms for political mobilization and conscientization for the masses towards national independence and exposing colonial subjugation (Ismail, 2011). The introduction of electronic media (radio), particularly *radio fusion* in 1932, and later, Nigeria Broadcasting Corporation in 1956, further expanded the space for critical media and nationalist movements.

Other European-dominated press during this period included *Lagos Times* and *Gold Coast Colony Advertiser* (1880), the name depicting a reflection of the joint administration of Nigeria (Lagos) and Ghanian proprietors; the *Lagos Observer* by John Payne Jackson (1891–1930), the *Lagos Observer* (1882–90), the *Eagle* and *Lagos Critics* (1883) owned by Emerick Macaulay, *Iwe Irohin* by Andrew Thomas (1888) and *Lagos Weekly Times* by John Payne Jackson (1890). A total of fifty-one newspapers were established between 1880 and 1937 including eleven dailies, thirty-three weeklies, three fortnightlies and four monthlies (Ismail, 2011).

According to Ismail (2011), the oppression of the media under colonialists started in 1891 with the promulgation of various legislations aimed at gagging critical media. The Official Secrets Ordinance No. 2 of 1891 and Newspaper Ordinance 1903 were introduced to control anti-colonial criticism, while the Seditious Publications Act of 1909 and Criminal Code of 1916 criminalized critical press publications. Notably, in 1916, journalist James Bright Davies, an editor of *Nigerian Times*, was convicted of sedition for writing that Nigeria would one day be free from Lugard's repressive colonial administration (Ismail, 2011). In 1921, journalist Thomas Jackson of *Lagos Weekly Record* was jailed for two months, while J. A. Olushora and Dr Caulcrick of *Daily News* were fined GBP50 each, and Albert Macaulay, the proprietor was jailed without an option of a fine for criticizing the colonial government.

Notably, this colonial era was characterized by state control of media by British colonists to serve the imperialist interests of British capitalism, particularly to undermine the independence nationalist struggle.

### *Post-independence era (1960–92)*

The Nigerian independence in 1960 after over one hundred years of colonization and nationalist struggle, was marked by the promise of democracy and human rights for all citizens. The era would, however, soon be hijacked by military coups, establishing brutal military regimes. Between 1966 and 1990 alone, Nigeria was under various military regimes. Although short-lived, intervention of the military government of General Aguiyi-Ironsi in 1966, was the beginning of a tyranny of brutal military repression of the press in post-independent Nigeria (Ekuma, 2012).

In 1966, General Yakubu Gowon, who succeeded General Aguiyi-Ironsi, promulgated the Army Emergency Decree of 1966, which made arrest and detention of citizens without warrant lawful and also empowered the Inspector General of Police and other officers of the same or higher rank to search any newspaper office or premises in Nigeria without warrant or notice. Using this Decree, in 1968, the police searched the *Daily Times* office (*Weekend Times*). The Decree was widely condemned for its ability to turn the Nigerian press into a 'captive press' (Ekuma, 2012). The administration also promulgated another Decree in 1967, titled the Newspaper Prohibition of Circulation Decree 1967, which empowered the Head of Federal Military Government to proscribe circulation of any newspaper in Nigeria where it was deemed detrimental to the interest of the federation or any state thereof within the federation. Offending this Decree attracted six months' imprisonment and or a N500 fine. In addition, General Gowon's administration promulgated the Amendment Decree No. 53 of 1969 which made it an offence for any person to 'publish in a newspaper, television or radio or by any means of mass communication, any matter which by reason of dramatization or other deflects in the manner of its presentation was likely to cause public alarm or industrial unrest'.

The rise of General Muritala Mohammed and General Olusegun Obasanjo's administration in July 1975, which brought General Gowon's administration to an end, worsened press freedom (Ekuma, 2012). In July 1978, the new administration banned the *New Breed Magazine* from circulation, evoking the Newspaper Prohibition from Circulation Decree of 1967. To cover up state corruption, on 8 April 1979, the administration further promulgated a Decree titled the Newspaper Public Official Report Decree which provided that

> any person who published or reproduces in any form whether written or otherwise; any statement, rumour or report alleging that a public officer has in any manner been engaged in corrupt practices or has in any manner corruptly enriched himself or any other person being a statement, rumour or report which is false in any material particular, shall be guilty of an offence and be liable on conviction to imprisonment for a term not exceeding 2 years without option of fine.

In a similar fashion of military political culture, the General Buhari-led Military administration introduced several repressive Decrees to muzzle the press and his political critics. In 1984, Decree No. 4 of 1984, called Public Officers {Protection against False Accusation} Decree 1984, was enacted. The Decree prohibited newspapers or any wireless telegraphy station in Nigeria from publishing or transmitting 'any message, rumour, report or statement which is false in particular that any Public Officer has in any manner corruptly enriched himself or any other person'. Individuals convicted of this offence were liable to imprisonment for a term not exceeding two years, without the option of a fine. Offending corporate bodies would be slapped with a fine not less than N10,000 for the same offence. As if this was not enough, the Decree also prohibited the circulation of any newspaper that may be detrimental to the interest of the federation or any part thereof, as well as empowered the Federal Military Government to revoke the licence granted to such wireless telegraphy stations under the provision of the Wireless Telegraphy Act 1961 or order the closure or forfeiture of such newspaper to the Federal Military Government. Interestingly, the Decree also targeted corporate leaders. It provided that, where the offence is committed by a Corporate Body, every person who at the time of the commission of the offence was the proprietor, publisher, general manager, editor, secretary or other similar officer of the body corporate or was purporting to act in any such capacity shall be deemed to be guilty of that offence unless they prove that the offence was committed without their consent or connivance and they had acted to prevent such an offence. Eventually, the *Guardian Newspaper* was convicted under this Decree of which two journalists, Mrs Nduka Irabor and Tunde Thompson, were jailed, and the paper was ordered to pay N50,000 as a fine. The two journalists were later pardoned by the General Ibrahim Babangida-led administration, following the fall of General Buhari military rule on 27 August 1985.

The messianic appearance of the Babangida administration was short-lived when he assumed power in 1985 on a human rights populist note. While his administration repealed Decree No. 2 of 1984, it reintroduced another Decree titled the State Security {Detention of Persons} Decree 2 of 1984 to ruthlessly clamp down on the press. The *NewsWatch Magazine* was prohibited for six months in 1985 and the administration was accused of being behind a bomb parcel that assassinated the Editor-in-Chief of *NewsWatch Magazine*, Dele Giwa, in October 1986. The administration also introduced the Nigerian Press Council Decree No. 85 of 1992, which established the Nigerian Press Council to deal with complaints by members of the public against the conduct of journalists in their professional capacity. On 9 April 1992, the administration further promulgated another Decree targeting Concord Newspapers, called Concord Group of Newspapers Publication {Proscription and Prohibition from circulation} Decree No. 14 1992. In the year 1993, the administration also proscribed the publication and prohibited from circulation various newspapers including the *Africa Concord Magazine*, *Weekend Concord*, *Sunday Concord*, *National Concord*, *The Punch*, *Saturday Punch*, *Sunday Punch*, *Daily Sketch*, *Sunday Sketch* and *Nigerian Observer* (Ekuma, 2012).

Unlike his predecessors, General Sanni Abacha, whose regime ruled between 1994 and 1998, did not bother with promulgation of draconian laws to repress the media – he had a different tactic. Instead, he harassed and jailed journalists as well as banning media houses, accusing them of conspiring in the execution of a coup. Some prominent journalists including Kunle Ajibade, Charles Obi and George Mbah, were secretly tried along with General Olusegun Obasanjo of conspiring to carry out the 1995 phantom coup and subsequently sentenced to life imprisonment, later commuted to fifteen years imprisonment each by General Abdulsalam Abubakar's regime.

Further, when General Abdulsalam Abubakar ascended to power following the sudden death of San Abacha, the new administration proscribed *Guardian Newspaper* and *Guardian Weekly Magazine* on 14 August 1994 through Decree No. 8 of 1994. In 1999, the administration also introduced a new Decree titled the Nigerian Press Council (Amendment) Decree No. 60 of 1999, which empowered the Council to regulate registration of journalists and newspapers as well as magazines annually and imposed heavy sanctions on the proprietors and publishers of any newspaper and magazine that failed to comply with the Decree. It is clear from this historical exposé that the post-independence era was marred by callous media clampdown and analogue shutdowns. The media controls served the interests of the military high command, a power retention strategy.

### *Democratic and digital age era (1999–2024)*

This is a democratic period which overlaps with the digital age. Instead of departing from oppressive military regimes, the succeeding civilian regimes have also exploited press freedom and free speech at the altar of narrow political interests.

Arrests and harassment of journalists and media censorship continued under the eight-year civilian reign of Olusegun Obasanjo between 1999 and 2007. For example, on 10 January 2008, journalists, namely Nnamdi Onyeuma, Emmanuel Okike-Ogah, Ogbonaya Okorie, Ademola Adegbamigbe and Igha Oghole, also Fidelis Mbah were arrested and detained in Ibadan for taking photographs of a controversial statue of an 'Unknown Soldier' erected to replace the statue of Chief Obafemi Awolowo by the Oyo State Government in a public place. Throughout his reign, Obasanjo also frustrated the freedom of information bill (FOI) which was introduced to the national assembly in 2003. The FOI bill was later passed into law by the administration of Goodluck Jonathan, in May 2011 (Ekuma, 2012).

The perception of governments to regain control or curb any attack through humanitarian blockades in war is a reality in many contexts. The same formula seems to be adopted in the context of internet restrictions during ethno-religious and other conflicts in Nigeria. Security challenges were documented by Freedom House (Freedom House, 2022), including the 'ethno-religious crisis, insurgency by the Boko Haram militant group, as well as communal and sectarian violence' in the Middle Belt region (Freedom House, 2022). The conflict climate in Nigeria has been sustained during the current review period regarding the incidence of internet shutdowns. The crackdown by the military on any publication perceived to be against the country or a state was a restriction imposed under the name of defence interest and seen in recent years manifesting in disruptions of internet access through directives that limit telephone and mobile services in a bid for retention of power. Human rights become relegated to the constitution's text while national interests are cited as the rationale for such limitation.

The preceding historical context affirms that media control did not begin with the internet. All administrations, from colonial, military and civilian, have exerted control over the media, including media blackouts and censorship.

## *Country case description*

In the digital age, the power of platforms like X, WhatsApp and Facebook has enabled an efficient way for human rights such as freedom of expression and access to information to be realized in Nigeria. Media freedom is anchored on internet access as a new media that enables diverse discourse. In January 2021, Nigeria recorded 104.4 million internet users, which number had since risen to 122.5 million internet users by January 2023, showing a rise in internet use. In 2021 there was an internet penetration of 50 per cent, and 33 million social media users, accounting for 15.8 per cent of the entire population. There were 187.9 million active cellular mobile connections, which had increased by 17 million from the previous year, 2020 (Datareportal, 2022). Social media platforms are used by many in Nigeria with 2.68 million Twitter users in Nigeria in 2020 alone (Statista, 2020). Anthonio and Roberts (2023) give an overview of the Nigerian context, highlighting the growing use of mobile internet services in Nigeria for digital citizenship, with X being cited as one of the most common forms of expression of

**Table 7.1** Internet Shutdowns in Nigeria

| Type of internet shutdowns in Nigeria | Dates/Period | Reasons proffered by the government | Affected community | Authority ordering internet shutdown |
|---|---|---|---|---|
| Mobile and Telecommunications network closure | May – July 2013 | Counter-insurgency strategy against Boko Haram terrorism | Adamawa, Borno, and Yobe | Nigerian Army |
| Twitter Ban | 4 June 2021–13 January 2022 | Protecting sovereignty | The entire Nigerian population | President Buhari |
| Mobile and Telecommunications network closure | 3 September – 19 September 2021 | Stability of Nigeria (national security) | Zamfara State | Nigerian Communications Commission |

Source: Authors.

digital civic duty. Nigeria has no history of blatant nationwide internet shutdowns cutting across all social media platforms. The Twitter ban incident in Nigeria was preceded by the #EndSars protests, which were largely facilitated by mobilization on X in October 2020 (Popoola, 2022).

The Twitter ban from 4 June 2021 to 13 January 2022 lasted about 222 days (Paradigm Initiative, 2022). In pushing back against the Twitter ban in Nigeria, Socio-Economic Rights and Accountability Project (SERAP), Media Rights Agenda, Paradigm Initiative for Information Technology Development (Paradigm Initiative), Premium Times Centre for Investigative Journalism, International Press Centre, Tap Initiative for Citizens Development, Patrick Eholor, Chief Malcolm Omokiniovo Omirhobo, David Hudeyin, Samuel Ogundipe, Blessing Oladunjoye and Nwakamri Zakari Appollo filed different suits against the government of Nigeria before the Economic Community of West African States (ECOWAS) Court, which were consolidated and a ruling passed to the effect that the government of Nigeria violated the rights to freedom of expression, access to information and the media by suspending Twitter on 4 June 2021 (ECOWAS, 2022).

## *Literature review*

This section reviews literature on internet shutdowns in Nigeria and concepts of technology, rights, agency, resistance, power and affordances to analyse the 2021 Twitter ban in Nigeria.

### *Types of internet shutdowns*

The definition of internet shutdown has evolved over the last decade owing to different technological contexts. An internet shutdown is: 'An intentional disruption of internet or electronic communications, rendering them inaccessible or effectively unusable, for a specific population or within a location, often to exert control over the flow of information over internet infrastructure' (Access Now, n.d). In analysing the Twitter ban in Nigeria in this chapter, this definition is applied to assess the concept of power exhibited and attendant impact on human rights. This definition broadly covers disruptions to any electronic communications, which encompasses social media platforms.

Internet shutdowns are also widely described as 'internet blackouts', 'network shutdowns', 'internet kill switches', or 'virtual curfews' (Access Now, n.d.). Internet shutdowns intend to deny someone's access to internet-enabled services and control the free flow of information, often used by states to disarm dissent. They include intentional shut-off or disruption of phone calls and text messaging services. Internet shutdowns habitually stem from state actors who give orders to private and state-owned internet service providers (ISPs) to deploy the 'kill-switch', but often deny complicity and an intentional violation of human rights. Oddly, state political interests have become the 'main-switch' of the internet.

Following the removal of a controversial tweet made by President Muhammadu Buhari in which he threatened to deal with those causing trouble in the country using 'the language they understand', referencing the experience of the 1967–70 civil war where millions of Nigerians were killed, the government of Nigeria ordered a Twitter ban that lasted for almost seven months (Al Jazeera, 2021). Oladapo and Ojebode mention how social media platforms are popular in Nigeria, including the growing use of hashtags such as #BringBackOurGirls, #EndSars and #Buharimustgo, started in 2014, 2017/2020 and 2019 respectively, as well as the reliance on Twitter, now known as X (Oladapo and Ojebode, 2021).

The incidence of internet shutdowns in Nigeria did not start in 2021 but other occurrences have been noted. In May 2013, mobile networks were suspended for about two months, affecting Adamawa, Borno and Yobe regions (Thumfart, 2024). Between 3 and 19 September 2021, the government of Nigeria in Zamfara State ordered a shutdown of mobile networks to address kidnapping incidents, restricting internet and mobile communications (CNN, 2021). In March 2021, the government restricted access to mobile network services in Zamfara state to address insurgencies, and reportedly, this was a welcome development, although the reasons are unclear (Thumfart, 2024). An assessment of the landscape in Nigeria reflects the rise in digital citizenship in Nigeria. Ojebode, Babatunde, Oladapo and Oosterom address the concept of ethno-religious fault lines and how they undermine digital citizens' collective resilience (Ojebode et al., 2023). They explore digital resilience and the ability of citizens to mount up collective action in a country which has the largest number of internet users (about 136 million) in Africa (Roberts and Bosch, 2023).

### *Types of shutdown*

In this chapter we apply Jigsaw's concept which stipulates six core methods that state actors often use to partially or fully implement internet blackout, depending on the scope, scale, target and level: (i) Throttling refers to the 'intentional slowing of an internet service/data bandwidth by an internet service provider (ISP).' Practically, the 'ISPs can slow – or "throttle" – connections to the point that loading websites becomes impractical or impossible.' Throttling is hard to detect as consumers may often mistake it for 'normal' connectivity glitches. (ii) Internet Protocol (IP) blocking is 'the targeted blocking of access to specific websites and platforms in specific geographical locations, based on IP addresses and/or application.' (iii) Mobile Data Shutoffs refer to 'the shutdown of mobile data services, especially on smartphones.' Both the IP blocking and data shutoffs are easily detectable. (iv) DNS Interference refers to 'The use of a DNS resolver to block access to names on a block list. Consequently, a resolver can be configured to "return no response, an invalid IP address, or the address of a different service entirely, redirecting the user to a location they didn't intend to reach".' (v) Server Name Identification Blocking is 'the blocking of a secure connection, from hypertext transfer protocol (HTTP) to Hypertext Transfer Protocol Secure (HTTPS), following a server name identification request to a targeted service'. (vi) Deep Packet Inspection (DPI) refers to 'the blocking of access to specific content using keywords and/or other content (filename, for example).' These technological means of restricting voices of the citizenry have the same effect of interrupting fundamental rights and freedoms (Jigsaw, 2021).

*Concept of rights*

The rights-based approach (also called a human rights-based approach) applied in this chapter looks at an internationally agreed set of norms 'backed by international law' and highlighted as 'providing a stronger basis for citizens to make claims on their states and for holding states to account for their duties to enhance the access of their citizens to the realization of their rights' (Cornwall and Nyamu-Musembi, 2004). Human rights are often regarded as privileges by repressive governments, yet they are the bedrock of human existence and should be respected without undue deviations, in accordance with international standards. Nigeria is a state party to the International Covenant on Civil and Political Rights (ICCPR, 1976) and the African Charter on Human and Peoples Rights (OAU, 1986) and is guided by a Nigerian constitution that has a bill of rights (Nigerian Constitution, 1999). As such, a human rights-based approach is critical in ensuring that concepts of power are subservient to human rights.

A human rights-based approach is similarly defined by the United Nations Sustainable Development Group (UNSDG) as

> a conceptual framework for the process of human development that is normatively based on international human rights standards and operationally directed to promoting and protecting human rights. It seeks to analyse inequalities which lie at the heart of development problems and redress African Charter discriminatory practices and unjust distributions of power that impede development progress and often result in groups of people being left behind.
>
> (UNSDG, n.d.)

This UNSDG definition is applied in the context of internet shutdowns in as far as they impede development and affect key human rights. This chapter particularly frowns on the unjust distribution of power that may be an impediment to human rights being realized. In the context of the Twitter ban in Nigeria, the unfettered power in the hands of the President, ordering a blanket Twitter ban for all Nigerian subscribers, was an unjust limitation of human rights.

### *Civil and political rights*

The Universal Declaration of Human Rights (UDHR) has established in Article 19 as follows:

> Everyone has the right to freedom of opinion and expression; this right includes freedom to hold opinions without interference and to seek, receive and impart information and ideas through any media and regardless of frontiers.

This has been similarly articulated in Articles 9 of the African Charter on Human and Peoples' Rights (African Charter) and 19(2) of the International Covenant on Civil and Political Rights (ICCPR), which provide for freedom of expression, drawing inspiration from the UDHR.

Freedom of expression is not an absolute right. In terms of Article 19(3) of the ICCPR, the exercise of the rights provided for in paragraph 2 of this Article carries with it special duties and responsibilities. It may therefore be subject to certain restrictions, but these shall only be such as are provided by law and are necessary: (a) For respect of the rights or reputations of others; (b) For the protection of national security or of public order (*ordre public*), or of public health or morals. This yardstick of limiting rights is applied in the analysis of the Twitter ban in Nigeria below.

Freedom of assembly and association are entrenched in Article 20(1) of the UDHR. The ICCPR in Article 21 provides that:

> The right of peaceful assembly shall be recognized. No restrictions may be placed on the exercise of this right other than those imposed in conformity with the law and which are necessary in a democratic society in the interests of national security or public safety, public order (*ordre public*), the protection of public health or morals or the protection of the rights and freedoms of others.

A case for rights is also premised on the Nigerian Constitution which entrenches freedom of expression and access to information in Article 39 and freedom of assembly and association in Article 40 (Federal Republic of Nigeria, 1999).

In the *Amnesty International Togo et al. vs the Republic of Togo* decision, the ECOWAS Court held that in the absence of the law, preventing internet access amounted to a violation of the right to freedom of expression by the Togolese Republic. The Court directed the Respondent State of Togo to take 'all necessary measures' to prevent the recurrence of internet shutdowns. The government of Togo was ordered to enact laws as part of addressing freedom of expression in accordance with international human rights standards and to pay each of the eight Applicants CFA2,000,000 (approx. USD3,500) in compensation (Global Freedom of Expression 2022). In the *Amnesty International Togo et al. vs the Republic of Togo* decision, the ECOWAS Court held that the right to access the internet is a right within the context of the right to freedom of expression, consequently requiring the protection of the law. This case aligns with the concept of rights and is referenced in the Twitter ban case in Nigeria.

### *Economic rights*

The right to pursue economic development is provided in Article 1 of the ICESCR which states as follows:

> All peoples have the right of self-determination. By virtue of that right they freely determine their political status and freely pursue their economic, social and cultural development.

Article 22 of the African Charter also echoes the same right and provides that:

> All peoples shall have the right to their economic, social and cultural development with due regard to their freedom and identity and in the equal enjoyment of the common heritage of mankind.

The rights entrenched in the ICCPR and African Charter are the basis of the rights-based approach applied in this chapter in assessing Nigeria's performance. With regard to the right to economic development in Nigeria, while not entrenched in the Bill of Rights, Article 16 of the Nigerian constitution articulates the objectives of the government not to prejudice the rights of any person to participate in the economy.

### *Business and Human Rights*

The United Nations has articulated in the Guiding Principles on Business and Human Rights the role of businesses in promoting human rights. While states have obligations under UN Treaties to adhere to human rights, businesses have responsibilities to safeguard human rights (UN, 2011). This normative framework provides as follows:

> In order to meet their responsibility to respect human rights, business enterprises should have in place policies and processes appropriate to their size and circumstances, including:

(a) A policy commitment to meet their responsibility to respect human rights;
(b) A human rights due diligence process to identify, prevent, mitigate and account for how they address their impacts on human rights;
(c) Processes to enable the remediation of any adverse human rights impacts they cause or to which they contribute.

In the context of internet shutdowns, the key business actors such as social media platforms and mobile network operators (MNOs) have a role to respect human rights, ensuring that they conduct due diligence in order to promote human rights and mitigate risks.

### *Concepts of power*

In this chapter, power is defined as a form of authority, control or domination (VeneKlasen and Miller, 2002). VeneKlasen and Miller break down power into a series of 'expressions of power'. Those with authority over others are considered to be relatively powerful, while those who are dominated are seen as relatively powerless. This kind of authoritarian power is referred to by VeneKlasen and Miller as 'power over', demonstrating repression. From a more positive angle the power to act collectively with others is referred to as 'power with' and the ability of individuals and groups to act in pursuance of their goals and objectives is referred to as 'power to', demonstrating resistance.

These concepts of power are useful for analysing the ability of citizens to effect change and to collaborate with others to hold those with 'power over' to account (VeneKlasen and Miller, 2002). In this chapter we use these concepts of power to analyse the actions of the President, the social media company Twitter, and the actions of Nigeria citizens in response to the Twitter ban. Other power concepts useful in analysing citizen resistance to 'power over' come from Foucault and Lukes. In assessing the resistance of citizens in Nigeria through their use of Twitter for digital activism and their harnessing of judicial process to push back against power, we borrow from Foucault's (1995) thoughts without delving into controversies around his concept of power, and he argues that 'resistance is inseparable from power – where there is power, there is resistance' (Kelly, 1994). Lukes then argues that agency exists inherently in all relationships of power, with agency referring to the ability a person has to act in the world (Lukes, 2005).

Whilst the government of Nigeria had indicated it occasioned the Twitter ban in Nigeria to protect its sovereignty, since Twitter was being used by a separatist leader to cause discord, the Applicants maintained that the suspension was in retaliation to a flagged tweet by President Muhammadu Buhari, for violating Twitter rules. The retaliation demonstrates the concept that those with authority are regarded as relatively powerful as in the case of President Buhari, whilst the citizens, in the shadow of political power, are relatively powerless.

The analysis of power plays, as mentioned in the introductory chapter, looks at different actors and the power they derive. Table 7.2 presents the power outlook in the case of Nigeria.

**Table 7.2** Power Interests in Nigeria

| Stakeholder | Power interests | Expression of power | Source of power | Manifestation |
|---|---|---|---|---|
| **President Buhari** | Retaining political power over the citizens and technology companies | Power over | State power | Twitter ban order /mobile and telecommunications network shutdown in Zamfara State |
| **Citizens using social media to protest** | Building collective power and agency over human rights | Power within | Inherent human rights and the collective resistance | Resistance though viral hashtags |
| **X (formerly Twitter) and mobile network operators (MNOs)** | Maximizing economic power | Power over | Economic power | Compliance as a way to maintain the market related interests |
| **Nigerian Communications Commission** | Balancing power interests | Power to | Legal | Effecting restrictions on mobile networks |

Source: Authors.

Nigerians have power derived from the Constitution which articulates their fundamental rights to protest and to freely associate on social media platforms through collective action. This is expressed through their ability to mobilize, seen through the various hashtags mentioned in earlier sections. The #EndSars protest is mentioned as a form of resistance that Nigerians used to the disbandment of the police unit abusing citizens.

### *Analysis of the Nigerian Twitter ban*

The internet shutdown is referred to as Internet Protocol (IP) Blocking and affected over 2.68 million users on Twitter (Statista.com, 2020). The preceding #EndSars protests had demonstrated the power of the citizens to act against a repressive SARS security unit unleashing police brutality on the citizenry. Through collective effort, Nigerians leveraged the power to mobilize and collaborate in protest action on Twitter, exercising their civil and political rights, in particular freedom of assembly entrenched in the ICCPR and Nigerian constitution. In the 2020 #EndSars protest, Twitter is credited with the honour of enhancing democracy and the connective power of the youth to curb repressive political power, which action is followed by a Twitter ban in June 2021 (Popoola, 2022).

The ordering of the Twitter ban was a clear show of impunity, occasioned by President Muhammadu Buhari without thought of the adverse human rights impacts. Triggered by the takedown of his tweet by Twitter for breaching community standards, he retaliated by banning the entire population from having access to the social media platform, the retaliation of a scorned Twitter user. Leveraging political power over the citizenry, his action carelessly violated human rights. The disproportionate measure of the conduct of former President Buhari failed to pass the limitations test of human rights as presented in Article 19(3) of the ICCPR where a limitation to freedom of expression must be presented by law, necessary and proportionate. Looking at the 325.4 thousand users on Twitter expelled from accessing the platform, the conduct of President Buhari could not be deemed necessary or proportionate. On one hand, former President Buhari's response of banning Twitter was a restriction interfering with Twitter access, while the restriction imposed on him as a removal of his Tweet from the public domain was only affecting him solely. This Twitter ban case study shows serious implications on the rights of the masses in Nigeria affecting political discourse, sharing and accessing information and other human rights (Anyim, 2021).

### *Technology for rights and power dynamics*

The internet has a special place in Nigeria, affording users the ability to exercise rights cutting across political participation and the ability to work and participate in their economy using online platforms. The expulsion of Nigerians from the internet has undeniable attendant impacts on labour rights and political participation. Furthermore, Twitter enhances political rights for Nigerians, and particularly young people who mostly rely on digital activism to effect change, advancing causes for girls to be saved through campaigns on Twitter and pushing back against police brutality. Technology affords citizens with agency to mount up resistance against power as seen through the cases consolidated in the ECOWAS Twitter ban case and reported under the SERAP cases where civil society organizations and individuals demanded their rights.

What makes the Nigerian Twitter ban peculiar is the fact that it was ordered following a removal of a Twitter post by President Buhari as highlighted in the country description. The government then proceeded to give a media statement saying the removal of the tweet was not the sole reason for banning Twitter and stated as follows (France24, 2021):

> There has been a litany of problems with the social media platform in Nigeria, where misinformation and fake news spread through it have had real world violent consequences.

The government assertions in media reports aimed at blaming Twitter for misinformation and fakes news after the President's own post had been taken down for violating Twitter's community standards showed a lack of transparency as to the actual reason for violating the rights of Twitter users, affecting their rights to share and receive information as well as to engage in business on the platform. The internet shutdown was an abuse of executive authority and, without a national law authorizing it and judicial oversight, proved to be a repressive demonstration of executive power. The clarion demand made on Twitter by the Nigerian government to be registered in Nigeria, appoint a designated Twitter representative in the country, to pay taxes and comply with applicable local media laws demonstrates the stringent action by the state to retain power over social media platforms. Twitter reportedly conceded to some of the government demands with Twitter highlighting that it would engage with the government (BBC, 2022). In this instance, the Nigerian Communications Commission exercised its power, enabled by its orders to dictate what should be the terms of operation of Twitter in Nigeria.

The Zamfara State shutdown of mobile networks attributed to addressing kidnapping incidents through restricting internet and mobile communications (CNN, 2021) is a mobile data shutoff as defined by Jigsaw, occasioned by the Nigeria Communications Commission. It demonstrates the power over the MNOs while the interests of MNOs to conduct business may place them in a weaker position, forcing them to comply with government directives. However, national security should be approached with caution, bearing in mind that a rights-based approach strives to assess the proportionality of state action where human rights are being limited by an existing law (UN, 1985). The blanket approach of shutting down the internet for a specific population violates freedom of expression (African Commission on Human and Peoples' Rights, 2019). Addressing business responsibilities, Twitter and any MNOs in Nigeria have to adhere to human rights standards, ensuring they are transparent with how they respond to directives, demonstrating clear commitments to human rights.

### *Citizen views*

In this chapter, respondents to a survey on internet disruptions who requested anonymity outline how internet shutdowns affect their human rights. We conducted a survey from 4 April 2024 to 20 April 2024 canvassing experiences of eleven victims of internet shutdowns in Nigeria who experienced shutdowns in Nigeria between 2020 and 2024. The views expressed in the survey include internet shutdowns experienced during the Twitter ban and mobile network shutdowns in various states mentioned in Table 7.1.

> 'I was unable to receive or share information via Twitter.' Respondent 1.
>
> 'It affected my work and access to information as Twitter was a major source of news and happenings around the world for me.' Respondent 2.
>
> 'It affected me because as a good citizen of my country, Nigeria, I also need to know what is going on concerning my country and use the internet for my personal business. During that period, I was unable to do anything on my computer and phone for an hour.' Respondent 3.

Respondents bemoaned the Twitter ban and echoed the role of the platform to enhance freedom of expression and access to information as well as the right to work and development as provided in the ICCPR, ICESCR and African

Charter. The rights of citizens to the enjoyment of their civil and political rights were affected, as well as their right to development. Twitter offered a platform for citizen participation in the economy, engaging in business. The loss of this platform affected their economic rights to work and participate in the economy.

*Impact on human rights: the rights-based approach*

Nigeria is a state party to the ICCPR, ICESCR and African Charter and so the expectations of a rights-based approach are within reasonable grounds. In the Twitter ban context, human rights were violated, mainly freedom of expression and access to information and potential threats to freedom of assembly and association. The platform was unavailable for almost 222 days and the youth could not exercise their power to act and express dissent with other like-minded communities if they so wished. The history of digital activism presented in this chapter showed the reliance placed on Twitter to facilitate digital activism, which reliance was sabotaged. Resistance is inseparable from power and we argue that without a platform to demonstrate resistance, there is no power to act.

*Civil and political rights*

In articulating a rights-based approach, a decision by ECOWAS in *SERAP v Nigeria (ECW/CCJ/JUD/40/22)* on the Twitter ban case highlighted the need for the government of Nigeria to respect human rights. In the case, several organizations including the Socio-Economic Rights and Accountability Project (SERAP), Media Rights Agenda and Paradigm Initiative filed cases against the government of Nigeria in the Community Court of ECOWAS Court claiming that the government of Nigeria had violated freedom of expression and access to information among other human rights (Global Freedom of Expression, 2022). The Community Court consolidated the cases and decided that the Nigerian government violated freedom of expression and access to information provided under Articles 9 and 19 of the African Charter on Human and People's Rights and the ICCPR, respectively.

The Community Court ruled that access to Twitter is a 'derivative right' that is 'complementary to the enjoyment of the right to freedom of expression'. In its decision the Community Court made an order for a lifting of the Twitter ban and a guarantee of non-recurrence. This progressive took a human rights-based approach to the decision, ensuring future preservation of freedom of expression and access to information, safeguarding the rights of victims of internet shutdowns in Nigeria.

Litigation has also been applied in Nigerian courts against telecommunications networks disruptions. SERAP filed a case *FHC/ABJ/CS/1323/2021* at the Federal High Court in Abuja asking the court to 'determine whether the shutdown of telecommunication networks in any part of Nigeria by the Buhari administration is unlawful, and a violation of the rights of access to correspondence, freedom of expression, information, and the press' (SERAP, 2022). Furthermore, SERAP sought for a decision that disruption of telecommunications networks is against the test of legality, proportionality and necessity, violating freedom of expression and access to information. This lawsuit was a case challenging telecommunications networks disruptions in Zamfara and Katsina State in Nigeria on grounds of addressing banditry and terrorism. SERAP argued that this conduct by the Nigerian government was collective punishment on the residents in the affected states in Nigeria, interfering with participatory democracy and their ability to engage in a wide discourse.

In the *Amnesty International Togo et al. vs the Republic of Togo* decision, the ECOWAS Court held that in the absence of the law, preventing internet access amounted to a violation of the right to freedom of expression by the Togolese Republic. This was similarly the outcome in the *SERAP v Nigeria* case on the Twitter ban.

Apart from advancing freedom of expression, freedom of assembly and association are fundamental and provide power to the citizenry to push back against state excesses. Platforms like Twitter provide a medium for citizen voices to be heard. This is witnessed in the #EndSars protests and rise in digital activism in Nigeria. In the case *of Media Rights Agenda et al. vs The Federal Republic of Nigeria* (2022), petitioners argued that the internet shutdown was not implemented in accordance with the law. In addition, it was not proved as necessary or proportionate action as envisaged by Article 19(3) of the ICCPR. In essence, the conduct violated human rights and could not meet the limitations test applicable in derogation from a human rights lens.

The Twitter ban in Nigeria took away a critical platform for subscribers to protest and call for accountability from the government as well as to associate with others on Twitter. In the *Registered Trustees of the Socio-Economic Rights and Accountability Project (SERAP) (Suing for & on behalf of concerned Nigerians) Plaintiffs v The Federal Republic of Nigeria* (*The Registered Trustees of the Socio-Economic Rights and Accountability Project (SERAP) v The Federal Republic of Nigeria*, 2021), Amicus Curiae submissions highlight that 'internet shutdowns, including blocking of social media services such as Twitter, which are often used to facilitate all of these activities, hinder online protests in a blanket manner'.

### *Economic rights*

Article 22 of the African Charter on Human and Peoples' Rights entrenches the right to economic, social, cultural development, which right is violated by internet shutdowns, causing losses. The effects of internet shutdowns on economic development are quantified, showing a clear case of economic sabotage by the government. The Twitter ban case in Nigeria cost the country's economy around USD6,919,069 using the Cost of Shutdown Tool (COST) which estimates the economic impact of an internet disruption, mobile data outage or app restriction using indicators from the World Bank, ITU, Eurostat and U.S. Census (NetBlocks, 2023). In the SERAP case against the Nigerian government, petitioners argued that the 'livelihoods and reputations of persons whose employment and businesses relied on the internet had been impacted, thereby causing extensive financial loss and hardships. Petitioners noted that this violated individuals' right to practise a profession.' This was affirmed by survey respondents who indicated that they could not conduct business during the Twitter shutdown.

*Relevance of the 3-part test*

Endong argues that the national security excuse by the governments of Nigeria and Cameroon should not be downplayed as the harm caused on social media platforms can be catastrophic (Endong, 2022). The argument posed is to the effect that some rationale exists where state power should prevail in curbing conflict. However, Endong accepts that internet shutdowns largely occur where there is no law authorizing internet shutdowns as in the Nigeria case. We argue that even if there is a law, it must still meet the test applied in the *Amnesty v Togo* case where three key elements should be present before limiting freedom of expression: a law, pursuing a legitimate aim and the means used to limit the right necessary and proportionate. With regard to limiting freedom of expression as previously highlighted, Article 19(3) prescribes that there should be a law and means used to effect the limitation necessary and proportionate. This approach, commonly known as 3-part test, is the yardstick ensuring human rights as the primary focus and not the exception. A limitation of human rights based on national security has to conform to this yardstick, which is also articulated in the Siracusa principles (United Nations, 1985). Principle 31 stipulates that 'national security cannot be used as a pretext for imposing vague or arbitrary limitations and may only be invoked when there exist adequate safeguards and effective remedies against abuse'. The safeguards provided by the ICCPR are aimed at ensuring that power is not abused by states to unjustifiably limit human rights.

*Recommendations*

It is critical that the government of Nigeria adopts a rights-based approach in addressing misinformation and fake news without resorting to blatant violations of human rights for segments or all of the Nigerian population or in the case of the Twitter ban, partial shutdowns targeting Twitter. There is a need to follow due process where judicial oversight is sought in any action to shut down the internet, as the judiciary is better placed to apply the legality, necessity and proportionality of a proposed action to shut down the internet in the preservation of human rights. The government should empower citizens to use social media platforms responsibly through awareness raising and exemplary conduct online within the confines of social media community standards. Beyond the call for governments to comply with human rights obligations, private companies must pursue economic interests from a rights-based approach, practising transparency as a due diligence process. It is critical for companies like Twitter to disclose how they respond to government requests adhering to their responsibilities under the United Nations Guidelines on Business and Human Rights (United Nations, 2011). The same practice should be implemented by MNOs, demonstrating a rights-based approach recommended in this chapter towards internet freedom.

## Conclusion

This chapter set out to address the questions: 'What are the forms of internet shutdowns in Nigeria? What power interests are served by them? What are their impacts on human rights? How have citizens pushed back to hold the government to account, end their occurrence and regain their rights?' Jigsaw's internet shutdown definition and a rights-based framework of civil, political and economic rights were used. Leveraging concepts of power, it is concluded that Twitter enables citizens to exercise the power to act individually and collectively while, on the other hand, pushing back against repressive power through litigation. Strategic litigation driven by civil society organizations and citizens led to a court decision that the shutdown was not lawful, necessary or proportionate, forcing the government to lift the ban.

Internet access in any form is essential to the realization of human rights such as freedom of expression, access to information, the right to development, freedom of assembly and association, labour rights and the right to education. The internet is a powerful tool for the citizenry to push back against repression, engage in diverse information sharing and enjoy being digital citizens. Threats to access subtract from the constitutional rights entrenched in the Nigerian Constitution and obligations Nigeria has under the African Charter, the ICCPR and ICESCR. It is imperative that state power be harnessed by international human rights standards to ensure a thriving environment which is rights-based.

## Bibliography

Access Now (n.d.), 'Internet Shutdowns and Elections Handbook', https://www.accessnow.org/guide/internet-shutdowns-and-elections-handbook/

Access Now (2020), '#ShutdownStories: How Chad's Fixation on Social Media Blackouts Hurts Citizens', https://www.accessnow.org/shutdownstories-how-chad-fixation-on-social-media-blackouts-hurts-citizens/

African Commission on Human and Peoples' Rights (2019), 'Declaration of Principles on Freedom of Expression and Access to Information', https://achpr.au.int/en/node/902

Al Jazeera (2021), 'Twitter Removes Nigerian President's "Abusive" Civil War Post', 2 June, https://www.aljazeera.com/news/2021/6/2/twitter-removes-nigerian-presidents-abusive-civil-war-post

Anthonio, F. and Roberts, T. (2023), 'Internet Shutdowns and Digital Citizenship', in T. Roberts and T. Bosch (2023), *Digital Citizenship in Africa: Technologies of Agency and Repression* (1st ed., pp. 85–115). London: Bloomsbury Publishing.

Anyim, W. (2021), 'Twitter Ban in Nigeria: Implications on Economy, Freedom of Speech and Information Sharing', Research Gate, https://www.researchgate.net/

publication/353827676_Twitter_Ban_in_Nigeria_Implications_on_Economy_Freedom_of_Speech_and_Information_Sharing

Balarabe, A., Kirfi, M. and Abdulsaam, Z. (2021), 'An Assessment of the Impact of Structures and Interinstitutional Collaboration on the Delivery of Security Services in the Bandits-bedeviled Zamfara and Sokoto States', *Journal of Relationship Marketing*, 9: 125–40.

BBC (2022), 'Twitter Agrees to Nigeria's Demands to End Seven-Month Ban', 13 January, https://www.bbc.com/news/world-africa-59958417

CNN (2021), 'Phone and Internet Shutdown in Nigerian State Enters Sixth Day as Security Forces Target Kidnappers', 9 September, https://edition.cnn.com/2021/09/09/africa/phone-services-suspended-zamfara-intl/index.html

Consumer Connect (2022, 14 January), 'Twitter Pledges Commitment to Nigeria as Consumers React to Restoration of Big Tech's Operations', https://consumerconnectng.com/19274

Cornwall, A. and Nyamu-Musembi, C. (2004), 'Putting the "Rights-Based Approach" to Development into Perspective', *Third World Quarterly*, 25 (8): 1415–37.

Datareportal (2022), 'DIGITAL 2022: NIGERIA', https://datareportal.com/reports/digital-2022-nigeria#:~:text=There%20were%20109.2%20million%20internet,percent)

ECOWAS Community Court of Justice (2022), '*Amnesty International Togo et al. vs the Republic of Togo*', https://www.courtecowas.org/wp-content/uploads/2022/08/JUD-ECW-CCJ-JUD-09-20-Amnesty-Int.-TOGO-7-ORS-vs.-REP.-OF-TOGO-25_06_20-vA.pdf

Ekuma, C. (2012), 'Press Freedom in Nigeria: Rundown from 1960–2012', *Rainbow Magazine*, https://www.academia.edu/40960056/PRESS_FREEDOM_IN_NIGERIA_RUNDOWN_FROM_1960_2012

Endong, F. P. C. (2022), 'Internet Blackouts in Africa', *UJ Press Journal*, https://journals.uj.ac.za/index.php/dps/article/view/1149

Federal Republic of Nigeria (1999), '*Constitution of the Federal Republic of Nigeria*', https://dullahomarinstitute.org.za/acjr/resource-centre/Nigeria%20Constitution.pdf

Foucault, M. (1995), *Discipline and Punish: The Birth of the Prison*, New York: Vintage Books.

France24 (2021), 'Nigeria Orders Media to Delete Twitter after Banning Site Nationwide', 7 June, https://www.france24.com/en/africa/20210607-after-ban-nigeria-orders-broadcasters-to-delete-accounts-from-unpatriotic-twitter

Freedom House (2022), 'Nigeria,' https://freedomhouse.org/country/nigeria/freedom-world/2022

Gibson, J. (1977), 'The Theory of Affordances', in R. Shaw and J. Bransford (eds), *Perceiving, Acting, and Knowing*, London: Oxford University Press.

Global Freedom of Expression (2022), 'ECOWAS Community Court of Justice *SERAP v. Federal Republic of Nigeria*', *14 July*, https://globalfreedomofexpression.columbia.edu/cases/serap-v-federal-republic-of-nigeria/

Hutchby, I. (2001), 'Technologies, Texts and Affordances', *Sociology*, 35 (2): 441–56.

ICANN (2023), '2023 Africa Domain Name Industry Study', https://itp.cdn.icann.org/en/files/stakeholder-engagement/2023-africa-domain-name-industry-study-15-12-2023-en.pdf

ICCPR (1976), International Covenant on Civil and Political Rights, New York: United Nations, https://www.ohchr.org/en/instruments-mechanisms/instruments/international-covenant-civil-and-political-rights

Ismail, A. (2011), 'The Nigerian Press: The Journey So Far', *Wilolud Journals*. https://www.academia.edu/879578/THE_NIGERIAN_PRESS_THE_JOURNEY_SO_FAR?auto=download&email_work_card=download-paper

Jigsaw (2021), 'The Internet Shutdowns Issue', *The Current*, Silicon Valley, Google Jigsaw, https://static.googleusercontent.com/media/jigsaw.google.com/en//static/images/current/04-internet-shutdowns/the-current-by-jigsaw-issue-004-internet-shutdowns.pdf

Kelley, M. (1994), *Critique and Power*, Cambridge, MA: MIT Press, https://www.scribd.com/document/342866528/Studies-in-Contemporary-German-Social-Thought-Michael-Kelly-Editor-Critique-and-Power-Recasting-the-Foucault-Habermas-Debate-The-MIT-Press-199

Lukes, S. (2005), *Power: A Radical View*, London: Macmillan, https://voidnetwork.gr/wp-content/uploads/2016/09/Power-A-Radical-View-Steven-Lukes.pdf

Media Rights Agenda (2022), 'MRA, Others Win Suit over Twitter Ban as ECOWAS Court Rules Nigerian Government's Action Unlawful', https://mediarightsagenda.org/media-rights-agenda-others-win-suit-over-twitter-ban-as-ecowas-court-rules-nigerian-governments-action-unlawful/

Mossberger, K., Tolbert, C. J. and McNeal, R. S. (2008), *Digital Citizenship: The Internet, Society, and Participation*, Cambridge, MA: MIT Press, https://direct.mit.edu/books/monograph/3275/Digital-CitizenshipThe-Internet-Society-and

NetBlocks (2023), 'Cost of Shutdown Tool', https://netblocks.org/cost/

News24 (2021), 'Nigeria Cuts Cellphone Network in Tense Northern State', https://www.news24.com/fin24/international/nigeria-cuts-cellphone-network-in-tense-northern-state-20210905

OAU (1986), 'African Charter on Human and Peoples' Rights', https://au.int/en/treaties/african-charter-human-and-peoples-rights

Ojebode, A., Ojebuyi, B., Oladapo, O. and Oosterom, M. (2023), 'Ethno-Religious Citizenship in Nigeria: Ethno-Religious Fault Lines and the Truncation of Collective Resilience of Digital Citizens: The Cases of #EndSARS and #PantamiMustGo in Nigeria', https://www.researchgate.net/publication/370959562_Ethno-religious_citizenship_in_Nigeria_Ethno-religious_fault_lines_and_the_truncation_of_collective_resilience_of_digital_citizens_The_cases_of_EndSARS_and_PantamiMustGo_in_Nigeria

Oladapo, O. and Ojebode, A. (2021), 'Nigeria Digital Rights Landscape Report', Institute of Development Studies, https://opendocs.ids.ac.uk/articles/online_resource/Digital_Rights_in_Closing_Civic_Space_Lessons_from_Ten_African_Countries/26430283?file=48079507

Onuoha, P. (2021), 'MAC 113: History of Nigerian Mass Media', https://nou.edu.ng/coursewarecontent/MAC%20113.pdf

Paradigm Initiative (2022), 'Press Release: Federal Government Reverses Twitter Ban in Nigeria after 222 Days', https://paradigmhq.org/press-release-federal-government-reverses-twitter-ban-in-nigeria-after-222-days/

Parkinson, J. (2020), 'Nigeria Protests: What's Happening and Why Are People Demonstrating Against SARS?' *The Wall Street Journal website*, https://www.wsj.com/articles/nigeria-protests-whats-happening-and-why-are-people-demonstrating-11603277989

Popoola, A. (2022), 'Twitter, Civil Activisms and EndSARS Protest in Nigeria as a Developing Democracy', https://www.tandfonline.com/doi/full/10.1080/23311886.2022.2095744

Premium Times Nigeria (2021), 'Why We Shut Down Telecommunications Networks in Zamfara – Governor', 6 September, https://www.premiumtimesng.com/regional/nwest/483366-why-we-shut-down-telecommunications-networks-in-zamfara-governor.html

Roberts, T. and Bosch, T. (2023), '*Digital Citizenship in Africa: Technologies of Agency and Repression*' (1st edn), London: Bloomsbury Publishing, https://www.bloomsbury.com/uk/digital-citizenship-in-africa-9781350324459/
SERAP (2022), 'SERAP Wants Court to Stop Buhari, Others from Shutting Down Telecoms', https://serap-nigeria.org/2021/12/05/serap-wants-court-to-stop-buhari-others-from-shutting-down-telecoms/
South African History Online (2019), 'Prime Minister Sir Abubakar Tafawa Balewa Is Killed in Nigeria's First Military Coup', 15 January, https://www.sahistory.org.za/dated-event/prime-minister-sir-abubakar-tafawa-balewa-killed-nigerias-first-military-coup
Statista (2021), 'Estimated Economic Impact of Twitter Ban in Nigeria Imposed on June 5, 2021, by number of days', https://www.statista.com/statistics/1242378/economic-loss-of-twitter-suspension-in-nigeria/
Statista (2024), 'Key Indicators of Nigeria's Economy – Statistics & Facts', https://www.statista.com/topics/6440/key-indicators-of-nigeria-s-economy/#:~:text=In%20 2022%2C%20Nigeria's%20GDP%20was,in%20terms%20of%20total%20GDP
Thumfart, J. (2024), 'Digital Rights and the State of Exception. Internet Shutdowns from the Perspective of Just Securitization Theory', *Journal of Global Security Studies*, 9 (1), https://doi.org/10.1093/jogss/ogad024
United Nations (1948), 'Universal Declaration of Human Rights', https://www.un.org/en/about-us/universal-declaration-of-human-rights
United Nations (1985), 'The Siracusa Principles on the Limitation and Derogation Provisions in the International Covenant on Civil and Political Rights', https://www.icj.org/wp-content/uploads/1984/07/Siracusa-principles-ICCPR-legal-submission-1985-eng.pdf
United Nations (1966a), 'International Covenant on Civil and Political Rights', https://www.ohchr.org/en/instruments-mechanisms/instruments/international-covenant-civil-and-political-rights
United Nations (1966b), 'International Covenant on Economic, Social and Cultural Rights International Covenant on Civil and Political Rights', https://www.ohchr.org/en/instruments-mechanisms/instruments/international-covenant-economic-social-and-cultural-rights
United Nations (2011), 'Guiding Principles on Business and Human Rights', https://www.ohchr.org/sites/default/files/documents/publications/guidingprinciplesbusinesshr_en.pdf
United Nations Sustainable Development Group (UNSDG) (n.d.), The 17 Goals, New York: United Nations, https://sdgs.un.org/goals
Usman, C. and Oghuvbu, E. (2021), 'The Impact of the Media on The #Endsars Protests in Nigeria', *International Journal of New Economics and Social Sciences*, 14 (2), https://ijoness.com/article/157330/en
VeneKlasen, L. and Miller, V. (2002), *A New Weave of Power, People and Politics*, Oklahoma: World Neighbours, https://justassociates.org/all-resources/a-new-weave-of-power-people-politics-the-action-guide-for-advocacy-and-citizen-participation/
VoA News (2022), 'Nigerian Authorities Lift Seven-Month Twitter Ban', 13 January, https://www.voanews.com/a/nigerian-authorities-lift-seven-month-twitter-ban/6395351.html
Worldometer (2024), 'Nigeria', https://srv1.worldometers.info/demographics/nigeria-demographics/

# Chapter 8

## Internet shutdowns in Chad

Qemal Affagnon

### *Introduction*

Shutting down the internet has become an increasingly popular strategy of governments looking to control the flow of information within their territory. In Africa and around the world, internet shutdowns are intentional disruptions of internet access within a specific location and for a specific duration. They are usually ordered by governmental officials, but involve a complex assemblage of actors, infrastructure, political drivers and regulatory discourses with national and transnational dimensions. If governments were using longer internet shutdowns in the past, they started to do it for short periods or within particular geographic areas as well. In the last decade, this strategy has been used in countries such as Syria (13 times since 2016), Turkey (9 times since 2016), Yemen (27 times since 2016), Iran (11 times since 2016), Iraq (24 times since 2016), Venezuela (14 times since 2016), Pakistan (40 times since 2016) but also in Algeria (11 times since 2016), Ethiopia (21 times since 2016), Sudan (12 times since 2016) and Chad in 2022 (Akhremenko et al., 2022).

In this chapter, we show how mapmaking and technology tools were used by authoritarian rulers to prevent and repress political action in Chad. In the central African landlocked country, these practices can increase the rulers chances of political survival. At the same time, they can deny citizens' rights to access information. Also, when the quality of information consumed by citizens is compromised, their ability to make informed choices is diminished and the essence of citizenship is threatened. From the same perspective, this not only creates a general risk-driven environment, encompassing a wide array of information vulnerabilities, in fact, it also exposes people to pervasive digital risks, such as bio surveillance, misinformation and e-democracy algorithmic threats. Given the political motives behind internet shutdowns and their opaqueness, one of the skills needed to fight against shutdowns is the ability to tackle real privacy challenges in a country like Chad. Within a specific location, these new types of shutdowns are used by governments as a matter of policy with the objective of exerting control over the free flow of information. Thus, it is also important to be aware of such practices to collect the technical evidence in critical periods such as elections or times of mass protest.

**Table 8.1** Internet Shutdowns Overview in Chad

| Type of shutdown | Duration | Date |
|---|---|---|
| Chad remained without internet and social network services during a long period. The situation returned to normal for a while after this long interruption in December the same year, although restrictions and blackouts were still observed after. | 235 days | 2016 |
| In March, authorities have restricted internet access, citing security reasons and the context of terrorist threats. | 30 days | 2018 |
| Chad cut access to social media platforms, including WhatsApp, Twitter, Facebook, Instagram and YouTube. | 472 days | Between 2018 and 2019 |
| The Chadian government blocked access to WhatsApp, and the authorities also cut off or slowed down internet access in certain parts of the country. | 192 days | Between 2020 and 2022 |
| Internet access, telephone calls and text messages sent from one telephone to another were disrupted for a fortnight. | 30 days | Between February and March 2021 |
| The internet network was reduced to 60% on 28 February, following a gunshot outside the home of opposition leader Yaya Dillo, which resulted in the death of his mother and son. | | 2021 |
| Internet was not totally cut, but the speed was so slow that even loading a Facebook page was very complicated. Internet blackout noticed in the 7th and 9th districts of the capital, as is part of the 6th. | 12 days | 2022 |
| On Tuesday 15 October, an internet disruption affected 4.18 million Chadian users in a digital blackout until Wednesday 16 October. | 235 hours | 2024 |

## *Background*

A landlocked Sahelian country in central Africa, Chad is of immense geostrategic importance, being the boundary between Arabs and sub-Saharan Africa. The country gained its independence from France in 1960 (Nicolaides, 2017) and immediately became ensnared in a morass of ethnic warfare (Hansen, 2011). In Chad, the Déby dynasty has been in power for over three decades. DeVore (2020) notes that Idriss Déby, the former President, has completely dominated the political and economic scene since 1990. On taking power in 1991 Idriss Déby promised to create a democratic society. Under his rule, political parties and a free press could be established. Six years after he came to power Chadians voted for a new constitution during a referendum. Moreover, Déby promised to be the right person who could assist Chad to develop as a democracy. The expectation was that, with the help of oil revenues, Chad could improve its undeveloped education and health system and build infrastructure and supply jobs. Instead, Déby used the oil revenues to secure his leadership. Part of the oil revenues went into strengthening the military and security forces. This enabled Déby to become a loyal ally of the French army on the Sahel battlefields against Islamist terrorism. Chad has been, for instance, the strongest supporter of Barkhane, the French military operation fighting jihadist groups in the Sahel. The Chadian army was also critically involved in the 2013 French-led military operation to defend Mali from a takeover by well-organized Islamic armed groups. The same year, Chad was also one of the top troop contributors to the United Nations peacekeeping operation in Mali through a stabilization mission. Despite its operational capacities abroad, May and Massey (2000) argue that the Chadian army was not able to build assurance with the citizens of Chad. The way the army was acting toward the civilian population, with frequent exactions, has limited its capacity to build up trust. Later, Buijtenhuijs (2000) explains the country nevertheless managed to organize the first elections in 1996. However, these elections were marred by allegations of fraud, a pattern that was to repeat itself in all future polls in the country. Furthermore, tensions with the political opposition started to increase rapidly. Ten years later, it is within this context that Chad used internet restriction to curb protests. In 2016, the internet was shut down following a disputed presidential vote. In July 2019, the Chadian government lifted a 16-month blockage on access to social media, which it had imposed in March 2018. Chad's shutdown began after a national gathering of politicians and traditional chiefs who disapproved constitutional changes, allowing Idriss Déby to rule until 2033. All in all, this notion is articulated around four distinct varieties of the concept: episodic, dispositional, systemic and constitutive. Rather than seeing these varieties as conflicting, he attempts to combine them in one pluralistic master concept, where each variety allows us to see a different facet of power. While doing so, Sattarov ends up with a book that at times seems to explain just about everything as some sort of power. Sattarov's approach shows also that power must be understood through other disciplines such as political theory, psychology and philosophy.

In his recent book, *Power and Technology*, Sattarov (2019) sets out to detail various notions of power while simultaneously showing how power and technology are related: 'phenomena of technology and power are becoming ever more inseparable.'

## *Country case description*

The State of Internet report by CIPESA (2019) reveals that Chad has experienced internet and social media disruptions since 2014. In November 2014, for instance, the government limited SMS, internet and money transfer services. This decision followed street demonstrations by students and teachers denouncing the high cost of living, fuel shortages and falling wages. Some of the communications disruptions were applied to specific civil society and leaders of democratic opposition parties, which technically revealed targeted filtering, combined with real-time surveillance of their communications. During these events, opposition members publicly denounced some attacks on their email accounts, Facebook accounts and telephone communications. Later in March 2015, the government briefly suspended SMS services for 24 hours. This situation happened during protests organized by some groups against the order for motorcyclists to wear helmets. For the presidential election of April 2016 in which Idriss Déby Itno was seeking a fifth consecutive term, mobile and fixed-line internet was disconnected on the morning of 10 April. This time, access to social networks and use of SMS messaging were also impossible. This situation contributed to limiting the public's access to information at a crucial moment in the nation's life. The government did not acknowledge ordering the disruption nor did telecom operators announce that they had blocked services. However, these measures of isolation and censorship prevented opponents from communicating with each other about the organization conditions of the ballot.

Since then, network disruptions have been systematically applied, mostly during public protests and around election times.

For several years now, Chad authorities have been voluntarily restricting the internet when critical voices are raised in the country. Alarmingly, in 2020, the internet was disrupted for 192 days. Between 2016 and 2021 for example, the observed restrictions amounted to two and a half years of internet outages or disruption. In total, we obtain since 2016 a cumulative figure of 911 days of intentional internet disruption. These figures include total disruptions to internet access and restrictions on certain social networks in Chad. In 2020 for instance, during the health crisis caused by the Covid-19 pandemic, WhatsApp access was restricted. Internet Sans Frontières sources in Chad and technical measurements carried out by the organization Netbloks confirmed that the WhatsApp messaging application had been blocked.

In 2024, the website https://tchadinfos.com/, the country's main online news platform, was inaccessible after it was suspended on Friday 26 July. This suspension followed a complaint from one of the former advisers to the Head of State, demanding the withdrawal of all articles about him, which Tchadinfos refused. This type of practice in Chad happened under colonialism, immediately after liberation, under one-party state, under military governments and even in more recent years. Chad is facing a succession of obstacles to press freedom which are undermining the public's right to news and information. Simultaneously, with press freedom restricted, the state of media freedoms is very dire and continues to be deteriorating in Chad. More than a dozen newspapers were suspended in 2020 under the new press law. In this law, defamation is punishable by up to three months in prison and, in this new text, it is mentioned that running a newsroom now requires a minimum level of qualification. It seems that this is done in an apparent desire to professionalize the media sector, but in reality, it could result in the elimination of many independent publications in Chad. During the elections organized in May this year, the High Authority for Media and Broadcasting banned all interactive broadcasts a few days before the start of the election campaign. During that period, Chad's media regulator had also improperly suspended two active media outlets, Al-Idath and Le Libérateur, although the former was subsequently allowed to resume publishing. In addition to banning interactive broadcasts, authorities in Chad also suspended another newspaper and prevented another from covering a political rally.

In 2018, another internet disruption occurred for twenty-four hours on January 25, ordered by the government to prohibit an anti-austerity protest. In March 2018, Chad authorities justified the internet restriction for security reasons in the context of terrorist threats. Following protests against changes to the constitution, the Chadian government decided to block access to social media networks including Facebook, Twitter, WhatsApp, Instagram and YouTube for sixteen months. Right after, in 2020, the country experienced 192 days of internet disruptions. In July 2020, access to social media was restricted, following the killing of a young mechanic in N'Djamena market by an army officer. For these new restrictions, authorities claimed measures were set temporarily to limit the spreading of hate messages and division. In February 2021, internet access was restricted again during a raid by security forces on the house of an opposition presidential candidate who had refused to respond to a judicial summons. One year later, as a result of some protests against the ongoing transition, people in the eastern and southern districts of N'Djamena noticed that they had lost access to the internet. This situation was affecting a proportion of internet users in the 6th district as well as in the 7th and 9th districts of the capital.

## *Literature review*

In modern societies, Sattarov (2019) argues, political democracy is overshadowed by the enormous power wielded by the masters of technical systems. Sattarov saw a situation coming where technology would be one of the major sources of public power in modern societies.

In the last decade, the African region has made substantial strides toward digital transformation, with hundreds of millions of people gaining access to the internet and productively utilizing a wide variety of digital services, such as mobile payments. In addition to being a means of payment, the mobile phone is widely used in sub-Saharan Africa to communicate. Sub-saharan Africa has been at the forefront of the mobile phone sector and continues to count for the majority of its growth. For example, the mobile phone sector plays an important role in accessing political information. Across urban or rural areas, mobile phones connect individuals to individuals, information, markets and services such as joining social networks.

African cities and their populations are integrating these innovations as best they can. These innovations play an important role in structuring power relations within societies. Across the continent, digital technologies facilitate access to government services. Over the years, expression through the internet is gaining contemporary relevance and is one of the major means of information diffusion throughout the African continent. The spread of new technologies and mobile connectivity improvement is enabling the proliferation of digital solutions that appear to make vital basic services more efficient, accessible and affordable. On one hand, this situation can contribute to improving the well-being of citizens.

Moreover, digitalization is changing the relationship between state and society significantly, gradually increasing the frequency and quality of interaction between citizens and government. Another major point is that, in the last two decades, political processes are also being transformed and modernized in parallel with the technological development. On the other hand, social control and digital authoritarianism have come to be part of the digital culture. For example, the Cambridge Analytica affair demonstrated how social media companies were able to build digital profiles of individuals through systematic and secret surveillance of online behaviour to covertly manipulate voters beliefs and behaviours. Corporate lobbyists and political parties are now able to buy such digital operations as a commercial service. There is also evidence that foreign and domestic online influence operations involving hired troll farms, bot armies and cyborg operations target key development policy issues. The use of technology for digital authoritarianism can also be observed during internet shutdowns in Africa through sophisticated techniques. With the help of these techniques, governments can shut down a single platform, as in the case of Nigeria's Twitter ban, or shut down specific districts, as in the case of Chad in 2022.

In the digital age, social control has come to be a more integral part of our lives.

Technology has become an important tool for controlling and manipulating people, especially those who are not supposed to have access to information or who stand out from the rest. In some ways, technology has made social control more efficient and easier, while in other ways it has created new challenges and opportunities for social control.

Across the continent, digital technologies have also given autocratic governments unprecedented possibilities to remain in power. In fact, while surveillance and propaganda have always been part of an autocrat's playbook, several technologies allow new types of political control that can be more pervasive, efficient and subtle. Armed with this capacity, authoritarian regimes have in their hands new tools to control their citizens, to restrict human rights and freedoms as well any harmful information flow.

The philosophical implications of this modern form of control have been explored by Sattarov (2019). Through the lines of his book, *Power and Technology*, Sattarov explores the technological construction of power. In this respect, the book aims to offer an empirically informed philosophical framework for understanding the technological construction of power, which allows for a differentiated vocabulary for describing various senses of technological power. The author also tries to show how the notions of power, rights and technology are interconnected.

By reading Sattarov, one interesting perspective of power appears: episodic power. When viewed from the episodic perspective, the episodic power is the ability, namely the capacity, to bring about significant outcomes from a situation. The episodic view of power highlights a specific aspect of power, namely the direct exercise thereof. This type of power can be used not only to control, but also to shape the behaviour of citizens via surveillance, repression, manipulation, censorship and the provision of services, in order to retain and expand political control.

Sattarov believes that episodic power can have an effect over people, by affecting their moods, decisions and actions. The episodic view of power entails that power occurs when one party exercises power over another, for example by means of force, coercion, manipulation or authority.

This may happen in a context where technology is used, like in Africa, to create an online presence during social movements or providing a forum for discussion. While digital divides persist within and between countries, civic engagement and debate, like political life, is increasingly happening online, thanks to mobile technologies.

Surfing on the mobile phone boom, the internet and social media platforms has become a critical part of civic space. Sometimes these platforms are even more open and accessible than actual physical civic space in countries where the opportunities to protest, organize and speak freely are limited.

Therefore, this type of power, coupled with the rise of Big Data, can be a dangerous instrument of subjection. In the same vein, it is important to underline other risks that can be caused by the lack of regulation of these new tools, as well as adequate and aware knowledge of their use. Examples of these implications can relate, for example, to how personality profiles can be used to tailor information in order to get individuals to vote a particular way or adopt a particular service.

As explained by Sattarov (2019), the episodic notion of power refers to a person being subject to the power of another. Also, episodic power raises the issue of inequality, as it views power as an asymmetrical relation between two or more agents, in which one agent with privilege exercises power over another agent with less power. Here, the underlying element of this form of relations between the person being subject to the power of another is the ability to move that person in an intended direction. This ability relies on the capacity of one of the actors to use structural resources that can determine the outcome for the stronger protagonist. These structural resources may also lead to a point where the most powerful protagonist can make threats and exert pressure on the weakest one. To proceed like that, deliberately vague notions of national security and social stability are typically invoked by some authorities, as in Chad. Under these circumstances, a variety of methods are used to control the flow of digital information. In a country like Chad, the administration was able to impose restrictions on electronic communication, the shutting down of internet connectivity, bans on entire social networks and applications, but also the suspension of telephone services, as well as more targeted censorship. In addition, authorities may also use other forms of restriction to the free flow of information online involving more targeted access restrictions, such as Internet Protocol (IP) address blocking, Domain Name System (DNS) filtering, and redirection or Uniform Resource Locator (URL) filtering. Sometimes such practices might also involve tapping and surveillance, chat room monitoring, discriminatory or prohibitive pricing policies, hardware and software manipulation, hacking into opposition websites and spreading viruses. In addition, we can also add the possibility of denial-of-service attacks that overload servers or network connections. Content filtering often relies on keyword matching algorithms that evolve as the internet's lingo changes, and filtering may occur at the levels of the internet service provider (ISP), the domain name, a particular IP address, or a specific URL. Most forms of filtering are difficult to detect technically: the user may not even know that censorship is at work. Most ISPs lack the ability to block transmission to an individual IP address or URL, so governments undertake this task in volume for this purpose. Because digital communication is crucial to civic, economic and educational participation, access to health services, and the flow of health-related data, internet shutdowns can have a significant negative impact on the lives and rights of citizens in Chad.

By proceeding like that, internet shutdowns can be seen as a new form of domestic power preservation. By using such tactics, the advantage for authoritarian regimes can be to curtail dissent within their borders. Sometimes, the sought effect can also be to monitor or shape online communications. In Africa, autocratic regimes use various methods to maintain their hold on power and control the narrative. Several tactics for censorship include internet filtering and blocking, content removal, surveillance and monitoring, online misinformation and propaganda. During critical political times, authoritarian regimes are compelling ISPs to deliberately reduce or restrict their services, a practice known as throttling. This action encroaches upon the freedom of expression, obstructs journalists from disseminating crucial updates to the public and hampers the unrestricted dissemination of information. The use of these tools and strategies by authoritarian regimes provides valuable insights into the ways in which power can be wielded in the digital age.

In fact, these elements can make it easy for governments to deploy their strength in order to control people's behaviour. They can use the take it, or even the take it or suffer strategy; the episodic perspective provides authoritarian regimes an opportunity to employ new technologies to strengthen their rule and counter opposition or civic challenges. Furthermore, the episodic perspective of power sheds light on emerging areas of contestation and highlights the complexities, urgency and dangers involved in the advance of digital technologies and their effects on politics. These trends cause growing concerns about how technology, politics and state authority will evolve.

The section that follows will explore the link between the notions of power and technology. We will use these concepts to explain how online censorship can reinforce hegemonic powers, cultivate a climate of fear, and prevent or minimize dissent in Chad.

## *Analysis*

Chad has a long-running history of information controls because of political instability. In Chad, the Government offers a wide range of reasons for closing the digital sphere. Authorities refer mostly to the goal of preserving the public good. Ayalew (2019) points out that autocrats generally frame these shutdowns as re-establishment of national security. In general, internet shutdowns constitute an exceptional measure and are associated by some governmental institutions with a securitization framework justified by the aversion of security threats. This also applies to Chad, where the government is still regularly attempting to stabilize its power through the imposition of internet shutdowns. Internet shutdowns can be understood in such a context as collective punishment. In a country like Chad, mobile internet shutdowns can have a severe effect because mobile internet use is often without an alternative.

In Chad, national security is the most cited reason where officials cited the importance of having a state free from danger. Besides this argument, officials also refer to the prevention of the spread of hate speech or fake news as reasons to intervene with internet shutdowns. The majority of the internet shutdowns were enacted as a pre-emptive measure on grounds of general security threats around mass events such as marches, strikes, protests or high-level political events. The defence of the government is most of the time based on security arguments. To explain their decision to shutdown the internet they tried to explain for instance that continuing protests can lead to the loss of human lives, injuries or the massive destruction of public and private properties. Thus, as a means of countering the effect of the protests, they had to contend with some form of control of the internet; other justifications used for implementing internet shutdowns include the importance of guaranteeing the physical integrity of citizens threatened by social media-fuelled riots.

Following the re-election of President Déby in 2016, over ten websites were blocked and the whole country experienced an internet shutdown for several weeks. This situation was followed by an eight-month disruption to social networks. At the time, authorities acknowledged that SMS services were restricted as a security measure but denied any interference with internet services, instead citing technical challenges. In Chad, social media is seen as a tool that encourages political indiscipline and engenders the production and circulation of alternative political narratives. Previous research has shown that they occur during protest movements (Howard, Agarwal and Hussain, 2011), to avoid mobilization (Wagner, 2018). In the African context, threats to the authorities can take the form of large-scale instability, but they may also take the form of strikes, riots and protest demonstrations, as seen in Chad.

During the 2016 presidential election, the Chadian regime took, for instance, some online isolation measures. These measures were taken to prevent opposition candidates from discussing between them the way the ballots were conducted. Furthermore, the blackouts had severe consequences for opposition groups' capabilities to use digital communication and information channels effectively.

Besides the effect on the political opposition, such isolation measures prevented ordinary internet users from accessing online news portals. By doing so, authorities in Chad were also able to use mapping services, like Google Earth and Google Maps, which can be useful to repress domestic populations. As explained by Wintrobe (1998), Gandhi and Przeworski (2006), Desai, Olofsgård and Yousef (2009), Besley and Persson (2010) and Boucekkine, Prieur and Puzon (2016), some politicians invest now in public goods and in means of coercion in order to contain the risk of popular revolutions. The typical assumption is that dissatisfied citizens have the capacity to stage revolutions successfully. Preventive repression, or repressive tactics that target the mobilizational capabilities are therefore more likely to lead to demobilization.

For this reason, political repression is used to quell the protesters that are contesting power and to prevent citizens from engaging in anti-government activities. In general, states are inclined to respond with more aggressive repression when protests increase in size and violence, protest activity is frequent and employs varied tactics, or when organizational capacity of dissident groups is high (Carey, 2006). This is easily understandable because the aim of political repression is to reduce dissent, especially in autocratic countries. For instance, the history of Chad shows that governments have the power to deter protests. The use of military strength also plays an important role in the repression – especially important here since autocratic governments like in Chad rely mostly on their military forces to maintain the status quo. Moreover, governments' repressive capabilities tend to be more intense and effective in oil-rich autocratic regimes because they can invest more heavily in remaining in power to continue to reap their lucrative oil income (Girod, Stewart and Walters, 2016). In addition, such countries receive more international support when they use repression because foreign countries that depend on the oil extracted from the repressive regime generally support the regimes to keep the oil flowing (Girod, Stewart and Walters, 2016).

Threats to the regime can take the form of large-scale domestic instability, such as civil war, as Poe and Tate (1994) suggest, but they may also take the form of strikes, guerilla warfare, riots and protest demonstrations, as pointed out by Davenport (1999: 102). Elite perceptions of the threat faced from a dissident challenge are – in large part a function of the fragility of the ruling government (Davenport, 1995). Where the threat is viewed as destabilizing, repression is more likely. Where the threat is not viewed in this way, repression is unlikely.

In Chad, repression is associated with direct targeting of certain groups or individuals (based, for example, on the likelihood of them opposing the government). In these terms, digital technologies can help autocrats to survive politically and to this end they act rationally (Gehlbach, Sonin and Svolik, 2016) not only to react to online actions, but also to carry out online tracking and to prevent any possible actions against their rule in the very preliminary phases of organizing dissent.

In 2022, if the internet was not completely cut off everywhere, the 7th and 9th districts of the capital were completely cut off, and part of the 6th. To proceed likewise, the regime was able to use some technology and mapping tools. These tools were provided by a branch of a French public institute: the National Institute for Geographic and Forestry Information. With the use of these technological and mapping tools, the authorities were able to slow down internet access in the political opposition's strongholds in the capital N'Djamena. The shutdown also severely limited Chadians' ability to organize and mobilize protests against this incident quickly and effectively, violating their right to peaceful assembly and following the previous pattern by the government of imposing internet shutdowns to evade accountability and suppress political criticism. In such circumstances, Chad police forces often use tear gas to disperse the gatherings in the streets.

In October 2022, protests broke out across Chad after new President Mahamat Déby declared his intentions to extend his rule by another two years instead of stepping down like he intended to when he took power. Hundreds of people answered the call of several opposition parties and civil society organizations. The protests were some of the most violent in the country's history, with hundreds of protesters being killed and thousands detained, injured or arrested.

Chadian authorities have been active in deploying internet shutdowns to quell mass protests and more recently cutting off conflict areas from the internet network. This situation has accumulated to almost two and half years of internet cuts or disruptions since 2016. If shutdowns are often justified as a tool to address security threats and protect the integrity of the electoral process, including impeding the spread of disinformation, there can also be noted a determination to control the political narrative on the Government side. In Chad and many other African countries, the internet continues to be seen by political leaders as a threat.

In a context where the stranglehold on the production and dissemination of information has always been an invaluable political tool, the internet disrupts older forms of government. However, in a number of African countries like Chad, the desire to control the internet is deeply rooted in authorities' determination to control the political narrative. While this perception affects freedom of expression, in particular it also interferes with multiple other rights, such as the right to association and peaceful assembly, public participation, privacy and non-discrimination.

Over time, the number of incidents involving state interference with internet infrastructure has increased. Some of these measures are taken at the behest of, or under legal compulsion from, the state; these incidents deployed by telcos and ISPs seriously threaten individuals' rights to freedom of expression. In some circumstances such demands are made applying pressure to, or by requesting the cooperation of, telcos and ISPs. This tactic allows not only the abuse of human rights under the cover of darkness but also the evasion of accountability from the authorities' side.

However, telcos and ISPs should not act on state orders that manifestly interfere with human rights unless such orders are issued by an independent judicial authority, and should exhaust all available remedies to challenge them. Telcos and ISPs should also ensure that their operations are consistent with internationally recognized human rights standards.

If the semi-desert nation interferes regularly with digital networks, Chad authorities use surveillance technologies to facilitate governance through social control. Chad authorities have bought surveillance technologies from the French National Geographic Institute. This specialized institution in aerial and ground surveys and maps is actually one of the foremost centres of mapmaking and geographic researching the world. However, these surveillance technologies could erode the fragile political culture of Chad. This can be explained because they can create major risks such as coercion and loss of freedom. Because these surveillance technologies are used against the beliefs, values and norms that citizens are expecting from their government, concerns regarding deep government interest toward greater centralized control must be taken into consideration. Furthermore, while the extremely invasive data compiled through these technologies can help the authorities to consolidate their power without transparency, there is also the fear of diminished privacy rights for future generations of Chadians.

In 2020, the country experienced a total of 192 days of internet disruptions. In the same way, following protests against constitutional changes, the Chadian government blocked access to social networks including Facebook, Twitter, WhatsApp, Instagram and YouTube for sixteen months. This was carried out from March 2018 to July 2019. While lifting the blockage, President Déby confirmed that his government had ordered the restriction of access to social networks to preserve national security. Without citing any law, he added: For a country like Chad which has had dark hours, it is not acceptable for the internet to be diverted for malicious purposes by some individuals with fatal intentions for peace and national unity.

If Chad was relying upon full internet blackouts in response to protests or political instability in the past, the authorities started to adopt more finely honed internet controls to block communication. As the data economy grows in power, these technological and mapping tools are making privacy increasingly difficult to preserve. In the data economy, the trading of personal data as a business model is being increasingly lucrative. Once translated into data, social activities of Chadians are the raw material of a surveillance economy. These data are then used as fodder for data vultures who collect it all, analyse it all, and sell it to the highest bidder.

Like in many places in Africa, people spend more time connected to their smartphones in Chad. Through their online activity, mobile phone users create new data all the time and there is a risk that citizens of Chad move through spaces under constant digital surveillance. In practice, in order to collect people's information, they must be observed. Through this observation, their pertinent information is discerned and translated into a notation system and organized. Each of these steps involves a surveillant gaze whose roots can be traced to military-industrial colonial expansion that relied on making use of indigenous populations through techniques based on visible measurement. This profit-oriented domination was further justified through European imperial knowledge systems such as medically proven inferiority which rationalized the existence of subject races.

Also, the user of data-driven insights to analyse social problems, typically framed around mitigating risk, performs a doubling of discriminatory frameworks through the asymmetrical representation of particular social problems that construct them precisely as problems. These various practices of surveillance-generating data could be processed, organized and, most importantly, mapped onto the expanding territories of empire.

In fact, we live in a datafied society in which a vast network of public and private entities collects and combines personal data. And those entities always want the most updated data. This surveillance society also has the potential to influence how political campaigns will be run in the future, the power that governments and private businesses may wield, the advancement of medicine, the pursuit of public health goals, the risks that will be exposed and whether people's rights will be respected, as based on the development of some form of authoritarianism in countries like Chad.

## Recommendations

In 2021, Déby died under murky circumstances two days after winning a sixth term in office. In April 2021, one of his sons, Mahamat Déby Itno was appointed head of a Transitional Military Council leading the country. General Mahamat Déby seized power and put the state on what was supposed to be an eighteen-month path to civilian government. At first, many found reason to hope that the country would find its way toward more democratic and inclusive governance without too much turmoil. In June 2021, however, the new strongman of Chad broke his promises by considering an extension of the transition and hinting at a possible candidacy in the next elections. Tensions started to boil as the national dialogue between the junta and the historical opposition ended in controversial circumstances. Its conclusions extended the transition (which was supposed to be coming to an end that month) for another two years, and declared junta members, including Déby, eligible to run in the next national elections, scheduled for 2024. Opposition demonstrations against the continuation in power for two more years of the transitional president were repressed in the capital, and in other cities of the country. In 2022, demonstrations against Mahamat Idriss Déby's transition took place in several districts of the Chadian capital. On 19 October, several parties and civil society organizations opposed to the transition had called for a day of peaceful protest throughout Chad on 20 October, the date on which the eighteen months of transition was supposed to end. The organizers of the protest said they rejected the announced 24-month extension of the transition. Thousands of Chadians took to the streets to protest on 20 October, triggering a brutal response. Calling the protest an armed insurrection, the authorities brought it to heel with considerable force.

## Conclusion

This chapter has attempted to sketch the internet shutdown's impact on human rights and the fundamental rights of people in Chad. The study also establishes that internet shutdowns are a policy concern. Even worse, they frequently provide cover for state and non-state actors to violate human rights with severe consequence. Internet shutdowns are a form of violence in themselves, stripping people's freedoms of expression, association, assembly and privacy. At times, striking a balance between the right to free speech and other human rights can be challenging and complex. This is the reason why more effort needs to be done to help promote and strengthen the right to online freedom of expression, right to access and right to freedom of association and assembly in Chad, by looking into issues that complicate this task and dismantling internal mechanisms. The internet is becoming an integral part of the majority of the population as it is closely knotted into the social, economic and cultural fabric of the society. In times of crisis, conflict and turmoil, blocking access to the internet makes it difficult for individuals to stay in touch with their loved ones, encourages the spread of untrue information and rumours and severely restricts the freedoms of assembly, speech and expression. Also, election-related interruptions undermine democracy by preventing voters from actively participating in the process and undermining confidence in the electoral outcome. The proliferation of shutdowns in a country such as Chad is particularly concerning, especially regarding the alarming number of of internet shutdowns. In such context, Chad runs the risk of using its information control policies as a test case and adopting its propensity for shutdowns, unless these disruptions are shown to be ineffectual. All this happens at a time when the government of Chad unveiled some digital initiatives with the goal of increasing internet access for all residents, even those living in remote locations, and providing basic services online. The overall goal is to ensure that digital technologies improve the lives of citizens of Chad, as well as digital technological capabilities in the country. However, this may be difficult to achieve as Chad is top of the internet shutdown list.

Given the potential of internet service, the government must safeguard the right to utilize these resources, rather than interfering with them in the name of security purposes. It was anticipated that the persistent expression of concerns by citizens and organizations in Chad regarding internet shutdown policy would draw lawmakers' attention to the problems with accountability. But Chad remains one of the worst performers in that area. It is high time to take action against the violation of the rights of people because single kill-switches affect the lives of millions of people.

## *Bibliography*


Akhremenko, A., Zheglov, S., Petrov, A. and Turobov, A. (2022), 'The Internet Shutdown during the Protest: a Model of Changing the Network Structure with an Adjustable Level of Continuity of Connections', *15th International Conference Management of Large-Scale System Development (MLSD)*, Moscow, Russian Federation, 2022, pp. 1–5, https://doi.org/10.1109/MLSD55143.2022.9934396

Ayalew, J. E. (2019), 'The Internet Shutdown Muzzle(s) Freedom of Expression in Ethiopia: Competing Narratives', *Information & Communications Technology Law*, 28(2): 208–24.

Banisar, D. (2010), 'Linking ICTs, the Rights to Privacy, Freedom of Expression and Access to Information', *East African Journal on Peace and Human Rights*, 16: 124–54.

Besley, T. and Persson, T. (2010), 'State Capacity, Conflict, and Development', *Econometrica*, 78(1): 1–34.

Boucekkine, R., Prieur, F. and Puzon, K. (2016), 'On the Timing of Political Regime Changes in Resource-Dependent Economies', *European Economic Review*, 88: 188–207.

Buijtenhuijs, R. (2000), 'The 1996–7 Elections in Chad: The Role of the International Observers', in J. Abink and G. Hesseling (eds), *Election Observation and Democratization in Africa* (pp. 211–227), London: Palgrave MacMillan, https://doi.org/10.1007/978-1-349-62328-0_10

Carey, S. (2006), 'The Dynamic Relationship between Protest and Repression', *Political Research Quarterly*, 59 (1): 1–11.

Carey, S. (2010), 'The Use of Repression as a Response to Domestic Dissent', *Political Studies*, 58(1): 167–86.

CIPESA (2019), 'Five Dimensions of Internet Shutdowns in Africa', https://cipesa.org/wp-content/files/briefs/report/Despots-And-Disruptions_March-20.pdf

Clark, J., Faris, R., Morrison-Westphal, R., Noman, H., Tilton, C. and Zittrain, J. (2017), 'The Shifting Landscape of Global Internet Censorship', Berkman Klein Center for Internet & Society Research Publication, Harvard Library, https://dash.harvard.edu/handle/1/33084425

Davenport, C. (1995), 'State Repression and Political Order', *Annual Review of Political Science*, 10, 1–23.

Davenport, C. (1999), *State Repression and the Domestic Democratic Peace*. Cambridge, UK: Cambridge University Press.

Desai, R. M., Olofsgård, A. and Yousef, T. M. (2009), 'The Logic of Authoritarian Bargains', *Economics & Politics*, 21(1): 93–125.

DeVore, M. R. (2020), 'Preserving Power after Empire: The Credibility Trap and France's Intervention in Chad, 1968–72', *War in History*, 27(1): 106–35, https://doi.org/10.1177/0968344518758359

Earl J., Maher T. V. and Pan J. (2022), 'The Digital Repression of Social Movements, Protest, and Activism: A Synthetic Review', *Science Advances*, 8(10), eabl8198. https://doi.org/10.1126/sciadv.abl8198

Freyburg, T. and Garbe, L. (2018), 'Blocking the Bottleneck: Internet Shutdowns and Ownership at Election Times in Sub-Saharan Africa', *International Journal of Communication*, 12: 3896–916.

Gandhi, J. and Przeworski, A. (2006), 'Cooperation, Cooptation, and Rebellion under Dictatorships', *Economics & Politics*: 18, 1–26.

Gehlbach, S., Sonin, K. and Svolik, M. W. (2016), 'Formal Models of Nondemocratic Politics', *Annual Review of Political Science*, 19 (1): 565–84, https://doi.org/10.1146/annurev-polisci042114-014927

Girod, D. M., Stewart, M. A. and Walters, M. R. (2016), 'Mass Protests and the Resource Curse: The Politics of Demobilization in Rentier Autocracies', *Conflict Management and Peace Science*, 35 (5), https://doi.org/10.1177/0738894216651826

Gupta, D. K., Singh, H. and Sprague, T. (1993), 'Government Coercion of 40 Dissidents', *Journal of Conflict Resolution*, 37: 301–39.

Gurr, T. R. and Lichbach, M. I. (1986), 'Forecasting International Conflict: A Competitive Evaluation of Empirical Theories', *Comparative Political Studies*, 19 (1): 3–38.

Hansen, K. F. (2011), 'Chad's Relations with Libya, Sudan, France and the US', NOREF Report, April. Oslo: Norwegian Peacebuilding Centre.

Howard, P. (2011), 'When Do States Disconnect Their Digital Networks? Regime Responses to the Political Uses of Social Media', *The Communication Review*, 14(3), 216–32.

Howard, P. N, Agarwal, S. D. and Hussain, M. M. (2011), '"The Dictators" Digital Dilemma: When Do States Disconnect Their Digital Networks?' *Issues in Technology Innovation*, 11. The Center for Technology Innovation at Brookings.

Joyce, D. (2015), 'Internet Freedom and Human Rights', *The European Journal of International Law*, 26: 498.

May, R. and Massey, S. (2000), 'Two Steps Forward, One Step Back: Chad's Protracted Transition to Democracy', *Journal of Contemporary African Studies*, 18 (1): 107–32.

Nicolaides, A. (2017), 'Examining the Role of France in the Colonial Inheritance of Chad up to 1997', *Insight on Africa*, 9(2): 196–214, https://doi.org/10.1177/0975087817710055

Poe, S. C. and Tate, N. (1994), 'Repression of Human Rights to Personal Integrity in the 1980s: A Global Analysis', *American Political Science Review*, 88 (4): 853–72.

Regan, P. M. and Henderson, E. A. (2002), 'Democracy, Threats and Political Repression in Developing Countries: Are Democracies Internally less Violent?', *Third World Quarterly*, 23 (1): 119–36.

Sattarov, F. (2019), *Power and Technology: A Philosophical and Ethical Analysis*, Lanham, MD: Rowman & Littlefield.

Suzor, N. (2019), *Lawless: The Secret Rules That Govern Our Digital Lives*. Cambridge, UK: Cambridge University Press.

Thompson, K. K. (2011), 'Not Like an Egyptian: Cybersecurity and the Internet Kill Switch Debate', *Texas Law Review*, 90: 465–495.

Vargas-Leon, P. (2016), 'Tracking Internet Shutdown Practices: Democracies and Hybrid Regimes', in F. Musiani, D. L. Cogburn, L. De Nardis and N. S. Levinson (eds), *The Turn to Infrastructure in Internet Governance: Information Technology and Global Governance* (pp. 167-88). New York: Palgrave Macmillan.

Wagner, B. (2018), 'Understanding Internet Shutdowns: A Case Study from Pakistan', *International Journal of Communication*, 12: 3917–38.

Warf, B. (2011), 'Geographies of Global Internet Censorship', *Geo Journal*, 76(1): 1–23.

Wintrobe, R. (1998), *The Political Economy of Dictatorship, Vol.* 6, Cambridge: Cambridge University Press.

# Chapter 9

## Internet shutdowns in Senegal

## How power interests prevail over citizen rights

Ababacar Diop

### *Introduction*

After nearly two decades of uninterrupted internet freedoms, Senegal experienced its first internet shutdown in the run-up to the presidential election scheduled for 2024. This chapter will analyse how the pre-electoral situation was marked by social and political unrest, which led to the restriction of internet access. Since 2021, Senegal has been engaged in a power struggle between two camps: those trying to retain the power of the incumbent party and those of the opposition forces contesting that power. The political power in place strives to preserve its interests by cutting off the internet, even to the detriment of the fundamental rights and freedoms guaranteed to citizens by the constitution and international treaties.

Certainly, Senegal has been going through a turbulent period since 2021. Finally, the presidential election, which was to be held on 25 February 2024, was postponed until 24 March 2024. At the same time, the fiercest opponent, the popular Ousmane Sonko, was imprisoned. This situation created serious political unrest, resulting in several deaths (TV5Monde, 2024).

It is in this context that the government has for the first time in the twenty-six years that Senegal has been connected to the internet used its position of power by ordering the closure of the internet. Indeed, it was through a press release by the Minister of Communication, Telecommunications and the Digital Economy that the political authority informed citizens of the internet shutdown. The government authority announced in the press release that 'mobile data internet is temporarily suspended in certain locations in the country and during certain time slots'. The reasons given by the minister responsible aim to put an end to the 'dissemination of messages of hatred and subversion in a context of disturbance of public order' (Thioubou, 2023). Subsequently, it is worth noting that the Senegalese government has repeatedly responded to protests perceived as threats to its power by imposing internet shutdowns.

This chapter examines the political nature of internet cuts in Senegal. It asks, 'What power interests explain the recent internet shutdowns in Senegal and how can citizens best respond to put an end to these violations of digital rights?' The chapter also assesses whether there is a legal basis for these shutdowns, and what constitutional and digital rights have been violated by these internet shutdowns, as follows: the next section provides the reader with a brief history of media controls in Senegal before detailing the current situation and describing the case study internet shutdowns that occurred in Senegal in 2023. A review of the existing literature is then used to identify concepts of power and rights to determine the political basis of recent internet shutdowns. The analysis will assess the consequences of internet shutdowns on digital rights and examine the forms of resistance developed by citizens to circumvent or fight against these internet shutdowns.

## *The context*

Senegal is a country colonized by France. During the colonial era, the French media served the interests of the colonial power to establish its power of domination over the colony. However, the media space has always been contested by opposing power interests. 'Since the creation of the first newspaper, in 1856, by the French colonial authorities, the Senegalese media have fought not to be the instrument of political power' (Barry, 2013). Indeed, from the colonial era to the present day, all of the different political powers that have succeeded one another in Senegal have continued to control the circulation of information through media censorship in the interest of preserving power.

After independence in 1960, President Senghor maintained domination and control of information through the use of media censorship. Even the cinematographic field was not spared from censorship. The control of information under the governance of President Senghor served to establish so-called independent power by directing opinion in the sense of defending the interests of political power.

It was not until the 1980s, under President Abdou Diouf, that a plurality of media appeared, through the creation of private newspapers and radio stations. The government of Abdou Diouf between 1981 and 2000 strived to open up the media to the private sector and the opposition to allow the expression of a plurality of opinions. This media opening coincided with the time when the wind of democracy blew through the countries of the French-speaking African region.

It was under the governance of President Abdoulaye Wade, who came to power in 2000, that Senegal resolutely committed itself to an era of offline and online media plurality with the development of the internet. It was at this time that private television diversified alongside radios and newspapers. During Abdoulaye Wade's presidency, we did not witness internet shutdowns or arrests for opinions expressed via the internet. The information age in Senegal was characterized under Wade's regime by the privatization of the national telecommunications operators and the liberalization of the telecommunications market.

Under the regime of President Macky Sall, from 2012, Senegal actively developed widespread use of information and communication technologies through its various national initiatives as described in its ‘Digital Senegal 2025’ strategy, supported by the development framework of the Emerging Senegal Plan (PSE), adopted in 2012. This is a long-term vision articulated around the slogan ‘digital for all and for all uses in 2025 in Senegal with a dynamic and innovative private sector in an efficient ecosystem’. Digital technology constitutes an important sector in the economic and social development of Senegal. It is an essential lever for multiplying productivity gains and increasing the competitiveness of all sectors of the economy, through the supply of digital goods and services.

In order to increase accessibility to mobile internet in the territory, the Senegalese government granted licences to three mobile and fixed telephone operators including Orange, Free and Expresso, which offer, among other things, call services, mobile and residential internet. These are supplemented by internet service providers (ISPs) such as ARC Telecom, WAW SAS and Africa Access, which have also provided internet access since 2018.

However, it was under the governance of President Macky Sall (2014–24) that we saw for the first time in Senegal that citizens were being imprisoned for the expression of their opinions on social networks. It was also during the presidency of Macky Sall that Senegal experienced its first internet shutdown. According to a report from the Telecommunications and Postal Regulatory Authority (2023), 97 per cent of Senegalese internet users use the internet connection via mobile data.

Analysing the state of digital media use in Senegal in 2023, the Datareportal Senegal (2024) concluded that Senegal had 3.05 million social media users in January 2023, or 17.4 per cent of the total population. A total of 20.13 million cellular mobile connections were active in Senegal at the start of 2023, equivalent to 114.8 per cent of the total population (DataReportal 2024).

Although this expansion of internet use has increased the importance of online platforms to social, economic and political life, it should be noted that internet accessibility remains a challenge. Senegal ranks 92nd in the world in terms of internet connectivity, according to the annual Digital Quality of Life Index (DQL) study; Senegal is ahead of only a few countries included in the ranking, numbering a total of 110. In Africa, Senegal occupies ninth place, out of a total of nineteen countries included in the study. Worse still, from 2020 to 2024 restrictions on internet access have become more frequent and regular in Senegal, a state considered inherently democratic, often under the pretext of fighting disinformation or ‘preserving’ national security.

Internet disruptions occurred in 2021 and 2023 in response to protests over the arrest of popular main opponent Ousmane Sonko. This is why internet shutdowns have become normal in Senegal. In addition to restrictions on access to social media platforms, media are controlled in Senegal. As an illustration, in March 2021, the National Audio-Visual Regulatory Council suspended Walf TV and Sen TV for 72 hours on the grounds that these two television channels had broadcast live images of demonstrations; the Council considered that, in doing so, they had engaged in an ‘apology of violence’ and ‘irresponsible coverage of the situation’ (Amnesty International, 2021).

## *Description of the country case*

This section provides a descriptive state of internet shutdowns in Senegal from the first in 2021 until the time of writing this chapter (end of 2024). Internet shutdowns are defined as intentional interruption of the internet or electronic communications, rendering them inaccessible or effectively unusable, for a specific population or in a specific location, often to exert control over the flow of information (Media Defense, 2021).

Repeatedly, from June 2021 to February 2024, the government of Senegal cut off the internet each time there was political or social unrest, this in the context of the pre-electoral process of the election of the President of the Republic that was scheduled to be held on 24 March 2024. The closures are summarized in Table 9.1.

On 5 March 2021, the internet was shut down in Senegal. Netblocks, an observatory specializing in monitoring internet disruptions and outages, told the world that social media and messaging apps are currently restricted in Senegal (AITN, 2021). 'To justify this measure, the Ministry of Communication, Telecommunications and the Digital Economy mentions "the dissemination of hateful and subversive messages in a context of disturbance of public order in certain localities of the national territory"' (http://www.osiris.sn/Coupure-de-l-internet-au-Senegal).

In June 2023, following an official announcement from the Minister of the Interior, the Senegalese government limited access to Facebook, Twitter, WhatsApp, Instagram, YouTube, TikTok, Telegram and other social media platforms from 1 to 6 June 2023 (https://polaris-asso.org/la-coupure-de-linternet-au-senegal-une-violation-de-la-liberte-dexpression-et-du-droit-a-linformation/). Regarding mobile internet the outage lasted three days. Added to this was the ban on broadcasting for a month by the private television channel Walfadjri. Concerning these internet access restrictions, the National Telecommunications Company (SONATEL) sent a message to its subscribers to clarify that 'the state has decided to cut off mobile internet' leading to 'disruptions among all operators', which directly determines that the state is mainly responsible for internet cuts in Senegal.

On 31 July 2023, the same practice of internet shutdown was observed in Senegal following the arrest of opponent Ousmane Sonko. These internet shutdowns were imposed by the government – they claimed, to counter the demonstrations and censor alleged hate speech. Telecommunications operators lost a significant daily income, which has not yet been quantified. In reality, it was a question of the shutdown having the effect of censoring the opinions and violating the freedom of expression of citizens, as well as reducing the civic space for protest and the free circulation of information (Pressafrik, 2023).

It should be noted that Senegal had never faced internet censorship of this magnitude since the introduction of the internet in the country in 1996. Internet freedom always existed in Senegal, despite social and political unrest until 2021. However, with the emergence and development of networks, citizens are increasingly using the internet to coordinate and mobilize opposition. This is why

**Table 9.1** Internet Shutdowns from 2021 to 2024

| Deadline | Type of cut | Extent of the cut | Duration of outages | Rationale/motivation |
|---|---|---|---|---|
| 5 March 2021 | Social media and messaging apps | National | Duration unknown | No motivation or press release from the state |
| 1 June 2023 | Social networks and mobile data | National | 7 days | The dissemination of messages of hatred and subversion in a context of disturbance of public order |
| 31 July 2023 | Social networks and mobile data | National | 8 days | The dissemination of hateful and subversive messages relayed on social networks |
| 4 February 2024 | Mobile data internet | National | 3 days | The dissemination of several hateful and subversive messages relayed on social networks in a context of threats of disturbances to public order |
| 13 February 2024 | Mobile data internet | National | 24h | Dissemination of hateful messages, likely to cause unrest |

Source: author adapted from TV5Monde (2024).

during large-scale social or political unrest, the government cuts off the internet, to counter the power of organization and coordination of demonstrators.

Furthermore, it is important to emphasize that Senegal is used to internet outages. For example, on 5 February 2024, a temporary outage was put in place, to be restored on 7 February. The Ministry of Telecommunications justified this decision by the dissemination of messages deemed 'hateful and subversive' on social networks, in a context of potential threat to public order. Furthermore, mobile data internet was again suspended on 13 February 2024 in Senegal. This suspension was the second after the postponement of the presidential election.

It is to this end that Rose Marie Diouf Baloucoune, general secretary of the Union of Postal and Telecommunications Workers declared that: 'From 2 June 2023 to 13 February 2024, Minister Moussa Bocar Thiam carried out 13 series of internet cuts mobile phones, on average the equivalent of a day and a half of internet outage each month' (Houeto, 2024).

Outages in Senegal have become recurrent and are raising concerns about freedom of expression and access to information.

### *History of internet cuts in Senegal in 2023*

Senegal did not experience any outages of its internet connection from 1996 to 2021. It was only from 2021, following political and social demonstrations, that the political powers began to cut off the internet, not only to prohibit hate speech, but above all to preserve their political interests of conserving power.

In 2023, the Senegalese authorities increased internet shutdowns from June for reasons, according to them, of security. They were first used in response to demonstrations against the conviction of opponent Ousmane Sonko. The government shut down social media platforms from 1 to 8 June 2023 and completely shut down mobile internet from 4 to 7 June 2023.

To justify these restrictions, the Ministry of Communication, Telecommunications and the Digital Economy indicated that 'due to the dissemination of hateful and subversive messages in a context of disturbance of public order in certain localities of the national territory that internet access has been suspended.' These restrictions on access to certain instant messaging platforms such as WhatsApp, Twitter, Facebook and Instagram and the YouTube application have been noted and could seriously undermine the right to public information guaranteed by the Constitution of Senegal and by most international legal instruments relating to human rights (Diouf, 2019).

Denouncing this practice, Seydi Gassama, a representative of Amnesty International (2023) in Senegal, declared that 'these restrictions on the right to freedom of expression and information constitute arbitrary measures, contrary to international law and cannot be justified by security requirements'.

Following strong mobilization of internet users on social media platforms, the government of Senegal once again imposed an internet shutdown, from 31 July to 7 August 2023 from 8.00 am to 2.00 pm. The reason given by the government was to stop the dissemination of hateful and subversive messages relayed on the internet. After the challenge to the postponement of the presidential election, which was scheduled for 25 February 2024, to an unknown date by President Macky Sall, whose electoral mandate officially ended on 2 April 2024, the mobile data internet was shut down again. The Ministry of Communication, Telecommunications and the Digital Economy informed citizens that 'mobile data internet is temporarily suspended from Sunday 4 February at 10.00 pm.' According to the press release, this cut was ordered due to 'the dissemination of several hateful and subversive messages relayed on social networks in a context of threats of disturbances to public order' (Gueye, 2024).

Following the decision to postpone the presidential election scheduled for 25 February 2024, and threats of protest from the populations, the Senegalese government once again cut off the mobile internet on Tuesday 13 February 2024, during a call to demonstrate against the postponement of the presidential election. The reason given by the Minister of Communication, Me Moussa Bocar Thiam, is the dissemination of hateful messages, likely to cause unrest. In his press release, he specifies: 'Due to the dissemination on social networks of several hateful and subversive messages which have already caused violent demonstrations with deaths and significant material damage, the internet of mobile data is suspended this Tuesday, 13 February 2024 depending on certain time frames' (Al Jazeera, 2024).

However, Muheeb Saeed, head of freedom of expression at the MFWA, responded: 'At a time of tension where citizens need to connect more and share information to ensure the safety and well-being of their parents and loved ones, the government has decided to worsen their feelings of anxiety with this regrettable decision.'

### *Political connotation of internet shutdowns*

In Africa, restrictions on internet access are generally motivated by political concerns. It is enough to refer to the case of Benin: in the middle of the legislative election, the Beninese authorities cut off the internet. Similarly, in Mali, the internet was disrupted on the eve of the first round of the presidential election on 29 July 2018 (Togora, 2018). Niger, Guinea and Gabon also implemented internet shutdowns during electoral periods (Essoungou, 2020).

For Guinea, the restrictions were imposed due to a security 'problem', according to Guinean authorities. They were lifted in a climate of growing social tension after the announcement of the dissolution of the government by the military junta in power for two and a half years.

It is clear from the above that government-initiated internet shutdowns restrict citizens' exercise of digital rights, but also economic, social and cultural rights, such as freedom of expression online; however, it also demonstrates that, particularly in Senegal, they serve to preserve the political power in place. The attack on digital rights, such as freedom of expression and citizens' right to access information, is a government policy established with the aim of defending the interests of the political power. The political reason for internet shutdowns is not controversial. To this end, the Senegalese government took its courage in hand with a press release from the Minister of Communication, Telecommunications and the Digital Economy, who announced that 'the internet of mobile data is temporarily suspended in certain localities of the country and during certain time slots'.

For all cases of internet cuts experienced by Senegal, the Minister publishes press releases each time. For example: 'dissemination of messages of hatred and subversion in a context of disturbance of public order' (Thioubou, 2023) are the reasons given to justify the internet shutdown. Furthermore, the reason given by the state for the internet shutdowns in July 2023 is 'the dissemination of hateful and subversive messages relayed on social networks'.

From the above, we see that the state of Senegal resorts to internet shutdowns in the event of demonstrations, during periods of political conflict, such as elections or social unrest. To this end, interruptions may be partial or total, temporary or prolonged. They can target specific social media platforms and relate to mobile data.

Motivated largely by political concerns of managing the electoral process with the aim of combating the political interests of the opposition and maintaining the existing political caste in power, in this pre-electoral period, the internet shutdowns ordered by the state in Senegal are multiplying, poised to become the 'new normal'. Worse still, the state uses the process of blocking internet access by ordering internet service providers to limit access to their subscribers.

The evolution of digital repression reveals a simple truth: shutdowns and political censorship are an indication of a government's weakness in the face of citizens who yearn for a change in political power. Weak governments, faced with growing political and citizen opposition, are cracking down on online activities they simply don't like (Roberts and Ali, 2021).

My analysis is that the government of Senegal often wrongly believes that internet shutdowns can end social unrest, curb the spread of misinformation, hate speech, or reduce cybersecurity threats. Whereas in times of socio-political tensions, it is more fundamental to guarantee access to information, access to the internet in order to appease populations who are often victims of manipulation and disinformation.

## *Digital rights violations*

All human rights, whether economic, social and cultural rights or civil and political rights, are interdependent. Digital rights are essentially human rights in the digital age, including rights related to our access and use of technologies, as well as how fundamental rights are exercised in the online environment. Internet restrictions have violated the rights of Senegalese people while stifling media freedom and freedom of expression in Senegal. Internet and social media restrictions deprive Senegalese citizens of the right to express themselves freely, access information and participate in public debate. In addition to infringing these fundamental rights, limitations imposed on the internet have considerable economic and social repercussions.

To this end, the African Commission on Human and Peoples' Rights (ACHPR, 2002) and the United Nations (UN) have both firmly established that the same rights enjoyed by people offline must also be protected online, particularly the right to freedom of expression. For example, Article 19 of the International Covenant on Civil and Political Rights of 16 December 1966 states that 'Freedom of expression includes the freedom to seek, receive and disseminate information and ideas of any kind, without distinction border, in oral and written form., in printed or artistic form and by any other means of one's choice, the right to freedom of expression applies without regard to borders and through any media of one's choice' (Article 19, 2023).

The Government of Senegal has international human rights obligations, including those set out in the ACHPR, the Universal Declaration of Human Rights (UDHR) and in the International Covenant on Civil and Political Rights (ICCPR), to which Senegal is a party. Freedom of expression, both online and offline, is an essential pillar of any democratic society. Mobile data internet outages deprive Senegalese citizens of the right to express themselves freely, access information and participate in public debate.

Internet shutdowns seriously undermine the public's right to information, guaranteed by the Constitution and most international legal instruments. For example, Article 9-1 and 2 of the African Charter on Human and Peoples' Rights which provides that: 'Everyone has the right to information; everyone has the right to express and disseminate their opinions within the framework of laws and regulations.' Internet disruptions constitute a flagrant violation of digital rights, in particular the right of access to information. The Constitution (Constitution, 2001) of Senegal guarantees to all on the basis of its Article 8 that: 'Citizens have fundamental individual freedoms, in particular the freedoms of opinion, expression, press, association, assembly, travel, demonstration.'

Article 5 and Article 2 of Law No. 2008–10 of 25 January 2008 on the information society orientation law[1] provide that 'the principle of freedom includes the fundamental right of every person to communicate, the right of every citizen to participate effectively in the information society, the right to free expression and the right to carry out electronic commerce actions and to receive information across borders in accordance with applicable laws and regulations'.

Free speech also allows citizens to question their government, which helps hold them accountable.

The Declaration of Principles on Freedom of Expression and Access to Information in Africa (ACHPR, 2019) provides that: 'States shall promote the enjoyment of the rights to freedom of expression and access to information online as well as the means necessary to exercise these rights. States recognize that universal, equitable, affordable and meaningful access to the internet is necessary for the realization of freedom of expression and access to information and the exercise of other human rights.'

It is in the same sense that the resolution of the Human Rights Council (HRC), 'unequivocally condemns measures aimed at preventing or deliberately disrupting access to information or the dissemination of information online in violation of international human rights law' (UNHRC Resolution, 2016). Furthermore, the United Nations considers that an internet shutdown, whatever the justification, constitutes a violation of civil and political rights. The right to access the internet is now considered a fundamental right, crucial for freedom of expression and access to information. The state of Senegal is therefore called upon to maintain access to the internet even in times of political unrest, in order to guarantee the rights of its citizens.

Internet shutdowns violate fundamental rights and freedoms. This is why the collective of unions of telecommunications operators, Sonatel, Free and Expresso, even recognizes the importance of digital rights. The collective declared its solidarity with the Senegalese population who are demanding their rights to communication, information, freedom of expression and their economic rights. It follows that freedom of expression is a fundamental principle of any democratic society as was enshrined in the Universal Declaration of Human Rights of 10 December 1948 and the Declaration of Principles on Freedom of Expression in Africa of 2002.

## *Violation of economic rights*

Internet shutdowns come at the expense of growth, as they have an immediate financial impact on a country's economy. The cuts cause a decline in economic activity, which leads to a decline in profits of local businesses, SMEs, tax revenues and GDP.

Restrictions on internet access also have detrimental consequences on the digital economy. This is why Sonatel and Expresso deplore the colossal economic losses for telecommunications operators, estimated at three billion CFA francs, not to mention the socio-economic damage for millions of customers (Internews, 2024).

Internet shutdowns are a violation of economic rights. From 2 June 2023 to 13 February 2024, Minister Moussa Bocar Thiam operated thirteen days of mobile internet cuts. The internet cuts have undermined the social rights of Senegalese by suspending family communications, and limiting citizens' access to precise information from government sources during political unrest. The social consequences are also harmful to the extent that it has become more difficult for citizens to contact their loved ones.

In the field of health and online education, internet outages have affected patients, students and training centres. Restrictions on internet access impact citizens' ability to coordinate and communicate effectively in the event of an emergency. Internet shutdowns harm individuals, countries and economies around the world. To this end, the general secretary of the National Union of Postal and Telecommunications Workers (SNTPT), Rose Marie Diouf Baloucoune, also underlines 'that despite the political crises which have caused all the successive regimes in Senegal to falter since independence, ICT have never been a weapon of deprivation of what they are supposed to facilitate: freedom of expression' (Houeto, 2024).

Better yet, the state could explore alternative, less restrictive means to prevent the dissemination of speech clearly identified as violent in such a situation. Safeguarding freedom of expression is essential for a democratic society, and any limitations on this right must be carefully assessed and justified within the framework of international human rights standards.

Furthermore, the current trend is towards the practice of internet shutdowns, restrictions on access to the internet in Senegal, motivated largely by political concerns and ordered by the government under the pretext of combating hate speech.

### *Forms of resistance developed by citizens to circumvent internet shutdowns*

In Senegal, citizens have made extensive use of virtual private networks (VPNs) to circumvent geographic restrictions and censorship imposed by the government or internet service providers. A VPN is a tool that allows users to browse the internet anonymously and securely.

In Senegal, Proton VPN saw a significant increase in usage during the shutdown. According to its new VPN Observatory, registrations have increased 2,800 per cent above the normal level since 31 July 2023. This increase appears to be the result of internet access restrictions, as well as the blocking of some popular social networks like TikTok in the country (*Le Parisien*, 2023). 'We saw two spikes last week, one following Senegalese authorities restricting internet access in response to violent protests following the arrest of opposition leader Ousmane Sonko, quickly followed by a second spike after TikTok blocking' (Cesarano, 2023).

VPNs have allowed Senegalese people to continue using social media to share information, organize protests and communicate with the outside world despite current restrictions.

Furthermore, organizations defending human rights, internet freedom and the media have, through a joint declaration (Article 19, 2023), strongly condemned the recent restrictions on internet access in Senegal, observed on the side-lines of public demonstrations, which took place following the conviction of opponent Ousmane Sonko to two years in prison for 'corruption of youth'; he was prosecuted for rape and death threats, although he pleaded not guilty.

Another joint statement was made in 2024 by civil society organizations (Access Now, 2023) strongly condemning the suspension of the internet mobile data in Senegal. This is a measure taken by the Ministry of Communication, Telecommunications and Digital Affairs, which cites the reasons for the dissemination of hateful and subversive messages relayed on social networks, in a context of threats and public order.

To circumvent and protest against internet shutdowns, the Court of Justice of the Economic Community of West African States (ECOWAS) was asked by ASUTIC, the association of ICT users in Senegal, to rule on the case of Senegal. To this end, the Senegalese pan-African organization for the protection of democracy and human rights 'AfricTivistes' and the Senegalese journalists Moussa Ngom and Ayoba Faye announced that they had brought the case before the ECOWAS High Court of Justice to denounce budget cuts to the internet by the Senegalese authorities in June, July and August 2023 (Medias Défense, 2024). This referral is currently pending before the Court of Justice of ECOWAS and the procedure is still ongoing. We wait to hear the decision of the Court of Justice.

'The appeal filed before the ECOWAS Court of Justice challenges the actions of the Senegalese government, highlighting the harmful impact on freedom of expression, media freedom and the right to work,' said the president of AfricTivistes, Cheikh Fall. He stresses that in times of political unrest, 'access to information is crucial, and internet shutdowns only deepen the darkness, hindering the flow of vital information and endangering the security of citizens'.

It is clear that internet shutdowns can prompt citizens to strengthen their offline information networks and, in the event of protests, to intensify their resistance. By denying people an online space to express their opinions, governments may actually push these energies into the streets, where they could cause violence. Even workers in the telecommunications sector – the Sonatel Workers' Union, the National Union of Postal and Telecommunications Workers, the National Union of Sentel Workers and the National Union of Postal and Telecommunications Workers – held a press briefing to denounce the repeated internet cuts in

Senegal: 'Once again, the Minister of Communication, Telecommunications and Digital Economy has just ordered the cutting of the mobile internet.'

## *Conclusion and recommendations*

Since the introduction of the internet in Senegal, there had been no internet shutdowns prior to 2021. But since 2021, political internet shutdowns have become a reality in Senegal. It is enough to refer to the internet shutdowns of 1 June 2023 and 31 July 2023, and the internet shutdown of February 2024 following the political decision of the President of the Republic to postpone the presidential election of 25 February 2024.

This chapter set out to address the question, 'What power interests explain the recent internet shutdowns in Senegal and how can citizens best react to put an end to these violations of digital rights?' It emerges from this study that internet cuts in Senegal are political in nature because they always occur in the pre-electoral period or in the event of popular citizen demonstrations. In Senegal, for simple political reasons or the defence of political interests linked to the preservation of political power contested by citizens, the government does not hesitate to infringe on digital rights, including the right to access the internet, the right to freedom of expression and the right to information through internet shutdowns. Whilst the cuts have an economic and social impact, this study showed that freedom of expression remains a fundamental principle that drives the political, economic and social dynamics of a country. Citizens must therefore be able to express themselves freely on any medium. Freedom of expression online and offline is a constitutional success in Senegal.

## *The following recommendations arise from this analysis*

The state must protect citizens' human rights by avoiding future internet shutdowns:

- The government of Senegal should promote citizens' digital rights by adoption of the Bill on Access to Information.
- It is up to the government to further involve civil society actors in the development of laws and regulations focused on the digital ecosystem.
- The government should commit to respecting fundamental rights and freedoms in accordance with the Constitution and to further guarantee freedom of expression, information and the right of access to the internet.
- It is up to civil society organizations in Senegal to strengthen their advocacy for the defence and protection of digital rights by guaranteeing the digital inclusion of all citizens and fighting against internet shutdowns.

Civil society organizations should work hand in hand with stakeholders, such as government, the private sector, the media and the general public, to promote digital rights, including freedom of expression, information and online opinion.

- It is up to civil society organizations to become more involved in strengthening their capacities to combat internet access restrictions in order to better understand the issues and challenges linked to internet shutdowns.

In the private sector, telecommunications operators should oppose illegal requests from governments to cut off the internet during political or social demonstrations or during election periods.

- It is up to the operators and internet access providers to permanently ensure citizens' access to the internet regardless of State requisitions.
- It is up to private companies to take into account respect for digital rights such as freedom of expression, the right to information, access to the internet and to customers' personal data.

## *Bibliography*


Access Now (2023), 'Civil Society Statement: Government of Senegal Must Stop Escalating Trend of Normalizing Internet Shutdowns', https://www.accessnow.org/press-release/civil-society-statement-stop-normalizing-internet-shutdowns-senegal/

ACHPR (2019), *Declaration of Principles on Freedom of Expression and Access to Information in Africa 2019*, https://achpr.au.int/en/node/902

Afex (2017), 'Internet Freedom in Africa: Baseline Study of Eight Countries', Report 2017, https://www.africafex.org/publication/baseline-study-on-internet-freedom-in-africa

African Commission on Human and Peoples' Rights (ACHPR) (2002), 'Resolution on the Adoption of the Declaration of Principles on Freedom of Expression in Africa', ACHPR /Res.62(XXXII)02 https://www.refworld.org/legal/resolution/achpr/2002/en/83570#:~:text=No%20one%20shall%20be%20subject,or%20her%20freedom%20of%20expression.&text=interest%20and%20be%20necessary%20and%20in%20a%20democratic%20society

AITN (2021), 'Political Tensions in Senegal: Internet Disruptions and Outages Reported', Afrique IT News, https://afriqueitnews.com/tech-media/tensions-politiques-senegal-perturbations-coupures-internet-signalees/

Al Jazeera (2024), 'Senegal Restricts Internet as Opposition Leader Formally Charged', https://www.aljazeera.com/news/2023/7/31/senegal-restricts-internet-as-opposition-leader-formally-charged

Amnesty International (2021), Annual Report, 'Heavy Threats to Freedoms in Senegal', https://www.amnesty.sn/rapport-annuel-2021-de-lourdes-menaces-sur-les-libertes-au-

Amnesty International (2023), 'Senegal: The Authorities Must Immediately Halt the Police Violence and Restore Social Media', https://www.amnesty.org/en/latest/news/2023/06/

senegal-les-autorites-doivent-immediatement-arreter-les-violences-policieres-et-retablir-les-reseaux-sociaux/senegal/

Article 19 (2023), https://www.article19.org/fr/resources/declaration-restrictions-internet-social-reseaux/

Barry, M. (2013), 'History of the Media in Senegal: From Colonization to the Present Day', in *African Societies and the Diaspora*, Paris: L'Harmattan, 351 pages.

Cesarano, A. (2023), 'Internet Censorship: The Use of VPNs Is Exploding in Senegal', *TechRadar 2023*, http://www.osiris.sn/Censure-sur-internet-l-usage.html

CIPESA, 'Dictatorships and Restrictions: Five Dimensions of Internet Shutdowns in Africa,' 2019 report, https://cipesa.org/wp-content/files/publications/Dictators-et-restrictions-Rapport.pdf

Constitution of January 7, 2001 (JORS, n° 5963 of January 22, 2001).

DataReportal 2024: https://datareportal.com/digital-in-senegal

Decree No. 2016-1987 Relating to the Terms and Conditions for Granting Infrastructure Manager Approval.

Decree No. 2016-1988 Relating to the Sharing of telecommunications infrastructure.

Diouf, A. (2019), 'Freedom of Expression on the Internet in Senegal', August 2019, https://ceracle.com/wp-content/uploads/2021/06/Liberte-dexpression-sur-Internet-par-Astou-DIOUF.pdf.2017 law establishing the press code.

Diouf, A. (2021), 'The Regulation of Digital Platforms and Freedom of Expression in West Africa', https://sn.boell.org/fr/2021/06/17/la-regulation-des-plateformes-digitals-and-freedom-of-expression-in-africa-from-0

Diouf, A. (2022), 'Data Governance: Data Localization, Biometric Database and Digital Identity', https://cipesa.org/2022/11/la-gouvernance-des-donnees-localization-des-donnees-base-biometric-data-and-digital-identity/

Essoungou, A-M. (2020) Manipulations numériques en Afrique, *Le Monde Diplomatique*, https://www.monde-diplomatique.fr/2020/09/ESSOUNGOU/62142.

Gueye, S. (2024), 'Senegal: Internet Mobile Data Temporarily Suspended, Says Minister', AllAfrica, https://allafrica.com/stories/202402050388.html

Houeto, C. (2024), 'L'évolution de la cybersécurité au Sénégal : Défis, réalisations et perspectives futures', *Africa Cybersecurity Magazine*, https://cybersecuritymag.africa/interview-evolution-senegal-en-cybersecurite-avec-cheikh-ahmadou-bamba-fall

Internews (2024), 'The Price of Disruption: Evaluating the Economic Impact of Senegal's 2023 Internet Shutdowns', https://internews.org/wp-content/uploads/2024/12/The-Price-of-Disruption-Internews-December-2024-English.pdf

Joint Declaration: Project to Regulate Social Networks in Senegal: We Are Alerting, http://jonction.e-monsite.com/

Joint Declaration for Maintaining an Open and Secure Internet During the Presidential Election of 24 February 2019 in Senegal, https://cipesa.org/2019/02/%EF%BB%BFdeclaration-conjointe-for-maintaining-an-open-and-secure-internet-during-the-presidential-election-of-February-24-2019-in-Senegal/

Joint Statement from the Global Network Initiative and the Telecommunications Industry Dialogue on Network and Service Outages. July 2016. http://globalnetworkinitiative.org/gni-id-statementnetwork-shutdowns/

Joint Statement on Internet Shutdown in Rakhine and Chin States by Digital Rights Organizations and Other Civil Society Organizations. June 2019. https://www.apc.org/fr/node/35556

Keep It On (2017), 'IFLA Calls for an End to Internet Shutdowns', August 2017, https://www.ifla.org/files/assets/faife/statements/ifla_internet_shutdowns_statement.pdfLaw 2018-28 of December 12 Relating to the Electronic Communications Code.

Law No. 2008-10 of January 25, 2008, Relating to the Orientation Law Relating to the Information Society (JORS, No. 6406 of May 3, 2008a, p. 419 et seq.).

Law No. 2008-12 of January 25, 2008 Relating to the Protection of Personal Data (JORS, No. 6406, of May 3, 2008b, p. 434).

Law No. 2016-29 of November 8, 2016 Amending Law No. 65,60 of July 21, 1965 on the Penal Code (JORS No. 6975).

Law No. 2016-30 of November 8, 2016 Amending Law No. 65,61 of July 21, 1965 on the Code of Criminal Procedure (JORS No. 6976).

*Le Parisien* (2023), 'Senegal: Suspension of Tiktok by Govt Allegedly Halters Freedom Of Expression & Information', https://www.business-humanrights.org/en/latest-news/senegal-the-govt-suspension-of-the-social-medial-tiktok-allegedly-halters-freedom-of-expression-and-information/

Media Defence (2021), 'Summary Modules on Litigation Relating to Digital Rights and Freedom of Expression Online', https://www.mediadefence.org/ereader/publications/introductory-modules-on-digital-rights-and-freedom-of-expression-online/

Medias Défense (2024), 'Media Defence and SLS's Rule of Law Impact Lab File Case Before ECOWAS Court Challenging Senegal Internet Shutdowns', https://www.mediadefence.org/news/senegals-internet-shutdowns/content/uploads/sites/2/2021/04/Module-2-Introduction-to-droits-numériques_FR_FINAL.pdf

Pressafrik (2023), 'Internet Shutdown: Economic Operators Speak of Losses Worth 3 Billion CFA Francs', https://www.pressafrik.com/coupure-d-internet-les-operateurs-economiques-parlent-des-pertes-d-une-valeur-de-3-milliards-de-francs-cfa_a268832.html

Regulatory Authority for Telecommunications and Posts (2023), 'Quarterly Report on the Electronic Communications Market, January–March 2023', https://artp.sn/sites/default/files/2024-03/2Rapport%20Observatoire%20T4%202023.pdf

Roberts, T. and Mohamed Ali, A. (2021), 'Opening and Closing Online Civic Space in Africa: An Introduction to the Ten Digital Rights Landscape Reports', in T. Roberts (ed.), *Digital Rights in Closing Civic Space: Lessons from Ten African Countries*, Brighton: Institute of Development Studies, https://doi.org/10.19088/IDS.2021.005

Sagna, O., Brun, C. and Huter, S. (2013), *History of the Internet in Senegal (1989–2004)*, Oregan: The Network Startup Resource Center (NSRC), University of Oregon, https://hdl.handle.net/1794/13061

Sénégal: la société civile dénonce les coupures d'Internet, https://www.ouestaf.com/senegal-la-societe-civile-denonce-les-coupures-dinternet/

Statement on Intentional Internet Shutdowns. African School on Internet Governance. October 2016, https://afrisig.org/previous-afrisigs/afrisig-2016/statement-on-an-intentional-internetshutdown/

Statements: Joint Letters to Keep the Internet Open and Secure (Multiple Countries). 2017–2019, https://www.apc.org/fr/tags/internet-shutdown.

Thioubou, M. W. (2023), 'Consequences of the Riots: The State Temporarily Suspends the Internet of Mobile Data', https://lequotidien.sn/consequences-des-emeutes-letat-suspend-temporairement-linternet-des-donnees-mobiles/

Togora, S. (2018), 'Attack on Freedom of Expression in Mali: Are We Still in a Democracy?' https://sahelien.com/atteinte-a-la-liberte-dexpression-au-mali-sommes-nous-encore-dans-une-democratie/#

TV5 Monde (2024), https://information.tv5monde.com/afrique/senegal-un-troisieme-mort-dans-les-manifestations-contre-le-report-de-lelection#

UNCHR (2016), 'The Promotion, Protection and Enjoyment of Human Rights on the Internet', A/HRC/RES/32/13, https://documents.un.org/doc/undoc/gen/g16/156/90/pdf/g1615690.pdf

# Chapter 10

## Internet shutdowns in Burkina Faso

## Technology, rights and power

Harold Adjaho

### *Introduction*

In November 2021, Burkina Faso experienced its first internet shutdown. Although it was just a mobile internet shutdown, it would be followed in January 2022 by two other similar shutdowns, following a restriction of access to social networks across the country.

This chapter examines these mobile internet shutdowns. Having affected more than 21 million connected devices used by more than 5 million internet users (Data Reportal, 2022), these shutdowns have highlighted various flaws in democracy in Burkina Faso, the 'country of honest people'. This chapter assesses the implications for democratic governance, the application of justice, respect for human rights and economic development in Burkina Faso.

An increasingly common practice in many countries in Africa, internet shutdowns are imposed by governments for supposed reasons of national security, preventing public disorder or controlling disinformation or hate speech. They can be partial or total, temporary or prolonged, and can target specific platforms, regions or an entire country. They have negative economic and social effects on the affected countries, particularly on small and medium-sized enterprises that increasingly rely on digital tools for their activities and growth (Agence Ecofin, 2023). They also constitute violations of the human, civil and political rights of users.

This chapter seeks to address the following questions: 'How and why did the internet shutdowns occur in November 2021 and January 2022 in Burkina Faso? What power interests motivated the 2021 internet shutdowns, and how do they affect the rights of Burkinabé citizens? What were the socio-political and economic consequences of the shutdowns for Burkinabé citizens?'

The remaining sections of this chapter will be organized as follows: the next section will provide a political history of media controls in Burkina Faso. It will also review existing publications about the 2021 and 2022 shutdowns in Burkina Faso, identifying gaps in the literature before reviewing the concepts of power, rights and technology that can be used to analyse internet shutdowns.

The results of a survey conducted with the assistance of the Burkina Faso Internet Society, which collected testimonies from eight people from various backgrounds affected by the Internet shutdowns, will be analysed. In addition, a desk research of official statements, policies and relevant reports, as well as a content analysis of social media, press articles and other online sources will be conducted. This case study will be analysed through the lens of technology, power and rights. The chapter will close with some tentative recommendations for key stakeholders and conclusions.

## *Background*

Burkina Faso, a landlocked country in West Africa, is situated at the crossroads between the Sahel and Sudanian regions. Known as the 'Land of Upright Men', a nickname symbolizing its values of dignity and integrity, it reflects the vision of Thomas Sankara. His reformist leadership instilled principles of honesty and social justice in the nation. With a rapidly growing population, estimated at more than 23 million inhabitants in 2023 and a growth rate of 3 per cent, Burkina Faso continues to evolve dynamically. French is the official language of the country.

Over the past sixty years, Burkina Faso has experienced various periods of political change, economic development, social challenges and media control and censorship. These can be summarized through several major phases. The Upper Volta, now Burkina Faso, had a tumultuous history during French colonization. Created on 1 March 1919, its territory was dismantled on 5 September 1932, and divided between Côte d'Ivoire, French Sudan (now Mali) and Niger, before being reconstituted in 1947 (UNIVERSALIS, 2011). This territorial and political instability hindered the development of the media.

### *Colonial era (1898–1960)*

During the colonial period, media in Burkina Faso (then Upper Volta) was heavily controlled by French authorities. The colonial government established French newspapers to serve its interests while suppressing local voices. The 1881 French law on press freedom restricted media ownership and content, requiring publications to be managed by French nationals (French law of July 29, Article 69, 1881). This control was not merely about censorship but was also aimed at shaping public opinion to align with French colonial interests. The media served as a tool for propaganda, promoting the narrative of civilizing missions while suppressing dissent and local voices. According to François Bassolet (1968), the 1921 decree prohibited the dissemination of any publication edited by Africans without prior authorization, further limiting freedom of expression.

*Post-independence (1960–74)*

After gaining independence in 1960, Upper Volta experienced a relative freedom of the press, but with intermittent periods of censorship and government control. The early years were marked by rapid development of state radio and television as instruments of sovereignty. The print media under the First Republic (1960–6) gave an 'impression of emptiness' except for *Carrefour Africain*, a pro-government newspaper (Yaméogo Lassané, 2021). This phrase, attributed to Marie-Soleil Frère, underscores that the press of this period was largely dominated by publications serving government interests, thus limiting the diversity of opinions available. Opposition parties were forced into clandestinity, along with their newspapers. Maurice Yaméogo, the first president after independence, quickly silenced opposition and confirmed Law No. 20 AL of 31 August 1959, granting the Ministry of the Interior full power to order the administrative seizure of print media that could threaten 'state security'. Three media outlets were affected by this law, including *L'Observateur*, which was closed for criticizing the government; *Le Journal du Peuple*, suspended for subversive content; and *Le Réveil*, banned for harmful information. Another law of 14 January 1960 further required the prohibition and repression of any publication that might create disturbances (Yaméogo Lassané, 2021). Limited strictly to civil servant journalists paid by the state, the media ecosystem primarily served as relays for official discourse. Under pressure from unions and the army, Maurice Yaméogo abandoned power on 3 January 1966 (Netafrique, 2017). General Sangoulé Lamizana then took power but maintained similar media control policies. For authorities, only state journalism could 'emerge and consolidate national identity in nascent states' (Achille Mbembe, 2013). The advent of the Second Republic on 14 June 1970, marked a return of opposition parties and led to new independent newspapers like *L'Éclair*, created by Joseph Ki-Zerbo's party 'Mouvement National de Libération – MNL' (Ki-Zerbo, 1972).

*Military rule and state control (1974–83)*

The year 1974 marked the end of the Second Republic and saw the establishment of the first journalism school in Upper Volta: the Centre de Formation Professionnelle de l'Information (CFPI). This political context significantly impacted media. As noted by Marie-Soleil Frère (2020), 'The press, radio, television transform or "are transformed" at the pace of ideological changes in their environment'. However, from 1974 to 1980, media were closely controlled by the state through Ordinance No. 63-68/PRES, which mandated pre-censorship. Newspapers were required to reflect official positions and avoid criticism. Founded in 1955, *L'Observateur* played a crucial role in civic engagement but faced censorship during Sankara's rise. In 1980, military coup leader Saye Zerbo attempted press reforms that led to relative freedom.

The changes during this period can be summarized as in Table 10.1.

**Table 10.1** Evolution of Media Landscape and Government Control in Burkina Faso (1974–82)

| Year | Type of media | Comments |
|---|---|---|
| 1974 | Radio / Television | Radiodiffusion-Télévision (RTB) du Burkina remains the only source of broadcasting with strictly controlled programming. |
| 1980 | Print media | Attempts at press reform and liberalization under Saye Zerbo. |
| 1982 | General media ecosystem | Brief period of media openness under Jean-Baptiste Ouédraogo. |

Source: Yaméogo Lassané, 2021.

### *Revolutionary period (1983–7)*

On 21 April 1982, Thomas Sankara famously declared during a live broadcast: 'Malheur à ceux qui bâillonnent le peuple!' ('Woe to those who silence the people!', statement by Thomas Sankara, 1982). He came to power in Upper Volta after a coup known as the Revolution on 4 August 1983, after having overthrown Jean Baptiste Ouédraogo (1982 to 1983) who had previously overthrown Saye Zerbo. Thomas Sankara had nationalized several media outlets to ensure they served revolutionary interests while placing private media under strict control. New publications promoting independence and self-sufficiency emerged alongside state newspapers like *Journal du Soir* broadcasting Sankara's speeches (Lassané, 2021). Despite some degree of freedom encouraged by Sankara's government, any criticism perceived as a threat was severely repressed; journalists faced arrest and censorship. *L'Observateur* was notably closed in 1984 due to its editorial line not aligning with revolutionary ideals.

### *Blaise Compaoré era (1987–2014)*

Following Sankara's assassination in 1987, Blaise Compaoré imposed strict controls over state and emerging private media. In his early years in power, Compaoré limited criticisms through censorship and intimidation of journalists (Freedom House, 2015). However, with international pressure for democratic reforms in the early 1990s, Burkina Faso adopted multi-partyism, leading to relative liberalization with new independent outlets like *l'Observateur Paalga* emerging after its ban during Sankara's regime. 'Paalga' means 'new' in Mooré, the language spoken by the Mossi. Despite this liberalization, repression continued; Norbert Zongo's assassination in 1998 marked a turning point that sparked protests against ongoing repression (Jeune Afrique, 2021). The 2000s were characterized by limited reforms and increased pressure for democratic change, culminating in protests that ultimately led to Compaoré's downfall in 2014 (International Media Support, 2015).

### *Transition Period (2014–15)*

After Blaise Compaoré's resignation in October 2014, Burkina Faso entered a political transition led by Michel Kafando, a former diplomat appointed as transitional president. This period focused on stabilizing the country and reforming institutions, particularly the media, in preparation for democratic elections. Key reforms included measures to enhance the independence and transparency of the Superior Council of Communication (CSC) and the adoption of new laws aimed at improving access to information for journalists. During this time, Burkinabé media experienced increased freedom to criticize the previous regime and engage in open discussions about the country's future. The transition also saw a rise in online media and social networks, providing platforms for citizens to express themselves and share information. Various training programmes were implemented to enhance journalists' skills, supported by international organizations (Betz, 2015). In preparation for the November 2015 elections, Kafando's government collaborated with civil society organizations to ensure balanced media coverage. Overall, this transition period was pivotal for reorganizing and liberalizing Burkina Faso's media sector, laying the groundwork for a freer and more professional press, essential for the country's democratic development.

### *Under Roch Marc Christian Kaboré from 2015 to 2022*

Roch Marc Christian Kaboré assumed office as President of Burkina Faso in December 2015, following the fall of Blaise Compaoré in 2014 and the transition of Michel Kafando (2015). His tenure focused on modernizing institutions, including the media sector, with significant reforms such as enacting new laws on press freedom to protect journalists from arbitrary arrests and establishing a Media Support Fund in 2017 to enhance journalistic quality. The government also supported efforts to integrate new technologies into journalism, leading to the launch of online platforms and an increase in activist blogs and social media channels.

However, despite these advancements, many media outlets struggled financially, and journalists faced ongoing pressures and intimidation, particularly in insecure regions. The second term (2020 to 2022) was tumultuous due to increased terrorist attacks, which justified restrictive measures, including censorship under the pretext of maintaining order. Noteworthy incidents included internet shutdowns in November 2021 and January 2022, officially justified as necessary to prevent misinformation but widely criticized as abuses of power and violations of communication rights.

Regarding surveillance and restrictions, the government intensified monitoring of social networks and digital platforms, using cybersecurity laws to justify restrictions, notably Law No. 059-2015/CNT on combating cybercrime. Bloggers and digital activists were targeted for their online criticisms.

Noteworthy examples of these restrictions included internet shutdowns in November 2021 and January 2022. Officially justified as necessary to prevent misinformation and maintain national security, these shutdowns were widely criticized as abuses of power and violations of citizens' communication rights.

*The digital era (2005–24)*

Several significant events have shaped the country's political and social landscape, such as the Burkinabé Spring in 2011, which refers to a series of protests that erupted in Burkina Faso and were widely organized and coordinated through social media platforms, particularly Facebook and Twitter (Wikipedia, 2023). Another notable example is the 'Balai Citoyen' (Citizen's Broom), a Burkinabé civil society movement that used social media since its inception in 2013 to mobilize citizens, share information and coordinate collective actions (Burkina 24, 2021). The popular uprising of October 2014, which led to the downfall of President Blaise Compaoré, saw widespread organization and coordination of protests via social media, using hashtags such as #BurkinaFaso and #Lwili.

To understand the various political and social developments in Burkina Faso better, it is crucial to focus on the popular uprising of October 2014, which was driven heavily by intense use of social media, notably through the famous hashtag #Lwili.

Initially, the citizen movement #Lwili emerged in response to a tense socio-political context marked by popular protests and social unrest. 'Lwili,' meaning 'bird' in Mooré, became a platform for mobilization and citizen demands, primarily on social media, especially Twitter. The hashtag played a significant role during the October 2014 uprising that ousted President Blaise Compaoré, marking the start of political change in Burkina Faso. Over time, #Lwili evolved into a symbol of the struggle for truth, justice and democracy. The years following 2014 were fraught with political and economic challenges, including tensions between the government and opposition, governance issues and socio-economic difficulties. The #Lwili movement is portrayed as a citizen tool responding to societal problems and injustices, activated mainly via social media. It has been pivotal in triggering large-scale social movements capable of inciting popular uprisings, which explains the government's reactions, such as cutting mobile internet access. Citizen mobilization via social media was notably observed during the 2020 presidential elections and subsequent calls for mobilization in 2021 and 2022.

These events underscore the importance of internet and social media use in citizen mobilizations, providing rapid access to information, facilitating large-scale citizen participation transcending geographical boundaries, and enabling coordination of collective actions. However, it should also be noted that they become prime targets in cases of censorship or repression of information by the authorities.

According to data from ARCEP (Regulatory Authority for Electronic Communications and Postal Services), by the end of 2021, the number of mobile internet subscriptions in Burkina Faso exceeded 13 million or 60 per cent of the population. The mobile internet shutdowns of November 2021 and January 2022, therefore, affected more than 13.4 million users by depriving them of access to the internet from their mobile devices (ARCEP Burkina Faso, 2021 and 2022).

Analysing this media ecosystem in Burkina Faso from the colonial period to the Roch Marc Christian Kaboré mandates reveals a complex dynamic of freedoms and repressions. The internet shutdowns of November 2021 and January

2022 have become synonymous with abuses of power and violations of citizens' rights, highlighting persistent challenges in press freedom, freedom of expression and digital rights in the country. Authorities used national security as a pretext to justify these repressive actions, limiting citizens' ability to access information and express themselves freely.

## *Description of the Burkina Faso case*

The various social movements during the digital era undoubtedly prompted the Burkinabé government in November 2021 to restrict access to mobile internet in anticipation of and in response to protests and social unrest, citing reasons of national security. This action was repeated in January 2022. These internet shutdowns sparked criticism from human rights defenders, the private sector and the international community, highlighting that such actions undermined citizens' freedom of expression, their right to information and the country's economy.

### *First mobile internet shutdown in Burkina Faso (20–28 November 2021)*

Burkina Faso experienced its first-ever internet shutdown lasting nearly nine days from 20 to 28 November 2021, setting a precedent. Citing the law 061-2008 on the general regulation of electronic communications networks and services in Burkina Faso, specifically Chapter IX, Article 44 titled 'Quality and security of networks and services and compliance with national defence and public security obligations', the government suspended mobile internet for approximately nine days, citing reasons of national security (Law 061, 2008).

Locally, the impact was immediate. In response to anti-government protests sparked by escalating jihadist threats in the country and the government's failures to address them, mobile internet data was shut down across Burkina Faso on the morning of 20 November. The government, through a statement from the Ministry of the Interior, announced that mobile internet would be unavailable for ninety-six hours (Lefaso, 2021). This initial shutdown lasted over a week, depriving millions of Burkinabé citizens access to online business services, banking services, health services, e-services, online educational resources and communication with loved ones via the internet.

Internet shutdowns during protests and citizen unrest impact citizens' ability to obtain accurate information from official government sources when they need it most. It also becomes more challenging for citizens to contact family members and friends in other regions of the country or abroad.

### *Second mobile internet shutdown (10–11 January 2022)*

On Monday, 10 January 2022, in the early afternoon, another disruption in mobile internet access occurred. This was the second shutdown of its kind within two months. Only wired internet remained functional. This new interruption occurred shortly after the Economic Community of West African States (ECOWAS) sanctions against Mali and just hours before the arrest of eight Burkinabé soldiers suspected of attempting to destabilize state institutions. ECOWAS imposed sanctions on Mali over the military government's decision to delay elections and extend its transition period. These sanctions included travel bans on members of the transitional government and military leaders, economic sanctions that suspended financial transactions with Mali, and diplomatic measures urging member states to withdraw their ambassadors from the country.

According to various reports after the shutdown, it was initiated following rumours of a coup d'état and armed insurrection. This shutdown, lasting approximately sixteen hours, mirrored the November 2021 event with almost no access to mobile internet via the data networks of the three mobile telecommunications companies in the country, namely Onatel (now Moov Africa Burkina Faso), Orange Burkina Faso and Telecel Faso Mobile; internet traffic was gradually restored overnight on 11 January 2022, stabilizing by 6.00 am.

### *Blocking of social media (10–23 January 2022)*

On 10 January 2022, in conjunction with the ongoing internet shutdown, Burkinabé authorities also ordered restrictions on access to social media, notably Facebook and its Messenger service, as well as the messaging application WhatsApp nationwide. This major blockage lasted more than twelve days, although WhatsApp became accessible after a few days following the decision.

To understand and substantiate this assessment, we rely on data analyses from the OONI platform.

Data from the Open Observatory of Network Interference (OONI) platform, measured between 11 January 2022 and 23 January 2022, suggests that access to Facebook Messenger was severely disrupted in Burkina Faso (OONI, 2022a).

Significant anomalies in data were observed on the country's two main mobile networks. These anomalies, detected over a longer period on the most used network, Orange Burkina Faso, than on Office National des Télécommunications (ONATEL), indicated unavailability of Facebook and Messenger applications between 11 January and 23 January 2022. These anomalies could suggest interference based on DNS, as OONI measurements showed that DNS queries did not resolve to Facebook's IP addresses during testing (OONI Explorer, 2022b).

The period of OONI measurement anomalies on Facebook Messenger (mainly between 11 and 23 January 2022) coincided with media reports that Burkinabé authorities had blocked access to Facebook for security reasons (Africanews, 2022). The authorities in Burkina Faso requested internet service providers to block Facebook Messenger and WhatsApp in January 2022 due to concerns over national security. This decision was justified as a means to prevent the spread of misinformation and maintain public order amid increasing terrorist attacks and political tensions. The government feared that these messaging platforms could be used to organize protests or social movements, which could further destabilize the country. This largely explains why authorities targeted ISPs to impose restrictions

**Table 10.2** Timeline and Impact of Internet and Social Media Shutdowns in Burkina Faso (2021–2)

| No. | Type of shutdown | Impacts | Duration | Dates | Financial cost |
|---|---|---|---|---|---|
| 01 | Internet shutdown | Mobile data shutdown | 9 days | November 20-28, 2021 | USD 1,863,715 |
| 02 | Social media block | Facebook Messenger; WhatsApp | 20 days | 10–22 January 2022 | |
| 03 | Internet shutdown | Mobile data shutdown | 16 hours | 10–11 January 2022 | USD 176,174 |
| 04 | Internet shutdown | Mobile data shutdown | 35 hours | 23–24 January 2022 | USD 359,688 |

Source: authors.

on accessing Facebook Messenger and WhatsApp, affecting approximately 93 per cent of the country's mobile internet users (Data Reportal, 2022).

### *Third mobile internet shutdown (23–24 January 2022)*

On 20 January 2022 violent demonstrations broke out, resulting in more than twenty-one casualties. The increasingly critical situation in Burkina Faso, facing security problems due to jihadist attacks, and the increasingly successful attacks against the country's defence forces ended up exacerbating the population who decided to demonstrate and protest. On 23 January 2022, following rumours of strikes, new civil movements including protest marches and potential security threats including a potential military coup, a third cut-off of mobile internet access and a blocking of the use of social networks were recorded nationwide.

This internet and social media shutdown was associated with an alleged attempt to prevent coordination of demonstrations and potential turmoil related to the tense political situation in the country.

Locally, this new shutdown, occurring twelve days after the previous one, once again prevented millions of citizens from accessing information or contacting their loved ones during the insurrectional turmoil. Likely linked to increasing tensions before the putsch that took place on 24 January 2022, led by Lieutenant Colonel Paul-Henri Sandaogo Damiba and his military forces, who took control of the country.

## *Literature review*

The internet shutdowns that occurred in November 2021 and January 2022 in Burkina Faso have been poorly documented, particularly regarding their implications for digital rights, governance issues, and the socio-economic landscape of the country. These events highlight the growing trend of using internet disruptions as a tool for political control.

### *Citizen resistance and adaptation*

Despite the shutdowns, citizens found ways to resist and adapt. The use of hashtags like #lwili, derived from local languages symbolizing resilience, became a rallying point for advocacy against digital blackouts (Internet Society Pulse, 2021). These hashtags facilitated international attention and solidarity through movements like #KeepItOn, championed by global organizations such as Access Now. Additionally, some citizens utilized circumvention tools like VPNs, although these were not fully effective during complete network outages.

### *Socio-economic and political impacts*

The blackouts disrupted essential services such as online banking, education and health communication. Businesses reliant on digital infrastructure reported significant losses, with estimates of $3.6 million in economic impact during the November 2021 shutdown (Netblocks, 2022). Politically, these actions stifled dissent and limited information flow during critical moments of unrest, raising concerns about human rights and the suppression of free expression. As noted by the Internet Society (2021), internet shutdowns harm economic activity by obstructing e-commerce and creating financial risks for businesses.

Alexi Sawadogo (Sawadogo, 2018), a doctor, spoke about feeling helpless in front of a bank:

> This disconnects us from our friends abroad, with whom we regularly communicate. Forced to visit a bank branch to check my account and ongoing operations, I understand the government's decision to cut off internet for security reasons, but it remains a valid reason that could explain why they shut down the internet, inviting the government to reconsider this strategy.

### *Global and regional implications*

Burkina Faso's internet disruptions reflect a broader trend in Africa where governments resort to shutdowns as a means of maintaining control over information and suppressing dissent. Advocacy groups and the international community have criticized these actions, emphasizing the need for robust discussions on internet governance, digital rights, and accountability in the face of state-enforced blackouts.

### *Power dynamics*

The analysis of these shutdowns can be framed through the concept of affordances, which highlights that the internet serves as an enabler for socio-economic and political rights; therefore, shutting it down restricts the realization of those rights.

Drabo Mahamadou, National Executive Secretary of the 'Save Burkina Faso Movement', noted that the government's insensitivity to public pain led to calls for protests, indicating widespread discontent with how authorities manage security and communication (VOA News, 2021).

The Burkinabé authorities demonstrated their grip on businesses by leveraging control over internet access as an expression of authority over both the private sector and the populace. This power dynamic mirrors situations in neighbouring countries like Benin, where compliance from private operators often stems from regulatory obligations and fear of government reprisals.

Ali Dayorgo, a university student, stated that the shutdown affected his ability to work and stay informed about current events (VOA News, 2021).

### *Human rights violations*

Reports during the shutdowns indicated an escalation of state actions against protests, including arbitrary arrests of demonstrators. This raises concerns about how internet restrictions serve not only as tools for information control but also as catalysts for broader human rights violations.

Serge BAMBARA 'Smockey', spokesperson for the citizen movement 'Balai Citoyen', criticized these measures as an 'authoritarian drift' (Burkina 24, 2021).

In conclusion, the mobile internet shutdowns in Burkina Faso illustrate significant challenges related to governance, human rights and economic stability. They highlight how state control over digital infrastructure can suppress dissent while also impacting citizens' socio-economic rights. The responses from civil society indicate a pressing need for advocacy around digital freedoms and accountability from government authorities.

## *Methodology*

This chapter is based on the implementation and application of documentary research on official statements, relevant policies and reports. A content analysis of social media, press articles and other online sources will be conducted.

A survey conducted with the assistance of the Burkina Faso chapter of the Internet Society allowed for the collection of testimonies from eight people from various backgrounds affected by the different internet shutdowns of November 2021 and January 2022, providing primary data that will be analysed.

## *Findings*

This investigation conducted in the writing of this chapter highlights several other testimonies from citizens from different categories who believe that the shutdowns have had negative consequences on their professional and social activities. To conduct this study on the three mobile internet shutdowns that occurred between 2021 and 2022 in Burkina Faso, several qualitative research methods were employed. I conducted a series of semi-structured interviews with members of the local chapter of the Internet Society. Additionally, a questionnaire was administered via an online form, gathering responses from citizens about the impacts of the mobile internet shutdowns. Among the eight respondents, I selected four individuals whose feedback was particularly relevant, reflecting notable professional diversity.

The choice of interviewees was motivated by their varied professional backgrounds, ensuring a rich and diverse representation of the impacts. The limited number of four participants was chosen to allow for a deeper qualitative analysis of their testimonies.

To ensure informed consent, all participants were informed about the study's objectives and the potential uses of their responses prior to participation, via a dedicated section of the form. Regarding the anonymity policy, each participant had the option to provide anonymous feedback or consent to the use of their first names only. This procedure was validated by the explicit acceptance of the terms of use at the beginning of the questionnaire.

Adama, a telecom expert and leader of a civil society organization responsible for internet issues, recounts:

> It was difficult for me to stay informed and carry out my professional activities. I struggled to reach my usual revenue figures, and the various actions we took with the organization I lead were in vain to restore internet access.

This testimony collected from a leader of a local civil society organization and professional in the telecommunications field describes the challenges faced during an internet shutdown in Burkina Faso, a situation that had significant impacts on professional and organizational activities. It underscores the importance of access to information for his daily work. Without internet, it is difficult for him to stay informed and accomplish his professional tasks. This is a violation of the right to work which is guaranteed on (ICESCR, 1976). The internet shutdown had a direct impact on his income, indicating that his work depends heavily on connectivity to achieve financial goals. Despite the actions taken by the Internet Society chapter he leads, they did not succeed in restoring internet access, highlighting institutional and technical challenges in managing their mission.

This testimony highlights the dependence of professionals in various sectors, especially telecommunications, on the internet. It shows that service interruptions can have serious economic and operational consequences. The organization's inability to restore the internet despite their efforts reveals the limits of their power and resources in the face of a national or regional shutdown. This imbalance underscores the pervasive influence of political state power, which often prioritizes its interests over those of workers and citizens. By leveraging internet shutdowns as a tool for control, governments assert their authority, frequently citing security or political stability as justification. However, such measures disproportionately affect the livelihoods of professionals and the broader public, who rely on stable internet access for economic productivity, education and civic engagement. This dynamic highlights a troubling disparity, where the state's pursuit of dominance undermines the agency and well-being of its constituents. It may also indicate structural issues within the country's telecommunications infrastructure, such as the lack of decentralization, inadequate investment in modern and redundant systems, or the heavy reliance on a single service provider. These vulnerabilities make the network more susceptible to disruptions and amplify the impact of intentional shutdowns. This testimony prompts reflection on the resilience measures that organizations and individuals must put in place to cope with such interruptions in the future, including diversifying access points and advocating for infrastructure reforms.

For Moussa, a Burkinabé entrepreneur who manages an online trading business:

> The mobile internet shutdowns were a real nightmare for my business. During these times, I couldn't process my clients' orders or communicate with them. This led to delivery delays and a lot of dissatisfaction. My turnover dropped by nearly 40 per cent during the weeks when the internet was cut off. I even had to lay off two seasonal employees, unable to pay their salaries. These shutdowns were extremely detrimental to me and many other economic operators who depend on the internet to conduct their activities. We feel like the authorities are playing with our tool of work, without caring about the consequences on our businesses and livelihoods. This is an unacceptable situation that seriously harms the country's economy.

The entrepreneur describes the internet shutdowns as a 'real nightmare', highlighting the extent of disruptions to his daily business activities. The shutdowns prevented order processing and client communication, resulting in delivery delays and dissatisfied clients, and a nearly 40 per cent drop in turnover during the shutdown weeks, demonstrating a direct and significant financial impact. The entrepreneur had to lay off two seasonal employees, showing the impact on employment. The entrepreneur criticizes the authorities for their lack of consideration for the economic consequences of internet shutdowns, accusing them of playing with the work tool of economic operators.

This testimony underscores the critical dependence of online trading businesses on the internet for their operations. Internet shutdowns directly affect these businesses' ability to function effectively. The drop in turnover and reduction in staff illustrate the negative effects of shutdowns on the local economy and employee well-being. This reflects a loss of customer confidence and a disruption in revenue streams. The testimony raises questions about how authorities manage telecommunications infrastructure and understand the needs of modern businesses. The perception of a lack of consideration for economic operators is a structural issue that needs to be addressed. The situation described seriously harms the country's economy, affecting not only individual businesses but also employees and customers. Shutdowns create an unstable and unpredictable economic environment. Economic rights encompass the ability of individuals and businesses to freely pursue economic activities without undue interference, ensuring access to resources and opportunities for livelihood. These rights are undermined when actions like internet shutdowns disrupt commerce, leading to financial losses, unemployment, and harm to the broader economy.

Zakaria, a journalist based in Ouahigouya in the northern region of Burkina Faso, testifies:

> It was difficult for me to stay informed and access information. While the direct impact on my work as a journalist was less pronounced despite the shutdowns, the inability to access online information sources was impossible, especially in the northern regions already suffering from unstable internet access.

The journalist highlights the challenges faced in staying informed and accessing online information, crucial for his work. While the direct impact on his work was less pronounced despite the shutdowns, he emphasizes the impossibility of accessing online information sources, limiting the depth and diversity of information he can obtain. He also notes that these difficulties are particularly severe in a region of the country already facing problems with stable internet access.

This testimony highlights the importance of the internet for the media in general and journalists in particular, not only for communication but also for access to information sources. The absence of internet limits their ability to conduct thorough research and verify information. The impact of shutdowns is thus amplified by regional conditions. In northern Burkina Faso, internet infrastructure is already inadequate, and any service interruption further exacerbates the situation. This testimony raises questions about the equity of access to information and digital infrastructure. Remote and less developed regions suffer more, creating a disadvantage for professionals working there.

Through these testimonies and reactions from citizens, several elements emerge related to research questions:

What power interests motivated the internet shutdowns in 2021 and how do they affect the rights of Burkinabé citizens? Power interests: authorities likely sought to limit the spread of critical information and restrict the organization of protests, which could undermine their power. Internet shutdowns were also used to prevent communication between opposition groups and human rights activists. With testimonies from the telecom engineer: 'We feel like the authorities are playing with our work tool' and the journalist: 'Access to online information sources was impossible', this reflects a strategy by the authorities to suppress dissent by disrupting communication means and also preventing journalists from disseminating independent and critical information.

What are the socio-political and economic consequences of the shutdowns for Burkinabé citizens? In terms of socio-political consequences, internet shutdowns limited citizens' ability to express themselves freely and organize peaceful demonstrations. They also made it nearly impossible for media outlets to access reliable information, affecting transparency and accountability. In economic terms, the shutdowns resulted in financial losses for businesses dependent on the internet, as illustrated by the testimony of the online trading entrepreneur. Businesses had to reduce their staff due to revenue losses caused by the shutdowns.

This can be explained by the testimonies of Moussa, the online trading entrepreneur: 'My turnover dropped by nearly 40 per cent … I even had to stop two seasonal employees,' and Adama, the telecom engineer: 'I struggled to reach my usual revenue figures.' This demonstrates the direct economic impact of the shutdowns on businesses and employment.

What are the broader implications in terms of digital rights, freedom of expression and democratic governance? Internet shutdowns undermine citizens' digital rights, including the rights to information and online communication. By restricting internet access, authorities violated the rights to freedom of expression and information, as stipulated in the UDHR and ICCPR. Internet shutdowns reveal an authoritarian trend, where authorities use technological means to control and suppress the population, thus undermining democratic governance.

## *Analysis*

### *Power interests and the internet shutdowns of 2021 and 2022*

During the shutdown from 20 to 28 November 2021, Burkina Faso's Minister of Communication and government spokesperson, Ousséni Tamboura, issued a statement on the suspension of mobile internet for ninety-six hours (Lefaso, 2021). No official communication was recorded regarding the 10 January 2022 shutdown from the authorities. However, when questioned on 11 January 2022, Maxime Koné, Minister in Charge of Security, responded as follows: 'We have no comment to make', according to private television BF1.

The Burkinabé government defended the mobile internet shutdowns of November 2021 and January 2022 by invoking national security concerns. These interruptions were primarily justified by the need to maintain public order, which the government claimed was necessary to prevent the spread of misinformation and calm social tensions. The shutdowns were also seen as a strategy to combat insurrections amid growing instability and protests against the government's inability to manage insecurity related to terrorist attacks. The shutdowns were perceived as a means to limit the coordination of protests via social media and to protect digital sovereignty: the authorities presented these shutdowns as tools to protect Burkina Faso from foreign influences or coordinated digital attacks.

As a result, the shutdown maintained the unavailability of mobile internet access for millions of citizens, affecting online businesses, banking services, healthcare and education.

However, a deeper analysis reveals that these shutdowns often serve to protect the political and partisan interests of the ruling elites. As in several other cases of internet shutdowns on the African continent, the Burkinabé government used these shutdowns to exercise narrative control and prevent citizens from accessing alternative or critical information about the regime. This includes restricting digital platforms where activists and journalists express their opinions. The shutdowns coincided with popular movements denouncing the government's management shortcomings, particularly in terms of security, revealing cases of repression of dissent. These interruptions aimed to disrupt protests and reduce citizens' ability to mobilize. These decisions are often made without public consultation or transparent legal advice, reflecting a power imbalance between the state and civil society.

The internet shutdowns had significant social and economic impacts, depriving citizens of crucial information about security and current events, which exacerbated collective anxiety. They also disrupted essential services such as healthcare, education, and digital commercial transactions, leading to considerable economic losses. Moreover, these interruptions violated digital rights, limiting freedom of expression, press freedom and the right to access information, all protected by regional instruments such as the African Charter on Human and Peoples' Rights.

### *The 2021 and 2022 internet shutdowns as an expression of power*

In November 2021 and January 2022, the internet shutdowns in Burkina Faso sparked strong reactions from civil society organizations and opposition political parties. These groups vehemently opposed the shutdowns, denouncing them as violations of fundamental freedoms and democracy, and as illegal acts by the government.

On the French television channel TV5 Monde, opposition leader Eddie Komboïgo stated:

> The government is scared and decides to cut off the internet to prevent civil society from protesting against its security policy. The government should have the courage to talk to civil society, which is asking to protest. It can supervise the protests rather than prevent them through illegal measures.

According to Komboïgo, the internet shutdown was the government's response to the fear of planned protests against its security policy, describing this measure as an infringement on individual freedoms.

Civil society organizations, such as the Burkina Faso chapter of the Internet Society and the 'Balai Citoyen' movement (Le Balai Citoyen, 2021), also expressed their outrage, calling on the government to immediately restore internet access and respect citizens' digital rights. These actions reflect widespread dissatisfaction with the government's authoritarian management and highlight the importance of freedom of expression in a context of political and security crisis. Several testimonies found in the media attest to the shock and strong disapproval of active citizens regarding these decisions. Legally, protests have arisen.

The National Human Rights Commission (CNDH) also expressed its concern, emphasizing that this suspension constitutes a violation of the rights to freedom of expression and information, which are essential in a democratic society (CNDH, 2021). The CNDH reiterated that access to the internet is a fundamental human right and called on the government to immediately restore mobile internet access to ensure citizens' communication and information.

However, it is important to recognize that these major protests from Burkinabé public opinion did not change the government's decision to restore the internet.

Lefaso (2022b) defines in an analysis by two academics, Dembélé S. Bertille and Tankoano Gnoari, doctoral students at Thomas Sankara University, the legal framework in Burkina Faso that obliges ISPs to comply with government directives, particularly regarding internet shutdowns, under the pretext of national security. This obligation is enshrined in Law No. 061-2008/AN and the ISPs' license agreements. Non-compliance with these directives can result in sanctions for companies, creating a dilemma between legal compliance and the protection of human rights. The shutdowns raise concerns about freedom of expression and the right to information, highlighting the need for a balance between public security and fundamental rights.

## *Affordances, citizen resistance and agency*

The November 2021 and January 2022 mobile internet shutdowns in Burkina Faso marked a pivotal moment in the intersection of technology, governance and civic activism. Through the lens of affordances, citizen resistance and agency, this analysis explores the implications of these disruptions, with a particular focus on the role of the hashtag #lwili as a tool of collective expression and mobilization.

### *Affordances*

The potential and limits of digital connectivity. The concept of affordances examines how technology provides opportunities and imposes constraints on action. In Burkina Faso, the internet is a critical enabler of socio-political and economic activities. Platforms like Facebook, Twitter and WhatsApp serve as key spaces for communication, coordination and information sharing, particularly during periods of civil unrest. The hashtag #lwili, rooted in local culture as a symbol of resilience and unity, emerged as a unifying digital marker during these crises. Citizens leveraged it to highlight abuses, amplify dissent and coordinate movements.

However, the government's deliberate shutdowns disrupted these affordances, curtailing the flow of real-time information and halting the digital economy. E-learning platforms, telemedicine services and internet-based businesses faced significant setbacks. The shutdowns underscored the duality of technological affordances: while they empower citizens, they are also vulnerable to state control, revealing the precarious balance between freedom and regulation in the digital space.

### *Citizen resistance*

Mobilization in the Face of Digital Suppression. Despite the state's efforts to suppress dissent through internet shutdowns, Burkinabé citizens exhibited remarkable adaptability and resistance. The hashtag #lwili became a rallying cry, transcending its digital origins to symbolize collective defiance. On social media, even with limited access, activists documented the impacts of the shutdowns, creating a digital archive of state overreach that resonated both locally and internationally.

In physical spaces, protests continued unabated, with the symbolism of #lwili carried on banners and spoken in chants. Citizens turned to alternative tools like SMS and offline networks to maintain coordination. Virtual Private Networks (VPNs) gained traction among tech-savvy users, allowing them to bypass restrictions and continue engaging online. This resistance highlights the resilience of civic actors in navigating and challenging technological suppression.

### *Agency*

Reclaiming Power in a Constrained Environment. The notion of agency refers to the capacity of individuals and groups to act independently, even under oppressive conditions. The Burkinabé experience during the internet shutdowns demonstrates a profound assertion of agency. Through #lwili, citizens redefined the narrative of the shutdowns, shifting the discourse from government-justified 'national security' to a broader critique of authoritarian overreach and digital rights violations.

Civil society organizations, legal advocates and international human rights bodies amplified these efforts, framing the shutdowns as breaches of fundamental freedoms. The agency of Burkinabé citizens extended beyond resistance to envisioning a digital future where access and rights are safeguarded. This was reflected in calls for transparency in governance and for the establishment of mechanisms to prevent similar abuses.

## *Conclusion*

The mobile internet shutdowns in Burkina Faso in 2021 and 2022 represent a multifaceted issue, intersecting security imperatives, political motivations and socio-economic implications. Analysing these events through the lenses of technological affordances, rights and power dynamics, and socio-political governance reveals critical challenges and areas for improvement.

These shutdowns highlighted the vulnerability of technological infrastructure to centralized and opaque decision-making processes. They also deepened inequalities in access to information, suppressed fundamental rights such as freedom of expression, and caused severe disruptions to economic and social activities. Businesses, citizens and public services bore the brunt of these disruptions, exposing the need for more transparent and inclusive policies.

### *Technological resilience*

Invest in robust and alternative digital infrastructures capable of mitigating the effects of future shutdowns. This effort should include public awareness campaigns to educate businesses and citizens about digital tools that enhance connectivity during disruptions.

*Legal and institutional frameworks*

Establish clear legal provisions to strictly regulate internet shutdowns, ensuring they are subject to judicial oversight and adhere to international standards of legality, necessity, and proportionality. Citizens should be empowered to understand and defend their digital rights.

*Governance and stakeholder involvement*

Foster transparency in decision-making processes and include key stakeholders – citizens, civil society, and private sector entities – in discussions about internet governance. Regional coordination with neighbours and bodies like ECOWAS can strengthen collective responses to digital rights challenges.

The internet shutdowns in Burkina Faso serve as a stark example of the tension between national security priorities and digital rights in fragile contexts. The lessons from these events underscore the importance of preserving the internet as a tool for development, inclusion and resilience rather than a mechanism for control and exclusion.

This chapter concludes with a call for unified actions to ensure that internet governance aligns with democratic principles and the needs of all stakeholders. By adopting these recommendations, Burkina Faso can set a precedent for balanced digital governance that respects fundamental rights while addressing national challenges.

The mobile internet shutdowns in Burkina Faso in November 2021 and January 2022 have revealed profound and varied implications for human rights, education, the economy and cultural participation. Analysing the violations of human rights, particularly in relation to the Universal Declaration of Human Rights (UDHR), the International Covenant on Civil and Political Rights (ICCPR), the International Covenant on Economic, Social and Cultural Rights (ICESCR), and the African Charter on Human and Peoples' Rights, highlights crucial issues of governance, transparency and accountability.

These shutdowns hindered freedom of expression, compromised access to education and essential services, and disrupted cultural participation, exacerbating social and economic inequalities. The actions of the Burkinabé government, justified on the grounds of national security, were deemed disproportionate and unnecessary by numerous human rights organizations, underscoring a lack of transparency and judicial oversight. It is therefore essential to have perspectives to prevent such unfortunate events from happening again in the future and to ensure that citizens can fully enjoy the internet without restrictions.

## Bibliography

Africanews. (2022, 20 January), Facebook Shut in Burkina Faso Due to Security Reasons. Africanews, https://www.africanews.com/2022/01/20/facebook-shut-in-burkina-faso-due-to-security-reasons/

Agence Ecofin (2023), 'Cinq pays d'Afrique ont perdu environ 225 millions $ depuis 2022 suite à diverses restrictions d'accès à Internet', *Agence Ecofin*, https://www.agenceecofin.com/internet/1701-104558-cinq-pays-d-afrique-ont-perdu-environ-225-millions-depuis-2022-suite-a-diverses-restrictions-d-acces-a-internet

Amnesty International (2021a), 'Burkina Faso: Authorities Must Respect Human Rights in Response to Protests', *Amnesty International.*

Amnesty International (2021b), 'Report of Burkina Faso', *Amnesty International*, https://www.amnesty.org/en/location/africa/west-and-central-africa/burkina-faso/

ARCEP Burkina Faso (2022a), 'Internet Market Reports'. *ARCEP Burkina Faso*, https://www.arcep.bf/le-marche-de-linternet

ARCEP Burkina Faso (2022b), 'Observatoire de l'internet 1er trimestre 2022', *ARCEP Burkina Faso*, https://www.arcep.bf/download/1e-trimestre-2022-observatoire-internet/?wpdmdl=38611&refresh=6631c4294cd131714537513

Bado, F. de S. (2011), 'Vers un printemps burkinabé ?'. *Revue Projet*, https://www.revue-projet.com/articles/vers-un-printemps-burkinabe/7627

Bassolet, F. (1968), *Evolution of Upper Volta, from 1898 to January 3, 1966*. Ouagadougou: Imprimerie Nationale de la Haute-Volta.

Bassolet, F. D. (2014), 'Évolution de la Haute-Volta, de 1898 au 3 janvier 1966'. *Cambridge African Studies Review*, https://www.cambridge.org/core/journals/african-studies-review/

BBC (2022), 'Tentative présumée de coup d'État au Burkina Faso: voici ce que nous savons', *BBC Afrique*, https://www.bbc.com/afrique/region-59964990

Betz, M. (2015), 'De la crise à la transition: les médias au Burkina Faso', International Media Support (IMS), https://www.mediasupport.org/wp-content/uploads/2015/02/publication_BurkinaFaso-ENG-jan2015-final.pdf

Burkina 24 (2021), 'Coupure de l'internet mobile au Burkina Faso: Une perte de plus de 20 milliards de FCFA', *Burkina 24*, https://burkina24.com/2021/11/25/coupure-de-linternet-mobile-au-burkina-une-perte-de-plus-de-20-milliards-de-fcfa/

Burkina 24 (2022), 'Restrictions des libertés: le balai citoyen prévoit un meeting le 19 février', *Burkina 24*, https://burkina24.com/2022/01/21/restrictions-des-libertes-le-balai-citoyen-prevoit-un-meeting-le-19-fevrier-2022/

Cloudflare (2022), 'Internet Disruptions Overview for Q1 2022', *Cloudflare Blog*, https://blog.cloudflare.com/q1-2022-internet-disruption-summary/

Commission Nationale des Droits Humains Burkina Faso (2021), 'Suspension d'internet mobile: la CNDH interpelle le gouvernement sur les violations des libertés d'expression et de l'accès à l'information', *CNDH Burkina Faso*, https://cndhburkina.bf/suspension-dinternet-mobile-la-cndh-interpelle-le-gouvernement-sur-les-violations-des-libertes-dexpression-et-a-linformationession-et-a-linformation/

Constitution du Burkina Faso (2019), 'Articles relatifs à la liberté d'expression et de presse', *ACCF*, https://cdn.accf-francophonie.org/2019/03/burkina-constitution-v2013.pdf

Data Reportal (2021), 'Digital 2021: Burkina Faso', *Data Reportal*, https://datareportal.com/reports/digital-2021-burkina-faso

Data Reportal (2022), 'Digital 2022: Burkina Faso', *Data Reportal*, https://datareportal.com/reports/digital-2022-burkina-faso

Dresch, J. (2017), 'Publications of the French Institute of Black Africa', *Cambridge Journals*, https://www.cambridge.org/core/journals/annales-histoire-sciences-sociales/article/abs/les-publications-de-linstitut-francais-dafrique-noire

Évolution du Burkina Faso (2020), '60 ans après l'indépendance', *Autre Terre*, https://www.autreterre.org/atm-bf-60-ans-apres-lindependance/

Faso 7 (2022), 'Burkina Faso: Le Balai Citoyen tient un meeting le 19 février 2022'. *Faso 7*, https://faso7.com/2022/01/21/burkina-faso-le-balai-citoyen-tient-un-meeting-le-19-fevrier-2022/

Fofana, H. (2023), 'La presse au service de la Révolution au Burkina Faso (1980-1987)'.

Freedom House (2015). 'Freedom of the Press 2015: Harsh Laws and Violence Drive Global Decline', Freedom House, https://web.archive.org/web/20160321170437/https:/freedomhouse.org/report/freedom-press/freedom-press-2015 and https://freedomhouse.org/sites/default/files/2020-02/FOTP_2015_Full_Report

Frère, M-S. (2020), 'Journalismes d'Afrique', De Boeck Supérieur, https://shs.cairn.info/journalismes-d-afrique--9782807331495?lang=fr

GSI (2014), 'The Lwili Revolution: Burkina Faso and Beyond', *GSI Articles*, https://gsi.s-rminform.com/articles/the-lwili-revolution-burkina-faso-and-beyond

Harsch, E. (2017), 'Burkina Faso: A History of Power, Protest, and Revolution', *Bloomsbury Publishing*, https://www.bloomsbury.com/uk/burkina-faso-9781786991379

Historique de la RTB (2020), 'Archives et documents sur l'évolution de la radiotélévision nationale'.

Human Rights Watch (2021a), 'Burkina Faso: Government Restricts Internet Amid Protests', *Human Rights Watch*, https://www.hrw.org/fr/world-report/2022/country-chapters/burkina-faso

Human Rights Watch (2021b), 'Sahel: Visite de la Haute-Commissaire de l'ONU aux droits de l'homme au Burkina Faso et au Niger', *Human Rights Watch*, https://www.hrw.org/fr/news/2021/12/01/sahel-visite-de-la-haute-commissaire-de-lonu-aux-droits-de-lhomme-au-burkina-faso

International Media Support (2015), 'From Crisis to Transition: Media in Burkina Faso', *IMS Publications*, https://www.mediasupport.org/publication/crisis-transition-media-burkina-faso/

Internet Society Pulse (2021), 'No Mobile Data in Burkina Faso', *Internet Society*, https://pulse.internetsociety.org/shutdowns/no-mobile-data-in-burkina-faso

United Nations. (1976), *International Covenant on Economic, Social and Cultural Rights (ICESCR)*, adopted by the United Nations General Assembly on 16 December 1966, and entered into force on 3 January1976, https://www.ohchr.org/en/instruments-mechanisms/instruments/international-covenant-economic-social-and-cultural-rights

Jeune Afrique (2021), 'Ce jour-là: le 13 décembre 1998, Norbert Zongo est assassiné au Burkina', *Jeune Afrique*, https://www.jeuneafrique.com/380728/politique/jour-13-decembre-1998-journaliste-burkinabe-norbert-zongo-etait-assassine/

Ki-Zerbo, J. (1972), *Histoire de l'Afrique noire: D'hier à demain*, Paris: Hatier.

Lassané, Y. (2021), Les précurseurs de la presse écrite voltaïque (1947–1974),https://oap.unige.ch/journals/rhca

Law No. 061-2008/AN of November 27, 2008, on the General Regulation of Electronic Communication Networks and Services in Burkina Faso.

Le Balai Citoyen (2021), 'Si cette coupure de l'internet est volontaire, c'est inacceptable', *Burkina 24*, https://burkina24.com/2021/11/22/le-balai-citoyen-sil-savere-que-cette-coupure-de-linternet-est-volontaire-et-concertee/

Lefaso (2021), 'Internet au Burkina: le Gouvernement admet officiellement avoir fait suspendre la connexion sur mobile', *Lefaso.net*, https://lefaso.net/spip.php?article109253

Lefaso (2022a), 'Coupure internet mobile au Burkina: Le gouvernement annonce la fin ce dimanche 28 novembre 2021 à 20h', *Lefaso.net*, https://lefaso.net/spip.php?article109410

Lefaso (2022b), 'Internet et droit: Retour sur les coupures emblématiques de l'accès à internet au Burkina Faso', *Lefaso.net*, https://lefaso.net/spip.php?article111879

Mbembe, A. (2013), 'Critique de la raison nègre', Paris: La Découverte, ISBN: 978-2-7071-7747-6.

Media Foundation for West Africa (2019), 'Media et Gouvernance Participative au Burkina Faso', *MFWA Publications*, https://www.mfwa.org/wp-content/uploads/2019/09/French-Bulletin-de-Politique-Media-et-Gouvernance-Participative-au-Bukina-Faso-1.pdf

Netafrique (2017), '3 janvier 1966: un soulèvement emportait le régime de Maurice Yaméogo', *Netafrique.net*, https://netafrique.net/3-janvier-1966-un-soulvement-emportait-le-regime-de-maurice-yameogo

Netblocks (2022), 'Internet Disruptions Observed in Burkina Faso Amid Coup Plot Arrests', *Netblocks Reports*, https://netblocks.org/reports/internet-disruptions-observed-in-burkina-faso-amid-coup-plot-arrests-1yPjl3AQ

Netloss Calculator (2022), 'Internet Disruption in Burkina Faso', *Internet Society Pulse*, https://pulse.internetsociety.org/fr/netloss/?country_code=BF

OONI Explorer (2022a), 'Facebook Messenger Is Likely Blocked | DNS Lookups Failed', https://explorer.ooni.org/m/20220111135735.605673_BF_facebookmessenger_1917aab9662116c6

OONI Explorer (2022b), 'OONI Measurement Anomalies on Facebook Messenger', https://explorer.ooni.org/search?since=2022-01-01&until=2022-01-25&failure=false&probe_cc=BF&test_name=facebook_messenger&only=anomal

Organization of African Unity (1981), 'The African Charter on Human and Peoples' Rights', *African Union*, https://au.int/sites/default/files/treaties/36390-treaty-0011_-_african_charter_on_human_and_peoples_rights_e.pdf

Reporters Without Borders (2021), 'Press Freedom in Burkina Faso', *RSF*, https://rsf.org/en/country/burkina-faso

Reuters (2021), 'Burkina Faso Government Extends Internet Suspension Amid Protests', https://www.reuters.com/world/africa/burkina-faso-government-extends-internet-suspension-amid-protests-2021-11-24

Sawadogo, A. (2018), 'Les stratégies de sortie de crises politiques au Burkina Faso', *Thèses HAL*, https://theses.hal.science/tel-02064752

United Nations Human Rights (1966a), 'International Covenant on Civil and Political Rights', *OHCHR*, https://www.ohchr.org/en/instruments-mechanisms/instruments/international-covenant-civil-and-political-rights

United Nations Human Rights (1966b), 'International Covenant on Economic, Social, and Cultural Rights (ICESCR)', *OHCHR*, https://www.ohchr.org/en/instruments-mechanisms/instruments/international-covenant-economic-social-and-cultural-rights

UNIVERSALIS (2011), 'Évolution politique du Burkina Faso depuis l'indépendance', *Universalis Encyclopedie*, https://www.universalis.fr/encyclopedie/burkina-faso/3-evolution-politique-depuis-l-independance

Voice of America (2022), 'Burkina Faso Internet Shutdowns: The Impact on Journalism and Freedom of Expression', https://www.voaafrica.com/a/burkina-faso-internet-shutdowns-the-impact-on-journalism-and-freedom-of-expression/6498121.html

Wikipedia contributors (2023), *2011 Burkina Faso protests*, Wikipedia, https://en.wikipedia.org/wiki/2011_Burkina_Faso_protests

World Bank (2021), 'Digital Development in West Africa: A Status Report', *World Bank Publications*, https://www.worldbank.org/en/news/feature/2021/09/02/digital-development-in-west-africa

World Wide Web Foundation (2021), 'Access Denied: The State of Internet Censorship in Africa', *Web Foundation*, https://webfoundation.org/2021/12/access-denied-state-of-internet-censorship-africa

World Wide Web Foundation (2022), 'The Effects of Internet Shutdowns on Democratic Processes', *Web Foundation*, https://webfoundation.org/2022/04/effects-internet-shutdowns-democracy

Xinhua News Agency (2021), 'Burkina Faso Government Extends Internet Shutdowns Amid Security Concerns', *Xinhua News Agency*, https://www.xinhuanet.com/english/2021-11/25/c_1310343654.htm

Young, J. (2022), 'Impact of Internet Shutdowns on Burkina Faso's Economy and Society', *The Africa Report*, https://www.theafricareport.com/104857/impact-of-internet-shutdowns-on-burkina-fasos-economy-and-society

# Chapter 11

## Algeria's internet shutdowns and school exams

Kassem Mnejja

### *Introduction*

The Algerian government claims to be advancing digital transformation; however, it has implemented week-long internet shutdowns for eight consecutive years, causing significant disruptions to social, economic and political life and infringing on fundamental human rights. This chapter critically examines the motivations behind these shutdowns, their multifaceted impacts, and provides recommendations to eliminate such practices and uphold digital rights in Algeria.

Algeria is distinctive in the region for its use of internet shutdowns, primarily – and almost exclusively – intended to prevent cheating during national examinations. This practice was instituted in 2016 following the online leak of baccalaureate exam questions, which led to the cancellation of the exams, which had to be retaken (Al Jazeera, 2016). This chapter delves into Algeria's unique reliance on internet shutdowns and broader restrictions in the online sphere. It explores the consequences of these shutdowns and seeks to address the following research question: 'How do internet shutdowns during exams affect individual rights, economic stability and broader societal dynamics in Algeria?'

The chapter employs a conceptual framework that integrates theories of media dynamics, power structures and digital rights, situating the discussion within Algeria's historical trajectory of media control, shaped by colonial legacies and post-independence governance. A human rights-based approach further underpins the analysis, comparing firsthand accounts from interviews with documented violations of rights, including those to work, education, healthcare, political association and freedom of expression, and their relationship to digital rights.

The chapter is structured as follows: the next section provides a historical overview of media control in Algeria, offering a foundation for understanding the contemporary drivers of internet shutdowns. The third section presents a detailed account of internet shutdowns in Algeria, outlining their dates, durations, types, scale and scope. The fourth section reviews the existing body of literature, synthesizing key studies and reports to contextualize the issue. The fifth section outlines the research methodology and analyses the consequences of internet shutdowns during exams through the dual lenses of power and human rights. Finally, the last section offers conclusions and actionable recommendations for addressing internet shutdowns and safeguarding digital rights in Algeria.

## *Media dynamics and historical legacies: understanding Algeria's internet shutdowns*

To understand the persistent use of internet shutdowns in Algeria, it is essential to analyse the country's political history, characterized by over a century of media censorship and authoritarian control. This legacy encompasses media repression during both colonial and post-colonial periods, extending into the digital age. This analysis focuses on key political epochs and their corresponding media controls: colonization (1830–1962), independence (1962–91), the civil war (1991–2002), and the digital era (2002–present). Each period is examined to uncover the characteristics of media regulation and the underlying power dynamics, shedding light on how historical precedents continue to shape Algeria's approach to media governance and its reliance on internet shutdowns.

### *The colonial era (1830–1962)*

During French colonization, Algeria's media landscape was heavily manipulated to support imperial objectives and suppress dissent. Media outlets were tightly controlled to maintain the colonial regime's grip on public opinion and stifle nationalist movements. Early colonial newspapers, such as *L'Estafette d'Alger* and *Le Moniteur Algérien*, functioned as propaganda tools, promoting imperial ideologies while marginalizing Algerian voices (Layadi, 2021). Scholars argue that the colonial regime used media to legitimize its rule, systematically denying Algerians the right to independent journalism and expression. Benammar (2021) observes that 'the press as a traditional media tool was also made part of the political events in Algeria since its emergence with the outset of French colonization in 1830'. This colonial precedent of media control set the stage for practices in independent Algeria, undermining the population's ability to organize and resist oppression.

### *The post-independence era (1962–91)*

Following independence, Algeria's media system remained under strict state control, mirroring colonial-era practices. The National Liberation Front (FLN) monopolized the media to consolidate power, using it as a tool for state propaganda. The 1982 Information Law institutionalized these controls, mandating a 'unity of perception and socialist thought' across media organizations (Layadi, 2021). Layadi argues that media managers effectively became state agents, ensuring that content aligned with FLN ideology through directives issued by the Ministry of Information and Culture.

The newly established government transformed the French Radio and Television Company into the national Radio and Television Company, launching fifty local radio stations and three national channels in Arabic, Tamazight and French, to educate a largely illiterate population with an 85 per cent illiteracy rate at the time (Layadi, 2021). However, the state maintained a monopoly over media and information, which took effect shortly after independence on 10 July 1962. This included banning certain publications, like *El Hourriya*, associated with the Algerian Communist Party, under the aim of preserving revolutionary unity. Subsequent nationalizations of newspapers such as *Oran Républicain* and *L'Écho d'Oran* further solidified state control over media, turning it into a vehicle for political propaganda (Scagnetti, 2012). This centralized media model mirrored colonial practices, reinforcing the role of media as a mechanism for political domination and restricting the rights of journalists and the public to access diverse viewpoints.

### *The civil war era (1991–2002)*

The Algerian Civil War marked a pivotal period for media freedom, characterized by intensified state repression and pervasive censorship. The government enacted sweeping controls under the pretext of national security, silencing media outlets critical of the regime. These measures often involved shutdowns of opposing channels and newspapers, setting a precedent for later internet restrictions. Journalists faced severe risks, with fifty-eight killed between 1993 and 1996, according to the Committee to Protect Journalists (CPJ, 1999). Amnesty International highlighted how the government weaponized censorship to suppress information and stifle freedom of expression, while non-state actors also targeted journalists with violence and intimidation (Amnesty International, 1996).

### *The digital era (2002–present)*

In the aftermath of the civil war, Algeria's media landscape remained under substantial state control, particularly in the audiovisual sector. While attempts at liberalization were made – such as the restructuring of the Algerian Radio and Television Establishment (RTA) in 1986 and the introduction of private broadcasting following the Arab Spring – these reforms did little to curtail state interference (AREACORE, n.d.; Layadi, 2021). The government retained oversight of broadcasting licences and imposed strict restrictions on critical reporting, further consolidating its influence over the media.

The shutdowns of Atlas TV and Al Watan TV in the mid-2010s, justified on legal grounds and for alleged licencing violations, underscore the persistence of media regulation rooted in historical precedents (Layadi, 2021). These actions highlight how colonial and post-independence practices of censorship and media control have continued to shape Algeria's media policies in the digital age. The enduring prioritization of state authority over press freedom reflects a broader resistance to allowing genuinely independent journalism to flourish.

This historical analysis underscores the entrenched nature of state control over media in Algeria, which has laid the groundwork for contemporary internet shutdowns. These shutdowns – ostensibly implemented to prevent exam leaks – serve as a continuation of longstanding efforts to suppress dissent and control societal narratives. By prioritizing state power over public rights, the Algerian government perpetuates a legacy of media repression that spans colonial, post-independence and digital eras. Understanding this context is crucial to addressing Algeria's current approach to digital restrictions and advocating for the protection of fundamental rights, including freedom of expression and access to information.

## *The evolution of internet shutdowns in Algeria: a comprehensive review*

This section examines Algeria's digital era (2002–present), focusing on the patterns and implications of internet shutdowns, particularly the annual week-long disruptions during school exams. It documents instances of shutdowns since 2016, categorizing them by type, duration and geographical impact to illustrate their trends and repercussions.

Algérie Télécom, established in April 2003, serves as the primary state-owned internet service provider (ISP), with a 'monopoly over the country's fixed-line and fibre optic networks' (International Trade Administration, 2023). The government has enacted laws to control internet access, often targeting journalists and activists (Euro-Med Human Rights Monitor, 2023). In the digital age, Algeria tightened restrictions on online spaces, introducing repressive media laws that continue to challenge press freedom (CPJ, 2012; RSF, 2020; ARTICLE 19, 2024).

Algeria's internet cafés – once thriving hubs of public internet access – became central targets in this crackdown. By the mid-2000s, the country ranked among the top African nations, alongside Egypt and South Africa, in the number of internet cafés (Kamel, 2005). Internet cafés, once central to public internet access, became targets of heightened surveillance. Following the 2007 terrorist attacks,[1] the government mandated that cafés collect customer IDs, monitor browsing histories and report suspicious activities, citing national security concerns (Bourouina, 2007; Chirazi, 2008; ONI, 2009).

Algeria has encountered significant challenges in recent years, leading to its classification as 'Not Free' in the 2023 Freedom House report, with a Global Freedom Score of 32/100 (Freedom House, 2023). This troubling trend of censorship and repression is underscored by the prosecution, arrest or detention of at least twelve journalists and media workers between 2021 and 2023 (Amnesty International, 2023). In 2023 alone, the organization reported that authorities 'shut down at least two media companies and suspended one media outlet for 20 days', illustrating the government's ongoing regulation of media and digital platforms in Algeria.

Algeria has faced increasing digital repression. Despite a growing online presence – 33 million internet users, a 73 per cent penetration rate, and 25 million social media users as of early 2024 (Kemp, 2024) – the government continues to impose restrictions, particularly during important periods like the baccalaureate exams.

As internet use expands and the Algerian economy grows more reliant on connectivity, the government is facing increasing pressure to end internet shutdowns. The economic repercussions are significant, disrupting businesses and undermining national competitiveness and investor confidence. As Younes Grar, CEO of Gecos, stated, 'the financial loss recorded by the Internet segment during the period reviewed [of the baccalaureate exams] was estimated at 50 billion dinars ($388 million)' (Ecofin Agency, 2020). Recently, there has been growing demand to call for uninterrupted internet access as a fundamental right. Although there has not been much action from local civil society, international civil society organizations have formed alliances, advocating for policies that reduce the likelihood of shutdowns to advocate for the broader rights to free expression and information.

The steady rise in internet users and penetration rates reflects Algeria's growing reliance on digital connectivity. With a penetration rate of 72.9 per cent in 2024, this trend demonstrates progress in digital infrastructure. However, it also underscores the wide-reaching impacts of deliberate internet shutdowns, such as those imposed during exams. Despite being framed as measures to curb cheating, these disruptions affect millions, interrupting businesses, education and essential communication. This contrast between expanding digital access and periodic blackouts highlights a persistent tension in Algeria's digital governance, where progress often competes with repressive policies.

### *Internet shutdowns during the Hirak movement protests*

Before addressing exam-related disruptions, it is essential to consider non-exam-related shutdowns, particularly during the Hirak movement protests. The Hirak movement, which began in February 2019, demanded political reforms and an end to corruption, sparked by then-President Abdelaziz Bouteflika's bid for a fifth term. In response, the government imposed internet shutdowns to suppress

**Table 11.1** Digital Connectivity and Social Media Penetration Trends (2017–24)[2]

| Year | Internet users (millions) | Internet penetration rate (%) | Social media users (millions) | Social media penetration rate (%) | Active cellular connections (millions) | Mobile connection rate (%) |
|---|---|---|---|---|---|---|
| 2024 | 33.49 | 72.9% | 24.85 | 54.1% | 50.65 | 110.2% |
| 2023 | 32.09 | 70.9% | 23.95 | 52.9% | 48.53 | 107.2% |
| 2022 | 27.28 | 60.6% | 26.60 | 59.1% | 46.57 | 103.5% |
| 2021 | 26.35 | 59.6% | 25.00 | 56.5% | 46.82 | 105.8% |
| 2020 | 22.71 | 52% | 22.00 | 51% | 49.48 | 114% |
| 2019 | 24.48 | 58% | 23.00 | 54% | 49.35 | 117% |
| 2018 | 21.00 | 50% | 21.00 | 50% | 49.70 | 119% |
| 2017 | 18.00 | 44% | 18.00 | 44% | 47.64 | 117% |

dissent. Access Now's #KeepItOn report for 2019 identified Algeria as a significant offender, documenting six shutdowns that year (Taye and Access Now, 2020).

On 1 March 2019, internet access was disrupted nationwide for an entire day, coinciding with protests demanding the resignation of President Abdelaziz Bouteflika, who had been in power since 1999 and was seeking a contentious fifth term in the upcoming elections (Internet Society Pulse, 2019a). State-run Algérie Télécom implemented targeted shutdowns, affecting key protest zones, including Tizi Ouzou, Bejaia and parts of Algiers (Dahir, 2019).

A few months later, on 14 and 15 September 2019, further internet restrictions were enforced during public demonstrations against military influence in Algeria's civic space. Algérie Télécom again restricted internet access in several regions, including Tizi Ouzou, Bouira, Sétif, Jijel and parts of Algiers (Internet Society Pulse, 2019b). Despite the widespread disruptions, authorities issued no official statements, leaving citizens and businesses to deal with the effects of the shutdowns in uncertainty.

*Exam-related internet shutdowns*

According to the Shutdown Tracker Optimization Project (STOP) methodology by Access Now, Algeria has implemented internet shutdowns annually since 2016 (Access Now, 2024). This recurrent strategy aims to curb exam cheating and protect exams from leaks (Reuters, 2016). The 2016 shutdown started a pattern of yearly internet disruptions aligned with baccalaureate exams,[3] determining university admissions. Subsequent years saw a week-long shutdown in 2017 and another in 2018, impacting mobile and landline connections (Al Jazeera, 2018). These actions underscore the government's efforts to prevent exam content leaks on social media, sometimes resulting in arrests and investigations (Atti, 2023).

In 2017, Algeria imposed nationwide mobile internet restrictions during the baccalaureate exams to prevent leaks of exam content. Despite this, reports of leaked questions still emerged, causing significant disruption. Minister of Education Nouria Benghabrit denied these claims, stating that the authorities 'are taking every necessary measure to ensure the integrity of the exams and protect against leaks' (*Middle East Monitor*, 2017). The shutdowns had economic consequences, particularly for providers like Algérie Télécom, highlighting the tension between exam security and economic stability.

From 2016 to 2018, Algerian authorities adopted increasingly stringent measures to maintain exam integrity. Starting with targeted social media restrictions in 2016, they moved to extensive mobile internet blocking in 2017. By 2018, the government imposed a complete broadband shutdown during exam hours from June 21 to June 25, with Facebook entirely inaccessible (Al Jazeera, 2018).

Algérie Télécom announced in advance that both mobile and landline connections would be disrupted for around two hours each morning during the baccalaureate exams. This measure applied to residential customers and telecommunications operators, except for economic operators, highlighting the government's resolve to prevent exam leaks (Algérie Maintenant, 2018). As the main telecommunications provider in the country and one controlled by the government, Algérie Télécom is in a precarious position, with little room to resist shutdown orders from state authorities. This monopoly over the telecommunications market not only amplifies government control but also stifles competition and innovation. Opening the market to other ISPs could mitigate such issues, providing users with more resilient connectivity options and reducing the risk of shutdowns being used as a tool for overreach.

In 2019, alongside the rise of internet usage and disruptions associated with the Hirak Movement, Algeria continued imposing internet restrictions during exams. These interruptions occurred during critical periods, affecting connectivity from 16 to 20 June and again from 20 to 25 June. Algérie Télécom stated that these cuts were 'in compliance with instructions from the government, aimed at ensuring the high school diploma tests run smoothly, a decision made

**Table 11.2** Timeline of Internet Shutdowns During Exams in Algeria (2016–24)

| Year | Dates | Type of shutdown | Impact and notes |
|---|---|---|---|
| 2016 | Baccalaureate period | Targeted shutdowns on social media | First instance; aimed to curb exam content leaks. |
| 2017 | June | Nationwide mobile internet restrictions | Week-long shutdown; significant disruptions in mobile and landline connectivity. |
| 2018 | 21–25 June | Complete broadband shutdown during exam hours | All-inclusive; Facebook blocked, with major disruptions reported (Al Jazeera, 2018). |
| 2019 | 16–20 June, 20–25 June | Planned internet blackouts | Three one-hour blackouts scheduled; focused on exam integrity amid rising Hirak Movement. |
| 2020 | 13–17 September | Daily blackouts during high school exams | Internet slowdowns prior to exams; DNS-level blockages detected (Sayadi and Samaro, 2020). |
| 2021 | June | Alternating complete blackouts and throttling | Shutdown during national exams for 731,000 students; marked curfew-style disruptions. |
| 2022 | 12–16 June | Targeted content-blocking approach | Shifted from broad shutdowns to restricting specific sites; minimal country-level traffic drops noted. |
| 2023 | 11–15 June | Targeted social networks and messaging platforms | Daily outages for several hours; significant anomalies in connectivity detected. |
| 2024 | 9–13 June | Selective content blocking, with nominal internet access | Less severe disruptions compared to previous years; targeted social media restrictions. |

by the telecommunications and education ministries' (France 24, 2018). The ISP published a shutdown schedule: three one-hour blackouts at the beginning of each baccalaureate exam on Wednesday, and two similar blackouts on Thursday, Friday, Saturday, Sunday and Monday (Henley, 2018).

In 2020, Algeria faced another internet shutdown from 13 to 17 September, coinciding with high school exams. According to Ali Sibai, reporting for SMEX on MENA countries' internet shutdowns, there were indications of internet slowdowns two days prior to the exams, suggesting intentional throttling to prevent early leaks (Sibai, 2020). During the exam period, a daily blackout occurred between 7.30 am and 6.00 pm, severely restricting website access, with Fing detecting a DNS-level blockage. Access Now highlighted that over half a million students took baccalaureate exams under Covid-19 conditions. To curb cheating, authorities implemented internet shutdowns during exam hours, although Algérie Télécom did not issue official statements regarding these disruptions (Sayadi and Samaro, 2020).

In 2021, Algeria marked its sixth consecutive year of internet shutdowns during national school exams in June. On 20 June, authorities enforced a shutdown from 8.00 am to 12.00 pm, coinciding with the first national exam session for 731,000 students. These disruptions persisted throughout the day, with alternating periods of complete blackouts during exam sessions and significant throttling between sessions, lunch breaks and overnight hours. The shutdown, characterized by its curfew-style[4] approach, impacted both mobile and broadband internet services (Mnejja, Fatafta and Anthonio, 2021).

During the 2022 baccalaureate exams from 12 to 16 June, the Algerian government shifted from wide-scale internet shutdowns to a more targeted 'content-blocking approach', despite earlier promises to avoid such disruptions. A content-blocking approach involves restricting access to specific websites or online services, such as social media platforms or communication tools, while keeping the broader internet available. David Belson, in his analysis, noted that authorities adopted this approach, with Cloudflare's data showing nominal drops in country-level traffic that coincided with exam sessions. This was further supported by traffic graphs from major Algerian network providers (Belson, 2022). Additionally, OONI Explorer detected anomalies[5] in web connectivity tests for communication tools and social networking sites during the exams (OONI, n.d.b,c).

In 2023, a shutdown began on 11 June, targeting social networks and messaging platforms to curb cheating. Officials identified these platforms as primary channels for students exchanging answers (Atti, 2023). The government instructed internet providers to restrict access to popular platforms like Facebook, due to its widespread use for sharing leaked content. Data from OONI highlighted the blocking of specific sites while keeping internet connections operational during the exam period. Between 12 and 14 June, disruptions to news media sites surged to 186 anomalies and 129 failures, compared to the previous week's 73 anomalies and 24 failures (Mitchell, 2023). The shutdown persisted until June 15, with daily outages from 11 to 15 June, featuring a four-hour morning outage from 8.00 am to 12.00 pm and a three-hour afternoon outage from 2.00 pm to 5.00 pm (TRT Afrika, 2023).

In 2024, Algeria continued its pattern of internet disruptions during the baccalaureate exams, which took place from 9 to 13 June (Mnejja, 2024). Despite previous reassurances from officials of minimal interference, two daily internet blackouts were observed during the exam period, each lasting several hours in the morning and afternoon. Cloudflare Radar recorded significant drops in traffic during these times, with TCP-based traffic particularly affected, although the disruptions were less severe than in previous years (Belson, 2024). The Open Observatory of Network Interference (OONI) detected anomalies in popular messaging apps like WhatsApp and Telegram, which coincided with the exam schedule (Mnejja, 2024). The disruptions appeared targeted, impacting access to social media and messaging platforms but not causing a total internet blackout. This approach mirrors the government's evolving strategy of selective content blocking, rather than wide-scale shutdowns, while maintaining nominal internet access.

## *Reviewing internet shutdowns in Algeria: literature, impact and advocacy*

Understanding the impact of internet shutdowns during exams in Algeria requires a thorough review of existing literature and reports. This section examines publications and analyses from civil society organizations like Access Now,[6] SMEX,[7] and the Internet Society (ISOC),[8] which have been focusing on internet shutdowns during exams in the Middle East and North Africa. Additionally, this review incorporates case studies and relevant insights from businesses and communities in Algeria. By exploring key findings from prior research and efforts on this issue, a nuanced analysis can be developed, complemented by evidence and data from specialized sources in internet documentation and measurement such as Cloudflare Radar, Internet Outage Detection & Analysis (IODA), and OONI, among others.

To analyse the impact of internet shutdowns systematically, one common conceptual lens is that of rights. This section will review a range of fundamental human rights that can be negatively impacted by internet shutdowns and form part of a framework for evaluating the impact of internet shutdowns. I focus on four key rights guaranteed to citizens in the Universal Declaration of Human Rights (UDHR 1948), the International Covenant on Civil and Political Rights (ICCPR 1976), and the International Covenant on Economic, Social and Cultural Rights (ICESCR 1976). This structured approach ensures a comprehensive understanding of how internet shutdowns undermine these fundamental rights and highlights the broader implications for society.

### *1 The right to work and business and economic costs of internet Shutdowns*

The right to work and conduct business is enshrined in Article 23 of the UDHR, adopted by the United Nations General Assembly in 1948. As a member of the United Nations, Algeria is committed to upholding its principles (UDHR, 1948). This right is further reinforced by Article 6 of the ICESCR, which Algeria signed on 10 December 1968, and ratified on 12 September 1989 (United Nations, 1966).

Internet shutdowns significantly disrupt economic activities, preventing businesses from accessing essential online services and communication tools. These disruptions lead to financial instability, job losses and substantial economic damage (GNI, 2016; Internet Society, 2019; OHCHR, 2022). Studies estimate that such shutdowns can cost millions in daily GDP losses. For example, Brookings estimated a global economic loss of USD 2.4 billion between 2015 and 2016 due to internet disruptions. In today's digital age, access to the internet is indispensable for job opportunities, professional communication and business operations. The increasing reliance on digital connectivity has made the right to work inextricably linked to digital rights, as evidenced by cases where internet disconnections directly resulted in lost income (Bajoria, 2023).

In Algeria, business owners have reported significant economic losses during periods of internet shutdowns. West (2016) explores the economic ramifications of such shutdowns, offering insights into Algeria and other affected nations. Published by the Brookings Institution, West's paper estimates that the economic toll of Algeria's shutdowns amounted to approximately USD 20 million for six days of disruptions in a single year (West, 2016). While these figures are conservative, West underscores the broader economic dimensions of internet shutdowns, shedding light on their severe impact on both the economy and individual businesses. His analysis provides a foundation for further research and policy discussions.

Data and analysis provided by Cloudflare Radar also contribute valuable insights into the dynamics of internet disruptions and shutdowns, offering critical data and trends for understanding this practice. In a recent article on widespread exam-related internet shutdowns by MENA governments, particularly in Iraq and Algeria, Belson (2023) highlights the significant financial toll these measures impose. He estimates losses in the millions of US dollars and questions the effectiveness of such shutdowns in curbing cheating (Belson, 2023). These findings align with other research, including estimates that the 2018 baccalaureate exam shutdowns in Algeria cost approximately 760 million dinars (5.5 million euros) for eleven hours of disruptions over five days (Rahmouni, 2018).

### *2 Right to education and internet shutdowns*

The right to education is enshrined in Article 26 of the UDHR and further supported by Article 13 of the ICESCR, both of which Algeria is committed to upholding (United Nations, 1948). In today's digital age, internet access is crucial for attending online classes, accessing educational resources, and communicating with educators. Internet shutdowns disrupt these activities, undermining the educational process and violating the right to education, which increasingly relies on digital connectivity. Efforts to combat exam cheating through shutdowns impact students nationwide who depend on uninterrupted internet access for their education, as will be explored further in this analysis.

Cupler (2022) contends that nationwide internet shutdowns are neither a proportionate nor effective response to exam cheating. She highlights the significant economic and social harm they cause, as well as their detrimental impact on reliance on the internet. Cupler argues that alternative, more proportionate methods exist that avoid the harmful consequences associated with shutdowns. If such alternatives can achieve the same goal without infringing on rights, then internet shutdowns fail the test of legality, necessity and proportionality (Privacy International, n.d.). To address this issue, Cupler recommends implementing 'strong security techniques such as encryption and access monitoring.' She also advocates for abolishing 'legal provisions that allow for shutdowns and government control over the internet infrastructure, and to enable regulators to act independently and in the interest of all internet users'.

Although authorities claim that internet shutdowns protect education by preserving the integrity of national examinations, testimonies suggest otherwise, with students at university level feeling that impact. Many students reported being unable to 'revise lessons' or 'complete courses on Zoom', particularly at the university level, where continuous internet access is essential (SMEX, 2022). These disruptions highlight the critical role of digital rights in ensuring educational access. By obstructing internet connectivity, shutdowns negatively affect students who are not sitting for the baccalaureate exams, thereby violating their right to education.

### *3 Right to healthcare*

The right to health is protected under Article 25 of the UDHR and Article 12 of the ICESCR, both of which Algeria upholds (United Nations, 1948). While specific literature on the health impacts of internet shutdowns during exams is scarce, it is reasonable to infer significant negative effects. Internet disruptions hinder timely access to health information and services, complicating the ability to contact healthcare providers, seek medical advice or utilize telemedicine services.

An illustrative example from Jordan demonstrates the broader consequences of exam-related internet shutdowns. During the 2021 Tawjihi exams – national secondary school examinations critical for university admissions – the shutdown disrupted the vaccination process in centres during the Covid-19 pandemic. Despite government efforts encouraging citizens to register online for vaccines, internet interruptions hampered operations at vaccination centres. According to Dr Riad Al-Shiyyab, Director of Health in Irbid, the internet disruptions slowed vaccination procedures across the city, causing significant crowding at vaccination centres (Amri, 2021). This incident underscores how internet shutdowns can undermine public health services and create ripple effects extending beyond their intended purpose.

### *4 Right to political association and expression*

The right to political expression and association is enshrined under Article 19 of the UDHR and Articles 19 and 21 of the ICCP. Disrupting internet access infringes on these rights by limiting communication, self-expression and access to vital information, thereby restricting freedom of expression (United Nations, 1948). It is essential to analyse how internet shutdowns in Algeria have historically impacted these fundamental rights.

A review of Algeria's shutdowns reveals that most were implemented during national exams, with notable exceptions in 2019, when disruptions coincided with political protests during the Hirak movement. The government employed internet shutdowns to stifle dissent and limit communication among protesters. Although justified as measures to prevent exam cheating, these shutdowns extended far beyond education, infringing on the social, economic and political rights of Algeria's 33 million internet users. This demonstrates how shutdowns have been used not only to safeguard examinations but also to suppress political expression.

Rydzak et al. (2020) question the effectiveness of internet shutdowns in suppressing dissent. Despite Algeria's significant internet penetration and active Facebook user base, the authors argue that the Bouteflika regime's attempts to disrupt connectivity around protest hotspots during peaceful demonstrations were largely ineffective in deterring mobilization. This finding challenges assumptions regarding the utility of shutdowns for suppressing political dissent. While this chapter focuses on internet shutdowns during exams, it is critical to consider their broader implications for freedom of expression and political association.

### *Digital transformation and internet shutdowns*

Cupler (2022) highlights a paradox in countries like Jordan, Sudan and Algeria, where efforts to advance digital economies coexist with frequent internet shutdowns, particularly during exams. These disruptions hinder innovation and growth, reflecting the competing interests of various stakeholders. Political leaders may perceive shutdowns as a means to address security concerns or counter challenges to their authority, while citizens rely on the internet for social, economic and political engagement. Meanwhile, corporations and businesses, driven by financial incentives to maintain connectivity, increasingly oppose government-imposed shutdowns.

In Algeria, technological solutions such as secure digital transmission of exam questions could address concerns about preserving exam integrity without resorting to shutdowns. However, challenges related to infrastructure, security and trust hinder their adoption. This tension underscores the potential for collaboration between civil society and the private sector. Telecommunications companies and civil society organizations, through shared interests in connectivity and economic stability, could join forces to challenge shutdown policies. Strategic efforts, including litigation, may pave the way for a digitally open, secure and resilient future aligned with both human rights and economic development.

Although several countries have successfully implemented secure systems for disseminating exam questions or utilized e-examination platforms to minimize risks of leaks, Algeria continues to face barriers to adopting these practices. Experts cite concerns about security, infrastructure limitations, and distrust of digital solutions, further exacerbated by poor internet connectivity and limited high-speed broadband access in rural areas. While 24.5 per cent of

Algeria's population resides in rural areas, 75.5 per cent live in urban areas where connectivity challenges persist (International Trade Administration, 2024). These systemic issues highlight the broader societal and economic repercussions of internet shutdowns during exams.

Khalfallah and Bendjelloul (2023) note that 'Algeria is one of the countries attempting to achieve the goals of digital transformation through its vision and initiatives in the field of digitization'. This includes efforts to digitize public services and achieve full-sector digitization by 2023 (Khalfallah and Bendjelloul, 2023: 34). However, the authors also argue that 'Algeria continues to lag behind', with recurring internet shutdowns directly contradicting its aspirations for digital transformation. Overcoming these contradictions is crucial for Algeria to embrace digital transformation fully and ensure exam integrity without resorting to measures that undermine both human rights and technological progress.

## *Methodology*

This section adopts a multi-method approach grounded in a human rights framework to examine how internet shutdowns during exams in Algeria affect individual rights, economic stability and societal dynamics. The study combines primary data from interviews with secondary analysis of existing literature. To address gaps in prior research on the experiences of students and business owners, interviews were conducted with seven individuals who either took their baccalaureate exams or worked in key sectors of Algeria's digital economy between 2016 and 2023. Purposive sampling was employed to select participants based on their firsthand experiences and ability to provide reflective insights. This qualitative methodology ensures the voices of those most affected by the shutdowns are captured (Palinkas et al., 2013). The findings presented in subsequent sections aim to provide a nuanced understanding of the broader implications of these shutdowns and offer recommendations for stakeholders.

## *Analysing the impact of internet shutdowns during exams in Algeria*

This section analyses the interviews to assess the human rights implications of internet shutdowns during exams in Algeria, focusing on their effects on education, work, healthcare, political participation and freedom of expression. By situating the interview findings within a broader rights-based framework, the section highlights how these disruptions extend beyond education, reflecting broader struggles over the control of digital spaces and power dynamics among the state, private companies and individuals.

### *Motivations behind internet shutdowns during exams*

The interviews revealed that many view the shutdowns as a measure to prevent cheating, with some acknowledging potential political motivations, particularly in the initial years. For instance, Leila and Khaled pointed to the political climate surrounding Minister Nouria Benghabrit, whose reforms faced opposition. One important addition from the interviews, not commonly discussed in the existing literature, is the belief that the 2016 exam leaks may have had political motivations. Several interviewees suggested that the shutdowns were intended as a 'sabotage' of the then Minister of Education, Nouria Benghabrit, who was perceived to have a direct and secular approach. As Leila, a former student who sat for the Bac exams during shutdowns, explained, 'many people thought this leak was to sabotage the work of the then minister, who was seen as trying to minimize religious influences in education'. Khaled, another former student, also initially believed these leaks might be politically motivated but added that 'the issue persists till now, so it may not be an isolated incident'. In 2018, Benghabrit herself acknowledged the uncomfortable necessity of shutdowns, saying, 'we are not comfortable resorting to shutdowns, but we must not give up in the face of such phenomena' (*Etudiant Algérien*, 2018).

Most interviewees believe the primary motivation behind these internet shutdowns was to prevent cheating and uphold exam integrity, with no alternative reasons suggested. Khaled, a former student, shared that 'the government saw this as the only viable solution at the time'. Similarly, Sara, another former student, noted that in 2016, authorities 'opted for the easiest solution without trying to find a more effective one'.

From a rights-based perspective, these actions raise significant concerns under international human rights law. According to Article 4 of the ICCPR, states may temporarily derogate from certain obligations only 'to the extent strictly required by the exigencies of the situation'. Such measures must adhere to the principle of proportionality, as underscored by the UN Human Rights Committee, which has stated that derogations must reflect 'the principle of proportionality, which is common to both derogation and limitation powers' (United Nations, 1976; UN Human Rights Committee, 2001).

By enforcing extensive, nationwide internet shutdowns, the Algerian government prioritizes its authority to control the population over its responsibility to safeguard individual and collective rights. These sweeping measures serve to reinforce state dominance in managing public life, framing such actions as indispensable for maintaining exam integrity while neglecting principles of proportionality and accountability rooted in human rights. This underscores a pattern of state power being exercised in ways that restrict freedoms while portraying these limitations as inevitable or justified.

Although authorities present these shutdowns as necessary to prevent cheating, their indiscriminate nature disproportionately affects all users, impeding access to essential information and emergency services. This renders the measures inherently disproportionate. A rights-based analysis suggests that while preventing cheating may constitute a legitimate objective, the broad and blanket application of internet shutdowns – particularly when less intrusive alternatives exist – fails to meet the proportionality requirements outlined under international law. Consequently, such actions unjustifiably infringe upon the rights to education, freedom of expression and access to information. These measures highlight the state's capacity to curtail digital spaces and essential services, affecting millions of citizens without demonstrating substantial evidence of their long-term efficacy.

Despite widespread frustration regarding the recurring nature of these shutdowns, some participants acknowledged government efforts to enhance the effectiveness of these measures. Amir, a digital transformation expert, remarked that 'there is improvement in the effectiveness of the measures taken'. Regarding efficacy, most interviewees argued that the shutdowns have been relatively successful in reducing widespread cheating. Omar, an entrepreneur, characterized them as 'very effective'. However, isolated incidents of exam leaks persist. Farid, a digital expert, noted, 'In 2019, there were leaks, which shows that the measures were not effective enough to prevent students from cheating'. Similarly, Omar described the measures as 'somewhat efficient at the moment, although not perfect as there are still occasional leaks'.

Many interviewees recognized the effectiveness of anti-cheating measures but emphasized the tension between preserving exam integrity and protecting broader societal and individual rights. Achraf, a start-up owner, stressed the rigorous application of these measures while critiquing Algeria's reliance on a single high-stakes exam to determine academic outcomes. He argued that 'transition[ing] away from this system' would reduce incentives to cheat, potentially eliminating the need for internet shutdowns during exam periods. Conversely, Omar recommended that 'the government … examine successful practices from other countries that allow life to continue during exams without significant disruption.' He maintained that while upholding exam integrity is essential, the current measures significantly infringe upon fundamental rights. These perspectives suggest that addressing structural issues, rather than implementing blanket shutdowns, could offer a more equitable and effective solution.

To date, no evidence substantiates claims that internet shutdowns during exams effectively prevent cheating or eliminate exam leaks. Although Algeria and other nations in the region continue to employ this practice, its impact on reducing academic malpractice remains unproven. Even if such measures were demonstrably effective, they would still violate the social, economic and political rights of over 33 million Algerians. Under international human rights law, restrictions on fundamental freedoms are permissible only if they are lawful, necessary and proportionate. These shutdowns fail to meet both the necessity and proportionality criteria, as viable alternatives exist for safeguarding exam integrity, such as securely disseminating exam materials shortly before exams commence. Ultimately, these measures infringe on individual rights, disrupt daily life and undermine economic stability, all while failing to address the root causes of academic malpractice.

### *Exam-related shutdown and impact on fundamental rights*

*Impact on the right to work and business* Internet shutdowns in Algeria, originally introduced to protect exam integrity, have caused significant disruptions to the economy and business operations. Achraf, a business owner, reported substantial losses, noting that his activities were halted for an entire week, severely impacting operations. Similarly, Omar, another entrepreneur, shared his frustrations, describing how his business 'suffered a lot' and now employs mitigation strategies such as working in advance and scheduling key meetings outside exam hours. These accounts underscore the considerable economic toll of internet shutdowns, including delayed operations, disrupted workflows, and the financial burden of implementing preventive measures.

From a rights-based perspective, these disruptions violate economic rights, including the right to work and participate in economic activities as outlined in Article 6 of the ICESCR. Moreover, the disproportionate impact on small businesses and marginalized communities, which often lack the resources to adapt to such interruptions, exacerbates systemic inequities and violates the principle of non-discrimination. Farid, a digital expert, highlighted these disparities, stating, 'In our company's office, we were not affected as we use a professional line', emphasizing unequal access to reliable connectivity and the inequitable consequences of shutdowns.

Private sector actors, particularly telecommunications operators (telcos) ISPs, play a central role in the implementation of these shutdowns. Governments compel compliance by issuing orders backed by legal mandates, penalties or threats to operating licences. This places telcos and ISPs at the intersection of state authority and corporate responsibility. While they are legally obligated to adhere to national regulations, they are also bound by the UN Guiding Principles on Business and Human Rights (UNGPs) to avoid complicity in human rights violations and mitigate adverse impacts. However, economic incentives often undermine these obligations, as companies prioritize government contracts and regulatory compliance over their commitments to human rights.

The Algerian government's emphasis on digital transformation and support for start-ups stands in stark contrast to the persistence of internet shutdowns. Khaled, a business analyst, remarked that 'the government is trying to support startups', yet businesses are forced to adopt coping mechanisms rather than focus on growth. For instance, Achraf plans vacations during expected shutdown periods, while Omar adjusts operations to 'anticipate problems and plan accordingly'. These adaptive strategies reflect a broader tension: the state's assertion of 'power over' digital spaces undermines the 'power to' of businesses and citizens to exercise economic agency (VeneKlasen and Miller, 2002).

Nonetheless, these disruptions have also sparked resilience and resistance. Businesses have demonstrated 'power within' by leveraging internal resources to navigate challenges (Cornwall, 2002). Furthermore, collective action through alliances among businesses, civil society, and citizens can generate 'power with', challenging the systemic dominance of state-imposed shutdowns and advocating for digital rights. Such coalitions transcend the limitations of individual rights-based approaches, promoting social justice and demanding accountability for policies that stifle economic growth and entrench inequality (Cornwall and Nyamu-Musembi, 2004; Gaventa, 2006).

This interplay of conflicting power dynamics highlights the pressing need for systemic change. Addressing the structural inequities perpetuated by internet shutdowns would enable Algeria to reconcile its digital transformation ambitions with the economic and human rights of its citizens and businesses. Such reforms would not only reduce economic harm but also foster a more equitable and sustainable digital ecosystem.

### *Education and exams: effects of internet restrictions*

The recurring practice of internet shutdowns in Algeria highlights the tension between state control and individual rights. Initially introduced to combat exam cheating following the 2016 baccalaureate leaks, these measures have significantly disrupted educational systems. Leila, a student at the time, recounted having to retake five exams, describing the experience as 'two baccalaureates in a single year', reflecting the frustration and upheaval caused by the policy during its early implementation. Over time, however, this practice has become normalized, embedding state authority into digital spaces with extensive and lasting consequences.

Although these measures ostensibly aim to safeguard the integrity of national exams, their impact extends far beyond their stated objective. Sara, now a teacher, described the challenges of reverting to pre-digital methods during shutdowns as a 'frustrating regression' that undermined her ability to teach effectively. Both students and educators experienced disrupted schedules and restricted access to essential resources, ultimately weakening the educational system rather than supporting it. As Cupler's research (2022) notes, even some educators were unable to conduct classes during these disruptions, further highlighting the policy's far-reaching implications.

The normalization of such measures represents a structural prioritization of state control over equitable access to digital tools and resources. Institutionalizing these disruptions perpetuates systemic inequalities, disempowering individuals and communities while prioritizing state-dictated solutions over personal agency. The accounts of Leila and Sara underscore the human cost of these policies, which not only disrupt daily lives but also discourage digital engagement, creating a chilling effect that further entrenches disparities in education and access to information. These dynamics epitomize the broader challenges of balancing governance, control and fundamental rights in the digital age.

### *Right to healthcare and freedom of expression amidst internet disruptions*

Although healthcare rights are not explicitly foregrounded in discussions about internet shutdowns, the challenges they pose during emergencies are profound. Omar recounted a family emergency that occurred while he was travelling, noting: 'My only means of contacting family and friends was through WhatsApp or Messenger. During that time, there was a family emergency, and I couldn't reach out immediately. I had to wait until after exam hours to connect again.' This account underscores the critical role of internet connectivity in ensuring timely communication during crises, directly implicating the right to health and safety by delaying access to emergency support.

The implications of internet shutdowns on political association and freedom of expression elicited mixed responses from interviewees. Some defended the measures as necessary for maintaining exam integrity rather than as instruments of censorship. Achraf remarked, 'I don't see it as a violation of human rights; rather, it's a necessary measure', while Amir argued that 'there is a purpose and reason behind such actions', suggesting that intent can justify the disruptions. However, under international human rights law, the legitimacy of such measures cannot rest solely on intent or perceived necessity. Instead, restrictions must satisfy the principles of legality, necessity and proportionality. Lawful restrictions must represent the least restrictive means available to achieve a legitimate aim, with no viable alternatives.

Other perspectives emphasized the adverse human rights implications of shutdowns. Leila observed that 'these practices don't consider human rights aspects or fundamental principles', while Khaled highlighted that 'this affects access to information, a fundamental right nowadays, more tied to information access than freedom of expression'. These concerns align with the positions of the Office of the High Commissioner for Human Rights (OHCHR) and recent UN resolutions, which condemn internet shutdowns for their detrimental effects on freedom of expression and access to critical information, especially during emergencies (United Nations, 2022).

Internet shutdowns are increasingly recognized as violations of international law. The OHCHR, alongside numerous UN resolutions such as UN Human Rights Council Resolution 47/16, has consistently denounced the intentional and arbitrary use of shutdowns to restrict access to information. Articles 19 of both the UDHR and the ICCPR protect freedom of expression, a right routinely undermined by these practices. The UN High Commissioner for Human Rights reiterated this concern, stating that 'switching off the internet causes incalculable damage, both in material and human rights terms' (United Nations, 2022). This global condemnation underscores the imperative for states to adopt alternative, rights-respecting measures that address security concerns without infringing on their international legal obligations.

### *Impact on internet shutdowns on daily life and what's next?*

Interviewees vividly detailed how internet shutdowns severely disrupted their lives, exposing profound infringements on rights protected under international conventions. One participant highlighted how the inability to use ride-hailing apps directly violated their right to freedom of movement under Article 12 of the ICCPR. For drivers reliant on these platforms, the shutdowns also obstructed their right to work, as guaranteed under Article 6 of the ICESCR (United Nations, 1976). These disruptions are sometimes far from minor inconveniences; they have significant economic consequences, undermining livelihoods, disrupting businesses, and deepening social inequalities.

Shutdowns also intensified feelings of frustration, isolation and disconnection, affecting the right to freedom of expression (Article 19, ICCPR) and participation in cultural life (Article 27, UDHR; Article 15, ICESCR) (United Nations, 1948; United Nations, 1976). Omar recounted the emotional toll, noting that 'this sparked a kind of anger and frustration. Over time, we need to stop these practices as they are counterproductive and create great discomfort and difficulties.' Similarly, Leila shared her experience of isolation, explaining how being unable to connect with friends or access content on YouTube left her feeling 'very isolated'. These accounts underscore the societal costs of shutdowns, such as the erosion of digital public spaces crucial for modern cultural and social participation and the weakening of social cohesion.

Perspectives on the future of these shutdowns were mixed among interviewees. Khaled expressed optimism, believing that 'they will stop implementing these shutdowns because many businesses have been affected', attributing potential change to public frustration and economic pressure. In contrast, Sara expressed scepticism, suggesting: 'I don't think they will stop but rather look for other solutions for people's work to not be impacted.' This division reflects the tension between mounting public pressure and entrenched state practices, suggesting that significant economic fallout and sustained advocacy are necessary for meaningful change.

These accounts reveal how internet shutdowns during exams in Algeria intersect with critical rights and state power dynamics. While authorities prioritize exam integrity, they do so at the expense of economic rights, freedom of expression and access to information. Business owners emphasized the financial harm and sense of powerlessness caused by these measures. Meanwhile, students and young people highlighted disruptions to education and exclusion from a connected society. Beyond the immediate impacts, these shutdowns represent a broader tool of control, raising pressing questions about accountability, equity, and the balance of power in policies that shape fundamental rights.

The following section will explore recommendations drawn from these findings, offering actionable strategies for governments, civil society and researchers. These strategies aim to balance exam integrity with individual rights and economic stability, ensuring a rights-respecting approach to governance in the digital age.

### *Recommendations for addressing internet shutdowns during exams in Algeria*

The recommendations from interviewees provide valuable insights for addressing internet shutdowns during exams in Algeria. Incorporating these suggestions with research-based strategies, this section explores actionable solutions to tackle the issue effectively.

Some interviewees proposed deploying signal jammers near schools to prevent cheating. Others recommended digitalizing the exam process to enhance security and efficiency. Amir suggested sending exam materials 'in an encrypted manner to prevent any manipulation', with questions distributed digitally and printed on-site shortly before exams begin. This method leverages encryption to securely transmit exam materials, minimizing reliance on physical transport and reducing risks of leaks or tampering.

Enhanced security at exam centres emerged as another key recommendation. Several interviewees called for stricter monitoring mechanisms and advanced technologies to deter cheating. Amir emphasized that 'analysing how exam centres organize the secure distribution of materials is essential'. He advocated for adopting technologies to securely transmit encrypted exam questions, delivered shortly before exams, as a practical alternative to shutdowns.

Educational reforms also featured prominently in recommendations. Achraf, a former student, criticized the reliance on the baccalaureate exam as the sole measure of academic standing, describing it as 'outdated'. He proposed transitioning to decentralized evaluations led by universities, stating: 'Shifting to a model where universities conduct their own exams could reduce the incentive to cheat and eliminate the need for internet blocks during exam periods.'

A holistic approach to addressing shutdowns was a consensus among interviewees. Solutions included banning electronic devices in exam rooms, increasing exam centre security, and incorporating educational reforms that emphasize academic integrity. Interviewees stressed reducing the pressures that drive cheating, coupled with rights-respecting measures like psychological support and positive incentives for honesty. Comprehensive training for educators and policies grounded in human rights principles were highlighted as essential steps. Algeria could also draw lessons from countries where academic integrity is upheld without infringing on students' access to information.

Efforts to resist exam-related shutdowns in the MENA region have been led by civil society organizations (CSOs), providing valuable lessons in advocacy and engagement. The #NoExamShutdown campaign has successfully united like-minded groups advocating for internet freedom, exploring various strategies to end these measures across the region (Access Now, 2023). In Jordan, the Jordan Open Source Association (JOSA) has taken a legal approach, arguing that such shutdowns violate the country's constitution, which explicitly prohibits blocking communication without a judicial order (Mahasneh, 2021). In Iraq, the Iraqi Network for Social Media (INSM) has engaged with ministries, delivered advocacy letters, trying to work closely with policymakers to push for change and end this practice (Iraqi Network for Social Media, 2024). In Sudan, legal action has become a prominent tool in challenging shutdowns, with organizations like the Sudanese Consumers Protection Association emphasizing the violation of consumer rights caused by these measures, resulting in some victories through coordinated efforts by civil society and legal experts (Radio Dabanga, 2019).

However, Algeria lacks similar civil society engagement. Drawing from other MENA countries' experiences, Algerian organizations could launch public campaigns, pursue legal challenges and engage with authorities to raise awareness about the human rights implications of internet shutdowns. These efforts would enhance accountability, protect consumer rights and foster public understanding of the economic and social harms caused by such measures.

Interviews highlighted that the persistence of internet shutdowns in Algeria revealed a multifaceted power struggle: the state's assertion of 'power over' digital spaces undermines the 'power to' of individuals to freely exercise their rights. However, the testimonies also highlight opportunities for resistance. Achraf and Omar's calls for alternative solutions, such as adopting modernized exam systems or learning from international best practices, reflect the potential for collective 'power with' to drive systemic change. Mobilizing alliances between businesses, civil society and citizens can counteract the structural dominance of state-imposed shutdowns. Such coalitions exemplify how agency and resistance can reclaim digital spaces, fostering a more equitable balance of power that prioritizes individual rights and social justice.

To resolve this issue, Algerian authorities should prioritize educational reforms and adopt non-intrusive anti-cheating measures, such as encryption, secure access monitoring and strict bans on electronic devices in exam halls. Transparent communication about anti-cheating policies is essential, as is avoiding unnecessary shutdowns that infringe on rights to information and free expression.

Policymakers must establish rights-based policies to prevent exam leaks and eliminate legal provisions that allow for shutdowns. Civil society should document shutdown cases, advocate for alternatives, and raise awareness of the broader human rights impact. Collaborative efforts among decision-makers, regulators, civil society and stakeholders are vital to balancing exam integrity with rights protections. Additionally, telecom companies should collaborate with authorities to develop strategies that ensure exam security without compromising access to digital spaces.

In conclusion, addressing exam-related shutdowns in Algeria requires a human rights framework grounded in collaboration, technological innovation and regulatory reform. By balancing exam integrity with the protection of fundamental rights, Algeria can uphold its commitment to fostering an equitable and connected society in the digital age.

## *Conclusion*

This chapter explores the impacts of internet shutdowns during exams in Algeria, focusing on their implications for individual rights, economic stability and societal dynamics. Framed within Algeria's history of media control and theories of digital rights and power, it situates these shutdowns within a broader pattern of state dominance over communication channels. While intended to preserve exam integrity, these measures come at a significant cost, as revealed through the experiences of students, business owners and citizens.

The findings highlight the state's exercise of 'power over' digital spaces, prioritizing exam security at the expense of internationally recognized human rights such as freedom of expression, the right to work, and access to information. Vulnerable groups bear the brunt of these shutdowns, exacerbating existing inequalities and destabilizing economic systems. Testimonies illuminate a range of adverse effects, from business losses to emotional distress and social disconnection, disrupting daily life and eroding social cohesion.

Despite these challenges, affected communities have demonstrated resilience, with business owners and individuals employing 'power within' to mitigate the impacts. Strategies such as rescheduling operations and planning around shutdowns showcase resourcefulness but also expose the inadequacy of such measures in addressing systemic inequities.

Signs of collective action, or 'power with', are also emerging. Stakeholders, including businesses and citizens, have started to demand accountability and rights-based alternatives to internet shutdowns. Civil society could play a pivotal role in fostering alliances to challenge the status quo and advocate for less intrusive measures, such as signal jammers or advanced monitoring technologies, which uphold exam integrity while respecting digital rights.

Case studies reinforce the conclusion that these shutdowns infringe on multiple rights, including the right to education, healthcare and economic stability, as well as freedom of expression. They disproportionately harm marginalized communities and compel businesses to adopt costly countermeasures. These findings align with global research on the human rights implications of internet disruptions, underscoring the urgent need for policy reforms and innovative solutions that mitigate harm while achieving security objectives.

Addressing the negative impacts of internet shutdowns in Algeria requires a comprehensive approach that integrates historical insights, technological advancements, and the perspectives of diverse stakeholders. Collaboration between the government, private sector, civil society and experts is essential to develop holistic strategies that minimize harm. Advocacy campaigns and transparency measures can further promote good governance and citizens' rights, contributing to a more equitable digital ecosystem.

By balancing its digital transformation goals with the fundamental rights and economic well-being of its citizens, Algeria can foster 'power to' – empowering individuals and institutions to drive systemic change through collaborative governance. This shift would reduce the harm caused by shutdowns, strengthen Algeria's digital infrastructure and support sustainable and equitable development.

## *Notes*

1 The 2007 terrorist attacks in Algeria involved coordinated bombings, including one at a government building in Algiers. The attacks killed forty-one people, including seventeen UN staff, and injured over 170 others.

2 The data presented in the table is sourced from reports published by DataReportal (DataReportal, 2024).

3 The baccalaureate exam, also known as the Bac, is a national examination in Algeria taken by students finishing secondary education. Success guarantees university admission, though not always in their preferred field. It serves as both a school leaving and university entrance test, originally stemming from the French academic system.

4 In the same resource, Access Now defines 'Curfew style' shutdowns as 'shutdowns present frequent disruption instances of one or multiple networks/services within a period of time'. They give the example of 'school exams' (Björksten and Access Now, 2022).

5 In OONI's definition, 'anomalies' are designated when there are indications of possible network interference, such as the blocking of a website or app. (OONI: Open Observatory of Network Interference, n.d.)

6 Access Now is an international organization that defends and extends the digital rights of people and communities at risk. See https://www.accessnow.org/

7 SMEX is a non-profit that advocates for and advances human rights in digital spaces across West Asia and North Africa. See https://smex.org/

8 The Internet Society is an organization working to promote the open development, evolution and use of the Internet for the benefit of all people throughout the world. See https://www.internetsociety.org/

## *Bibliography*

Access Now (2023), 'Tell MENA Authorities: #NoExamShutdown', Access Now, https://www.accessnow.org/campaign/no-exam-shutdown/

Access Now (2024), 'Tracking Internet Shutdowns: Our STOP Methodology', Access Now, https://www.accessnow.org/guide/shutdown-tracker-optimization-project/

Al Jazeera (2016, 20 June), 'Algeria: Over 500,000 Students Resit Exams After Leaks', Al Jazeera, https://www.aljazeera.com/news/2016/6/20/algeria-over-500000-students-resit-exams-after-leaks

Al Jazeera (2018), 'Algeria and Iraq Shut Down Internet to Prevent Exam Cheating', Al Jazeera, https://www.aljazeera.com/news/2018/6/21/algeria-and-iraq-shut-down-internet-to-prevent-exam-cheating

Algérie Maintenant (2018), BAC 2018 : L'internet sera suspendu pendant la première heure de chaque épreuve. Algérie Maintenant, https://fr.algeriemaintenant.dz/2018/06/19/bac-2018-linternet-sera-suspendu-pendant-la-premiere-heure-de-chaque-epreuve/

Algérie Télécom (n.d.), 'Présentation du GROUPE TÉLÉCOM ALGÉRIE', Algérie Télécom, https://www.algerietelecom.dz/fr/page/presentation-du-groupe-telecom-algerie-p107

Amina, N. (2023), 'Digitization and Higher Education in Algeria', *Proceeding Book of 2nd International Conference on Recent Academic Studies ICRAS 2023*, http://dx.doi.org/10.59287/as-proceedings.34

Amnesty International (1996), 'Algeria: Fear and Silence: A Hidden Human Rights Crisis', Amnesty International, https://www.amnesty.org/en/documents/mde28/011/1996/en/

Amnesty International (2023), 'Algerian Government Must Halt Crackdown on Rights, Release Journalists', Amnesty International, https://www.amnesty.org/en/latest/news/2023/09/algeria-government-must-halt-crackdown-on-rights-and-immediately-release-detained-journalists/

Amri, A. (2021), انقطاع الإنترنت عن مراكز التطعيم في إربد وازدحامات غير مسبوقة بسبب "فايزر" و"التوجيهي" فيديو وصور. *Roya News*, https://beta.royanews.tv/news/250205

ARTICLE19 (2024), 'Algeria: Mitigate Human Rights Threats of New Media Laws', ARTICLE 19, https://www.article19.org/resources/algeria-mitigate-human-rights-threats-of-new-media-laws/

Atti, B. E. (2023), 'Algeria Blocks Internet to Stop Cheating During Final Exams', *The New Arab*, https://www.newarab.com/news/algeria-blocks-internet-stop-cheating-during-final-exams

Bajoria, J. (2023), 'No Internet Means No Work, No Pay, No Food', Human Rights Watch, https://www.hrw.org/report/2023/06/14/no-internet-means-no-work-no-pay-no-food/internet-shutdowns-deny-access-basic

Belson, D. (2022), 'Exam Time Means Internet Disruptions in Syria, Sudan and Algeria, The Cloudflare Blog, https://blog.cloudflare.com/syria-sudan-algeria-exam-internet-shutdown/

Belson, D. (2023), 'Exam-related Internet Shutdowns in Iraq and Algeria Put Connectivity to the Test', The Cloudflare Blog, https://blog.cloudflare.com/exam-internet-shutdowns-iraq-algeria

Belson, D. (2024), 'Exam-ining Recent Internet Shutdowns in Syria, Iraq, and Algeria, The Cloudflare Blog, https://blog.cloudflare.com/syria-iraq-algeria-exam-internet-shutdown/

Benammar, S. K. (2021), 'Mass Media in Algeria', in *Routledge Handbook on Arab Media* (pp. 11–21). London, New York: Routledge, http://dx.doi.org/10.4324/9780429427084-3

Björksten, G. and Access Now (2022), 'A Taxonomy of Internet Shutdowns: The Technologies Behind Network Interference', https://www.accessnow.org/wp-content/uploads/2022/06/A-taxonomy-of-internet-shutdowns-the-technologies-behind-network-interference.pdf

Bourouina, F. (2007), الجزائر: أجهزة الأمن تعلن الحرب على مقاهي "الانتر نت" لإحباط مشاريع خلايا نائمة إرهابية. جريدة الرياض. https://www.alriyadh.com/246175

Business & Human Rights Resource Centre (n.d.), 'UN Guiding Principles', Business & Human Rights Resource Centre, https://www.business-humanrights.org/en/big-issues/governing-business-human-rights/un-guiding-principles/

Chirazi, K. (2008), طوارئ في الجزائر ضدّ مقاهي الأنترنت. إيلاف. https://elaph.com/ElaphWeb/Politics/2008/3/317444.htm

Committee to Protect Journalists (CPJ) (1999), '58 Journalists Murdered in Algeria Since 1993', Committee to Protect Journalists, https://cpj.org/1999/01/58-journalists-murdered-in-algeria-since-1993/

Committee to Protect Journalists (CPJ) (2012), 'In Algeria, New Media Law Stifles Free Expression', Committee to Protect Journalists, https://cpj.org/2012/01/in-algeria-new-media-law-stifles-free-expression/

Cornwall, A. (2002), 'Making Spaces, Changing Spaces: Situating Participation in Development', IDS Working Paper 170, Brighton, Institute of Development Studies.

Cornwall, A. and Nyamu-Musembi, C. (2004), 'Putting the 'Rights-based Approach' to Development into Perspective', *Third World Quarterly*, 25 (8): 1415–37.

Cupler, S. (2022), 'Internet Shutdowns to Prevent Cheating During Exams: The Impact on Society and Economy in the MENA Region' (SMEX and A. Abrougi, eds), SMEX, https://smex.org/wp-content/uploads/2022/09/ISOC-report-Final_Eng.pdf

Dahir, A. L. (2019), 'Algeria Has Blocked the Internet Days Before Its Ailing President Files to Run for a Fifth Term, Quartz, https://qz.com/africa/1563958/algeria-shuts-internet-amid-anti-bouteflika-election-protests

DataReportal (2024), 'Digital in Algeria', https://datareportal.com/digital-in-algeria

DIA-Algérie (2016), 'Rapport ARPT 2015 : 43 millions abonnés mobile et 18,5 millions abonnés internet', Dia-Algérie, https://dia-algerie.com/rapport-arpt-2015-43-millions-abonnes-mobile-185-millions-abonnes-internet/

Ecofin Agency (2020), 'Algeria: Internet Restriction During the Baccalaureate Exam Cost Nearly $388mln', Ecofin Agency, https://www.ecofinagency.com/telecom/2109-41838-algeria-internet-restriction-during-the-baccalaureate-exam-cost-nearly-388mln

El Atti, B. (2023), 'Algeria Blocks Internet to Stop Cheating During Final Exams', *The New Arab*, https://www.newarab.com/news/algeria-blocks-internet-stop-cheating-during-final-exams

*Etudiant Algérien* (2018), 'Nouria Benghabrit: "Toutes les dispositions prises pour le bon déroulement du baccalauréat"', *Etudiant Algérien*, https://etudiant-algerien.com/amp/nouria-benghabrit-toutes-les-dispositions-prises-pour-le-bon-deroulement-du-baccalaureat/

Euro-Med Human Rights Monitor (2023), 'Algeria: New Bill Tightens Restrictions on Journalists, Increases Media Censorship', Euro-Med Human Rights Monitor, https://euromedmonitor.org/en/article/5595/Algeria:-New-bill-tightens-restrictions-on-journalists,-increases-media-censorship

France 24 (2018), 'Algeria Goes Offline to Stop Students Cheating', FRANCE 24, https://www.france24.com/en/20180620-algeria-goes-offline-stop-students-cheating

France 24 (2019), 'Algeria Announces Presidential Election for December 12', FRANCE 24, https://www.france24.com/en/20190915-algeria-presidential-election-fixed-december-12-says-bensalah-bouteflika

Freedom House (2023), 'Algeria', Freedom House, https://freedomhouse.org/country/algeria/freedom-world/2023

Gaventa, J. (2006), 'Finding the Spaces for Change: A Power Analysis', *IDS Bulletin*, 37 (6): 23–33.

Global Network Initiative (GNI) (2016), 'New Report Reveals the Economic Costs of Internet Shutdowns', Global Network Initiative, https://globalnetworkinitiative.org/new-report-reveals-the-economic-costs-of-internet-shutdowns/

Henley, J. (2018), 'Algeria Blocks Internet to Prevent Students Cheating During Exams', *The Guardian*, https://www.theguardian.com/world/2018/jun/21/algeria-shuts-internet-prevent-cheating-school-exams

International Trade Administration (2023), 'Algeria – Information & Communications Technologies', International Trade Administration | Trade.Gov., https://www.trade.gov/country-commercial-guides/algeria-information-communications-technologies

International Trade Administration (2024), 'Algeria – Digital Economy', International Trade Administration | Trade.Gov, https://www.trade.gov/country-commercial-guides/algeria-digital-economy

Internet Society (2019), 'Policy Brief: Internet Shutdowns', Internet Society, https://www.internetsociety.org/policybriefs/internet-shutdowns/

Internet Society Pulse (2019a), 'Algeria – March 1, 2019', Pulse.Internetsociety.Org. https://pulse.internetsociety.org/shutdowns/shutdown-41

Internet Society Pulse (2019b), Algeria – september 14, 2019. Pulse.Internetsociety.Org. https://pulse.internetsociety.org/shutdowns/shutdown-177

Iraqi Network for Social Media (2024), انسم – رسالة مفتوحة إلى السلطات العراقية للمطالبة بوضع حد لحجب الانترنت في العراق أثناء الامتحانات, Insm-Iq.Org, https://insm-iq.org/archives/1079

Kamel, S. (2005), 'Assessing the Impacts of Establishing an Internet Café in the Context of a Developing Nation', Conference: Information Resources Management

Association International Conference (IRMA) on Managing Modern Organizations with Information Technology: San Diego, CA, Volume 16, https://doi.org/10.13140/2.1.2217.0249
Kemp, S. (2024), 'Digital 2024: Algeria – Datareportal – Global Digital Insights', DataReportal – Global Digital Insights, https://datareportal.com/reports/digital-2024-algeria
Khalfallah, H. and Bendjelloul, K. (2023), 'The Reality of Digital Transformation in Algeria: An Analysis of International Indicators', مجلة البحوث الاقتصادية والمالية, *Journal of Economic and Financial Research*, 10(1), 776–802.
Layadi, N. E. (2021), 'Algeria: The Costs of Clientelism', in A. Bouifer (Trans.), *Arab Media Systems* (pp. 285–302), Cambridge: Open Book Publishers, https://books.openbookpublishers.com/10.11647/obp.0238/ch17.xhtml
Mahasneh, I. (2021), عن حجب الإنترنت في التوجيهي مجددًا, JOSA, Ngo, https://josa.ngo/blog/122
McGee, R. (2020), 'Rethinking Accountability: A Power Perspective', in R. McGee and J. Pettit (eds), *Power, Empowerment and Social Change*, London: Routledge.
*Middle East Monitor* (2017), 'Algeria Blocks Internet Access to Prevent Exam Cheats', *Middle East Monitor*, https://www.middleeastmonitor.com/20170612-algeria-blocks-internet-access-to-prevent-exam-cheats/
Mitchell, R. (2023), 'Algeria: Exam Season 2023 Internet Shutdowns', Internet Society Pulse, https://pulse.internetsociety.org/blog/algeria-exam-season-2023-internet-shutdowns
Mnejja, K. (2024), 'Why #NoExamShutdown Should Be Every Country's Class Motto', Access Now, https://www.accessnow.org/why-noexamshutdown-should-be-the-motto/
Mnejja, K., Fatafta, M. and Anthonio, F. (2021), 'Internet Shutdowns During Exams: When MENA Governments Fail the Test', Access Now, https://www.accessnow.org/mena-internet-shutdowns-during-exams/
Nossiter, A. (2019), 'Algeria Protests Grow Against President Bouteflika, Ailing and Out of Sight', *The New York Times*, https://www.nytimes.com/2019/03/01/world/africa/algeria-protests-bouteflika.html
OHCHR (2022), 'Internet Shutdowns: UN Report Details "Dramatic" Impact on People's Lives and Human Rights', OHCHR, https://www.ohchr.org/en/press-releases/2022/06/internet-shutdowns-un-report-details-dramatic-impact-peoples-lives-and-human
OONI: Open Observatory of Network Interference (n.d.-a), 'Interpreting OONI Data', OONI, https://ooni.org/support/interpreting-ooni-data/#anomalies
OONI: Open Observatory of Network Interference (n.d.-b), 'OONI Explorer – Open Data on Internet Censorship Worldwide', https://explorer.ooni.org/search?probe_cc=DZ&since=2022-06-12&until=2022-06-16&failure=false&only=anomalies&category_code=GRP
OONI: Open Observatory of Network Interference (n.d.-c), 'OONI Explorer – Open Data on internet censorship worldwide', https://explorer.ooni.org/search?probe_cc=DZ&since=2022-06-12&until=2022-06-16&failure=false&only=anomalies&category_code=COMT
Palinkas, L. A., Horwitz, S. M., Green, C. A., Wisdom, J. P., Duan, N. and Hoagwood, K. (2013), Purposeful Sampling for Qualitative Data Collection and Analysis in Mixed Method Implementation Research', *Administration and Policy in Mental Health and Mental Health Services Research*, 42 (5): 533–44, https://doi.org/10.1007/s10488-013-0528-y
Privacy International (n.d.), 'Legality, Necessity and Proportionality', Privacy International, https://privacyinternational.org/our-demands/legality-necessity-and-proportionality

Radio Dabanga (2019), 'Sudan Internet Shutdown: Another Court Case Filed', Dabanga Radio TV Online, https://www.dabangasudan.org/en/all-news/article/sudan-internet-shutdown-another-court-case-filed

Rahmouni, Z. (2018), 'Bac 2018 en Algérie: La coupure Internet plombe l'activité des entreprises – Jeune Afrique.com', JeuneAfrique.Com. https://www.jeuneafrique.com/583689/societe/bac-2018-en-algerie-la-coupure-dinternet-plombe-lactivite-des-entreprises/

Reporters Without Borders (RSF) (2020), 'Algeria Blocks Access to Three More News Sites', RSF, https://rsf.org/en/algeria-blocks-access-three-more-news-sites

Reuters (2016), 'Algeria Blocks Facebook, Twitter to Stop Exam Cheats – State Media', Reuters, https://www.reuters.com/article/us-algeria-media-idUSKCN0Z50JX/

Rydzak, J., Karanja, M. and Opiyo, N. (2020), 'Dissent Does Not Die In Darkness: Network Shutdowns and Collective Action in African Countries', *International Journal of Communication*, 14: 4264–87, https://ijoc.org/index.php/ijoc/article/view/12770/3185

Sayadi, E. and Samaro, D. (2020), 'Internet Shutdowns in Algeria and Sudan: Damaging Practices During Exceptional Circumstances', Access Now, https://www.accessnow.org/internet-shutdowns-in-algeria-and-sudan-damaging-practices-during-exceptional-circumstances/

Scagnetti, J.-C. (2012), 'État, médias et émigration en Algérie sous l'ère Boumediene (1965–1978)', *Cahiers de La Méditerranée*, 85: 59–70, https://doi.org/10.4000/cdlm.6667

Sibai, A. (2020), '#NoExamShutdown: 4 MENA Countries Shut Down the Internet So Far "to Fight Cheating!"', SMEX, https://smex.org/noexamshutdown-4-mena-countries-shut-down-the-internet-so-far-to-fight-cheating/

SMEX (2022), 'Internet Shutdowns and Their Impact on Society', SMEX, https://smex.org/internet-shutdowns-and-their-impact-on-society/

Taye, B. and Access Now (2020), 'Targeted, Cut Off, and Left in the Dark', The #KeepItOn Report on Internet Shutdowns in 2019, https://www.accessnow.org/wp-content/uploads/2020/02/KeepItOn-2019-report-1.pdf

The Arab-European Association for Media and Communication Researchers (AREACORE). (n.d.), 'Private Broadcasting in Algeria – script (en) – AREACORE', https://www.areacore.org/ims/private-broadcasting-in-algeria/private-broadcasting-in-algeria-script-en/

The OpenNet Initiative (2009), 'Algeria', OpenNet Initiative, https://opennet.net/research/profiles/algeria

TRT Afrika (2023), 'Algérie: Démarrage des épreuves du baccalauréat, l'accès à internet perturbé', TRT Afrika, https://www.trtafrika.com/fr/africa/algerie-demarrage-des-epreuves-du-baccalaureat-lacces-a-internet-perturbe-13577416

UNESCO (2020), 'Diversification des chaines radiophoniques: developpement et numerisation du reseau radiophonique national', https://Www.Unesco.Org/.https://www.unesco.org/creativity/en/policy-monitoring-platform/diversification-des-chaines-radiophoniques-developpement-et-numerisation-du-reseau-radiophonique

United Nations (1948), 'Universal Declaration of Human Rights (UDHR)', https://www.un.org/en/about-us/universal-declaration-of-human-rights

United Nations (1966), International Covenant on Economic, Social and Cultural Rights. OHCHR. https://www.ohchr.org/en/instruments-mechanisms/instruments/international-covenant-economic-social-and-cultural-rights

United Nations (1976), 'International Covenant on Civil and Political Rights (ICCPR)', https://www.ohchr.org/en/instruments-mechanisms/instruments/international-covenant-civil-and-political-rights

United Nations (1976), 'International Covenant on Economic, Social and Cultural Rights (ICESCR)', https://www.ohchr.org/en/instruments-mechanisms/instruments/international-covenant-economic-social-and-cultural-rights

United Nations (2021), https://www.ohchr.org/sites/default/files/2022-01/NV-shutdowns-call-for-inputs.pdf (Office of the United Nations High Commissioner for Human Rights, Ed.).

United Nations (2022), 'Internet Shutdowns: UN Report Details 'Dramatic' Impact on People's Lives and Human Rights', OHCHR https://www.ohchr.org/en/press-releases/2022/06/internet-shutdowns-un-report-details-dramatic-impact-peoples-lives-and-human

UN Human Rights Committee (HRC) (2001), 'CCPR General Comment No. 29: Article 4: Derogations during a State of Emergency', CCPR/C/21/Rev.1/Add.11, https://www.refworld.org/legal/general/hrc/2001/en/30676

VeneKlasen, L. and Miller, V. (2002), *A New Weave of Power, People and Politics*, Oklahoma: World Neighbours.

West, D. M. (2016), 'Internet Shutdowns Cost Countries $2.4 Billion Last Year', Center for Technology Innovation, https://witnessradio.org/wp-content/uploads/2016/10/intenet-shutdowns-v-3.pdf

# Chapter 12

## Uganda's 2021 election

## Platforms versus the state versus citizens

Juliet Nanfuka

### *Introduction*

This chapter will focus on a unique series of events that contributed to the internet shutdowns during Uganda's 2021 election, marked by a social media shutdown that was swiftly followed by a complete internet shutdown. While these disruptions were not unexpected, they underscored a disturbing and evolving pattern of digital repression that has been employed in Ugandan elections since 2006. Over the years, authorities have strategically weaponized disruptions to digital communications to stifle citizens' ability to assemble online, build or support movements, express opinions and access vital resources during critical moments such as during protests or elections – ultimately reinforcing their grip on power. Thus, this chapter delves into these dynamics with a focus on the intricate nature in which power and rights have been increasingly challenged by technology – and in more recent years by increasing access to social media. With a specific focus on the five-day internet shutdown that occurred in February 2021, this chapter reflects upon the interplay between state power and citizens' rights, and what the implications of the action of shutting down the internet have on power structures and rights in the country. The chapter draws from key informant interviews with journalists, political aspirants, representatives from state authorities and members of civil society, and an online survey, complemented by desk research, a review of news reports and social media posts, and offers a comprehensive view of these dynamics. It is also guided by John Gaventa's 'powercube' framework (Gaventa, 2006) which allows for an analysis of power and how it operates, including in digital spaces.

With increasing access to the internet and growth in social media use, citizens have grown to possess the ability to amplify narratives in ways that were previously unseen – and are consequently challenging power. In environments where traditional media is suppressed, online content, particularly on social media platforms, has emerged as a key avenue for filling this void. More importantly, for Uganda, social media is a place where political, social and economic tensions play out, particularly during times of national crisis such as public protests and elections.

Uganda, with its increasingly youthful and often discontented population, finds itself at a critical juncture. Long-standing political power interests are clashing with shifting social-economic dynamics, competing power agendas and pressures to align with global best practices. These tensions are particularly evident in the digital society, where digital citizenship issues of access, control and governance are increasingly contested.

Various forms of information control have been employed in Uganda since the 1900s, often as a response to shifting power dynamics and changing social, political and technological contexts. These measures have evolved alongside advancements in communication technologies and shifts in societal and political landscapes, reflecting the state's efforts to adapt its control mechanisms to maintain authority and influence. In a country marked by a history of kingdoms, colonial rule and a struggle for independence, Uganda's post-independence period was marked by optimism and the promise of self-governance. However, in the years that have since followed, the country has faced significant challenges, including political instability, ethnic tensions and economic difficulties.

Currently, Uganda is ranked as a 'hybrid regime', a state that combines democratic characteristics with autocratic ones. This description of regime-type is mirrored by the country's categorization as 'partly free' state in the 2023 Freedom on the Net ranking (Freedom House, 2023). It was listed as one of the countries that have implemented various forms of online censorship and information controls including the blocking of websites that hosted political, social or religious content deemed contrary to state interests, restricting access to social media platforms, engaging in documented pro-government online manipulation, enforcing restrictive laws and arresting journalists critical of the regime – key markers of an authoritarian mentality.

Uganda's population has grown from an estimated 32 million in 2011 to the current 45.5 million (State House, 2023). Alongside the population growth has been the consistent growth in internet access and use over the years which in 2011 stood at 4.8 million internet users, 21.5 million internet users in 2021, and 27.7 million internet users in 2023 (UCC, 2023). While internet penetration has been on the rise, the growth in liberal media in the 1990s has seen traditional media formats like radio, television and print also seek presence in online spaces.

## *Methodology*

This study comprises a mixed methods approach that included desk research, a short online questionnaire, complemented by key informant interviews (KII); in total, fifteen individuals contributed insights. Combined, this represented a diverse mix of academics, journalists, government representatives, business owners, civil society representatives and students. Each experienced internet shutdowns including the 2021 shutdown and provided unique interpretations and accounts of the event – as well as other prior network disruptions. The online survey aimed to capture general experiences, perceptions and impacts of internet shutdowns across a diverse demographic. The KIIs provided detailed and nuanced accounts of internet shutdowns offering insights into their personal and professional experiences. Extensive desk research was undertaken to contextualize and supplement the primary data. The desk research involved reviewing policy documents, reports, academic literature and media articles to analyse patterns, and the evolution of information controls in Uganda over the years.

## *Background*

To understand current practices in digital disruptions and information controls through internet shutdowns, one has to track back to a pre-digital era in Uganda. A time shaped by colonial rule and jostling with local leaders and communities as Uganda's media landscape evolved into one informed by growing regulation of information flow. Analog methods such as censorship of media and restrictions on political communication laid the foundation for power interests to be maintained through information controls.

**The rise of the media:** Media restrictions in Uganda have been commonplace for decades with documented cases going as far back as the pre-colonial era. Uganda was declared a British protectorate in 1894 by Sir Gerald Portal on the back of vicious religious wars involving Anglicans, Catholics and Muslims. As such, religion was one of the tools utilized by the British as an avenue for control to extend colonial power. This merged into the power interests of the colonialists being served through print publications, before shifting to the interests of Ugandan citizens being served by print publications authored by Ugandans.

This shift in the role of print publications and their alignment with power interests is reflected in the surge of newspapers that began slowly in the early 1900s, then expanded rapidly in the 1950s and 1960s, and slowed down in the late 1970s. By the end of 1976, only fourteen of the original eighty-four newspapers established over the last seven decades still existed (Isoba, 1980). This decline mirrored the broader transition from colonial rule to indigenous governance, highlighting how changes in political power directly influenced the rise and fall of some forms of media publications in Uganda.

In 1900, the Church Missionary Society (founded by the Church of England to send missionaries to Africa and other parts of the world) published the first newsletter in the country. Over the coming years, a series of religious publications would emerge including the *Mengo Notes* (1902), *Ebifa mu Buganda/News* in Uganda (1907) and in 1911, a monthly Luganda language newspaper called *Munno/Our Friend* (1911). While these publications served religious interests (though some fostered early political consciousness among Ugandans, e.g. Munno) and loyalty to the British Empire, in 1920 the nature and content of publications started changing with the arrival of *Sekanyolya* which is lauded as the 'first independent African newspaper' and was started by Ugandans working as clerks, teachers and printers in Nairobi, Kenya (*Daily Monitor, 2021*). It would be the first of several other publications that would emerge and challenge the protectorate (a pre-colonial power structure), class, religion and the use of kingdoms for social influence.

**Media restrictions:** However, with the British colonial government realizing the growing threat to colonial interests and power, they introduced the first restrictions on free press in 1910 by issuing Surety Ordinance No.9 which stated that, 'no person or company shall print or publish or cause to be printed or published within the protectorate unless executed and registered in the office of the Registrar of Documents under the Registration of Documents Ordinance a bond in the sum of shs.6000 with one or more [surety]' (African Center for Media Excellence, 2011). Four years later, the Press Censorship Ordinance No. 4 of 1915 was published granting powers to the governor to 'at any time establish a press censorship and may at any time revoke such order'. As criticism of colonial rule and demands for independence grew stronger, so did Britain's repressive media legislation.

By 1927, the monthly publication called *Gambuze* was already questioning free labour and class structure in the protectorate. These concerns would go on to intensify as the publication called *Buganda Nyaffe* challenged the colonial practice of pursuing policies aimed at exploiting Africans through sinister tactics, especially in the cotton industry. In 1944, the founder of the publication, who was also the president of the Uganda Growers Co-operative Union, was arrested and 'charged with publishing a seditious document and fined Shs. 100 for breach of war-time censorship regulations' (Gariyo, 1992). Despite the arrest, more publications would emerge to challenge imperial power interests, expressing grievances and casting a light on socio-economic concerns that would otherwise have remained unknown.

In 1949, narratives emerged criticizing the King of the Buganda Kingdom (Kabaka) for failing to address these concerns, which benefited the interests of colonial authorities at the expense of the local population. This discontent led to a series of riots and press reports that highlighted the growing strife among the people. As such, publications like *The Uganda Star*, *Mugobansonga* and *Munyonyozi* contributed to the introduction of The Press Censorship and Publications Act of 1949 that served to limit circulation of these papers before altogether banning them. Parallel to this was the arrest and conviction of the editor of *Dobozi lya Buganda* for criticizing the Kabaka (Lugalambi and Tabaire, 2010). By 1950, the Penal Code (ULII) would go on to provide for the offences of 'seditious conspiracy and libel, possessing seditious documents, and publishing a false report'. It would also allow for police to arrest suspects without a warrant.

These comprised the early framework of tactics through which colonial power structures would use the law to enable information control measures, which would evolve as the media landscape grew, access to education improved and media-related technologies evolved. During the 1950s and early 1960s there would be more arrests of journalists who criticized the Protectorate Government. It would also be during this time that language such as 'fostering confusion' would be used against the media, while the practice of banning print publications would become even more commonplace as a tool to teach newspapers to be 'responsible and objective' in their reporting (Lugalambi and Tabaire, 2010).

As more Ugandans became exposed to broader world views through education, travel and interaction with other Africans and people outside the continent, they began to question the logic of colonial rule as well as discrimination, oppression and exploitation. They questioned the logic of restricting Africans from carrying out lucrative import and export trade, the middleman's role of the Asian traders and businessmen and land grants to white settlers in Uganda. In 1961, a standout publication, *The Transition*, founded by Rajat Neogy, a Ugandan of Indian Bengali descent would go on to become a key pan-African literary and political journal, building upon its beginnings as an intellectual magazine during a time of radical changes across the continent (*The Transition,* 1961). However, the space for publishing critical opinion was shrinking. This included the 1956 banning of the publications *Uganda Express* and *Uganda Post* by the British colonial authorities for alleged sedition and which also saw the publisher, J. W. (Jolly 'Joe') Kiwanuka, being jailed. In 1968 Abu Mayanja, a critic of the colonialists for their approach toward a proposed East African federation was arrested as a consequence of the publication in *The Transition* of a letter from him to Neogy, the editor of *The Transition*. Neogy would also be arrested. Upon release, Neogy would shift the publishing of *The Transition* from Uganda to Ghana in response to the shrinking space for critical opinion in Uganda (Tabaire, 2007) and the necessity to maintain power interests at physical and ideological levels.

The Penal Code has been described as 'the mother of all Colonial media legislations in the Protectorate, with implications for post-independent Ugandan media the Colonialist may possibly never have conceived, was the passage of the Penal Code in 1950' (Kakooza, 2012).

The trends established and enabled by the Penal Code aimed at information controls would continue to be used in post-colonial rule and would see publications like *Sekanyolya*, the Luganda-language newspaper promoting Buganda interests, being banned in 1966 and in 1981; the Obote government would go on to ban five of the main newspapers in one month (March) alone (Tabaire, 2007).

**The evolution of politics:** Uganda gained independence from colonial rule on 9 October 1962. Of early post-colonial rule period, Lugalambi and Tabaire write that 'any criticism (of the government) had to be "constructive," with the leaders retaining the right to define what the phrase means or should mean'. The state encouraged the press to restrict itself to questions of development not politics, as if the two were mutually exclusive, arguing that nation-building was the national goal and that criticism is counter-productive of that goal (Lapček-Neogy, 1997). This marked a continued need for power interest to be served even though there had been a change in leadership. It also highlights the unequal power relationship between the state and the media in favour of the former.

While print had been a dominant media form, radio would be introduced in Uganda in 1954, and television would later arrive in 1963. Politicians would seek to control these new media using justifications that echoed language from the earlier ruling regime. In 1962, Milton Obote of the Uganda People's Congress (UPC) party, was elected as Prime Minister. The Obote regime would continue with the practice on clamping down on the media and would target the popular '*The Transition*' publication due to its criticism of government policy. Obote became less and less tolerant of criticisms. Through a coup d'état, in 1971 Obote was overthrown by General Idi Amin who would be described as one who 'embraced the media and understood its power … he had a great sense of how media could amplify his ego and his political will' (Burke, 2019). As media technology advanced during Amin's rule, he used it to articulate his populism and radical ideologies to maintain his grip on political and military power. So shrewd was Obote in his understanding of the media that Tabaire (2007) writes,

> when Idi Amin overthrew Milton Obote in 1971, he cited lack of freedom to air views as reason number three, out of 18, for his action. Many were happy. The happiness did not last. Within a year, the killing of journalists had started. Munno editor Fr Clement Kiggundu, John Serwaniko, also of Munno, news photographer Jimmy Parma, and TV journalist James Bwogi were all murdered. Many more were jailed. Others chose exile. The news business as we know it died. So did Uganda.

In 1980, Amin was overthrown by Obote and for a moment it appeared as though the press had revived in the years that followed. However, under this second rule of Obote, press freedom and control would only worsen as, in 1981 alone, seven newspapers would be shut down due to the content they posted including reporting about military killings of civilians.

In 1986, Yoweri Museveni overthrew Obote and made promises of democracy and fundamental change. Many of the banned newspapers would resurface with the change of guard. However, during this period into the early 1990s, the government would drag at least one journalist to court a year. The Museveni government would use more sinister tactics against the media; when it wasn't using legislation to harass the media, it was using administrative means such as withholding state advertising from publications. Nonetheless, the practice of banning media remained commonplace despite an increasingly liberal and pluralistic media landscape.

> The *Weekend Digest* was banned by Museveni within six months of taking power. The newspaper had carried a story claiming the opposition Democratic Party was planning to oust the government with the support of the West Germans and Italians. The government declared the paper a front being used by its enemies to 'destabilise the country'. Then, starting in March 1986 through to 1992, the government hauled before the courts at least a journalist a year. Sedition was the charge of choice, although there was a sprinkling of criminal libel and defamation.
>
> Extract from The Press and Political Repression in Uganda: Back to the Future? by Bernard Tabaire (2007).

During this period, the state demonstrated its capacity to grant or withdraw power strategically. By reinstating some media houses, the state created the appearance of restoring visible power to these media houses – allowing them to operate within a space they have been invited into by the state. This action projected an impression of inclusion and accountability. However, this reinstatement came with constraints, such as self-censorship or alignment with state interests, thereby transforming these invited spaces into mechanisms of hidden power. Media houses were silenced not through overt suppression but by shaping their operating conditions and limiting their capacity to challenge the status quo. The state's actions reinforced invisible power by normalizing the idea that control over media is a privilege granted by the state, not an inherent right.

The press control tactics employed in Uganda's earlier years as a protectorate, then as a colonial and post-colonial state have been employed and extended beyond the media to political opposition actors, civil society and state critics. It is during Museveni's rule (from 1986 to the time of writing) that the media and technology landscape has greatly evolved, presenting unique challenges – and opportunities for control – including through digital telecommunications blocks and shutdowns.

In its early years, the National Resistance Movement (NRM) with Museveni at the lead had created a 'no-party democracy' which banned competing political parties. However, a decade into his rule, the first multiparty election was held in 1996. This was marred by widespread claims of voter intimidation and election rigging. In accordance with the 1995 constitution, Uganda has held six national elections (1996, 2001, 2006, 2011, 2016 and 2021) all of which have resulted in the re-election of President Yoweri Kaguta Museveni, marking nearly four decades of presidency.

However, it should be noted that as the media landscape evolved with liberalization, internet penetration figures also grew steadily in the country. This added a new intensity to the need to maintain control over the flow of information, not only by the media, but also by the public who had gained a new power form enabled by social media tools that allowed them room not only to express themselves but also to demand accountability and transparency. As such, while a myriad of rights could be enabled by online tools including Access to Information (ATI), Freedom of Expression, Press Freedom, Freedom of Assembly and Association (FoAA) and many others, the need to exert power would mean that these rights would be withdrawn when state power was challenged.

## *The turning point in 2011*

Over the years, various efforts have gone into regulating and managing the flow of analogue and digital information in Uganda. Some may argue that more sinister tactics such as increased taxation (A4AI, 2018) on digital access are also tools employed as information controls and a show of power.

**Table 12.1** Network Disruptions in Uganda

| Platform | Dates | Circumstances | Key opposition actor |
|---|---|---|---|
| Multiple websites affected by the blocking of RadioKatwe.com | 2006 | The first documented case of internet censorship was applied to RadioKatwe.com a website critical of the state – the action would affect nearly 700 several other websites hosted under the same internet protocol (Freedom House, 2012). The website would later be closed by its administrators. | Dr Kizza Besigye<br>• Turned to social media as a tool for social commentary and movement building in 2011 with the walk to wine campaign. |
| Short Message Services (SMS) | 17 February – unclear, 2011 | In the wake of the 2010 Arab Spring, ahead of the 18 February, elections, government banned text messages/SMS that included words like 'Egypt', 'dictator', 'teargas' and 'people power'. | |
| Social media (Facebook and Twitter) | 14 – 17 April 2011 | The social media platforms received a 24-hour ban while media houses were banned from screening '#WalkToWork' protests | |
| Social media, messaging tools like WhatsApp and mobile money | 18–21 February 2016 | Election day | |
| Social media | 11–12 May 2016 | Swearing in of incumbent Yoweri Museveni | |
| *Social Media Tax | June 2018 | A social media tax (Over-The-Top – OTT tax) was introduced that initially forced off some 5 million users from the internet (Nanfuka, Social Media Tax Cuts Ugandan Internet Users by Five Million, Penetration Down From 47% to 35%, 2019). Numbers slowly recovered to pre-OTT tax levels. In 2021, government introduced a direct 12% levy on the net price of internet data, after which a Value Added Tax (VAT) of 18% would apply. | |

| Platform | Dates | Circumstances | Key opposition actor |
|---|---|---|---|
| Social media | 9–18 January 2021 | Led to 14 January 2021 Election day which was marked with pre-election violence, arrests of opposition actors and media. Shutdown commenced with download platforms like Google Play and Apple's App Store being blocked. By 11 January, social media platforms such as Facebook, Twitter, Instagram and WhatsApp also started being blocked. While rising numbers of users are relying on Virtual Private Networks (VPN) to stay connected, the government is understood to have ordered that several VPN providers be blocked too. | Robert Kyaluganyi (Bobi Wine)<br>• Emergence of opposition actor channels aimed at supporting his campaign<br>• Strategic use of social media as a tool for commentary<br>• Rise in prevalence of bots aimed at supporting opposition narratives including through disinformation |
| Facebook | 13 January 2021 | The platform was shutdown alongside other platforms but remain inaccessible without a VPN to date | |

Source: Author.

## *A selective 'kill switch'*

The 2010 Arab Spring marked a key event in the digital ecosystem the world over. The realization that movement building through online tools could not only be a catalyst for change but also contribute to the downfall of entrenched regimes sparked fear into other authoritarian regimes across the continent, including in Uganda.

Up until 2011, the practice of disrupting communications through internet shutdowns was not a regular occurrence; however, the blocking of select websites alongside longstanding practices such as the arrest of journalists, and the silencing of civil society actors through arrests and threats as forms of controlling the flow of information had served the power interests of the state. However, in early February 2011, the government through the Uganda Communications Commission (UCC) ordered telecommunications service providers to intercept all text messages (SMS) with words or phrases including 'Ben Ali', 'Tunisia', 'UPDF' (Uganda Police Defence Force), 'army', 'dictator', 'gun', 'police' and 'teargas', 'Egypt', 'bullet' and 'people power' ahead of the 18 February 2011 elections. While not a complete shutdown of digital communication, the move still constituted a disruption to digital communications – albeit, selectively. A statement provided by the UCC indicates that the measure was taken as the content had the potential to 'promote hatred and create discomfort among the public'. This was the beginning of what would eventually morph into fully fledged internet shutdowns in later years including in 2021, the focus year of this chapter.

Following the 2011 elections, protests would erupt following the broadcasting of the arrest of opposition actor and presidential challenger, Dr Kizza Besigye. Broadcasters were instructed to stop live coverage of the anti-government protests and some media houses found that access to their websites was disrupted (African Center for Media Excellence, 2011). These blocks to information were attributed to government interference including by instruction from the communications regulatory authority, the Uganda Communications Commission (UCC). A verbal instruction was issued by the national communications regulator, the UCC to various broadcast media houses with an instruction that if any of the TV stations that had been carrying live coverage refused to heed the directive, they risked their license being revoked (African Center for Media Excellence, 2011). This demonstrated the state's use of power through its regulatory frameworks – specifically the licensing system – as a tool to exert control over media houses.

Critics noted that Uganda's heavy-handed response to the service delivery protests organized by opposition actors did more to undermine the legitimacy of the government than the controversial 2011 presidential elections themselves (Africa Center, 2011). The disruption to digital communications during this period would serve to undermine the state's legitimacy in future elections as well.

## *Silencing social media*

The tension between political parties and opposition actors – in particular Dr Kizza Besigye and Yoweri Museveni – remained rife in the period between 2006 and 2016. The occurrences of affronts to press freedom and access to information marked this period which saw a decline in access to information/press freedom amidst rising internet penetration in the country. In recognition of the latter, it must be noted that, in 2013, the government released social media guidelines which sought to enhance access to information held by the various Ministries, Departments and Agencies (MDAs). The Guidelines required that all MDAs open a social media account – Twitter (now X) and Facebook – noting that 'The main benefit of social media for governments is that well-considered and carefully implemented social media can create greater transparency, an interactive relationship with the public, a stronger sense of ownership of government policy and services, and thus a greater public trust in government' (National Information Technology Authority-Uganda (NITA-U), 2013).

Ironically, in the lead up to the 18 February elections in 2016, concerns over whether digital connectivity would remain accessible became a key point of public discussion, especially in reference to the government's apparent shift towards embracing the use of online tools for accountability and civic engagement. It was also in 2016 when the first ever pre-election presidential debate was hosted and televised ahead of the elections which also contributed to an increase in online engagement specific to the elections. Nonetheless, on the morning of the 2016 elections, citizens would find themselves locked out of social media platforms including Facebook, X (then Twitter) and WhatsApp (Nanfuka, 2016). Further, the popular mobile phone-based financial transaction service commonly known as mobile money was also offline. The block would last two days and would be followed by another social media ban in May as the re-elected Museveni was being sworn in. The president noted that the move was necessary as 'steps must be taken for security to stop so many (social media users from) getting into trouble; it is temporary because some people use those pathways for telling lies' (Butagira, 2016). However, opposition candidates popularized the use of Virtual Private Networks (VPNs) to circumvent the shutdown. Meanwhile, the use of VPNs could not help with the block placed on mobile money transactions which stunted most citizens due to Uganda's nature as a largely unbanked economy, leaving millions of customers stranded without access to funds including for payments for services such as electricity, water or even airtime to make calls. Due to the elections being declared a public holiday alongside fears of election violence, mobile money users topped-up their accounts to maintain some level of liquidity.

These decisions marked a blatant show of power over citizens where the state could invite citizens into digital spaces, and even economic spaces, but at the same time retract that invitation. Meanwhile this illustrated a power over telecommunication services providers, for if they did not follow suit with the instruction to shutdown access, they risked having their licences revoked.

## *The 2021 elections: platforms versus the state*

In 2021, the internet shutdown that occurred was in the wake of a tense pre-election environment shaped by Covid-19 restrictions and increased online activity as a result of heavy restrictions to physical public movement in a bid to curb the spread of the virus. The pandemic forced a shift to what the government termed a 'scientific election' (Ministry of ICT and National Guidance, 2020). The approach would rely on digital engagement and smaller gatherings rather than large gatherings typical of campaign rally seasons. The heightened online activity would also see the rise of rampant disinformation – not only about the pandemic, but also about the campaigns related to the elections that were set to take place in February of that year.

The presence of Covid-19 ultimately provided an opportunity for the militarization of enforcement of pandemic control and preventive measures and would see the heavy-handed responses of security forces documented by the public and shared online (BBC Eye, 2021). The election would be marked with a heavy presence of support for musician turned politician, Robert Kyaluganyi (stage name Bobi Wine). Both pro-government and opposition actors would employ disinformation as a tool to sway narratives in their favour, with Facebook and Twitter being the primary platforms upon which this would occur. Hashtags like #StopPoliceBrutalityInUganda and #StopHooliganism (Roberts and Karekwaivanane, 2024) underscored the intense clash of narratives. Closer to the elections, a series of protests erupted and authorities responded with violence, as police used tear gas and live bullets to disperse the presidential candidate's supporters following his arrest (Al Jazeera, 2020). Various incidents were widely documented online including on YouTube channels newly created as an avenue to disseminate information in the wake of the arrests and threats of journalists covering the opposition candidate campaign trail. One standout incident occurred on 18 November 2020 when Bobi Wine was arrested during which the aftermath would be shared on social media, providing crucial data for a *BBC Africa Eye* report. The *BBC* programme would document in an investigative feature the zealous use of live ammunition against mostly unarmed citizens and bystanders (BBC Eye, 2021). To justify this use of police violence, the state claimed that the peaceful demonstrations had turned violent. Although legitimate cases of 'hooliganism' were documented such as video and pictures of a female police officer being beaten by citizens, the investigation revealed that, contrary to the pro-ruling party disinformation, there was no evidence that any of the civilians shot on the streets of Kampala city (as documented in the BBC Eye report) were rioting on that day – they were simply going about their daily business. Following the screening of the investigation, the Criminal Investigations Department summoned Uganda-based editors on allegations of 'criminal libel, incitement to violence, and false news publication' (BBC, 2021). It is ironic that having been caught deploying disinformation the state arrested the editor on charges of 'false news publication'. The summoning echoed familiar state power plays over the media seen throughout

Uganda's history, including actions taken during colonial rule and the early post-colonial period.

Amidst these developments, the government harboured increasing anxiety about the nature of content on platforms like Google's YouTube, Facebook and X (then Twitter) and the extent of the actions these platforms were taking. An example of this is documented in a letter submitted by the UCC on 9 December 2020 to Google requesting the company to take down seventeen YouTube accounts that focused on publishing pro-Bobi Wine content. Among the accounts was one belonging to Bobi Wine himself. By mid-December 2020, the channels had amassed over 59 million views and 300,000 subscribers (URN, 2020). The UCC argued that the channels did not meet the minimum broadcasting standards and were sensationalizing news reports, resulting in riots that led to the loss of several lives. They further argued that the channels were broadcasting without broadcasting licences and were thus in violation of the law. However, in response, the Google Head of Communication and Public Affairs for Africa, Dorothy Ooko, stated that 'it is very hard to just have a channel removed due to a government request' (*The Independent*, 2020). This marked a direct challenge of state power – a challenge unwitnessed before in the history of power structures in the country. It rendered the typical tactic useless as the platforms were not domiciled in Uganda where legislation, arrests, threats could be utilized as they have been for other stakeholders who have challenged the state.

However, where opposition actors turned to foreign-owned social media platforms, according to the African Center for Media Excellence (ACME), the incumbent Museveni got more time on television news than Kyagulanyi, with some television stations heavily tilting the scale in the former's favour. This was similar for print media. Radio broadcasts, however, featured more content on Kyaluganyi than Museveni (ACME, 2021).

## *The shutdown*

On 11 January 2021 Facebook suspended the accounts of a number of government officials associated with the ruling party for what it described as coordinated inauthentic behaviour aimed at manipulating public debate ahead of the presidential elections. Twitter also suspended similar accounts. Facebook removed 220 accounts, thirty-two pages, fifty-nine groups and 139 Instagram accounts which according to the platforms had links with the media arm of the government – the Government Citizens Interaction Center (DFR Lab, 2021).

The action taken by the platforms to remove the state-linked accounts that violated their terms of use sparked a debate on who has the authority to curate online content, especially where government content is involved. President Museveni's press secretary, Don Wanyama (whose Facebook and Instagram accounts were also suspended), took to Twitter and accused Facebook of trying to influence the elections. He stated, 'Shame on the foreign powers who think they can impose a puppet government on Uganda by disabling the online accounts of NRM supporters'. Wanyama's account was among those that shared anti-opposition narrative.

On 12 January, forty-eight hours before polling opened, reports of social media being blocked in Uganda started emerging. Eventually a nationwide internet shutdown was implemented. The election slated for 14 January would be conducted in a complete internet blackout. The state's communication regulatory authority, the Uganda Communications Commission instructed ISPs to block internet access (Nanfuka, 2021). Internet access would start its journey back to restoration on 18 January. All sites would be made accessible, except Facebook. Similarly to 2021, a power dynamic would play out, one that entailed the power relationship between the state, the regulator and private companies.

## *The kill switch: casting a dark cloud on rights*

In Uganda, power – its access, control and retention – has shaped not only the political and media landscape but also the evolving digital sphere. The government has continued the power dynamics established during the colonial era by asserting its power over the media and exerting political influence over state bodies including ministries, departments and agencies (MDAs).

Indeed, even in its early years as a democracy, the internet marked a significant change in the way citizens engaged with information or built movements – which when combined, introduced a new way of challenging state power, demanding

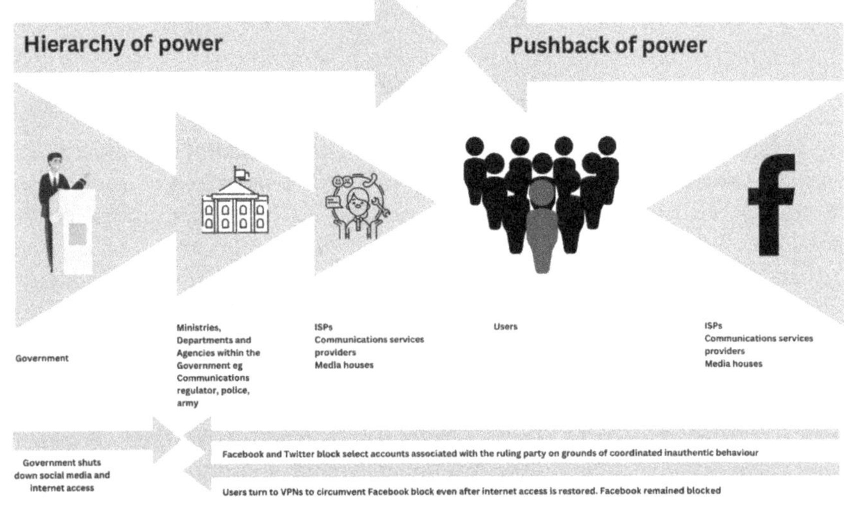


**Figure 12.1** Power Interests of Internet Shutdowns.

Source: Author.

accountability, and simultaneously the internet also provided an almost direct avenue for responses from the state.

While the internet was evolving into an indispensable part of modern life, shaping and informing much of the human experience and affecting both those online and offline, it was also redefining power structures between the state and citizens – granting citizens the power to demand more transparency and accountability, including through movements built online. Indeed, online movements, an extension of offline structures would evolve to become key avenues through which the state would be challenged in the public domain.

Through an analysis of John Gaventa through the structure of the 'power cube', Uganda presents a strong case for the interactions of spaces, levels and forms of power (2006). While internet shutdowns present an invisible act of power by disconnecting citizens or internet users from their basic rights of access to information and freedom of expression, in many instances, the display of power has also been accompanied by visible acts such as arrests of journalists – an act which also serves to limit press freedom and access to information.

The invisible acts of power have been met with equally unseen forms of resistance such as the use of VPNs to counter disruptions to the social media shutdowns in 2016 and 2021, and the 2021 complete internet shutdown. However, in 2021 when platforms (Meta and X) exercised their invisible power by blocking state-affiliated accounts, the state responded by blocking social media and eventually entire access to the internet.

The three dimensions of levels, spaces and forms of power prove to be useful in analysing internet shutdowns. It may be that the people imposing shutdowns are global, national or local powerholders; their decisions may be very visible or hidden or deploying invisible power and may take place in closed or invited spaces. Citizens may be claiming new spaces to resist shutdowns, mobilize counter-power and campaign at local or global levels. In some countries shutdowns have become so frequent that they are normalized, leading to what we might term 'shutdown realism', where citizens internalize shutdowns as normal and justified, and where a 'chilling effect' results in citizens self-censoring their online comments to those they feel are acceptable to powerholders.

In the case of disruptions to digital communications, one has to ask to what extent power exists before it is exercised; whether an actor already has the potential to exercise their power, or whether power is only realized when it is exercised (Avelino, 2021)? However, questioning power associations is challenged by Giddens who notes that power is characterized as being 'generated in and through the reproduction of structures of domination' which resonates with Gaventa's position on power dimensions of levels, spaces and forms (Giddens, 1984), thus reinforcing the idea that the areas in which power is exerted or displayed are not neutral, and neither are they static (Gaventa, 2006). Indeed, the different arguments on power offer an opportunity to understand the power dynamics in Uganda specific to internet shutdowns.

When considering power alongside rights in the Ugandan digital access ecosystem one realizes that the undercurrent of human and digital rights is a constant presence. Access to the internet is recognized by the United Nations as critical for the realization of rights and freedoms – and as an enabler of access to power by citizens. As such, even the Ugandan legal framework acknowledges that citizens should have access to power, as it is a party to international standards such as those prescribed in both the Universal Declaration of Human Rights (UDHR 1948) and the International Covenant on Civil and Political Rights (ICCPR 1976), as well as in the African Charter on Human and Peoples' Rights (ACHPR), which gives the individual the right to information and expression. At a national level, Uganda's existing legal framework has laws that provide for the realization and enjoyment of digital rights and internet freedoms. For instance, the 1995 Constitution provides for the freedom of expression in Article 28, privacy in Article 27 and access to information in Article 41.

While these legal frameworks appear to enable citizens with various rights including access to information and freedom of expression, the state has maintained or introduced laws that have often been used to shrink civic space and restrict rights and freedoms in the online space. These moves have also served as extensions of pre-colonial and post-colonial ruling party power dynamics, reinforcing an unequal relationship and continuing structures of domination over citizens. The laws that have been used in recent times to curtail civic rights and shrink civic powers emerged in tandem with the growing popularity of the internet and in the wake of the 2010 Arab Spring. These include laws such as the Regulation of Interception of Communications Act 2010, Computer Misuse Act 2011 and its 2022 amendment, the Uganda Communications Act 2013, the Anti-Terrorism Act of 2002 (as amended in 2015, 2016 and 2017), and the Public Order Management Act 2013. These laws have been used to limit or curtail access to the internet during critical times such as in elections and have been used to justify wanton directives and limitations such as internet disruption by the state.

## *Power and rights: online access affordances*

In the wake of the January 2011 election – and indeed in the elections that have followed – the power dynamics evolved from visible actions of power such as arrests and blocks to physical campaigns by deploying a military presence which has affected critical voices from the opposition, human rights defenders and the media; to invisible demonstrations of power which have included disruption of digital communications, including by websites, blocking of select words in SMS messages (as witnessed in 2011), through to the blocking of social media websites and access to platforms that support powerholding such as VPN download sites (which would otherwise allow citizens to reclaim their power and online movement).

The Arab Spring showed how collective movements could shift power from the state to citizens, using online tools to counter state control. In Uganda and other authoritarian countries, this movement gave citizens the impression of gaining an upper hand.

The Arab Spring illustrated how collective movements could not be held by borders and could indeed shift from the state to citizens using online tools to counter power. It marked a fleeting moment where citizens in mostly authoritarian countries including Uganda assumed they had an upper hand as powerholders. Despite Ugandan citizens making earlier attempts in 2006 towards demanding accountability from the state by holding power such as through the #WalkToWork campaign, the attempt was countered by the state reclaiming power swiftly alongside the display of both visible and invisible forms of powerholding. By 2011, the state increased its powerholding using frameworks in contravention of international, regional and even national human rights standards, which would feature in all election periods from the Arab Spring.

In the years that followed and by the 2021 elections, the chilling effect deployed by the state use of its power had led to a culture of 'shutdown realism'. This was exemplified by actions like the arrest of journalists (ACME, 2021) who reported on police brutality using social media posts (BBC Eye, 2021) as evidence in the lead-up to the elections and the announcement from earlier years that social media is a place of gossip.

By the 2021 elections, the state's use of power had created a chilling effect, resulting in a culture of 'shutdown realism' as outlined in this book's introduction. Roberts and Anthonio (2025) define shutdown realism as when shutdowns have become so frequent that they become normalized. Roberts and Anthonio argue that 'citizens internalise shutdowns as normal and justified, resulting in a "chilling effect" with citizens self-censoring their onlinle comments to those they feel are acceptable [to powerholders]'. When put in practice at times of national importance such as elections, this marks a key reduction of power and civic agency, and the loss of rights – despite elections being a moment to exercise power.

However, by virtue of elections being a space in which citizens are invited, a power dynamic remains as elections remain a space into which citizens are invited (Gaventa, 2006) to participate under the structures and regulations of the state, who ultimately set the terms of engagement for citizens, including through their laws and regulations, visual show of power (visible military presence, beatings and arrests) and invisible shows of power (network disruptions, limited access to funds – blockage to mobile money services).

While technology, its availability and access can facilitate credible democratic engagements and participation as it enhances effectiveness, efficiency, accountability and transparency of elections, the disruption of digital communications via the internet led to doubt in the credibility of the process, underscored by the civic loss of power.

## *Power interests: platforms versus the state, citizens versus the state*

The 2021 internet shutdown in Uganda served as a key example of the battle of power interests. This conflict was framed under the guise of combating disinformation, revealing deeper tensions over control and influence in the digital space.

Public commentary on the network disruption has often placed the burden of blame on the Uganda Communications Commission (UCC) for the internet shutdown. This, however, has been challenged by officials who argue that they have often tried to engage with platforms not only on matters of disinformation but also on other concerns users face on platforms. Despite these attempts, they claim that platforms have often been unresponsive.

An interview with a high-ranking official (KII05-10, 2024) from the communications regulator, noted:

> We started engaging with platforms (Facebook and Twitter) back in October 2020. We were trying to get support to help us address growing problems with fraud, impersonation and hate speech on the platforms – mainly Facebook. We reported through the public reporting facility. We never got any response. We'd even struggle to find whom to write to as the contact us email had no actual person to contact. We never got responses .... We felt that as regulators, we were losing control over our mandate. We couldn't help the victims of these crimes.

Although efforts to meet with Facebook were pursued by the UCC via email and in some instances in-person, no real action appeared to be taken. Meanwhile, ahead of the 2021 elections, the UCC received reports from the National Security Council that, 'people were mobilizing online – on Facebook – to undermine the elections'. However, there were concerns that, since Facebook had failed to address the earlier reports lodged by the Commission, 'how sure are you that they will act when we report these concerns? What if they don't and trouble happens in this country? Who will be responsible? Would it be responsible for the government to say it did not act because a platform didn't respond? But Facebook is not the government. It is not the regulator. Who is the regulator of Facebook?' (KII05-10, 2024).

The interviewee (KII05-10, 2024) further argued that it is within the mandate of the UCC to 'monitor, inspect, licence, supervise, control and regulate communications services' as per section 5B of the Uganda Communications Act. 'Facebook falls outside of the mandate of the UCC and that of others across the world'.

In pursuit of adhering to its mandate and acknowledging the concerns raised by the National Security Council – the UCC responded to a directive issued on the grounds of national security concerns to suspend Facebook in the country. The respondent noted that 'It wasn't just UCC creating a scenario. There were real issues documented and written by the powers that be. So, we acted.'

The respondent (KII05-10, 2024) further noted, 'maybe, they don't take our concerns seriously', musing on how Facebook was more likely to appear before Congress to address matters than it was to appear in an African Parliament to do the same.

There was also an acknowledgement of the power struggle between platforms and the state that comes at the cost of citizens' rights.

> Uganda recognizes digital rights and that's why in all this, closing and suspension of access to the internet is never the first option. It's usually a last resort. However, it's not the only right in our bill of rights, the government has to deal with balancing the enjoyment of digital rights vis-à-vis other rights. The government has to make the difficult balance as to which one right has to be deemed superior to the other for the good of everyone and that's why some of these rights are suspended for the greater good.

When considering these arguments through a human rights lens, it is important to note that human rights are interrelated, interdependent and indivisible (UN, 2024). Citizens are all equally entitled to these rights without discrimination. However, during internet shutdowns – or in arguments justifying them – certain rights appear to be prioritized over others, often reflecting the interests of the state. This thus forces citizens to trade certain rights – unwillingly – despite the state obligation and duty to protect and promote both rights.

### *Social and economic rights: the cost of freedom*

In all instances of internet shutdowns in Uganda, mobile money transactions have also been affected. It was noted that the action to also suspend this key channel of financial inclusion is to quell the movement of funds aimed at undermining the state through payments for activities such as burning tyres and 'mobilizing and paying allowances to the youth to go to the streets' (KII05-10, 2024).

Mobile money, a key economic tool in the country, serves as an important means of livelihood for a largely unbanked population. By shutting down this platform, powerholders leverage visible power to impose direct restrictions on financial flows, with the goal of silencing opposition and grassroots groups by cutting off their economic lifeline. However, caught in the power struggle is a large population that isn't online as well as the telecommunications sector, who by virtue of the contracts of their licences are obligated to adhere to shutdown instructions from the state. For the latter, an invisible power play weaved within operating licences and the right to conduct business in the country.

Citizens are thus affected by the loss in communication and access to financial transactions to meet basic needs such as buying airtime to make calls or send messages (SMS), and for paying for basic utilities such as water and electricity, and needs such as household shopping and school fees. Blocking mobile money transactions not only disrupts economic activity but also undermines civic participation and shrinks the civic space for democratic deliberation. Ultimately, power is used to infringe on fundamental rights to expression, association and assembly, further entrenching authoritarian control. Moreover, it serves to reinforce state overreach in critical democratic processes, framing it as a necessary intervention for stability or security. This narrative diminishes citizens' agency, making it harder for them to see financial freedom and civic participation as interconnected rights worth defending.

### Power over the press

While blocking mobile money can be framed as a tool for controlling who participates in public life, it also illustrates how economic control translates into political dominance. A similar argument can be made for the media – society's watchdog – a key stakeholder during times of public interest. The block to social media and the internet disrupted established processes that the media use to collect and deliver timely information to the public.

A freelance journalist (KII03-07, 2024), interviewed for this chapter noted: 'It became challenging for the media to play its watchdog role of disseminating information to the public or give real time updates on events surrounding the elections and the aftermath of the voting period. Many had to rely on traditional communication methods such as phone calls. Information dissemination to the public became a slow and cumbersome process.'

They also noted that,

> Unlike previous elections where only social media platforms were blocked, 2021 saw a total internet shutdown. This meant that even Virtual Private Networks (VPNs) could not be used to circumvent the blockade as most VPN sites had also been blocked. Most media organizations therefore resorted to phone calls and SMSs to gather information and reach out to sources. Radio and television also became key platforms for sharing election-related information to the public.

Meanwhile the complete block to the internet shrunk media avenues for information gathering considerably – narrowing sources and limiting a necessary media diversity.

> There was wide coverage of the social media shutdown shortly after it had been implemented. Most of the coverage focused on voices from the government justifying the shutdown, namely that it was done to prevent the spread of fake news and disinformation related to the elections. The government also stated that the shutdown was necessary to mitigate election-related violence resulting from fake news.

The interviewee added that, 'News gathering and dissemination in real time became challenging majority of media houses did not have access to their journalists who were deployed at various polling stations to provide updates on the voting process' (KII03-07, 2024).

Indeed, the state used invisible and visible power forms to control the media. The kill switch affords government the possibility to prevent accountability while also limiting transparency during a time when both are necessary especially as the state in democratic theory is supposed to be held accountable by voters and by the media.

The placement of the media at a disadvantage is further entrenched by visible actions such as arrests and intimidation – actions that fuelled self-censorship –

and served the power interest of the state. Meanwhile basic rights of access to information and freedom of expression were trumped.

## *Power over civil and political rights*

In Uganda, a key stakeholder group during elections is civil society who also often get caught in the fray when it comes to ensuring that specific power interests are maintained. A civil society organization leader (K1104-06, 2024) noted that:

> the shutdown sent a chilling effect on not just CSOs' digital rights but for all Ugandan citizens. Most affected were the right to access information, and freedom of expression, association and assembly. With these rights suppressed, it meant that CSOs working on issues such as election integrity could not exercise their mandate. With limited and almost no access information on voting processes, CSOs could not fully monitor and report on any election fraud or election violence thus affecting election transparency. On the right to freedom of expression, CSOs could not speak out, report or document any election injustices experienced at that time.

Meanwhile CSOs had to rely on foreign actors to disseminate information. Unlike the 2011 election which saw SMS/text messaging blocked, the 2021 election would see this avenue become primary for the distribution of information where possible. However, it relied on mobile money to ensure access to the text messaging service. 'CSOs worked with parties outside Uganda to issue statements condemning the shutdown while urging the Uganda government to respect international human rights' (K1104-06, 2024).

Although in this instance, CSOs had the power to utilize the technical affordances of basic communication tools (SMS and phone calls) to build 'power with' international organizations who consequently had the opportunity to use their internet access to share developments with their audiences, this tactic afforded CSOs in Uganda some form of 'power to' hold government powerholder to account. However, for CSOs to operate in the country, they remain at the mercy of the state who grant them the 'permission' to perform their tasks as civil society in line with the Uganda National Bureau for Non-Governmental Organizations which in the wake of the 2021 elections would go on to ban fifty-four entities for 'non-compliance' (*Daily Monitor*, 2024). This clearly illustrated that while the state can invite one into a perceived position of power, it can withdraw that power at any time – regardless of how that power is claimed – including by utilizing alliances outside of Uganda.

Meanwhile, an interviewee (KII02-06, 2024) with a background in multilateral affairs stressed that the shutdown 'narrowed the voices and perspectives of citizens, regarding matters of public affairs and governance of the country', while the regime ensured a specific narrative was maintained. However, there have previously been actions taken to challenge the state when it comes to restricting digital access.

> There were efforts by civil society actors such as the Unwanted Witness Uganda, who challenged the constitutionality of the shutdowns by the government. They argued shutdowns violated constitutional rights to freedom of expression, and that the actions of the state were unjustified, disproportionate and greatly affected the livelihoods of citizens when mobile money services – a means of survival for many Ugandan micro businesses – were shut down by the state. The petition, as far as I remember, was dismissed by the state unfortunately.

Indeed, in 2016, a petition was submitted to the Constitutional Court challenging the social media shutdown and mobile money block (*The Independent*, 2021). The petition was dismissed five years later – in the wake of the 2021 election – on the grounds that, 'the suspension was done in good faith and for purposes of securing the country against the reasonably suspected risk of incitement of violence by publishing unregulated content on social media, which is permissible under article 43 of the constitution' (*The Independent*, 2021). This illustrated that even at the judicial level, there isn't a clear separation of power as the legal regime has positioned itself as one that appears to maintain particular power interests which benefit the state more than they do civic rights.

Respondents noted that there were more repressive laws enacted in the lead up to the elections which granted the state more power and control over citizens and the flow of information such as the Computer Misuse Amendment Act 2022 which had gross implications for human rights.

## *Recommendations*

Further to the insights that emerged from this chapter, the following are recommendations to different stakeholders to address internet shutdowns as witnessed in 2021. These are crucial as the country heads into yet another controversial election in 2026.

**To the government of Uganda:** There is a need for legislative reform that makes more explicit the necessity and proportionality of internet shutdowns. The reforms should ensure that digital rights are not overridden by other rights. Further, the government needs to aim for more transparency and accountability enabled by digital access. This should be guided by increased multi-stakeholder engagement with the multi-stakeholder community: more dialogue is required with the greater multistakeholder community on solutions that balance security with digital rights, particularly at times or moments of special public interest, to ensure a balance of power interests.

**To technology platforms:** With the rise in disinformation, platforms need to prioritize disinformation in African digital spaces better, recognizing the constantly evolving manifestations of disinformation and its use by both ruling and opposition actors and the actions necessary to address it. Further, more dialogue and responses are required by platforms in response to government concerns as not all submissions are politically motivated, such as online fraud and impersonation. Further, platforms need to enhance their internal capacities to identify disinformation and provide more detailed accounts of government requests for takedowns or investigations as well as the platform responses.

**To civil society actors:** Advocacy and litigation need to continue being used as tools against internet shutdowns. The documentation of the evolving nature of disruptions is contributing to a growing body of evidence and public campaigns, strengthening the case against shutdowns. Further, these efforts support the continued need to push back against repressive laws and pursue collaborative policy development built upon evidence to protect consumer rights and digital rights better, and prevent arbitrary shutdowns.

**To media:** There is a need for more media houses to develop strategies for more resilient reporting during internet shutdowns. Further, journalists need to increase reporting on the impact and consequences of internet shutdowns which sometimes persist far beyond the duration of the shutdown.

## *Bibliography*

A4AI (2018, 6 June), 'Uganda: New Social Media Tax Will Push Basic Connectivity Further Out of Reach for Millions', https://a4ai.org/news/uganda-social-media-tax/

ACME (2021), 'Uganda Media Coverage of the 2021 Elections', https://acme-ug.org/wp-content/uploads/Uganda-Media-Coverage-of-the-2021-Elections-DESIGNED-JANUARY-REPORT-_FINAL.pdf

Africa Center (November 2011), 'ACSS Special Report, Africa and the Arab Spring', https://africacenter.org/wp-content/uploads/2016/06/ASR01EN-Africa-and-the-Arab-Spring-A-New-Era-of-Democratic-Expectations.pdf

African Center for Media Excellence (2011, 15 April), 'Uganda Government Bans Live Broadcast of Protests', https://acme-ug.org/2011/04/15/uganda-government-bans-live-broadcast-of-protests/

Al Jazeera (2020, 18 November), Deadly Protests in Uganda after Bobi Wine Arrested Again', https://www.aljazeera.com/news/2020/11/18/bobi-wine-uganda-opposition-presidential-candidate-arrested

Anthonio, F. and Roberts, T. (2025), *Internet Shutdowns in Africa: Technology, Rights and Power*, London: Bloomsbury.

Avelino, F. (2021), 'Theories of Power and Social Change: Power Contestations and Their Implications for Research on Social Change and Innovation', *Journal of Political Power*, 14(3): 425–48.

BBC (2021, 15 January), 'Uganda Social Media Ban Raises Questions Over Regulation in Africa', https://www.bbc.com/news/world-africa-55618994

BBC Eye (2021, 31 May), *Three Killings in Kampala – BBC Africa Eye documentary*, https://www.youtube.com/watch?v=g7d2AvLEPyA

Burke, J. (2019, 7 October), 'Idi Amin's Mastery of Media Revealed in Newly Published Photos', *The Guardian*, https://www.theguardian.com/world/2019/oct/07/idi-amins-mastery-of-media-revealed-in-newly-published-photos

Butagira, Tabu (2016, 18 February), 'Yoweri Museveni Explains Social Media Shutdown', *The Nation*, https://nation.africa/kenya/news/Yoweri-Museveni-explains-social-media-mobile-money-shutdown/1056-3083032-8h5ykhz/index.html

*Daily Monitor* (2021, 21 February), 'How Native Media Influenced Issues in Pre-independence Uganda', https://www.monitor.co.ug/uganda/magazines/people-power/how-native-media-influenced-issues-in-pre-independence-uganda-3299230

*Daily Monitor* (2024, 16 October), 'Suspended NGOs Speak Out Against Govt Crackdown Ahead of 2026 Elections', https://www.monitor.co.ug/uganda/news/national/suspended-ngos-speak-out-against-govt-crackdown-ahead-of-2026-elections-4795694

DFR Lab. (2021, 12 January), 'Social Media Disinformation Campaign Targets Ugandan Presidential Election', https://medium.com/dfrlab/social-media-disinformation-campaign-targets-ugandan-presidential-election-b259dbbb1aa8

Freedom House (2012), 'Freedom on the Net', https://www.freedomhouse.org/sites/default/files/Uganda%202012.pdf

Freedom House (2023), 'Freedom on the Net', https://freedomhouse.org/sites/default/files/2023-10/Freedom-on-the-net-2023-DigitalBooklet.pdf

Gariyo, Zie. 1992, *The Press and Democratic Struggles in Uganda, 1900-1962*. Working Paper No. 24, Kampala: Centre for Basic Research.

Gaventa, J. (2006), 'Finding the Spaces for Change: A Power Analysis', *IDS Bulletin Volume*, 37: 23–33.

Giddens, A. (1984), *The Constitution of Society: Outline of the Theory of Structuration*, Berkeley, CA: University of California Press.

Isoba, J. C. (1980), 'The Rise and Fall of Uganda's Newspaper Industry, 1900–1976', *Journalism Quarterly*, 57(2): 224–33.

Kakooza, M. (2012), *Revisiting the Media Freedom Debate at Uganda's Independence*, Research Report, Kampala: Konrad-Adenauer-Stiftung.

K1104–06 (2024, 2 September), Civil society leader (Author, Interviewer).

KII02–06 (2024, 15 June), Multilateral affairs expert (Author, Interviewer).

KII03–07 (2024, 24 July), Interview with Kampala-based freelance journalist (Author, Interviewer).

KII05–10 (2024, 21 June), Key informant interview with a communications regulator official (Author, Interviewer).

Lapček-Neogy, B. (1997), 'The Transition,' *The Anniversary Issue: Selections from Transition, 1961–1976*, 244–8.

Lugalambi, G. W. and Tabaire, B. (2010), 'Overview of the State of Media Freedom in Uganda, Research Report', Kampala: ACME.

Ministry of ICT and National Guidance (2020, 21 June), 'Call to Embrace the Scientific Campaign Road Map', https://ict.go.ug/wp-content/uploads/2020/06/Press-Statement-on-Scientific-Electoctions-Road-Map.pdf

Nanfuka, J. (2016, 12 May), 'Uganda Again Blocks Social Media to Stifle Anti-Museveni Protests', CIPESA, https://cipesa.org/2016/05/uganda-again-blocks-social-media-to-stifle-anti-museveni-protests/

Nanfuka, J. (2019, 31 January), 'Social Media Tax Cuts Ugandan Internet Users by Five Million, Penetration Down from 47% to 35%', CIPESA, https://cipesa.org/2019/01/%EF%BB%BFsocial-media-tax-cuts-ugandan-internet-users-by-five-million-penetration-down-from-47-to-35/

Nanfuka, J. (2021, 13 January), 'Uganda's 2021 Election: A Textbook Case of Disruption to Democracy and Digital Networks in Authoritarian Countries', CIPESA, https://cipesa.org/2021/01/ugandas-2021-election-a-textbook-case-of-disruption-to-democracy-and-digital

*National Information Technology Authority-Uganda (NITA-U)* (2013, July), Government of Uganda Social Media Guide, https://ict.go.ug/wp-content/uploads/2019/12/Government-of-Uganda-Social-Media-Guide.pdf

Roberts, T. and Karekwaivanane, G. H. (2024), *Digital Disinformation in Africa: A Critical Approach*, London: Zed Books.

State House (2023, 13 December), 'President Launches National Population Census-2024', https://statehouse.go.ug/president-launches-national-population-census-2024/

Tabaire, B. (2007), 'The Press and Political Repression in Uganda: Back to the Future?', *Journal of Eastern African Studies*, 1 (2): 193–211, https://doi.org/10.1080/17531050701452408

*The Independent* (2020, 16 December), 'Google Requires Court Order to Delete YouTube Channel-Africa Spokesperson', https://www.independent.co.ug/google-requires-court-order-to-delete-youtube-channel-africa-spokesperson/

*The Independent* (2021, 20 April), 'Constitutional Court Dismisses Petition Challenging Internet, Mobile Money Shutdown During Elections', https://www.independent.co.ug/constitutional-court-dismisses-petition-challenging-internet-mobile-money-shutdown-during-elections/

*The Transition* (1961), 'Our Story', https://transitionmagazine.fas.harvard.edu/our-story/

The Uganda Communications Commission (2023, 1 June), 'Industry Snapshot June 2023', https://www.ucc.co.ug/wp-content/uploads/2024/03/UCC-Market-Report-for-June-2023-FY-4Q22-3.pdf

Uganda Penal Code Act (1950, 15 June), Uganda Legal Information Institute (ULII), https://ulii.org/akn/ug/act/ord/1950/12/eng@2024-12-23

United Nations (2024), *What Are Human Rights?* https://bangkok.ohchr.org/what-are-human-rights/

URN (2020, 17 December), 'Lawyers Amazed at UCC "Ignorance" as Google Tells Regulator to Go to Court', https://observer.ug/news/headlines/67794-lawyers-amazed-at-ucc-ignorance-as-google-tells-regulator-to-go-to-court

# Chapter 13

## Conclusions on critical internet shutdown research

Tony Roberts and Felicia Anthonio

This is the first book to bring together case studies of internet shutdowns from across Africa. It is the first collected edition by African authors analysing the impact of internet shutdowns on digital rights and power relations. In this collected volume we have extended the existing rights-based analysis of internet shutdowns beyond civil and political rights, to include a consideration of their impact across a range of social, economic and political rights and to identify the specific power interests they serve and advance. The study set out to answer *why* internet shutdowns happen, *which* human rights they violate, *what* power interests are served, and *what* can be done to mitigate and prevent them. In pursuing those questions, the authors of the preceding chapters have produced the most comprehensive account to date of the frequency, duration and types of internet shutdowns taking place across the continent of Africa. We have then used a framework of technology affordances, digital rights and power interests to provide the most sustained analysis of those shutdowns to date. This new body of rich case studies provides a valuable platform on which we hope other researchers will build. In this final chapter we present the main findings of the overall study and offer a framework for 'critical studies of internet shutdowns' for other researchers to adapt and improve.

**The shutdown landscape is uneven.** The experience of internet shutdowns across Africa is neither uniform nor static. The in-depth case studies show that there are radical differences between countries on the continent when it comes to internet shutdowns. Ethiopia has imposed thirty internet shutdowns in the nine years from 2016 to 2024; Sudan has imposed twenty-one and Algeria fourteen in the same period. However, fourteen African countries have never experienced a single internet shutdown and another twelve countries on the continent have only ever experienced one in their history. There are also good examples where a history of internet shutdowns now appears to have ended (see for example the DRC chapter in this book). The point here is that the duration, frequency and types of shutdowns vary significantly across the continent, which means that continued empirical research is necessary to monitor and understand this dynamic variation and complexity.

**The task is urgent.** The number of internet shutdowns in Africa in 2024 was an all-time high involving twenty-eight countries. It remains commonplace for African governments to shut down the internet especially during protests and contentious elections. In some countries a form of 'shutdown realism' has set in where they are viewed as normal. Yet as the chapters in this book graphically illustrate, each internet shutdown violates fundamental human rights, damages the economy and destroys trust in democratic systems. An internet shutdown deprives millions of citizens and businesses of access to information and communication tools that have become essential to social, economic and political life. To advance our understanding of this problem, this book has provided three things: (i) the most extensive documentation to date of the detail, dates and duration of internet shutdowns in Africa; (ii) the deepest analysis so far of the impact of internet shutdowns on human rights; and (iii) the first sustained analysis of the power relations that both give rise to internet shutdowns and are impacted by them.

**Gaps in the literature.** In the introduction of this book, we began by reviewing what was already known about internet shutdowns from prior publications. This review identified several gaps in the existing literature that provide an agenda for further research, which we sought to address in this study. Those under-researched areas were (a) the historical and political context that provides the precedents for internet shutdowns, (b) the technological affordances that shape internet disruptions, (c) a disaggregation of who benefits and who is negatively impacted by internet shutdowns, (d) analysis of the full range of human rights impacts extending beyond civil and political rights, (e) an examination of the role of the private sector in internet shutdowns, (f) power analysis of the interests giving rise to internet shutdowns and the impact of shutdowns on those power interests and (g) study of the forms of resistance and collective agency designed to mitigate and end shutdowns. The following sections summarize what we learned in these regards.

**History matters.** In our initial literature review we found that internet shutdowns were analysed without reference to the historical context of previous media shutdowns. However, we found that in every one of the eleven African countries we studied, internet shutdowns had been preceded by other forms of media shutdown. Chapter authors documented historical newspaper shutdowns including in Algeria, Burkina Faso, Nigeria, Sudan, Uganda, Zambia and Zimbabwe. The chapters on the DRC, Zambia, Senegal and Chad are among those to detail radio and TV shutdowns. Authors even evidenced a fax machine shutdown in Sudan, and the emergence of SMS text messaging shutdowns including in the chapters on the DRC and Ethiopia. This is important because this long history of pre-digital media shutdowns provides current powerholders with a cultural and political precedent for imposing internet shutdowns. This is important because the field of science of technology studies (STS) teaches us that when the study of technology is abstracted from its historical and political context there is a tendency to draw technologically deterministic conclusions about the causes of technological harms, and to mistakenly prescribe technosolutionist initiatives to tackle them. To guard against this technological fallacy, we asked chapter authors to include the historical and political context of internet shutdowns in their analysis.

**The colonial roots of internet shutdowns.** By taking historic context into account we found that media shutdowns were introduced to African countries by colonial powers. Authors were able to evidence that the first media shutdowns in their countries were imposed by colonial powers to serve imperialist interests, by suppressing the emerging power interests of anti-colonial movements. The chapters also showed that, after liberation, post-colonial governments often imposed newspaper, radio and TV shutdowns of their own to repress the emergence of opposition political parties that threatened the hold on power of one-party states and military regimes. And now, in contemporary African settings, some governments use internet shutdowns to preserve their power. Our research shows that internet shutdowns in these eleven countries are most often imposed during protests and elections when the threat of opposition power is most present.

**Shutdowns are power politics.** When accounts of internet shutdowns omit the history of media shutdowns, the idea that internet shutdowns are a technical phenomenon is more believable. By providing a history of media shutdowns chapter authors demonstrate that internet shutdowns are only the latest instance of a long-established political phenomenon of elites to retain power. Chapter authors catalogue the claims of powerholders that internet shutdowns are a necessary response to social media disinformation and hate speech but courts are providing clarity that internet shutdowns are never 'legal, necessary and proportionate', the threshold in international law required to abrogate fundamental human rights. This historical approach is important because it helps get to the 'why' of internet shutdowns. Including the political and historical context in the analysis helps researchers to excavate a little deeper in their quest to identify the underlying root causes of internet shutdowns. Having documented the history of media shutdowns in their countries, researchers were invited to use power analysis to identify their motives and to use their findings to diagnose political and policy solutions that address the causes as well as the symptoms of internet shutdowns.

**Technology matters.** Despite the historical continuities of media shutdowns from the colonial age right through to the digital era we also found significant discontinuities between the experience and impact of 'traditional' media shutdowns and 'modern' internet shutdowns. We found theories of technology affordances to be most useful for analysing these qualitative distinctions. The affordances of the internet are radically different from the affordances of a newspaper or other traditional media. State-owned newspapers afford little opportunity to opposition groups trying to share critiques of existing powerholders or promote policy alternatives. The affordances of the internet and social media platforms are radically distinct in that they provide any user with the ability to disseminate text, image and video messages instantly, repeatedly, globally, at low cost. Worried about these developments, especially after the so-called Facebook revolution in Egypt, authoritarian governments became keen to have power over this new channel of online assembly and free expression.

**Authoritarian affordances.** The flip side of social media's utility to activists is that internet technologies also provide powerful new action possibilities to authoritarian states for new kinds of digital repression. Governments are now able to use the 'kill switch' to implement internet shutdowns and instantly remove citizen access to key elements of social, economic and political life that have migrated online. Powerholders can shut down all mobile and internet communications nationwide or they may choose to impose a narrower shutdown in a specific region or to just cut off a particular social media platform (see for example the Twitter ban in the Nigeria chapter or the Facebook ban in the Uganda chapter). The affordances of shutdown technologies are providing repressive states with the new action possibility of 'targetability', imposing shutdowns on those that they see as a threat. Chapter authors evidence shutdowns that target specific geographies during protests or war (see for example the Ethiopia chapter) as well as throttling bandwidth when opposition supporters are rallying (see for example the Zimbabwe chapter). This raises the possibility of deliberately disadvantaging citizens living in areas of high opposition support while allowing uninterrupted internet to continue in 'loyal' areas and in the central business district. The increasing sophistication of shutdowns as power politics is a clear trend evidenced in this book, and it is one that we expect to continue. In the future we can expect to see what we call 'micro-targeted shutdowns' that disrupt specific neighbourhoods, networks, groups or individuals. The use of hashtags or keywords for targeting is likely to be combined with the use of throttling or shadow-bans to micro-target shutdowns for political effect.

**Who is (dis)advantaged?** The impact of internet shutdowns is uneven within countries. Beyond the point that internet shutdowns are designed to advantage powerholders and disadvantage opposition groups, the impact is experienced unevenly. This is clear when an internet shutdown targets one region and not others (see for example the Tigray region in the Ethiopia chapter). However, in all countries, internet access is greater among high-income men in urban centres when compared to low-income women in rural areas. There remains a gender digital divide in most of the countries studied. Chapter authors in this book have made efforts to produce some clarity about the differentiated impact on, for example, the income of online workers and digital businesses; the educational impact on students; the health-seeking behaviour of citizens; in addition to the more often documented impact of disconnecting online journalists and political activists. Much more research is necessary to disaggregate the experience of internet shutdowns across different demographics to develop a more sophisticated understanding of the uneven impact across different parts of the population.

**Extended rights analysis.** The chapters in this book provide evidence of the impact on citizens' fundamental human rights when an internet shutdown is imposed, including the right to free expression, the right to work and the right to education online. Our initial literature review found that the impact of shutdowns on citizens' civil and political rights is perhaps the most well documented and that comparatively little research attention has been paid to assessing the impact on economic, social and cultural rights. In order to contribute to addressing this imbalance we asked authors to go beyond documenting impacts on rights covered in the International Covenant on Civil and Political Rights and to also include the impact on the rights covered in the International Covenant on Economic, Social and Cultural Rights. In the Sudan chapter interviewees provide testimony about losses caused by the shutdowns and the right to work as well as being unable to continue online studies and the right to education. In the DRC chapter interviewees explain how their access to online healthcare and family communication impacted their access to cultural rights and to the right to health. We understand why research to date has legitimately focused on civil and political rights but argue that further research needs to be carried out on the full range of fundamental human rights that are violated by internet shutdowns.

**Private companies implement shutdowns.** Authors in this book have explained that when African leaders impose internet shutdowns, they need private mobile phone companies and private telecoms companies to implement the shutdown. Although those private companies have a pecuniary interest in keeping the internet on, and an obligation to protect and promote human rights law, the government's power interest prevails. This is because it is the government that licenses mobile and internet companies to operate. The state is able to exert 'power over' the companies forcing them to implement internet shutdowns despite it otherwise being in the companies' self-interest to resist the orders. There has been little power analysis in the existing literature about these competing powers and further research could be valuable in identifying opportunities between companies, civil society organizations and citizens to build collective 'power with', designed to resist, litigate against and ultimately end internet shutdowns.

**Platform accountability.** Digitalization has been the handmaiden of privatization, which has removed transparency and democratic accountability of core utilities. In the eleven African countries that we studied, traditional media and telecommunications were originally state owned, and state regulated. Since the turn of the century state media and telecommunications companies have been largely replaced by private social media and mobile phone companies that are often headquartered outside of the continent. This has reduced the ability of citizens and governments to control key infrastructure or to exercise influence or accountability. The social media companies used by the majority of African citizens are owned by private companies based in the United States and to a lesser extent in China. These companies now often have more data and influence over users than local elected leaders or public institutions. It has proven impossible for African citizens or politicians to regulate, tax or hold these foreign powers accountable. Anger about these power interests contributed to the Twitter ban in Nigeria and to the Facebook ban in Uganda covered in those two chapters.

**Power analysis needed.** Our initial literature review suggested that to date the primary focus of research on internet shutdowns has been on the immediate first-order effects of shutdowns: and especially their negative impact on human rights. This is understandable as the right place to begin an inquiry, but it does not necessarily produce an understanding of the underlying causes. So, in this book we also set out to examine the second-order effects that those rights violations have on power relations. We asked authors to investigate *why* powerholders violate citizens' rights by imposing internet shutdowns. We did so to excavate the root causes of this form of repression and to shed light on what needs to be done to prevent them.

**Internet shutdowns as power over**. All internet shutdowns take place across power divides. Shutdowns are implemented by small powerful elites and are imposed on millions of less powerful citizens. With the exception of internet shutdowns aimed at preventing cheating in school exams (see chapter on Algeria), most of the internet shutdowns examined in this book can be interpreted as a tactic deployed in a wider contestation of power between powerholders in government and opposition actors. In the analysis of chapter authors in this book, internet shutdowns are most often imposed by incumbent political leaders to protect vested power interests.

**National interests or ulterior motives?** In most of the chapters in this book, governments claimed to be imposing internet shutdowns in the 'national interest' (or 'national security' and similar formulations). However, the chapter authors were largely sceptical and identified other motives. In no cases in this book did the authors conclude that internet shutdowns served the 'national interest' of the whole population. The research evidence documents damage to the national interest in terms of economic costs, rights violations and opportunities lost. The power analysis conducted by researchers in this study concludes that internet shutdowns serve the much narrower interests of an incumbent political party, ethnic group or military elite. Authors document that most common triggers for internet shutdowns in Africa are elections, protests or military or political conflict to serve sectional and partisan interests. By plotting the sequence of events from historical context and triggering events, through first-order and second-order effects (as illustrated in the Introduction Figure 1.1), it becomes clear that, despite public statements about 'national interests', the evidence suggests that the ulterior motive for internet shutdowns is to respond to a perceived threat to incumbent leaders' hold on political power by disrupting the power of communication and mobilization of opposition groups.

**Power analysis.** Understanding how power operates in digital spaces and platforms requires applying tools of power analysis to the study of digital authoritarian practices. Chapter authors used the powercube (Gaventa, 2006) and concepts 'expressions of power' (VeneKlasen and Miller, 2002) alongside other theories to begin this process of power analysis. From this perspective, state-imposed internet shutdowns can be understood as crude expressions of state 'power over' opposition groups as well as over internet and mobile phone companies. In authoritarian contexts, offline civil space can be shrunk using police violence and arrests. Chapter authors explain how citizens claimed and created new online spaces to build countervailing power. These 'created spaces' (Cornwall, 2002; Gaventa, 2019) are relatively safe and afford new action possibilities to build 'power with' rehearsing counter-narratives, sharing circumvention tactics and deploying strategic litigation. The chapters on Nigeria and Zambia document citizens' building 'power to' make rights-claims and to hold those responsible for internet shutdowns accountable online or in the courts.

**Resistance is fertile.** African citizens have not been passive in the face of internet shutdowns. Each chapter documents the range of creative agency deployed by individuals and civil society organizations in circumventing, protesting and mounting strategic litigation to end internet shutdowns. Authors demonstrate that the collective power of civil society continues to grow as organizations develop and deploy new ways to challenge internet shutdowns. Citizens across Africa are proving themselves able to deploy their own technologies to detect, circumvent, evade and escape internet shutdowns. They are using strategic litigations to take their own government to court and obtain legal rulings ordering the internet to be switched back on, and to demand the 'non-re-occurrence' of rights-violating shutdowns (see Togo ruling in the Nigeria chapter). Collective citizen action has been successful in obtaining commitments from government to #KeepltOn, including in countries where they used to be common (see for example DRC chapter). This has been achieved through awareness raising, advocacy, strategic litigation and by replacing repressive governments with more open and democratic ones. This is important because understanding this evolving landscape of resistance is essential to guide future action to mitigate the harms of Internet shutdowns and prevent them reoccurring. The authors of the country chapters in this book have contributed toward this aim by documenting the tactics and practices of resistance that are gaining traction in different territories.

## *Limitations*

We acknowledge several limitations of study and acknowledge that further research needs to be carried out. We know that our contribution is modest. In many respects we are learning as we go, but we hope that by 'showing our workings' other researchers will point out our blind spots and find this framework useful scaffolding.

**Research limitations.** A limitation of any study like this is that, by isolating just one practice of digital authoritarianism like internet shutdowns, we lose sight of other authoritarian practices also being deployed. The African Digital Rights Network has conducted separate studies of Digital Disinformation in Africa (Roberts and Karekwaivanane, 2024) and Digital Surveillance in Africa (Roberts and Mare, 2025). This study, *Internet Shutdowns in Africa*, will be accompanied by two other studies of digital authoritarian practices: *Biometric Digital-ID in Africa* and on *Public Space Surveillance in Africa* (forthcoming 2026). Although there is a logic to isolating these distinct practices for the purposes of analysis, further research needs to be done on how these tools work alongside each other in repressive settings. To support this end, single-country studies should be conducted to understand how the full range of digital authoritarian practices are combined as repressive apparatus to inform analysis of what action is necessary to mitigate and overcome their effects.

**Participatory action research.** Another limitation of research to date is that it has been carried out primarily by external experts. In the next phase it will be important to commission participatory action research carried out with and by those people with the most direct experience of digital authoritarian practices – both to provide new insights but also to develop their critical agency to resist and overcome the practices. This will help build more research capacity embedded in local civil society, both to document shutdowns, but importantly to analyse the underlying root causes of digital authoritarian practices, and the viability of potential tactics to circumvent, challenge and end reoccurrence.

**Symptoms vs causes.** First responders should focus on firefighting and treating wounds. Tackling immediate and practical needs should be the first order of priority. However, if 100 per cent of our time and attention is always dedicated to treating the symptoms of a problem it is inevitable that our children and grandchildren will be condemned to fight the same fires. To ensure non-recurrence, it is also necessary to dedicate a percentage of our limited resources to identifying and removing the root causes. Protesting the human-rights violations that flow from internet shutdowns is essential work that helps unite activists, lawyers, academics and policymakers around a key issue and builds counter-power. We also need to address the underlying causes.

We argue that power analysis can make an important contribution as one empirical tool researchers can use to identify the specific political, ethnic or partisan interests that give rise to internet shutdowns, as well as improving our understanding of how they affect those power relations. The studies in this book have shown that understanding this requires situated qualitative analysis by local researchers able to draw on contextual knowledge. Detection of internet outages by technical experts in foreign observatories is indeed important, as is the development of circumvention and personal security tools, but we argue that it needs to be complemented by qualitative research by African researchers able to interview those affected in African languages and analyse findings in the light of their lifelong understanding of local political dynamics and power relationships.

We offer the following framework to researchers to adapt and to improve.

## *Critical studies of internet shutdown: a framework*

In this book we adopted a novel and critical approach to the study of internet shutdowns. Based on our previous studies, *Digital Disinformation in Africa* (Roberts and Karekwaivanane, 2024) and *Digital Surveillance in Africa* (Roberts and Mare, 2025), and further informed by this study, *Internet Shutdowns in Africa*, we argue that six elements are useful in framing a critical analysis of internet shutdowns – or other digital authoritarian practices:

1. **Historical context:** by situating each study in the local historical, political and economic contexts to surface the contextual drivers of internet shutdowns.
2. **Technological affordances:** by analysing the affordances of specific shutdown technologies that make possible new possibilities for the repression of communication and networking.

3. **Impact disaggregation:** by being attentive to exactly who is (dis)advantaged by internet shutdowns, including along intersecting dimensions of gender, ethnicity, class, age and sexuality.
4. **Power interests:** by analysing who benefits and which power interests are being served, and distinguishing between partisan political interests, economic interests, military interests, etc.
5. **Rights and justice**: by having clear normative commitments to rights, equity and social justice.
6. **Guide action:** by guiding practical action to end injustices including by making actionable recommendations and building power to mitigate and overcome rights-violating practices.

In this book this critical approach is reflected in the chapter structure, opening with locating internet shutdowns in their historical context, analysing the affordances of the technologies, impacts on citizens in relation to both human rights and power interests, and concluding with documentation of forms of resistance and guidance in the form of actionable recommendations to circumvent, mitigate and ultimately end internet shutdowns. We found this approach to be helpful in developing a more critical approach to the study of internet shutdowns and we invite other researchers to adopt and improve the framework.

## *Bibliography*

Cornwall, A. (2002), 'Making Spaces, Changing Spaces: Situating Participation in Development', IDS Working Paper 170, Brighton: Institute of Development Studies.

Gaventa, J. (2006), 'Finding the Spaces for Change: A Power Analysis', *IDS Bulletin*, 37: 23–33.

Gaventa J. (2019), 'Applying Power Analysis: Using the "Powercube" to Explore Forms, Levels and Spaces', in R. McGee and J. Petit (eds), *Power, Empowerment and Social Change*, pp. 117–38, London: Routledge.

Roberts, T. and Karekwaivanane, G. H. (2024), *Digital Disinformation in Africa: Hashtag Protest, Power and Propaganda*, https://www.bloomsburycollections.com/monograph?docid=b-9781350319240&st=digital±disinformation

Roberts, T. and Mare, A. (Eds) (2025), *Digital Surveillance in Africa: Power, Agency and Rights*, London: Zed Books.

VeneKlasen, L. and Miller, V. (2002), *A New Weave of Power, People and Politics*, Oklahoma: World Neighbours.

# Index